UNDERSTANDING GLOBAL SOCIAL POLICY

Also available in the series

Understanding poverty, inequality and wealth
Policies and prospects
Edited by Tess Ridge and Sharon Wright

"This volume provides a timely and much-needed critical account of the inter-relationship between 'the problem of poverty' and 'the problem of riches'. Combining both conceptual, empirical and policy perspectives and a UK and global focus, it offers rich pickings for students and all who are concerned about poverty and inequality."
Ruth Lister, Loughborough University, author of *Poverty* (Polity Press, 2004)
PB £19.99 (US$34.95) ISBN 978-1-86134-914-9
HB £60.00 (US$80.00) ISBN 978-1-86134-915-6
240 x 172mm 352 pages June 2008 tbc

Understanding immigration and refugee policy
Contradictions and continuities
Rosemary Sales, Middlesex University

"This book provides a much needed overview to the key concepts and issues in global migration and the development of immigration and asylum policy. The book is thought provoking and deserves to be read widely."
Alice Bloch, City University London
PB £19.99 (US$34.95) ISBN 978-1-86134-451-9
HB £60.00 (US$80.00) ISBN 978-1-86134-452-6
240 x 172mm 296 pages June 2007

Understanding health policy
Rob Baggott, De Montfort University

"This book by aleading commentator on health policy breaks new ground in understanding how health policy is made and implemented."
Martin Powell, University of Birmingham
PB £18.99 (US$34.95) ISBN 978-1-86134-630-8
HB £60.00 (US$80.00) ISBN 978-1-86134-631-5
240 x 172mm 292 pages June 2007

Understanding health and social care
Jon Glasby, University of Birmingham

"This is an ambitious and wide-ranging book which provides a valuable historical perspective, as well as a forward-looking analysis, based on real experience. It will be a valuable tool for leaders, policy makers and students." Nigel Edwards, Policy Director, The NHS Confederation.
Nick Ellison, University of Leeds
PB £18.99 (US$34.95) ISBN 978-1-86134-910-1
HB £60.00 (US$80.00) ISBN 978-1-86134-911-8
240 x 172mm 216 pages June 2007

Understanding the mixed economy of welfare
Martin Powell, University of Birmingham

"This book provides an up-to-date account of welfare pluralism that is both accessible to students and likely to revitalise an important debate within Social Policy. A must-read for academics and students alike."
Kirk Mann, University of Leeds
PB £22.99 (US$39.95) ISBN 978-1-86134-759-6
HB £60.00 (US$80.00) ISBN 978-1-86134-760-2
240 x 172mm 272 pages February 2007

For a full listing of all titles in the series visit www.policypress.org.uk

SOCIAL POLICY
ASSOCIATION

www.policypress.org.uk

INSPECTION COPIES AND ORDERS AVAILABLE FROM:
Marston Book Services • PO Box 269 • Abingdon • Oxon OX14 4YN UK
INSPECTION COPIES
Tel: +44 (0) 1235 465500 • Fax: +44 (0) 1235 465556 • Email: inspections@marston.co.uk
ORDERS
Tel: +44 (0) 1235 465500 • Fax: +44 (0) 1235 465556 • Email: direct.orders@marston.co.uk

UNDERSTANDING
GLOBAL SOCIAL POLICY

Edited by Nicola Yeates

First published in Great Britain in 2008 by

The Policy Press
University of Bristol
Fourth Floor, Beacon House
Queen's Road
Bristol BS8 1QU
UK

Tel +44 (0)117 331 4054
Fax +44 (0)117 331 4093
e-mail tpp-info@bristol.ac.uk
www.policypress.org.uk

© The Policy Press and the Social Policy Association 2008

British Library Cataloguing in Publication Data
A catalogue record for this book is available from the British Library.

Library of Congress Cataloging-in-Publication Data
A catalog record for this book has been requested.

ISBN 978 1 86134 943 9   paperback
ISBN 978 1 86134 944 6   hardcover

Cover design by Qube Design Associates, Bristol.
Front cover: photograph kindly supplied by www.jupiterimages.com
Printed and bound in Great Britain by Hobbs the Printers, Southampton.

Contents

Detailed contents   vi
List of tables, figures and boxes   xi
List of abbreviations   xiii
Notes on contributors   xvii
Foreword   xx
Acknowledgements   xxiii

one   The idea of global social policy   1
          Nicola Yeates
two   Global and regional social governance   25
          Bob Deacon
three   The global transfer of social policy   49
          Rob Hulme and Moira Hulme
four   Business and global social policy formation   73
          Kevin Farnsworth
five   International trade and welfare   101
          Chris Holden
six   Global labour policy   123
          Robert O'Brien
seven   Global health policy   149
          Meri Koivusalo and Eeva Ollila
eight   Global housing and urban policy   179
          Sunil Kumar
nine   Global pensions policy   207
          Mitchell A. Orenstein
ten   Global migration policy   229
          Nicola Yeates
eleven   Global population policy   253
          Sarah Sexton, Larry Lohmann and Nicholas Hildyard
twelve   Conclusion   279
          Nicola Yeates

Appendix: Glossary of terms   291

Index   311

Detailed contents

one   The idea of global social policy   1
Overview   1
Key concepts   1
The global turn in social science   2
Social policy responds   8
The development of definitions of global social policy   11
Rethinking theory and concepts   15
The importance of contextualisation: history and place   16
The aims and structure of this book   18
Reading and using this book   21
Summary   22
Questions for discussion   23
Further reading and electronic sources   23
References   24

two   Global and regional social governance   25
Overview   25
Key concepts   25
Introduction   26
Conceptualising and understanding global social governance   26
International organisations and national social policies   29
Global redistribution, regulation and rights   34
Global social governance reform   36
Conclusion   43
Summary   44
Questions for discussion   44
Further suggested activities   44
Further reading   45
Electronic resources   45
References   45

three   The global transfer of social policy   49
Overview   49
Key concepts   49
Introduction   50

What is policy transfer?   51
Policy sociology: a global perspective   59
Travelling and embedded policy   59
Policy communities and local policy settlements   61
Evidence into policy: the political nature of decision making   62
Making the global local: divergence within Britain   64
Conclusion   65
Summary   66
Questions for discussion   67
Further reading   67
Electronic resources   67
References   68

four   **Business and global social policy formation**   **73**
Overview   73
Key concepts   73
Introduction   74
Globalisation and business power   75
The globalisation of corporate harm   79
The emergence of corporate-centred global social policy   81
Corporate social responsibility and corporate codes of conduct   85
Global business interest associations and social policy   90
Conclusion   93
Summary   94
Questions for discussion   95
Further suggested activities   95
Further reading   96
Electronic resources   96
References   96

five   **International trade and welfare**   **101**
Overview   101
Key concepts   101
Introduction   102
Economics, trade and welfare   102
The development of the trading system   105
Global institutions and policy processes   107
The welfare state and trade   110
Trade in welfare services   115
Conclusion   117
Summary   118
Questions for discussion   119

Further suggested activities	119
Further reading	119
Electronic resources	119
References	120

six	**Global labour policy**	**123**
Overview		123
Key concepts		123
Introduction		124
Global labour conditions		125
Actors in global labour policy		126
Policy issues in global labour policy		136
Conclusion		143
Summary		144
Questions for discussion		144
Further suggested activities		144
Further reading		144
Electronic resources		145
References		145

seven	**Global health policy**	**149**
Overview		149
Key concepts		149
Introduction		149
Global health governance		151
Global health policy agendas		162
Regulation, rights, redistribution and the politics of global health policy		167
Conclusion		168
Summary		169
Questions for discussion		170
Further suggested activities		170
Further reading		171
Electronic resources		171
References		172

eight	**Global housing and urban policy**	**179**
Overview		179
Key concepts		179
Introduction		180
Poverty and housing in an urbanising world		181
Global actors and housing policy change		183

Housing and urban development in the 21st century 194
Conclusion 199
Summary 200
Questions for discussion 200
Further suggested activities 201
Further reading 201
Electronic resources 201
References 201

nine **Global pensions policy** **207**
Overview 207
Key concepts 207
Introduction 208
The new pension reform phenomenon 208
Historical background: the ILO and post-war global 211
  pensions policy
The rise of the new pension reforms 211
Methods of policy diffusion 214
Country examples 215
Limits of global pensions policy 217
Emerging debates in global pensions policy 220
A bottom-up perspective 221
Conclusion 221
Summary 222
Questions for discussion 223
Further reading 223
Electronic resources 223
References 223

ten **Global migration policy** **229**
Overview 229
Key concepts 229
Introduction 230
Global migration flows 231
Transnational social welfare: cash and care 235
The migration of welfare workers and global care chains 238
Towards a global migration regime? 241
Conclusion 246
Summary 246
Questions for discussion 247
Further suggested activities 247
Further reading 248

Electronic resources   248
References   250

eleven **Global population policy**   **253**
Overview   253
Key concepts   253
Introduction   254
The origins of population control thinking   255
Malthusian transformation: eugenics   258
Population policies in the 20th century   259
Population policies in the 21st century   265
Population control as counter-insurgency   267
Conclusion   272
Summary   273
Further reading   273
Electronic resources   274
References   275

twelve **Conclusion**   **279**
Introduction   279
Global social policy   280
Ideas, discourses, actors, agendas and practices of   281
  global social policy
Global policy actors and forces 'from above' and 'from below' 284
The importance of history and geography   286
Global social policy: final reflections   289
References   290

List of tables, figures and boxes

Tables

1.1	Typology of transnational entities	6
1.2	Conceptual premises of transnationalism	7
1.3	The extended welfare mix	16
2.1	International organisation approaches to national social policy	34
2.2	Elements of global social policy	36
3.1	The global knowledge economy: competing discourses for education	54
4.1	Global business interest associations and their links with IGOs	78
4.2	Globalisation and corporate harm	82
4.3	OECD guidelines for multinational enterprises and the UN Global Compact	87
6.1	Divergent state interests	129
7.1	International variations in child and adult mortality rates, 2005	151
7.2	WHO's estimates of the direct economic impact of selected infectious disease outbreaks between 1990-2003	155
8.1	Population of slum areas at mid-year by region: 1990-2005 and annual slum growth rate	184
8.2	Proportions of slum dwellers by shelter deprivation in developing country regions, 2003	185
9.1	New pension reforms worldwide by type	213
10.1	Migrant population, 2005	232
12.1	Dimensions of global social policy	282

Figures

7.1	US and war on the WHO	153
8.1	Proportion of WB spending on urban housing, 1972-86 and 1987-2005	189
8.2	Proportion of IDB urban spending, 1970-2003	190
10.1	Net immigration map	233

10.2   Net emigration map   233

Boxes

1.1   Contrasting approaches in social science   2
1.2   Dimensions of enmeshment   3
1.3   Some possible effects of globalisation on social policy   9
1.4   Global social policy   11
1.5   Embedded transnationalism   14
1.6   Globalising social policy concepts   16
3.1   Perspectives on the global movement of social policy   52
3.2   UNESCO and the making of global education policy   56
4.1   Distinguishing business and business organisations   74
4.2   Business power: structure and agency   75
4.3   Aim of the UN Global Compact   86
5.1   Trade protection   103
5.2   Services: 'modes of supply'   115
6.1   Deadly toys   135
6.2   Codes versus practice   141
7.1   UN health-related human rights and social rights   156
        stipulations
7.2   Declaration of Alma Ata   163
8.1   Poverty in an urbanising world   180
8.2   The challenges of an urbanising world   180
8.3   Urbanisation   182
8.4   Slum improvement, sites and services   187
8.5   The WB and UNDP urban policy papers compared   190
8.6   WB housing policy of the 1990s: enabling markets to work
        191
8.7   The urban ladder   193
8.8   Cities in transition   194
10.1   Global care chains   238
10.2   The human rights of migrant workers and their   243
        families
10.3   Migration-related trade rights in the GATS   243
11.1   Thomas Malthus's theory of population   255
11.2   Global policy transfer: the export of Malthusianism   256
        to British colonies
11.3   India's population policies since 1994: the resurgence   263
        of neoliberal coercive population control
11.4   Green Revolution agriculture   268

List of abbreviations

ADB	Asian Development Bank
ASEAN	Association of South East Asian Nations
ASEM	Asia–Europe Meeting
BIAC	Business and Industry Advisory Committee to the OECD
CARICOM	Caribbean Community
CEO	Chief executive officer
CLIFF	Community Led Infrastructure Financing Facility
CSO	Civil society organisation
CSR	Corporate social responsibility
DAC	Development Advisory Committee
DELSA	Directorate for Employment, Labour and Social Affairs (OECD)
DfID	Department for International Development, UK (prior to 1997, known as the Overseas Development Administration)
EAC	East African Community
EC	European Commission
ECLAC	Economic Commission for Latin America and the Caribbean
ERT	European Round Table
ESCAP	Economics and Social Commission for Asia and the Pacific
ETI	Ethical Trade Initiative
EU	European Union
FAO	Food and Agriculture Organization
FDI	Foreign direct investment
FLA	Fair Labour Association
G8	Group of 8
G20	Group of 20
G77	Group of 77
GASPP	Globalisation and Social Policy Programme
GATS	General Agreement on Trade in Services
GATT	General Agreement on Tariffs and Trade
GAVI	GAVI Alliance, formerly the Global Alliance for Vaccines and Immunization
GBIA	Global business interest associations
GCC	Global care chain

GCIM	Global Commission on International Migration
GDN	Global Development Network (World Bank)
GHPPP	Global Health Public–Private Partnership
GM	Genetically modified
GPPN	Global Public Policy Networks
GUF	Global Union Federation
HAI	Health Action International
HfA	Health for All
IBRD	International Bank for Reconstruction and Development
ICC	International Chambers of Commerce
ICFTU	International Confederation of Free Trade Unions
ICPD	International Conference on Population and Development
IDA	International Development Association
IDB	Inter-American Development Bank
IFC	International Finance Corporation (WB)
IFI	International financial institution
IFPMA	International Federation of Pharmaceutical Manufacturers and Associations
IGO	International governmental organisation
ILO	International Labour Organization
IMF	International Monetary Fund
INGO	International non-governmental organisation
IO	International organisation
IOM	International Organization on Migration
IPPF	International Planned Parenthood Federation
ITUC	International Trade Union Confederation
IUD	Inter-uterine device
KNET	Knowledge network
MDG	Millennium Development Goal
MEI	Multilateral Economic Institution
MERCOSUR	Mercado Común del Sur (Southern Core Common Market)
MFN	Most favoured nation
MNC	Multinational corporation
MSF	Médecins sans Frontières
NAFTA	North American Free Trade Agreement
NGO	Non-governmental organisation
NIEO	New International Economic Order
NSDF	National Slum Dwellers Federation (India)
ODA	Overseas development aid

OECD	Organisation for Economic Co-operation and Development
OFSTED	Office for Standards in Education
PHM	People's Health Movement
PISA	Programme for International Student Assessment (OECD)
PPP	Public–Private Partnership
PRSP	Poverty Reduction Strategy Paper
PWC	Post–Washington Consensus
SAARS	South Asia Association for Regional Cooperation
SADC	Southern Africa Development Community
SDI	Shack/Slum Dwellers Federation (South Africa)
SEWA	Self Employed Women's Association
SIDA	Swedish International Development Agency
SMEs	Small and medium-sized enterprises
SPARC	Society for the Promotion of Area Resource Centres (an Indian NGO)
SWAp	Sector-wide approach
TAA	Trade Adjustment Assistance
TJM	Trade Justice Movement
TNC	Transnational corporation
TRIPS	Agreement on Trade-Related Aspects of Intellectual Property Rights
TTC	Transnational Tobacco Corporation
UEAPME	European Association of Craft, Small and Medium-Sized Enterprises
UN	United Nations
UNCESCR	United Nations Committee on Economic, Social and Cultural Rights
UNCHR	United Nations Commission on Human Rights
UNCHS (Habitat)	United Nations Centre for Human Settlements (renamed UN-HABITAT)
UNCTAD	United Nations Conference on Trade and Development
UNDESA	United Nations Department of Economic and Social Affairs
UNDP	United Nations Development Programme
UNEP	United Nations Environment Programme
UNESC	United Nations Economic Security Council
UNESCO	United Nations Educational, Scientific and Cultural Organisation
UNFPA	United Nations Population Fund

UN-HABITAT	United Nations Human Settlements Programme
UNHCR	United Nations High Commission for Refugees
UNICE	Union of Industrial and Employers' Confederations of Europe
UNICEF	United Nations Children's Fund
USAID	United States Agency for International Development
WB	World Bank
WEF	World Economic Forum
WHO	World Health Organization
WRC	Worker Rights Consortium
WSF	World Social Forum
WTO	World Trade Organization

Notes on contributors

Bob Deacon is Professor of International Social Policy at the University of Sheffield. His most recent books are *Global Social Policy and Governance* (Sage, 2007) and, with Paul Stubbs, *Social Policy and International Interventions in South East Europe* (Edward Elgar, 2007). He is an elected fellow of the UK Academy of Social Sciences and has worked as a consultant to a number of international organisations on matters of global social policy. He is director of the Globalism and Social Policy Programme (GASPP) and founding editor of the journal *Global Social Policy*.

Kevin Farnsworth is Lecturer in Social Policy at the University of Sheffield. He has published widely on the issues of globalisation, and business power and its influence on social and public policy.

Nicholas Hildyard has worked as an activist on environmental, development and human rights issues since 1976.

Chris Holden is Lecturer in Global Health in the Centre on Global Change and Health at the London School of Hygiene and Tropical Medicine. He has published widely on international trade in health services and corporate involvement in social policy. He is a member of the executive committee of the UK Social Policy Association and joint editor of *Social Policy Review*.

Moira Hulme is a research fellow in the Faculty of Education, University of Glasgow. She is currently working on a number of projects researching teacher education in the UK.

Rob Hulme is Professor of Education at the University of Chester. He has published for a number of years on the international movement of ideas and practices in social policy, particularly education. His most recent work focuses on the integration of service provision for children and young people.

Meri Koivusalo is Senior Researcher in the Finnish National Research and Development Centre for Welfare and Health and a member of GASPP. She is co-author (with Eeva Ollila) of *Making a Healthy World: Agencies, Actors and Policies in International Health* (Zed Books, 1997) and (with Maureen Mackintosh) *Commercialisation of Health Care* (Palgrave, 2006). She is co-editor (with Nicola Yeates and Robert O'Brien) of the journal *Global Social Policy*.

Sunil Kumar lectures on the MSc in Social Policy and Development at the Department of Social Policy, London School of Economics and Political Science. He is an urban social planner with interests in housing, poverty, livelihoods and informal institutions. He has undertaken work for the United Nations Centre for Human Settlements and the UK Department for International Development. He has written widely on housing and housing tenure – for example, *Social Relations, Rental Housing Markets and the Poor in Urban India* (LSE, 2001). He is currently working on social security and social protection in relation to people working in the informal economy in India.

Larry Lohmann has worked for the past 20 years in Thailand, the UK and the US on issues of land, forest and atmospheric rights as well as racism and the discourses of economics and development.

Robert O'Brien is LIUNA/Mancinelli Professor of Global Labour Issues and Chair of the Department of Political Science at McMaster University in Canada. He teaches courses in international relations and is co-editor (with Meri Koivusalo and Nicola Yeates) of the journal *Global Social Policy*. Recent publications include *Solidarity First: Canadian Workers and Social Cohesion* (UBC Press, 2008), *Globalization and Economy: Globalizing Labour* (with Paul James, Sage, 2007) and a second edition of *Global Political Economy: Evolution and Dynamics* (with Marc Williams, Palgrave, 2007).

Eeva Ollila is Senior Researcher in the Finnish National Research and Development Centre for Welfare and Health and a member of GASPP. She is co-author (with Meri Koivusalo) of *Making a Healthy World: Agencies, Actors and Policies in International Health* (Zed Books, 1997). She has also worked with the WHO, the EU and the Finnish Ministry of Social Affairs and Health. She has published on global health, pharmaceuticals and population policies.

Mitchell A. Orenstein is S. Richard Hirsch Associate Professor of European Studies at Johns Hopkins University School of Advanced International Studies in Washington, DC. His publications include *Privatizing Pensions: The Transnational Campaign for Social Security Reform* (Princeton University Press, 2008), *Pension Reform in Europe: Process and Progress*, co-editor (World Bank, 2003), and *Out of the Red: Building Capitalism and Democracy in Postcommunist Europe* (University of Michigan Press, 2001).

Sarah Sexton has worked as an editor and researcher with a range of women's, development, environment and human rights groups in South East Asia and Europe for the past 20 years.

Nicola Yeates is Senior Lecturer in Social Policy at the Open University. She has published widely on matters of globalisation, social policy and migration. Among her publications are *Globalization and Social Policy* (Sage, 2001; Italian translation published in 2005), *Social Justice: Welfare, Crime and Society* (with J. Newman, Open University Press, 2008) and *Migrant Workers and Globalising Care Economies: Explorations in Global Care Chains* (Palgrave, forthcoming). She is co-editor (with Robert O'Brien and Meri Koivusalo) of the journal *Global Social Policy*.

Foreword

Peter Townsend

In the last 30 years people have become more familiar with cross-border features of their lives. Continental travel has become cheaper and more frequent; goods in the shops arrive from countries across the world; the consumption of particular fruit and vegetables is much less seasonal; and long periods of life are spent in different countries, whether as students, members of international organisations or as employees of transnational corporations and their subsidiaries, and in both work and retirement.

These are not the only examples of structural economic and social change. Cross-border marriages and family relationships are breaking down cultural and ethnic specificity. More people identify with two or more countries. More people have debts and allegiances in two or more countries. Partly as consequence, although partly as cause, companies, countries and administrative organisations of many kinds are becoming more multinational, and the biggest of them have been growing fast and are assuming exceptional power.

The acceleration of structural changes of a global kind has become hard to monitor and absorb – as much by scientists and politicians as by the general public. The 'catch-up' element of knowledge and personal disposition is a profound and very awkward feature of modern life.

Understanding Global Social Policy is one gallant and impressive attempt to readdress the stock assumptions of the great majority of people about the necessary scope of activity of professional social scientists. Those assumptions were, and unfortunately still are, predominantly governed by the boundaries of the nation state. In calling for a globalist analysis of social policy, Nicola Yeates and her team argue methodically for a revolution in the way we need to analyse and resolve social and economic problems.

One way into this revolution is via recognition of the power now exercised by global organisations like the international financial institutions and the transnational corporations, as well as by the groups of politically strong rich countries, like the G8 and the OECD. For example, the largest transnational corporations have far greater resources than most nation states and, in the phrase used on page 81 by Kevin Farnsworth, 'corporate-centred global social policy' now needs to be resolutely investigated and publicly assessed. Again, international financial institutions, such as the World Bank and the International Monetary Fund, exert huge power – as many of the chapters in this book show. Their policies are politically conditioned and are very influential.

However, these financial agencies, especially the World Bank and the International Monetary Fund, have not contributed as much to the diminution of the extreme poverty experienced by a billion and a half people as they would wish member governments of the UN to believe. The World Bank loans approximately $22 billion a year – $2.4 billion of which is estimated to be for social protection. However this sum is less than five hundredths of 1% of world gross domestic product (GDP), and is dwarfed by the sum spent internally every year by each rich country on social protection (or social security). Today public expenditure on social security (such as on child benefit, sickness and disability benefit and pensions for the elderly) amounts to 13.6% of GDP (2005) in the average OECD country compared with between 1.0% and 3.0% in most low-income countries, for example, 1.5% in India. Because the redistributive mechanisms of social security are not in place even for groups who cannot be expected to gain earnings through employment, there cannot be effective 'trickle-down' from economic growth.

The World Bank has set out for low-income countries a series of 'safety-net' anti-poverty programmes as one condition for agreeing loans for their economic development. In the 1980s it adopted policies which tended to override local initiatives and plans. Structural Adjustment Programmes (SAPs) were introduced and extended by the early 1990s to many countries including 40 of the 56 countries of Africa. The declared intention was to stabilise national economies and promote growth by freeing imports from tariffs, general deregulation, reduced public expenditure and privatisation. But serious criticisms led first to a Programme of Action to Mitigate the Social Cost of Adjustment (PAMSCAD) and in successive years to variations in the nominal anti-poverty programmes such as the Poverty Reduction Strategy Programme (PRSP) and the Social Fund.

Many observers have come to believe that the World Bank's frequent replacement of anti-poverty programmes has been to give the impression of major change and correction when little has in fact changed in the real meaning and content of those programmes. The succession of differently described programmes has amounted to very little alteration in the strategy directed towards the entrenchment of free market policies, with small redistribution of resources being allowed to, or within, the low-income countries, and conditional loans being balanced by rates of repayable interest that largely reverse the flow of aid. This example of global social policy has led to cutbacks in domestic social investment, the privatisation of social programmes and the abandonment of social planning.

This is just one example of global social policy overtaking national social policy. But it helps to suggest why global policy analysis must now attract the predominant part of academic analysis of economic and social structural change.

I happen to believe that sooner or later economists will be obliged to return to renewed appreciation of Keynes' criticisms of the economic policies of the depression years of the 1930s and of his formulation of the proposals for post-war recovery and the Bretton Woods institutions. He had a vision of economic and social justice that is of lasting practical value. Today that means investigating and analysing the declared, but also implicit, international social policies being followed by the international financial institution's and the transnational corporation's and constructing global alternatives. It means building organisations to collect international tax, and to establish a successor international welfare state that insists on automatic cross-national subsidies for basic social services and social security in all the present low-income countries and regions. This is very different from current preoccupations with corporate self-regulation and the UN's Global Compact, and can develop Joseph Stiglitz's ironic witness of the 'revolving door' relationship between business and the World Bank.

Economists will be obliged to return to Keynes because of the inherent need to democratically control global market developments and restore marked redistribution of wealth and income, so as to redress poverty and ensure the survival and health of the world's populations. They will also be obliged to return to Keynes because in wrestling with deeper inequalities they will have to deal with the accompanying crises of war and civil conflict, shortages of oil and water and growing concern about global environmental damage, which are beyond the capacities of the global market either to control or understand.

Throughout history different ideas – usually captured in a phrase or a single word – have been seized to characterise the nature of economic and social changes being experienced at the time. Globalisation has become of common concern today, like centralisation and urbanisation a hundred years ago. But it has also become the fundamental contradiction of the early 21st century – carrying mixed messages both of hope and destruction. Most people, including social scientists and politicians, invest in the golden promise of change rather than in the mixed reality of that change when belatedly discovered. They are slow to anticipate in any detail the accompanying structural changes and especially the harm that may be wrought. It is the potential harm and not only the benefits to peoples and individuals of global social and economic policy that needs now to be brought more regularly into the frame of attention.

Understanding Global Social Policy is of the first importance in setting out what global policy analysis entails and how the structural changes determining the conditions under which the world's population now live can be addressed.

Acknowledgements

I am first and foremost grateful to all of the authors of this book for willingly agreeing to make room in their busy schedules to contribute a chapter, for not baulking – too much – at my various editorial interventions and requests, and for responding promptly to meet our deadlines. Thanks to you all.

I would also like to acknowledge various other people without whose support this book would not have seen the light of day. The idea for the book was prompted by the lack of a student text on global social policy, and I was encouraged (indeed, challenged) by Saul Becker to put one together for the Understanding Welfare series. I also have the anonymous reviewers to thank, whose thorough and critically constructive comments on the shape of the book overall and the draft chapters were much appreciated. Staff at The Policy Press – Leila Ebrahimi, Laura Greaves, Jessica Hughes, Jacqueline Lawless, Alison Shaw and Emily Watt – as ever displayed a wonderful combination of encouragement, practical support, flexibility and efficiency throughout the production process. Thanks also to Hilary Brown for editing the book, Alison Farrell for proofreading it and Caroline Wilding for the index. The study leave facilities of the Open University were important in enabling me to progress this book, and I owe thanks to my colleagues in particular – Ross Fergusson, Mary Langan, Esther Saraga and Mike Saward – who showed both an interest in, and enthusiasm for, the book. Finally, thanks to Tomás Mac Sheoin for helping out in putting the final touches to the glossary.

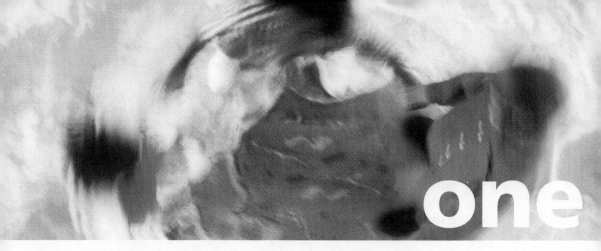

The idea of global social policy

Nicola Yeates

Overview

This chapter introduces global social policy as a field of academic study and as a political practice. It contrasts different approaches to the study of social policy in a global context, setting out the essence of globalist approaches to social policy that lie at the heart of this book. The chapter goes on to discuss different perspectives within the field of global social policy itself and emphasises the importance of historicising global social policy and attending to the different ways in which global policy plays out across the world. Finally, the chapter reviews key themes and debates within the field of global social policy and points to how these are taken up in the ensuing chapters. It then provides a brief guide to using this book, ending with a summary of the key points covered in the chapter. Some questions for discussion and some suggestions about how to keep up to date with developments in the field are also included.

Key concepts

Global social policy; globalisation; methodological transnationalism; methodological nationalism

The global turn in social science

The 'global turn' in social science poses fundamental challenges to the idea that the social world, institutions, policies and experiences can be understood exclusively in terms of what happens 'inside' the borders of particular countries. Global approaches prise open the core tenets and premises of **methodological transnationalism** that have had such an enduring influence on social science, setting out an alternative methodology to the study of processes of social change and development. Methodological transnationalism starts from different underlying assumptions and premises from the **methodological nationalism** that has long prevailed in social sciences generally including in social policy (***Box 1.1***).

> **Box 1.1:** Contrasting approaches in social science
>
> Methodological nationalism – emphasises the institutions, links, activities and social processes occurring within countries.
>
> Methodological transnationalism – emphasises the institutions, links, activities and processes cutting across countries.

Methodological transnationalism rejects the conflation of the nation state and society that characterises much of social science. This approach emphasises that society and social life operate across varied spaces and scales, of which the nation state is just one. It focuses on interactions, processes and institutions – be they 'from above' or 'from below', institutionalised or non-institutionalised, formal or informal – that transcend nation states and the formal (governmental) relations between them.

In emphasising the existence of social phenomena that transcend nation states and the variety of socio-geographic spaces and scales other than the national political unit, methodological transnationalism has opened up alternative ways of studying society and its key institutions. Indeed, this approach has proved a productive lens through which a range of contemporary phenomena have been explored: from the border-spanning flows of capital, goods, services, people and ideas, to social formations that channel these flows and interactions, links and ties connecting people and places in more than one country, to modes of consciousness that reconstruct a sense of place and locality and give rise to the experience of the world as a single, shared place. In inviting us to question and rethink the ontological foundations of social science, methodological transnationalism fundamentally reframes understandings of the contemporary world away from one made up of a multitude of bounded national social systems and towards a global social system that links populations and places in different parts of the world and comprises various global and sub-global hierarchies and networks of border-spanning connections, interactions and effects.

Globalisation studies is perhaps the clearest expression of a global approach to social science. While there is a great deal of controversy over the concept of **globalisation** and its onset, causes, effects and universal applicability (for further discussion of this see Yeates, 2001; 2007), at its core is an emphasis on the ways in which the conditions of human existence are characterised by dense, extensive networks of interconnections and interdependencies that routinely transcend national borders. These networks and links take a range of forms: flows of capital, goods, services and people; the global integration of business activities; flows of images, ideas, information and values through media and communications; the worldwide spread of ideologies such as consumerism and individualism; international movements of people (for leisure and work). They also take the form of 'new' collective responses, expressed in political cooperation and action across borders, as in the emergence of global political movements directing their action at multilateral organisations in an attempt to shape how territories and populations are governed. Not only is this interconnectedness said to be more extensive in scope than in previous historical periods, but the interconnections are also said to be more intensive and the speed at which such interactions occur increasing (***Box 1.2***). Globalisation is, then, characterised by an increasing *enmeshment* of the lives of people and places around the world, expressed in ways that appear to 'bring together' geographically distant places and peoples around the world.

Box 1.2: Dimensions of enmeshment

Extensity – the degree to which cultural, political, social and economic activities are 'stretching' across national borders to encompass the world.

Intensity – changes in magnitude and regularity of interconnectedness.

Velocity – changes in the speed of global interactions and processes.

Source: Held et al (1999)

There is now a large literature that outlines and debates the varied social, economic, political and cultural dimensions and consequences of globalisation processes. One of the main consequences emphasised is how events happening in one part of the world are able to quickly produce effects in other parts of it. New technologies are significant in these developments: advances in travel technologies make it easier and quicker to get to far-flung corners of the world, while communications technologies enable geographically distant people to keep in close, frequent contact. Technology enables the transmission of information around the world within seconds, with the result that what seem to be 'local' events can soon have worldwide impacts. For example, currency fluctuations in one economy reverberate around the world within the context of global financial markets based on open trading. As the Asian financial crisis of 1997 proved, currency markets soon have an impact on the 'real' economy, jeopardising millions of people's jobs and incomes worldwide. The 'sub-prime' mortgages fiasco in the US in 2007 also reverberated in particular ways in the housing and financial markets of a range of countries worldwide, including the UK, assisted by communications technologies on which global financial and information systems are premised. Acknowledging the significance of technologies in globalisation processes is not the same as assigning them a determining role, since political, economic, social and cultural contexts mediate their use and effects. However, technological advances are clearly a major factor in increasing knowledge of events and conditions around the world, and in shaping sense of the world as an enmeshed, shared place – a so-called 'global village'. Of course, it would be incorrect to argue that this heightened knowledge applies to everyone everywhere, but there is a growing awareness of how human activity, events and risks 'there' have impacts on us 'here' in tangible and significant ways.

Globalisation studies is often criticised for its inattention to history, both in terms of overemphasising the newness of the phenomena that it claims are qualitatively different from previous periods, and the extent to which it purports to break from academic traditions in ways of understanding the world. In fact, globalisation studies builds on existing traditions of thought that understand the world as a single global system. For example, the development of ecology as a science since the 1950s has seen ecological processes as planetary in scale, with changes in ecological conditions in one part of the planet affecting other parts of it. Here, the impact of human activity on ecological systems was also seen to have a planetary impact, in that toxic chemicals and pollution released in one locality are transported to and have 'impacts on' other proximate and distant parts of the world. Branches of sociology, too, integrated a global perspective into their analyses long before 'globalisation' in the 1990s was invented. In the 1960s world-systems and dependency theories, for example, were mapping the global systems and mechanisms of unequal exchange that tie the social fates and fortunes of populations in very different parts of the world (Wallerstein, 1979). In contrast to globalisation studies, with its emphasis on changes affecting certain western countries and populations over the past half century, world-systems theory dates the existence of these global social systems back several hundred years.

A further body of thought that invokes methodological transnationalism is transnational studies. Transnationalists focus on cross-border processes and connections by state and non-state actors, conceptualising these actors as transnational entities. While transnationalists and globalists share a common interest in actors, entities and processes that transcend the nation state, transnationalists do not necessarily adhere to the globalisation concept or its various theoretical claims. They also tend to focus on the actual transactions involved in transnational processes and assign a greater role to issues of agency power. They distinguish themselves from globalists in the following way:

> ... 'globalist' scholarship is far too often not fine-tuned enough to capture cross-border agents, structures and interactions at different scales, ranging scopes, varying units and multiple levels that are not worldwide, global or transplanetary.... Furthermore, agents are often understood to be either so heavily constrained that acting against universalistic systemic forces is under-theorised, or are so heavily constituted that they are just enacting scripts, or are just plain 'institutionalised others'. (Khagram and Levitt, 2005, p 8)

Various types of transnational entity have been identified along with the predominant or central motivation (*Table 1.1*), while Vertovec (1999) usefully isolated six conceptual premises underlying the use of transnationalism, along with their main elements and examples (*Table 1.2*).

Transnational entities and dynamics have been invoked in a wide range of studies – of communities, capital flows, citizenship, corporations, intergovernmental agencies, non-governmental organisations, trade, political activism, services, social movements, social networks, families, migration circuits, identities, public spaces and public cultures (Vertovec, 1999). These studies highlight that no new claims can be made for the existence of transnationalism: people, ideas, symbols, capital, goods and services have routinely 'travelled' across the borders of nation states, facilitated by developments in communications and travel technologies and channelled by globe-spanning institutions and networks. Furthermore, transnational activities, interactions and ties are expressed in multiple ways across socio-cultural, economic and political arenas; they affect everyday lives, impact on individual and collective subjectivities, shape major

Table 1.1: Typology of transnational entities

Type	Definition	Motivation	Examples
Epistemic communities	Experts in different countries linked through the production and dissemination of knowledge	Scientific ideas	Think tanks, international consultancy firms, research institutes
Transnational advocacy networks, transnational social movements	Individuals in different countries linked through a common concern	Moral ideas	Labour, human rights, gender justice, nuclear disarmament
Transnational corporations	Economic entities in different countries linked through the pursuit of economic gain	Profit	Nike (footwear), Shell (oil), Ford (automobiles), Fyffes (bananas)
Transnational criminal networks			Trafficking and smuggling of humans and commodities such as drugs, tobacco
Transnational professions	Professionals in different countries linked through knowledge and expertise that is not owned by any single society	Technical expertise	Medicine, nursing, accountancy, law, engineering
Transnational governmental networks	Governmental actors in different countries linked through a common issue or concern	Common public mandates	G8, G77, G20; networks of ministers of social development, trade, finance and so on

Source: Adapted from Khagram and Levitt (2005)

social institutions and influence social outcomes in ways that, although not always immediately perceptible, are nevertheless significant. In highlighting the multiple and diverse ways in which activities, links and ties of a wide range of social actors transcend nation states, transnationalists emphasise that such processes are integral, not incidental, to contemporary social organisation and lived experience. Transnational processes cannot be relegated to the status of non-permanent 'external' shocks or intervening variables in an otherwise 'national' frame of reference: they are woven into the social fabric itself.

A turn towards the transnational, then, entails the injection of additional geographical frames of reference into social (policy) analysis, since it draws attention to the different spatial dimensions of social, political, economic and cultural structures and flows – the ways in which 'social spaces could extend over more than one of the coherent geographic container spaces of different national societies' (Pries, 2001, p 3) and the ways in which organisational

Table 1.2: *Conceptual premises of transnationalism*

Transnationalism as ...	Main elements and examples
Social morphology	Social formations spanning borders (for example, ethnic diasporas and networks)
Type of consciousness	Identity, memory, awareness; dual/multiple identifications and awareness of multi-locality
Mode of cultural reproduction	Fluidity of constructed styles, social institutions and everyday practices, often channelled through global media and communications (creolisation, hybridity, cultural translation as seen in fashion, music and film)
Avenue of capital	Networks that create the paths along which transnational activities flow (transnational corporations, transnational capitalist class, migrant remittances)
Site of political engagement	Global public spaces and fora (international non-governmental organisations, transnational social movement organisations, ethnic diasporas and transnational communities)
Reconstruction of 'place' or locality	Social fields that connect and position some actors in more than one country; creation of translocal understandings – 'translocalities' – and transnational social spaces

Source: Vertovec (1999, p 447)

structures (networks, fora, institutions) and social subjectivities extend beyond the confines of the nation state.

Social policy responds

Methodological nationalism has had far-reaching and enduring consequences for the way that social policy is studied; indeed, it has framed and defined the development of the discipline since the outset. Welfare states have been studied as national phenomena, the result of coalitions and compromises among different domestic actors. Cross-national comparative analyses have built on this premise, treating each country's welfare system as a self-contained unit to be compared and contrasted against other such 'units'. Histories of welfare state development have similarly tended to focus on the domestic actors, institutions and contexts shaping the development of national welfare states as a whole or particular sectors thereof (health, housing, **social protection** and so on) over time. While not denying the importance of 'domestic' contexts and the balance of power between different actors and interests, such approaches pay little attention to the global context and transnational processes affecting the emergence and development of social policies or to the forms of social welfare financing, regulation and provision that transcend the nation state. Thus, such narratives typically overlook the ways in which governments are directly and indirectly influenced by international norms and laws, ideas and ideologies. They overlook the ways in which non-governmental organisations, whether for profit or not for profit, have long acted in coalition with overseas equivalents, or how non-governmental organisations (NGOs) take part in policy-making processes in international fora in order to lever reforms at home or abroad. These narratives overlook the ways in which European states have constructed welfare states for resident nationals, while simultaneously pursuing policies that have impeded the development of welfare provision in 'developing' countries and colonies.

In response to the global turn in social science, social policy has begun to examine the ways in which policy processes and outcomes are shaped by transnational and globalisation processes. This has given rise to an expansive and expanding literature on the impacts of globalisation(s) on welfare states and social policy formation. There is a growing debate about the extent to which globalisation processes are implicated in changes to the aims, characteristics and outcomes of welfare states and social policies. This literature emphasises a wide range of possible effects of globalisation processes (***Box 1.3***), from the demise of welfare states due to the spread of neoliberalism to their resilience due to institutional and political resistance against neoliberal policies; from an emphasis on probable convergence to an emphasis on continued actual divergence across welfare states (see Yeates, 2007 for an extended discussion).

Box 1.3: Some possible effects of globalisation on social policy

- Sets welfare states in competition with each other. This is said to threaten comprehensive systems of public service provision where they exist or stall their future development where they do not. Among the anticipated effects are:
  - lowering of social and labour standards;
  - privatisation of public services;
  - creation of global health and welfare markets;
  - growing reliance on voluntary and informal provision.
- Raises the issues with which social policy is concerned to the level of supranational institutions, agencies and fora, both world-regional (for example, the European Union (EU)) and global (**World Bank** (WB) and so on).
- Brings new players into the making of social policy (for example, Bretton Woods institutions; various United Nations (UN) agencies; development banks; international commercial, voluntary and philanthropic organisations).
- Generates 'new' political coalitions within and between countries (regionally and globally) concerned with social policy reform.
- Creates new/additional social risks and opportunities for individuals, households, workers and communities.

Source: Yeates (2007)

This body of literature is highlighting the need to fundamentally rethink the conditions and processes of social policy formation, as well as core social policy concepts and the ways social policy concerns are framed. For example, a global(isation) perspective questions the very idea of a 'national' welfare state. It challenges the idea that the forces shaping the social organisation of welfare services are uniquely or primarily local and national ones, and that the entities involved in formulating and implementing social policy operate purely on a national basis. It also challenges the assumption that social policy exists within a contained national space, impermeable to wider geo-political and social systems in which it is embedded, untouched by developments and events elsewhere in the world or unaffected by the policies and actions of **international governmental organisations, international non-governmental organisations, global social movements** and **transnational advocacy campaigns**. A globalisation perspective is also 'stretching' the scope of scholarly enquiry to recognise the variety of welfare arrangements that exist worldwide together with the ways in which 'national' systems are interconnected. It is also challenging the rethinking of constructs, such as the welfare mix, social equity, justice, citizenship and altruism that were originally developed within the methodological nationalist tradition.

Social policy analysis has responded to the challenge of 'the global' in the following three ways:

1. Extending studies of national social policy to a wider range of countries worldwide than those traditionally the object of analysis. In this sense, 'global' is little more than a synonym for extended internationalism. It is *internationalist* because the methodological stance still analyses social policies and welfare arrangements as national phenomena. This internationalism is *extended* because the investigative gaze extends beyond the usual 'developed' countries (those belonging to the Organisation for Economic Co-operation and Development (OECD)) to examine 'developing' low- and middle-income countries. In this usage, it does not signal any engagement with the methodological tenets of global(isation) studies or transnationalism and is a thoroughly misleading use of the term 'global'. Examples of this usage are *Handbook of Global Social Policy* (Nagel, 2000), and the Center for Law and Social Policy (CLASP) global social policy programme (www.clasp.org/publications.php?id=38), both of which examine varieties of national social policy without reference to the broader global processes in which these policies and systems are embroiled.

2. Analysing social policy formation in cross-border and multilateral spheres of governance. These spheres of governance may be world-regional (EU, SADC, ASEAN, Mercosur) trans-regional (ASEM) or global (WB, UN, **International Monetary Fund** (IMF) and so on). In practice, the focus of analysis often falls on intergovernmental fora, since these are the clearest institutional expression of a transnational social policy, but it also embraces non-governmental fora such as the World Social Forum (WSF) or the World Economic Forum (WEF).

3. Focusing on cross-border flows of people, goods, services, ideas, finance as they relate to the provision, finance and regulation of social welfare, social policy making and governance processes and the impacts of social policies on human welfare.

Both of these latter two approaches are consistent with methodological transnationalism and are therefore rightfully included within **global social policy** (*Box 1.4*). In the following section we take a look at these in more detail, tracing how definitions of global social policy have developed over the past decade.

Box 1.4: Global social policy

- Examines how social policy issues are increasingly being perceived to be global in scope, cause and impact.
- Examines how cross-border flows of people, goods, services, ideas and finance relate to social policy development.
- Examines the emergence of transnational forms of collective action, including the development of multilateral and cross-border modes of governance.
- Examines how these modes of governance and policy making shape the development and impacts of social policy around the world.

The development of definitions of global social policy

Over the past decade, the definition of the scope of global social policy has developed in substantial ways. Initially focusing on the practices of an elite set of institutions and policy actors and the ways they impact on national ones, it has come to embrace a more embedded notion of transnationalism to include a wider range of global social policy dialogues taking place around the world in national, sub-national and transnational fora.

Global social policy as a practice of elite global institutions and actors

The emergence of global social policy as an identifiable field of academic study and research is commonly dated back to the work of Bob Deacon and colleagues (1997, p 195). They defined global social policy as:

> a practice of supranational actors [which] embodies global social redistribution, global social regulation, and global social provision and/or empowerment, and ... the ways in which supranational organisations shape national social policy.

The focus of this definition lay with intergovernmental institutions such as the WB, IMF and UN, international non-state actors such as Oxfam working around social development issues and consultancy companies providing policy and technical advice. This definition has proved productive, introducing an innovative approach to the analysis of welfare state restructuring and social policy reform. The work was informed by the authors' study of changes to the welfare systems in central and eastern Europe, where a range of international actors were vying to influence the direction of national policy reforms. It successfully drew attention to a highly active set of political forces and policy actors that had either been omitted from explanations of national policy change or relegated to the status of 'context'. In focusing on these supranational global agencies, Deacon and his colleagues' work effectively demonstrated how the battle over ideas and policy was being waged at the global level and how national political and policy actors were faced with competing policy reform prescriptions (Yeates, 2008).

Although this work was innovative in the social policy context, it resonated with other literatures that were also emphasising the ways in which decisions made in transnational (global or world-regional) institutions were shaping domestic policy reforms. The notion of multi-level governance was, for example, being used in the EU context to show how although relatively few powers were transferred to supranational institutions in the social policy domain, processes of European integration were having a tangible effect on the shape of social policy development across EU member states.

Hierarchies are implicit in this vocabulary of level and tier – with supranational entities placed at the top of the hierarchy and city authorities at the bottom, with power and authority travelling 'downwards'. Recent work has, however, since come to emphasise how these different levels are parts of an overall system in which all parts affect each other, with influence 'travelling' multi-directionally rather than just from the top down. It is therefore as appropriate to ask questions about the ways in, and extent to, which actors located in domestic arenas influence the formation of supranational policy as it is to ask questions about the ways in which supranational agencies and actors shape the course of national social policy (Yeates, 2007).

Deacon et al's definition, and the work that built up around it subsequently in the Finnish-funded Globalism and Social Policy Programme (GASPP), had a strongly normative – indeed political – inflection to it, in the sense that the authors were not only trying to assess the extent to which global social policy could be said to actually exist but also identify the kinds of reforms that would be needed to ensure that social democratic principles were embodied in international governmental organisation (IGO) policies. Thus, for Deacon and his colleagues in GASPP, global social policy is not only about analysing the extent to which global social democracy exists – as 'measured' by the extent to which global social redistribution, global social regulation and global social rights are promoted by IOs – but also about the kinds of reforms needed to achieve it.

Global social policy embraces a wider range of global social policy dialogues

In an article published in 1999, I drew attention to the narrow focus on institutional and policy elites in the Deacon et al/GASPP approach to global social policy, arguing that the political forces involved in global social policy formation and the arenas through which it was being played out were wider than those being focused on at the time. I argued that the scope of global social policy analysis therefore needed to be broadened to include the range of social dialogues taking place outside the boardrooms and bureaux of international governmental organisations (IGOs). This wider definition included the activities of non-elites in global social politics and policy making, notably social movement and non-governmental organisations operating in the numerous shadow congresses and social fora that accompany international governmental meetings. It also opened up the possibility of including NGO campaigns against (for example) local branches of multinational corporations as a site of global social governance. This analysis drew attention to the ways in which global social governance was not only multi-tiered, as in the institutionalist approach to global social policy, but also multi-sphered in the sense that it encompassed the wider social regulation of economic and political globalisation processes themselves – the activities of corporations and institutionalised political and bureaucratic elites. This work (developed in Yeates, 2001) located the emergence of global social policy within increased social and political conflict worldwide that has accompanied contemporary globalisation processes. Extending this focus on a broader range of sites of global social policy and governance, Mitchell Orenstein (2005) defined global policies as 'those that are developed, diffused and implemented with the direct involvement of global policy actors and coalitions at or across the international, national or local levels of governance' (2005, p 177). Thus, social policies enacted nationally and sub-nationally may also be considered 'global' to the extent that they are codetermined by global policy actors and are transnational in scope (2005, pp 177-8).

Both these works connect with literatures that reject conceptualisations of 'the global' as something 'out there', 'above' the state or society, or something that is done to 'us' by 'them'. Moreover, they are consistent with literatures that emphasise the ways in which the global is 'in here', 'within' the nation state and something that involves 'us'. This embedded transnationalism does not draw a strict demarcation between the national (that is, internal) sphere from the transnational or global (that is, external) one, and is informed by a recognition of the existence of transnational spaces within nation states and the playing out of transnational processes within national territories as well as across them. As the extract in **Box 1.5** suggests, transnationalism can be found in 'national' identities, social institutions, economic interactions and political processes as well as in the more visible border-spanning structures and 'high-level' fora and processes.

> ### Box 1.5: Embedded transnationalism
>
> There are forms and fractions of capital that are already (or wish to be) international or transnational within the 'national' space of nation states. There are political blocs and projects that propound the necessity or desirability of becoming 'global' within the 'national' political formation. Similarly, there are 'national' citizens who actively seek aspects of international, transnational and global politics and culture ... and there are transnational citizens who seek to locate themselves in more than one national space. (Clarke, 2005, p 409)

This embedded transnationalism is emphasised in global social policy in its inclusion of the 'globalising' strategies of a wide range of social policy actors, whether they be firms and business executives (planning efficiency reforms involving the shedding of staff and relocation of production to another country or sub-contracting production to other firms), trade unions (protesting about the offshoring of jobs overseas), consumer movements (initiating campaigns against child labour used in the production of commodities or price fixing by cartels) or households (recruiting mothers from poorer countries to provide social care for their children or elderly parents, or sending a member of the family to work overseas). This attention to bottom-up processes involved in the globalisation of social policy effectively brings to the fore the ways that social relations of power and authority, of connectedness and responsibility, are structured across distant and proximate geographies. These global actors are as much part of global social policy and governance as political, bureaucratic and economic elites operating within cross-border, high-level institutions of global governance.

Global social policy analysis has come to embrace a variety of sites, spheres and scales of socio-political collective action to influence social policy. While a core focus on IGOs remains, there is increasing focus on the *multiple socio-spatial sites and scales* across which social policy formation occurs, the wider range of global policy actors and the 'everyday' transnationalisations of social welfare provision and policy making. This attention to a wider range of transnational entities and relations involved in social policy making has brought a welcome focus on the role of sub-global formations such as regional groupings of countries (ASEAN, Mercosur), the role of non-elite transnational policy actors and their campaigning networks and a wide range of ways in which social regulation, financing and provision take place across borders. Overall, global social policy has broadened and invigorated the study of social policy itself and has undergone substantial developments itself, bringing in a new range of concerns and a new set of theoretical, conceptual and methodological approaches to understanding social policy and welfare provision.

Rethinking theory and concepts

We have so far looked at how a global perspective 'stretches' the scope of social policy analysis to embrace additional sites and scales of policy formation and welfare provision and recognise the de facto interconnectedness of peoples, social institutions and places around the world. We now turn to consider what effect it has on existing theoretical and conceptual constructs.

By way of a preface, it is important to note that, in many regards, academic work has barely begun on 'globalising' the bodies of sociological, political, philosophical and economic theory. These disciplines are all strongly rooted in methodological nationalism, although there are, of course, discernable elements within them that have globalist sensibilities. Sociology, for example, has world-systems theory to call on, while political science has developed useful theoretical positions on global governance. However, these remain to be applied to global social policy formation. Moreover, there is no theory or set of theories of global social policy formation in the same way as there is for national social policy, such as functionalist or conflict theories. This is not to say that these are not possible, only that the theoretical basis remains less developed in global social policy. For this reason, some would argue that global social policy is 'atheoretical'. To be fair to global social policy, this is also a criticism levelled at globalisation studies and even social policy itself on occasion. This absence of a unified theory does not mean, however, that global social policy has no theoretical underpinnings or that theoretical claims are not possible. Indeed, there is a range of implicit and explicit theoretical frameworks deployed in global social policy research, as the ensuing chapters make clear, and work on this area is in progress.

It is perhaps in the realm of concepts that progress has been more visible (***Box 1.6***). This reconceptualisation has not meant jettisoning existing concepts and replacing them with new ones. Instead, existing concepts have been adapted, expanded and refashioned. In some cases, this has involved a quite fundamental rethink of concepts such as citizenship, justice, efficiency and altruism to see how they might be globalised. In other cases, it has been a relatively easy task to globalise concepts. ***Table 1.3*** provides an illustration of how one central social policy concept, the welfare mix (or mixed economy of welfare), might be adapted for our purposes.

Box 1.6: Globalising social policy concepts

The classical concerns of social policy analysts with social needs and social citizenship rights becomes [sic] in a globalized context the quest for supranational citizenship. The classical concern with equality, rights and justice between individuals becomes the quest for justice between states. The dilemma about efficiency, effectiveness and choice becomes a discussion about how far to socially regulate free trade. The social policy preoccupation with altruism, reciprocity and the extent of social obligations are put to the test in the global context. To what extent are social obligations to the other transnational? (Deacon et al, 1997, p 195)

Table 1.3: *The extended welfare mix*

	Domestic	Global
State	National government, regional government, local authorities, town/city councils	International governmental organisations, regional formations; national donors
Market	Domestic markets; local/national firms	Global markets; transnational corporations
Intermediate	National service NGOs, consultancy companies	International non-governmental organisations (charitable and philanthropic bodies); international consultancy companies
Community	Local social movements, neighbourhood associations	Global social movements, diasporic communities
Household	Household strategies	Transnational household survival strategies, international migration

Source: Yeates (2007)

The importance of contextualisation: history and place

Before moving on to an outline of the aims, structure and context of this book, we take a look at the place of history and place in global social policy. One of the criticisms of globalisation studies is its 'presentism', in that it tends to portray contemporary arrangements and conditions as qualitatively different from those that existed in the near past. Global social policy can also be criticised on these grounds: with the emphasis on contemporary institutions there comes the possibility of exaggerating breaks with the past. Moreover, it is reasonable to argue that it has never been appropriate to think of welfare states and social policies as first and foremost the outcomes of national ideas and forces or divorced from geo-politics.

For example, during the 19th and 20th centuries, the forces behind welfare state building and the social regulation of capitalism operated within a world order characterised by extensive international trade and migration, transnational corporations and developed international monetary and exchange rate regimes. While much recent commentary focuses on contemporary transnational political mobilisation in the 'anti-globalisation movement', there are, in fact, examples of political mobilisation dating back two centuries that were international and extended beyond Europe. Two such examples are the Anti-Slave Trade Movement (1787-1807) and the Movement Against Congo Colonisation (1890-1910). Thus, international cooperation and action on social policy issues long predate the recent concern with globalisation. International NGOs resulting from private initiatives can be traced back to 1863 when the precursor to the Red Cross, the International Committee for the Relief of the Military Wounded, was founded. This led to the signature in 1864 of the Geneva Convention for the Amelioration of the Wounded in Armies in the Field, which is recognised as the beginning of international humanitarian law (Yeates, 2007).

Colonialism (and slavery) provides another example of the way in which social policy is best understood in global and historical terms. The accumulation of wealth that underpinned the development of the British welfare state, for example, is an example of global social policy. The historical development of the British welfare state is intricately tied up with Britain's status as a colonial power: labour from its various colonies – Ireland, Australia, Canada, India, Hong Kong and many African countries – sustained its economic foundations, constituted a destination to which criminal classes and other 'social deviants' could be exported, and formed a labour pool from which Britain drew extensively to staff its welfare services. In turn, these countries' colonial histories influenced the development of their social policies, as Britain 'exported' welfare ideologies and systems (the legacy of which these countries still bear today), influenced their social and political structures and, together with local elites, subsumed their economic development to British interests – often with disastrous results for the welfare of the colonised countries' populations and those countries' socioeconomic development more widely (Yeates, 2007).

This need to historicise global social policy is matched by a need to 'geographise' it. The recognition of political and economic geography is central to a sense of place in global social policy analysis. Countries and regions have varied histories, traditions, systems and circumstances, varying in terms of the nature and strength of ideologies, cultural and religious values and traditions, social, religious, political and environmental movements, the strength and balance of political power between political parties, and between labour, civil associations and capital, and the political compromises between them. All of these factors shape global social policy formation and its impact on them. The experiences of, for example, African countries differ from those in East Asia, which differ again from those in Central America. Many African countries, for example, have experienced the effects of global actors in very particular ways, either being ignored by the globalising strategies of corporations or being the subject of intense scrutiny and coercive policy prescriptions by international financial institutions (IFIs). These geographical variations help explain both why it is, for example, that some countries are more embracing of neoliberal ideas and policies than others, and why it is that some countries appear to have successfully resisted them – why it is essentially that some countries, whether acting unilaterally or collectively, have been able to follow alternative strategies to those prescribed by Bretton Woods institutions and Northern governments. What we see, then, is global social policies playing out in very different ways across different countries and regions of the world. This recognition of place is necessary to avoid the inappropriate universalising tendencies some claim to see in global social policy.

The aims and structure of this book

Having set out some of the key constituents of global social policy, what do students and scholars of global social policy actually focus on? The answer to this question is defined by the definition of global social policy set out in this chapter (see page 11 and *Box 1.4*) as well as in the content of this book. The 10 remaining substantive chapters emphasise the transnational dimensions of social policy formation, identifying key issues and debates across a range of areas within global social policy. We do not claim to have exhausted the full range of all possible subjects and perspectives within global social policy, but what we provide is a comprehensive and accessible collection of research-based chapters exploring in some depth major areas, issues, debates and themes in contemporary global social policy studies.

In Chapter Two, Bob Deacon approaches global social policy from the perspective of governance. Beginning with a review of concepts that help us comprehend the complexity of global social governance, Deacon then reviews the key international organisations involved – international financial institutions, UN bodies and many others. Having briefly outlined issues of global redistribution, social regulation and social rights, he reviews some recent proposals to reform global social governance. In Chapter Three, Rob Hulme and Moira Hulme review some key perspectives on how ideas and practices 'move' across the world and influence policy making. Drawing in particular on education policy, their focus on global policy transfer serves to illuminate the complex relationships between the different levels and scales at which policy formation occurs, showing how the use the concepts of 'travelling' and 'embedded' policy help us understand how policy is contested, interpreted and mediated.

In Chapter Four, Kevin Farnsworth turns looks at one particular influence on global social policy formation – that of business interests and organisations. He reports a variety of results of globalisation – increasing corporate power, including stronger business influence on policy formation combined with an increased awareness of corporate harm and social risks resulting from lack of global regulation of corporate activity – and concludes that global social policy as a political practice has shifted closer to the interests of business in recent years. In Chapter Five, Chris Holden looks at the interaction of international trade and welfare, providing a clear guide to the development of the world trading system and noting the key role the welfare state has played in allowing capitalist economies to adjust to global conditions, while protecting workers from the worst risks of the market and ensuring some redistribution. He concludes with a brief consideration of a major area that has occupied many global social policy analysts – the possible effects of international trade agreements on the provision of health, education and welfare services.

These chapters helpfully set out overarching themes and concerns within global social policy: the institutional architecture of global social policy; the ways in which ideas and policies travel around the world; the role of economic (business organisations and trade) interests in shaping social policy. The next part of the book turns to examine four social policy areas from a global perspective: labour and employment (Chapter Six); health (Chapter Seven); housing and urban development (Chapter Eight); and pensions (Chapter Nine). These chapters pick up on many of the different themes identified in the first five chapters.

In Chapter Six, Robert O'Brien notes that while labour policy has benefited from the existence of an IO dedicated to promoting key labour rights (the **International Labour Organization**) for the best part of a century, the majority of the world's working population does not enjoy adequate labour or social protection. He examines how a varied group of policy actors – states, IOs, transnational corporations and civic actors, including trade unions – have mobilised to address this global issue and influence global labour policy. The chapter teases out a number of issues in global labour policy, such as 'core' labour standards and corporate self-regulation, and ends with a critical consideration of a recent attempt to advance global labour policy – the UN Global Compact.

In Chapter Seven, Meri Koivusalo and Eeva Ollila consider what is perhaps one of the most visible areas of global social policy – health – where a set of commonly agreed commitments and a legal framework exist. They review the variety of actors aiming to influence the shape of global health policy – including the UN, IFIs and other IGOs as well as NGOs, business corporations and other private interests. They also examine developments and changes in global health policy, including three specific policy agendas – Health for All, health reform and access to pharmaceuticals – and end with a consideration of the priorities for global health governance.

In Chapter Eight, Sunil Kumar examines the role of global housing and urban policy, a relatively neglected area of global social policy so far. Kumar traces changes in this global policy arena over in the post-war period, looking at how policies have shifted from a model of state provision of housing to governments as enablers, from shelter to housing finance and finally to broader concerns about city development. He considers the rise of alliances of the poor and other non-state actors in housing policy and provision, including in partnerships with governments and IOs, but notes the limitations of these 'public–private' partnerships. Kumar concludes that the main challenges in this policy area are political ones and emphasises that issues of land tenure and land distribution need to be addressed in order to make serious headway into global problems of housing insecurity and shelter deprivation.

Mitchell Orenstein's study of global pensions policy in Chapter Nine shows how global policy actors have had an increasing influence on pension policy globally. He shows how, through a transnational campaign for new pension reforms, the WB has supplanted the ILO in global pensions policy. Orenstein's case study details the transfer or diffusion of these pension reforms to over 30 countries worldwide through indirect coercive and persuasive methods. Importantly, he shows that domestic actors can resist these reforms under certain circumstances. Despite these successful examples of resistance, Orenstein concludes that the new pensions reform trend will continue to influence pensions policy globally in the years ahead.

The final two chapters examine illustrate how new areas are being introduced into social policy as a result of the development of global social policy. In Chapter Ten, Nicola Yeates provides an overview of global migration trends and issues as it pertains to social policy and welfare. This focus brings in a new set of global actors that are often overlooked in the more institutionalised conceptions of global social policy – the **migrants** themselves and their households. She shows the connections between migration and social policy in two case studies, which examine **transnational social welfare** through migrants' long-distance care practices and the migration of care workers globally, relating them to concepts such as global social reproduction and cosmopolitan citizenship. The chapter also looks at different policy approaches of IOs in their attempts to protect the human rights of migrants while fostering development, and reviews some attempts to construct a more coherent global migration policy.

In Chapter Eleven, Sarah Sexton, Larry Lohmann and Nicholas Hildyard examine global population policy as one of the oldest forms of global social policy. They trace the changing concerns and manifestations of population policy over two centuries, examining Malthusian and neo-Malthusian ideas as essentially global ideas. From their origin in England, these ideas were quickly taken up in that country by elite groups and soon spread across the world aided by colonialist global political formations, facilitated in the 20th century by northern governments through their overseas development assistance as well as by IOs such as the WB and UN agencies. The authors also highlight the enduring influence of discourses of over-population and show how these are taken up in a wide range of policies ranging from crime control to the control of women's fertility to national security.

In Chapter Twelve, I conclude the volume by briefly reviewing the chapters in terms of the key themes of the book. All the chapters show how a variety of global policy actors, whether governmental or non-governmental, struggle to influence global social policy in different policy areas, arenas and fora. They show that the making of global social policy is a contested area that different interests attempt to manipulate for their own benefit – often with disastrous outcomes for the quality of life of the people whom social policy is ostensibly supposed to benefit. They also show the increasing – although not uncontested – influences of global policy debates and prescriptions on national policy making and reform. Finally, the volume addresses the more recent substantial focus on the 'bottom-up' globalisation processes – the transnational entities and interactions at the level of families, communities, social movements and NGOs – that complement the existing focus in global social policy on the top-down processes associated with intergovernmental fora and institutions.

Reading and using this book

This book is designed to be as accessible as possible for non-specialist readers looking for an informative way in to key approaches, debates and issues in global social policy, both as a field of academic study and a political practice. To this end, each of the chapters starts with a brief overview of its contents and ends with a summary of the key points covered. The chapters make good use of examples and case-study material from research, campaigns and policy and incorporate plenty of illustrative and visual material to aid understanding. At the end of each chapter you will find a list of questions for revision and/

or discussion that will help you to check your understanding of the chapter contents. Each chapter also suggests some activities to follow up your reading, together with some key resources for further reading and research on the particular topic. Global social policy, like many academic subjects, makes frequent use of abbreviations and acronyms and you will find a full list of those used in this volume at the front of the book. This field is also rife with specialist terms that can be a little off-putting, so a comprehensive glossary of all the key terms used in the book has been included (see the Appendix on p 291). Note that the terms in this glossary are highlighted in bold in each of the chapters the first time they are used. A comprehensive subject index has also been compiled to help you locate particular issues or topics.

Finally, the authors use varying terms to describe the divisions of the world – North and South; Global North, Global South; rich and poor; developed and developing; western and non-western; core and periphery. Each of these is associated with particular theoretical and political positions, but, in practice, usage of many of the terms are effectively synonymous. Accordingly, the Editor has not attempted to impose uniformity in this area.

Summary

- The global turn in social science opens up alternative ways of approaching social phenomena in general and social policy in particular. At the heart of this global turn is a methodological transnationalism that recognises the processes, ties and links between people, places and institutions that routinely cut across nation states.
- At the heart of global social policy as a subject of academic study is attention to transnational entities and processes involved in the provision, finance and regulation of social welfare and the making of social policy on a global scale.
- Global social policy is concerned with the competing interests and pressures on social policy formation and with the different applications and impacts of global ideas and policies on welfare systems and people around the world.
- The traditional emphasis on global institutions and actors such as IOs and global policy elites is now complemented by attention to 'bottom-up' social policy formation, involving diverse social actors operating across various spheres, at different levels and on a range of scales.
- The historicisation of global social policy highlights how earlier global formations were 'carriers' of social ideas, policies and practices centuries before the existence of present-day global organisations, as well as changes in the policy aims and prescriptions of these organisations in the more recent period.

Questions for discussion

- What is meant by methodological transnationalism, and what are its implications for the study of social policy?
- How does a globalist approach to social policy analysis differ from an internationalist approach?
- Why is it important to historicise and geographise global social policy?
- What are the implications of global social policy analysis for the study of social policy making and welfare formations?

Further reading and electronic sources

Keeping up to date with political and policy developments in any one country's social policies is a substantial task at the best of times. In some ways this is amplified in global social policy because of the scope of the subject, the breadth of issues covered and its relative lack of coverage in the mainstream media and academic journals. Happily, there is a range of materials available on global social policy in general and on specific issues and policies. As noted above, each of the chapters provides a list of further resources, including electronic sources, that will enable you to follow latest developments in particular areas. In addition to these, we recommend you regularly consult *Global Social Policy: Journal of Public Policy and Social Development* published by Sage Publications. This provides the best available source of up-to-date information for anyone seeking to keep abreast of academic and policy developments in global social policy. It has a range of full-length and shorter articles on various aspects of global social policy, as well as Reviews and Digest sections.

The Digest section of *Global Social Policy* provides a helpful summary of key policy developments, events and publications during the year, so is one of the best ways of keeping up-to-date with developments in the field. Global Social Policy Digest is organised around five main sections: (i) global social redistribution, regulation and rights, which takes a thematic perspective on developments in global social policy; (ii) developments in global social governance which covers issues of global institutional reform; (iii) sectoral policies, covering health, social protection, education, habitat, land and housing; (iv) trade and social policy; and (v) southern voices, which highlights the contributions and events organised by southern and pro-southern actors. Each section contains hyperlinks to relevant websites and documents. Digest can be accessed at http://gsp.sagepub.com or at your library, providing it has a subscription to *Global Social Policy*. Alternatively, a pre-publication version of Digest is available from http://gaspp.org or http://icsw.org.

References

Clarke, J. (2005) 'Welfare states as nation states: some conceptual reflections', *Social Policy and Society*, vol 4, no 4, pp 407-15.

Deacon, B. with Hulse, M. and Stubbs, P. (1997) *Global Social Policy: International Organisations and the Future of Welfare*, London: Sage Publications.

Held, D., McGrew, A., Goldblatt, D. and Perraton, J. (1999) *Global Transformations*, Cambridge: Polity Press.

Khagram, S. and Levitt, P. (2005) *Towards a Field of Transnational Studies and a Sociological Transnationalism Research Program*, Hauser Center for Non-Profit Organizations, Working Paper No 24, available at http://ssrn.com/abstract=556993.

Nagel, S. (2000) *Handbook of Global Social Policy*, London: Routledge.

Orenstein, M. (2005) 'The new pension reform as global policy', *Global Social Policy*, vol 5, no 2, pp 175-202.

Pries, L. (2001) 'The approach of transnational social spaces: responding to new configurations of the social and the spatial', in L. Pries (ed) *New Transnational Social Spaces: International Migration and Transnational Companies in the Early Twenty-first Century*, London: Routledge, pp 3-33.

Vertovec, S. (1999) 'Conceiving and researching transnationalism,' *Ethnic and Racial Studies*, vol 22, no 2, pp 447-62.

Wallerstein, I. (1979) *The Capitalist World-economy*, Cambridge: Cambridge University Press.

Yeates, N. (1999) 'Social politics and policy in an era of globalisation', *Social Policy and Administration*, vol 33, no 4, pp 372-93.

Yeates, N. (2001) *Globalization and Social Policy*, London: Sage Publications.

Yeates, N. (2007) 'Globalisation and social policy', in J. Baldock, N. Manning and S. Vickerstaff (eds) *Social Policy* (3rd edn), Oxford: Oxford University Press, pp 627-53.

Yeates, N. (2008) 'Supranational agencies and social policy', in P. Alcock, M. May and K. Rowlingson (eds) *The Student's Companion to Social Policy* (3rd edn), Oxford: Blackwell.

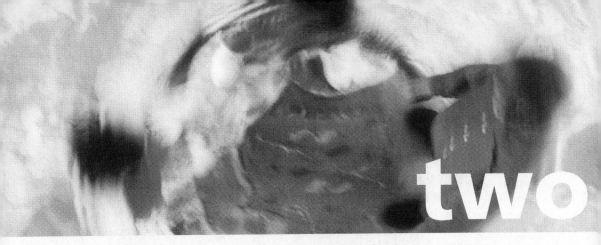

two

Global and regional social governance

Bob Deacon

Overview

This chapter approaches the subject of global social policy from the point of view of its governance. Governance is a concept that allows for the recognition that a range of different actors and organisations are involved in shaping, overseeing and implementing social policies. The chapter first introduces some key concepts that help us understand the complexity of the global social governance process. It then outlines the key international organisations involved in global social governance and reviews progress in the development of global social rights, redistribution and regulation. Finally, it reviews several suggestions about how the current system of global social governance might be reformed, attending to both global and world-regional structures.

Key concepts

Complex multilateralism; global policy advocacy coalitions; global public–private partnerships; politics of scale; regional social policy; global social governance; global redistribution; global social regulation; global social rights

Introduction

This chapter provides an account of the institutions and actors that are engaged in the process of governing global social policy. This process is referred to as **global social governance**: *global* because the policy issue we are addressing is worldwide in nature, involves transnational processes and cross-border fora (see Chapter One); *social* because we are concerned with health, social protection, education and other social welfare issues; and *governance* because there is no one locus of elected government power, rather a number of actors and agencies all contributing to a complex process of influence, decision making and administration. Before we examine those institutions and actors, the chapter first provides a guide to some concepts that help us understand the role of those organisations in the structures and processes of global social governance.

Conceptualising and understanding global social governance

At the outset, we have to point to the existence of the dispute within the international relations literature between those 'realists' who continue to insist that there is no such thing as *global* governance and 'cosmopolitans' (Held and McGrew, 2002), who argue that genuinely transnational policy processes now exist in an interconnected world. For 'realists', what exists in terms of international institutions such as the United Nations (UN) and World Bank (WB) are, precisely that – *inter*national institutions whose policies and programmes are shaped in the main by states. Cosmopolitans, on the other hand, argue that **international organisations** and other international actors have some autonomy from states and are engaged in a genuinely transnational policy-making process. A formulation that attempts to reconcile these two extremes is the concept of 'complex multilateralism' (O'Brien et al, 2000). This captures the extent to which states and inter-state bargaining exists alongside genuinely transnational policies and policy-making processes, whereby the professional staff and secretariats of international agencies dialogue with global social movements and **civil society organisations**.

In addition to states and formal international organisations, a whole host of other actors and players are engaged in shaping and administering global social policy. First, the influential part that **non-state international actors** are increasingly playing in world politics and global governance has been recognised by a number of international relations scholars. Josselin and Wallace (2001) usefully reviewed this literature in a volume that examined the part played by the global knowledge elite (international experts associated with global think tanks), transnational corporations, the Catholic Church, international trade unions, global diasporas and other trans-border actors in specific policy fields. This work reiterated the ways in which global social policy formation and governance occur outside the realm of international governmental organisations as well as within them (see Yeates, 1999, and Chapter One of this volume). Second, within this context have emerged a number of new **global public–private partnerships** engaged directly in the mechanisms of **global redistribution** and **global regulation**. The Global Fund to Fight AIDS, Tuberculosis and Malaria (the 'Global Fund'), for example, was established in 2002 as a public–private partnership with a secretariat housed in the **World Health Organization** (WHO) but with the WB managing the funds as a trustee. Income is derived from donor governments and philanthropic organisations such as the Bill & Melinda Gates Foundation.

At the global level, therefore, there are diverse actors with a stake in shaping global social policy. These actors are engaged in a struggle to define the nature of the social problems and effect their preferred societal visions in policies. The term struggle is used because there are competing and overlapping institutions and ideas about what makes effective social policy. First, the WB and, to a lesser extent, the **International Monetary Fund** (IMF) and **World Trade Organization** (WTO), are in competition for influence with the UN system. WB's health, social protection and education policy for countries is not always the same as that of the WHO, International Labour Organization (ILO) or the United Nations Educational, Scientific and Cultural Organization (UNESCO), respectively. While the world may be said to have one emerging Ministry of Finance in the shape of the IMF (with lots of shortcomings) and one Ministry of Trade in the shape of the WTO (which is highly contested), it has two Ministries of Health, two Ministries of Social Security and two Ministries of Education. Then again, the UN social agencies (WHO, ILO, the United Nations Children's Fund (UNICEF) and UNESCO) are not always espousing the same policy as the United Nations Department of Economic and Social Affairs (UNDESA). Moreover, the Secretary General's initiatives such as the Global Compact and the Millennium Project may bypass or sideline the social development policies of UNDESA. Quite apart from conflict between the UN and WB and within the UN system, there is also the G8, G20, G77 and other regional groupings of countries that need to be considered. This struggle among many different global actors for the right to shape policy and for the content of that policy is what passes for a system of global social governance.

Because so many players are engaged in this complex process of global social governance, it is has been argued that transnational or **global policy advocacy coalitions** (Orenstein, 2005) and **transnational knowledge networks** (Stone and Maxwell, 2005) play a major part in shaping global policy formulation. Such actors organise alliances between some of the large number of players identified above and, often because the debates between the big organisations are stalemated, such advocacy coalitions and knowledge networks can get things done more quickly. A key example of such a global policy advocacy coalition is the global pension policy story, discussed in Chapter Nine.

A further preliminary remark is required regarding the concept of **multi-level governance** that is often used to capture the idea of layers of governance at sub-national, national, world-regional, and global levels. It is better to approach this issue using the concept of scale rather than level. The politics of scale literature suggests that it is not adequate to attempt to capture the complexity of transnational policy making by thinking in terms only of discrete layers or levels of government or governance. What is important here is not only that policy making is taking place at different levels of governance but also that key policy players operate at different levels at any one moment. The politics of scale therefore better captures the ways in which the policy-making process is multi-sited, multi-layered and multi-actor at the same time (Yeates, 1999), and how individual policy actors operate in the policy spaces that exist between levels and organisations (Wedel, 1998; Lendvai and Stubbs, 2007). Those who are better able to travel between these scales – consultants, INGO experts, policy entrepreneurs and so on – are better placed to influence global and indeed national social policy. Thus, national policy about poverty reduction in Tanzania is made by international WB consultants and **international non-governmental organisation** (INGO) representatives acting in global, national and sub-national fora alongside consultants and non-governmental organisations (NGOs) operating in the domestic sphere (Gould, 2005).

The issue of global social governance generates intense debate between those holding different political positions and representing different interests. Marxian analysts dismiss existing global social governance as a smokescreen to manage global capitalism in the interests of global capital (Soederberg, 2006). Social democrats (Monbiot, 2003) want to reform existing global social governance to make it more effective at tackling global social problems. Some on the political right (Ohmae, 1990) dismiss existing global governance as an interference in both markets and national interests and want less of it, while others in that side of the political spectrum want an effective global governance to maintain stability and peace necessary for capital accumulation without too many concessions to social policy questions. Finally, many in the Global South (Bello, 2004) regard existing structures and processes of global social governance as skewed in favour of the interests of the Global North and want to decommission much of it. Here the project of world-regional social governance emerges as an alternative 'global' reform strategy.

This chapter now proceeds to:

- elaborate on the idea of global social governance as an arena of contestation, illustrated by the contest of the social policy advice offered by international organisations (IOs) to countries;
- outline the emergence of supranational social policies of redistribution, regulation and rights; and
- review the major arguments and proposals for global social governance reform, including an outline of the alternative scenario of world-regional social governance.

International organisations and national social policies

World Bank

The WB (in terms of its component bodies – the International Bank for Reconstruction and Development (IBRD) and the International Development Association (IDA)), under the guise of being *the* world's anti-poverty agency played the major role in shaping – and damaging – national social policy in developing and transition countries in the 1980s and 1990s. Its earlier insistence on user charges or cost recovery, through the process of policy conditionality whereby money is lent on condition of policy change, often prevented access by people living in poverty to education and health services. Its demonstration that public spending often benefited those other than the poor was used to undermine the embryonic welfare states of Latin America, South Asia and Africa that had been built to serve the interests of the state-building middle classes. WB social policy essentially became a safety net policy for people living in poverty and fostered private commercial services for the better off. There are some signs that the ongoing intellectual struggle inside the WB between those who still favour safety nets for the poor and private services for the better off and those more attuned to the European story of building cross-class alliances to create good public service for all might be tilting in favour of the latter. Indeed, one reading of WB's *World Development Report* of 2006 is that concern with the institutional and political barriers to equity is also now centre stage in the WB (Deacon, 2007). The problem, however, for those within the WB who have struggled long and hard to reform its social policies in a more progressive direction is that they are working in an institution that does not enjoy global legitimacy. In particular, the WB is regarded by the South as serving Northern interests (Bello, 2004). Also, we need to distinguish between the more progressive elements within the WB and the regressive ones: the WB's International Finance Corporation (IFC) in particular continues to encourage private investment in health and education (Deacon, 2007).

International Monetary Fund

The thrust of IMF social policy in the 1970s, '80s and '90s was also the 'safety net' comprising targeted subsidies, cash compensation in lieu of subsidies, or improved distribution of essentials such as medicine. The IMF also insisted on these in the process of policy-conditioned structural adjustment lending. Although criticism of the IMF's structural adjustment facility led to its replacement by the poverty reduction and growth facility, critics continue to point out the contradictions between the IMF's short-term concerns with macroeconomic stability and long-term poverty reduction goals. In particular, they point out that IMF fiscal targets often lead to diminished social spending. However, in terms of the IMF's own account of its social policy prescriptions for countries, there has been a significant shift from the 'old' structural adjustment days. It now approvingly cites evidence of social spending in countries that have received IMF support, claiming that real spending on education and health has increased (Deacon, 2007).

World Trade Organization

The WTO, formed in 1995, is also a key institutional actor in global social policy, and is influencing national social policy formation in diverse and controversial ways. This is especially the case in terms of boosting global private (commercial) service providers through the General Agreement on Trade in Services (GATS) and in terms of the constraints of the Agreement on Trade Related Aspects of Intellectual Property Rights (TRIPS) protecting drug company patents, which affects the cost of drugs in poor countries. The part played by the WTO is discussed further in Chapter Five in the context of international trade and welfare, and in Chapter Seven in the context of global health.

Organisation for Economic Co-operation and Development

The Organisation for Economic Co-operation and Development (OECD), an international organisation of the richest developed countries, also plays a part in the global social governance process. The social policy advice of the OECD occupies a position somewhere between the market opening and liberalising push of the WB, IMF and WTO on the one hand and the concern of UN social agencies on the other to protect public services. It has argued that globalisation creates the need for more, not less, social expenditure and has been fairly even-handed in its advice about social policy, although Armingeon and Beyeler (2004) emphasise the neoliberal tendencies of the OECD's social policy advice to member countries (see also Chapter Seven in the context of health).

There is a difference of emphasis within the OECD, with the Directorate for Employment, Labour and Social Affairs (DELSA) favouring adequate public services and the Department of Financial and Enterprise Affairs encouraging private provision (Deacon and Kaasch, 2008).

International Labour Organization

The ILO is the longest-established international governmental organisation (IGO) concerned with social questions. It was a major player in helping developing countries build state pension and social security systems between 1930 and the early 1970s. Although the WB took over the global leadership role in the 1980s and 1990s in the social protection domain, arguing for and securing the rolling back of state systems in favour of privatised and individualised ones, especially in the area of pensions, the ILO fought back. It sought to expose what it regarded as the flaws in the dominant WB thinking on pensions by arguing that there was no demographic imperative leading to privatisation, that the European-type schemes were reformable and sustainable, and that the privatisation strategy was merely a cover to increase the share of private capital savings (see Chapter Nine for further discussion).

Just as in the WB, so in the ILO there were other tendencies. The ILO's socioeconomic security programme had taken a broad brief to examine those 21st-century policies that might contribute to universal citizen (and resident) security in the context of global labour flexibility. This programme argued for the emergence of a new universalism 'from below', embodying, for example, universal cash income benefits conditional on a child's attendance at school or universal categorical pensions. These ideas are now largely mainstreamed within the ILO and, under the leadership of its Social Security Department, considerable effort is being made to form alliances with the European Union (EU), United Nations Development Programme (UNDP), WHO and others to advance this agenda.

World Health Organization

The shadow cast over the role of the WB also touched the WHO in the 1980s and 1990s, so much so that the last but one Director General, Gro Harlem Bruntland, attempted to rescue the WHO from the margins of international influence and establish it as an agency able to compete with, or at least stand alongside, the WB as an authority on global health issues and national health policies. To do this, she believed it necessary to shift the WHO discourse from a purely normative one about health for all to one that engaged with economists. Health expenditures were to be encouraged not because they were morally desirable but because they were a sound investment in human capital. However, in subsequent work on comparing healthcare systems, the WHO came under heavy criticism for ranking countries and has lost some ground to the OECD where analytical work on health services is expanding rapidly with EU support (see also Chapter Seven).

United Nations Educational, Scientific and Cultural Organization

One of the smallest IOs concerned with social policy is the Paris-based UNESCO. WB versus UN social agency issues arose also with regard to education and the role of UNESCO. In the context of the Education for All campaign with which UNESCO is centrally connected, the big question of money was in effect left to the WB to manage the fast-track initiative and the global education fund for education. UNESCO remains concerned rather more with the content of education, giving emphasis to its social and humanising purposes, and has promulgated a set of guidelines to regulate global private education. It has good links with ministers of social development in Africa, Latin America and to a lesser extent Asia, with whom it has been encouraging a south–south regional social policy dialogue.

United Nations Children's Fund

UNICEF, which is funded in large part by popular donations and operates with a degree of independence from the rest of the UN system, focuses on the welfare and rights of children and in so doing addresses a wide range of social policy issues. Its professional staff have often been in the forefront of criticisms of the residual social policy approach of the WB. For example, it was first to argue (Cornia et al, 1987) for structural adjustment with a 'human face'. It is broadly in favour of universal child support policies.

United Nations Development Programme and United Nations Department of Economic and Social Affairs

For the future of social policy in developing countries, perhaps the new major struggle for influence centres on how countries will plan to meet the Millennium Development Goals (MDGs) set by the UN and agreed by the WB, IMF and OECD in 2000. Planning for meeting these goals to halve poverty, get children into school and improve access to health with the support of increased aid from richer countries requires countries to construct social development plans that are overseen by the UNDP. The UNDP operates in countries to support development but has far fewer resources than the WB. On the one hand, countries are required to bring these UNDP plans into line with the WB-directed Poverty Reduction Strategy Papers, which are still evaluated through the lenses of its safety-net approach, while on the other hand they are being advised in the shape of new social policy guidance notes issued by UNDESA (Ortiz, 2007) to build universal and inclusive forms of provision linked to adequate job creation. However, UNDESA, as the Secretariat of the UN Economic and Social Council in New York, does not have an adequate operational capacity in countries to drive its new guidance notes, which – crucially – are not endorsed by UNDP.

United Nations Committee on Economic, Social and Cultural Rights (UNCESCR)

This relatively weak sub-committee of the relatively ineffective UN Economic and Social Council has responsibility for overseeing and reporting on violations by countries of the UN's 1966 International Covenant on Economic, Social and Cultural Rights. In principle, this covenant is very progressive in social policy terms, stating that parties to the covenant recognise everybody's right to social security, including social insurance, and to an adequate standard of living (see Social Watch, 2007). There are, however, no enforcement mechanisms, no means of legal redress at the global level and no individual right of appeal against any failure of governments to protect social rights (Deacon, 2007; Dean, 2008). Similar limitations apply to the more recent 1989 Convention on the Rights of the Child.

In sum, ideas about desirable national social policy argued for by the major IOs suggest something approaching a 'war of position' between those agencies and actors within them. This struggle is essentially between those who have argued for a more selective, residual role for the state together with a larger role for private actors in health, social protection and education provision and those who take the opposite view. This division of opinion often reflects a disagreement as to whether the reduction of poverty is a matter of targeting specific resources on the poorest or whether it is a matter of both providing universal services and effecting major social and political-institutional change, involving a shift in power relations and a significant increase in redistribution from rich to poor. In other words, we can say that international agencies propagate social policy ideas in keeping with one or other of the three worlds of welfare identified by Esping-Andersen (1990). It does seem that the tide *may* have begun to turn in 2007 against both the targeting and privatising view (liberal welfare state policy) and the Bismarckian approach (conservative corporatist welfare state policy) towards a more universal approach (social democratic welfare state policy). The opportunity now exists for the UN, working with sympathetic donors such as the Scandinavians and some other

European countries, to begin to undo the damage wrought by the WB over the past decades. *Table 2.1* summarises some of this discussion.

Table 2.1: *International organisation approaches to national social policy*

International organisation	Dominant approach to social policy
WB (IBRD and IDA)	Residual – becoming more universal
WB (IFC)	Residual – strongly favours private (commercial) health and education
IMF	Residual – becoming supportive of increased social spending
WTO	Residual – favours international markets in private welfare
ILO	Bismarckian – becoming universal
UNICEF, UNESCO, WHO	Universal public services
OECD	Mixed views – with DELSA emphasising the value of public services
UNDESA	Comprehensive universal social policy
UNDP	Not clearly explicated

To conclude this section, it is finally worth noting that the policy space afforded to some African countries by unconditional lending now coming from China might help here in supporting more comprehensive provision. However, some are concerned that in its unconditional lending policy China does not give adequate attention to the human and social rights issues of the countries to whom it lends money.

Global redistribution, regulation and rights

As we have seen, there are diverse and competing views among IOs regarding what they see as the preferred social policy model. In terms of global social policy understood as supranational social policy at the global level, the world is stumbling towards articulating a global social policy of **global redistribution**, **global social regulation** and **global social rights** and creating the institutions necessary for the realisation of such policies in practice.

Global redistribution

In terms of international north–south transfers, in addition to the recent increases in overseas development aid provided by rich countries to poorer ones we must note the birth of new global funds for health, education and social protection. The most well-known example is the Global Fund. Poorer countries may now access limited global resources on certain criteria of social need. This fund has its critics, who suggest in the case of health that improved health outcomes needs to extend beyond pharmaceutical and technical programmes to include broad-based public health programmes. The fund's accountability is also called into question (see Chapter Seven for further discussion of these issues). We are also witnessing the move from purely North–South support for within-country social development to the articulation of the concept of **global public goods** such as disease eradication, water provision and social stability through social protection that may need to be funded out of taxes on international air travel (Kaul et al, 2003).

Global social regulation

In terms of social regulation of the global economy, global business is being asked by the UN through its social compact, the Global Compact, to act in a socially responsible way. Businesses that sign up to this 'contract' are required to show that they are taking action on one or other area of labour or environmental or anti-corruption standards. There are no 'teeth' to this social compact, and the idea of voluntary codes rather than enforceable rules prevails for now (see Chapters Four and Six). Neither is there a social clause in international trade deals, which would otherwise have meant that countries could refuse to trade with those not respecting international labour standards, because many in the Global South objected to a possible undermining of their comparative advantage and a consolidation of **trade protectionism** by the Global North (see Chapter Five). However, there is now a wide expectation on all countries who are members of the ILO to uphold core labour standards concerning the right to organise, the right to equal treatment and the right to no forced labour and no 'worst forms' of child labour whether they have chosen to sign up to them or not (see Chapter Six). Concern, however, continues to exist about the underdevelopment of global regulatory capacities in the health, education and social care markets (see Chapter Five).

Global social rights

Despite continued controversy about aspects of global social rights and the weakness of the UN agencies, the existence of the UNCESCR and its promulgation by the UN enables others to campaign for their realisation in countries where governments have hitherto been reluctant to concede them. The international community has also confirmed, despite a strong attempt by the US to persuade it otherwise, its commitment to the MDGs, which are in effect a minimum set of global social standards in education, health and poverty alleviation. Of course, the global institutions to ensure these are met are not yet strong enough, and the MDGs are only benchmarks around which there will be continued struggle. But the important point is that the language and discourse has changed from that used in the heyday of global neoliberalism and the Washington Consensus. It is no longer the dominant belief that global markets left to themselves will secure the meeting of human and social needs. Just as within one country the market has to be embedded in a set of political institutions to secure social justice, so does the meeting of global human and social needs.

Table 2.2 summarises the existing elements of supranational global social policy.

Table 2.2: *Elements of global social policy*

Aspect of global social policy	Examples of global social policy
Global redistribution	Overseas development assistance, global funds, airline ticket tax, differential drug pricing
Global regulation	Core labour standards, UN Global Compact, UNESCO guidelines for private higher education
Global rights	UN International Covenant on Economic, Social and Cultural Rights; UN Convention on the Rights of the Child

Global social governance reform

The previous section indicates that the political climate in the early 21st century differs in many ways from two decades ago, in that the question is now less whether there should be a global social policy than how such a policy should be realised. In this regard, ideas and proposals abound as to what kinds of reform are required to bring about a more coherent and effective system of global governance necessary for the development of global social policy.

Ideas from the radical right, the radical left and the radical South would rather tear up the existing institutions. The radical right in the US is increasingly irritated by the need to make international policy in the shadow of the WB and UN, whose influence they would wish to see reduced. The US has not supported the setting up of the International Criminal Court and it has withdrawn its support for the Global Warming Treaty and attempted to get reference to the MDGs removed from the outcome of the 2005 UN Summit. In this scenario, the US becomes even more obviously the global superpower 'exercising global governance' in its own interests, unmediated by any sense of belonging to an international community or membership (with all that that implies) of international organisations.

On the other hand, the '50 years is enough movement' among radical NGOs called for the abolition of the Bretton Woods organisations for different reasons. Here the wish is to strengthen the UN as *the* main agent of global social governance by raising global taxes on international currency transactions through the agency of a UN-run Global Tax Authority and instituting an Economic Security Council mirroring the existing Security Council to oversee global policy (Patomaki and Teivainen, 2004). The UN would be made more accountable not only to national governments but also, and more directly, to global 'citizens' by means of a second chamber of parliamentary representatives or civil society representatives.

At the same time, and leading in a quite different reform direction, there has been the growth of the civil society-influenced **anti-globalisation movement** (Mac Sheoin and Yeates, 2007). The deglobalisation strand would replace long-distance trade and global markets with local production for local use that would nurture local economies and sustain ecological systems. Colin Hines (2000) represents such a strand. Walden Bello (2000, p 61) has argued that 'multilateral structures entrench the power of the Northern superpowers under the guise of creating a set of rules for all.... The fewer the structures and the less clear the rules, the better for the South', while Martin Khor of the Third World Network (www.twn.org) shares some of this view but tends to put more importance in the strengthening of the UN as a whole. He emphasises the need for a South–South policy dialogue and coordination linked to joint work to strengthen the UN (Khor, 2000, 2001).

Not surprisingly, these radical reforms face considerable resistance due to outright opposition of powerful states, or because of a lack of sufficient political will or capacity among their advocates. However, a number of more limited, but nonetheless significant, reforms to the institutions and processes of global social governance are in train. Among these are moves to:

- strengthen the UN's role in economic and social policy;
- increase inter-organisational cooperation, policy dialogue and synergy;
- create more social policy 'space' for the Global South;
- extend the use of global public–private partnerships;
- reform the WB; and
- construct world-regional formations with a social policy dimension.

A stronger United Nations?

Moves to strengthen the UN's role in economic and social policy were formalised in the Report of the Secretary General to the 57th session of the UN in 2002 (UN Secretary General, 2002). It recognised (para. 19) the growing role of the UN in helping to forge consensus on globally important social and economic issues and called for the corresponding strengthening of the principal organ concerned with those issues, namely the Economic and Social Council (ECOSOC). Some (Haq, 1998; Falk, 2002; Nayyar, 2002; Dervis, 2005) have argued differently, positing that the role of the UN in the management of the world's economic and social affairs would be strengthened by the creation of an Economic Security Council (UNESC). UNESC would operate rather like a reformed Security Council, but with a few members who could better direct global economic and social matters. Most recently, Kemal Dervis, Director of the UNDP, argued (Dervis, 2005) for a UNESC with six permanent members (EU, US, Japan, China, India, Russian Federation) and eight others, two each from Asia, Latin America, Canada and the Caribbean, the Arab League, Africa and Other Europe. Voting would be weighted by population, gross domestic product and financial contribution made towards global public goods. It would be the strategic governance umbrella for the WB, IMF, WTO and UN system.

Others, including Johan Scholvinck, the Director of the Division for Social Policy and Development within UNDESA, argue that it is better to concentrate reform efforts on ECOSOC, although even this will not be easy (Scholvinck, 2004). The role and function of the ECOSOC was addressed in the Secretary General's report to the UN Summit in September 2005. *In Larger Freedom: Towards Development, Security and Rights for All* (UN Secretary General, 2005) praised the work of ECOSOC to date and asserted that a reformed Council 'could start to assert leadership in driving a global development agenda' (para. 179). It should 'hold annual Ministerial-level assessments of progress towards agreed development goals, particularly the MDGs. These assessments could be based on peer reviews' (para. 176) and 'it should serve as a high-level development cooperation (biennial) forum' (para. 177). The final agreed outcome of the summit (UN, 2005) did indeed 'recognise the need for a more effective ECOSOC as *a* (not *the*) (my emphasis) principal body for coordination, policy review, policy dialogue and recommendations on issues of economic and social development, as well as for implementation of the international development goals agreed at the major United Nations summits and conferences, including the MDGs' (para. 155). It went on to endorse the specific procedural recommendations of the Secretary-General and these changes will now take place.

More significant still was the setting up of a High-Level Panel on United Nations System-Wide Coherence in the areas of Development, Humanitarian Assistance and the Environment. The panel reported in November 2006. Among its main points were that the UN should 'deliver as one' at country level; establish a UN Sustainable Development Board as an oversight body of core agencies; refocus UNDP's operational work on the policy coherence of UN country teams; appoint the UNDP administrator as development coordinator reporting to the Sustainable Development Board working with UNDESA's chief economist; set up a multi-year funding mechanism for 'One UN Country Programmes'; and establish a Global Leaders Forum (L27) within ECOSOC to upgrade its policy coordination and leadership role on economic, development and global public goods issues. Broadly welcomed by Northern governments and INGOs, it has been criticised by the G77 for reducing the UN to a development agency and sidelining its work in trade (United Nations Conference on Trade and Development (UNCTAD)) and global finance.

International organisation dialogue and synergy

Strengthening the role of the UN in international social and economic affairs by means of giving more power to ECOSOC might be one way of curtailing the global influence of the WB. Another approach is to call for inter-organisational cooperation and policy dialogue between the WB and UN agencies. This was perhaps the most important conclusion of the ILO-sponsored World Commission on the Social Dimension of Globalisation, which reported in 2004 (ILO, 2004). Thus, 'international organizations should launch *Policy Coherence Initiatives* in which they work together on the design of more balanced and complementary policies for achieving a fair and inclusive globalization' (ILO, 2004, paras. 608-11). The first of these, it said, should address the question of global growth, investment and employment creation (para. 611). These proposals for policy dialogue between IOs can find reflection in the initiative of the UN Secretary General discussed in the last section to win agreement at the September 2005 UN Summit for ECOSOC to hold a biennial global policy forum on development issues. Progress towards a more formal collaboration between the WB, OECD, ECOSOC and other agencies is also more likely to develop around joint monitoring of progress towards meeting the MDGs. Indeed, in April 2002 the Joint Development Committee of the World Bank and IMF agreed that the WB, in 'collaboration with staff of partner agencies', would produce an annual Global Monitoring Report on progress towards meeting the MDGs. The first report appeared in 2004, with the second appearing in September 2005 (WB, 2005).

More policy space for the South

The reclaiming by the Global South of the right to make social policy and social development policy choices is a movement that is gaining impetus. In the 1980s and 1990s, the WB, through its policy conditions attached to loans, shaped social policy thinking in the Global South. This is now less overtly the case, and the conditions are more about the process of countries having in place *any* poverty reduction strategy. At the same time, development aid from Northern donors is now less likely to be tied to the condition that it is spent on goods and services from donor countries. More aid is going to country budgets to support their policy-making processes. The increased unconditional aid flows from China may also liberate space for Southern policy choices. The UNCTAD provides one forum where some Southern governments have been able to debate an alternative developmental path from the export-orientated and privatising path laid down by the Washington Consensus. According to Charles Gore (2000), work within UNCTAD combined with thinking within at least two of the UN Regional Economic Commissions (ECLAC in Latin America and ESCAP in East Asia) has generated a 'Southern consensus' or a 'coming paradigm shift'. In broad terms, this implies an approach to development that involves strategic integration of a country's economy into the international economy with appropriate sequencing and sector-only opening; productive development policy, focusing on areas of comparative advantage, in addition to macroeconomic policy; building or retaining a pragmatic developmental state; and the management of the distributional consequences of development 'primarily through a production-orientated approach rather than redistributive transfers' (Gore, 2000, p 798).

Global networks and global public–private partnerships

We may be witnessing a shift in the *locus and content* of policy debate and activity from those more formally located within the official UN and WB policy-making arenas to a set of practices around networks, public–private partnerships and projects that in some ways bypass these institutions and debates and present new possibilities for actually making global change in particular social policy arenas. As Ngaire Woods (2002, p 42) has argued:

> The global governance debate is focused heavily on the reform and creation of international institutions ... yet global governance is increasingly being undertaken by a variety of networks, coalitions and informal arrangements which lie a little further beyond the public gaze and the direct control of governments.

Among examples of these networks, partnerships and projects are:

• the UN Secretary General's Millennium Project, involving 10 task forces to consider the implementation of the MDGs;

- GAVI, established in 2000 with a major donation from the Bill & Melinda Gates Foundation to encourage other public and private donations to achieve the goal of increased vaccination against preventable diseases in developing countries; and
- the UN Secretary General's Global Compact with Business.

The details and issues of these are taken up in later chapters (in particular, Chapters Four, Five Six and Seven), but for present purposes it is worth noting that the essence of this emerging networking and partnership form of policy development and practice shifting through a focus on specific projects is the collaboration between stakeholders in IOs, the global corporate sector, INGOs and civil society organisations. Charlotte Streck (2002) argues for Global Public Policy Networks (GPPNs) that bring together governments, the private sector and civil society organisations. Such GPPNs can set agendas and standards, generate and disseminate knowledge and bolster institutional effectiveness. It has been argued that IOs have a particular role to play in GPPNs as convenor, platform, networker and sometimes partial financier (www.globalpublicpolicy.net).

A key question is how intervention in these tasks, projects and networks might be anything other than opportunistic, self-interested or pragmatic. A major concern of critics (Boas and McNeill, 2003; Martens, 2003; Ollila, 2003; Richter, 2004) of these developments – and especially of the public–private partnerships – has been that the corporate sector might start dictating UN policy and that the ad hoc processes and mechanisms are not accountable to UN democratic processes. As Martens (2003, p 25) argues, 'the creation of more satellite funds outside the UN system may not only end up weakening the United Nations, it may at the same time impede cross-sector development strategies aimed at implementing the MDGs'.

Accountability of the World Bank

The question of the accountability of the WB and the IMF not only to their shareholding customers (that is, donor governments) but also to the countries they lend money to has been a long-standing concern to elements of global civil society. The concerns relate to three areas: the apportionment of voting rights, the composition of the executive boards and the selection of organisation staff (Christian Aid, 2003a, 2003b; Martens, 2003). Voting rights currently largely reflect the principle of 'one dollar, one vote' rather than 'one county, one vote' (as is the case in the WTO) so that countries with more gross national income, trade flows and currency reserves get a bigger say. Reforms would centre on reducing the weight attributed to economic size and give a greater weight to the one country, one vote principle. In terms of the executive boards, industrialised countries currently have an absolute majority. The EU in particular is over-represented, with EU member states currently appointing to the IMF seven out of the 24 executive directors, with the Asian countries appointing four and the African, Latin American and Arab groups appointing two each. It has been proposed therefore that the EU should appoint three at most to even up the membership. In terms of staff, the concern is the appointment of large number of US-trained orthodox economists to the WB who tend to support particular ways of thinking about economic and social development.

World-regional social policy

Some in the Global South (Bello, 2004) regard this focus by largely Northern and European scholars and civil society activists on reforming the existing institutions of global social governance as essentially mistaken. The point is not so much to reform and strengthen institutions that operate in the interests of the north but to undermine and outflank them by creating new countervailing sources of power serving the interests of the Global South more effectively. This is where the construction and strengthening of regional formations of countries that have a partly Southern protectionist purpose enters the picture. Rather than seeking to develop a case for a single global social policy of redistribution, regulation and rights that, proponents such as Bello and others argue, must also imply a strengthening of Northern-oriented and Northern-based institutions, the focus should perhaps be on building several world-regional social policies of redistribution, regulation and rights. Equally, rather than seek to win the WB over to a European progressive perspective on social policy so that the WB and the UN concur on the advice to national governments about the best social policies, the point should be to liberate a policy space where Southern governments and civil society can make their own policy choices. Reforming global social governance should perhaps imply building a world federation of regions each with competence in their own locations.

Several emerging trading blocks and other regional associations of countries in the south are already beginning to confront in practice the issues of the relationship between trade and labour, social and health standards and the question of how to maintain levels of taxation in the face of international competition to attract capital. In this context, the potential advantage for developing countries of building a social dimension to regional groupings of countries has been commented on by policy analysts (Room, 2004; Yeates, 2005, 2007; Yeates and Deacon, 2006; Deacon et al, 2008) and is being acted on within several world regions. In relation to the rest of the world, such an approach affords a degree of protection from global market forces that may erode national social entitlements and can create the possibility of such grouped countries having a louder voice in the global discourse on economic and social policy in UN and other fora. Internally, through intergovernmental agreement, world-regionalism would make possible the development of regional social *redistribution* mechanisms that can take several forms, including regionally financed funds to target particularly depressed localities or to tackle particularly significant health or food shortage issues; regional social and labour *regulations*, including standardised health and safety regulations to combat a within-region race to the bottom; regional social empowerment mechanisms that give citizens a voice to challenge their governments in terms of regional supranational social *rights*; and regional *intergovernmental cooperation* in social policy in terms of regional health specialisation, regional education cooperation, regional food and livelihood cooperation and regional recognition of social security entitlements.

There are signs of such a regional approach to social policy emerging in the Global South. Mercosur has developed regional labour and social security regulations and has a mutual recognition of educational qualifications. SADC (Southern Africa Development Community) has approached health issues on a regional basis and its gender unit has made progress in mainstreaming these issues across the region. ASEAN has declared that one of its purposes is to facilitate the development of 'caring societies' and has a university scholarships and exchange programme. SAARC (South Asian Association for Regional Cooperation) has included social issues on the agendas of its summits and in 2002 signed a regional convention for the promotion of child welfare and a regional convention on the prevention of trafficking of women and children for prostitution. At its summit in November 2005, it resolved on a Decade of Poverty Alleviation, a regional food bank and a Poverty Alleviation Fund. The Andean Community agreed in 2004 a regional Integral Plan for Social Development that involves technical cooperation on social policy among Andean countries, including the exchange of good practice, regional monitoring of the MDGs and a number of regional social projects. Some similar developments are emerging at the level of the African Union and in regional groupings of countries in West and East Africa.

Conclusion

This chapter has shown that the process of global social policy governance is best understood as a fragmented system involving contest and struggle between multiple international actors for the right to influence the development of global social policy and its content. Key IOs are often in competition with each other, with the WB being more influential than the UN agencies. Several ideas for the reform of the system have been reviewed, including those to strengthen the UN and alternative scenarios to develop a more 'devolved' – world–regional – basis for global governance.

Summary

- The system of global social governance is a mosaic of international organisations often competing with each other to shape policy.
- A large number of non-state international actors compete to influence the social policies of the formal intergovernmental organisations.
- Sometimes a number of actors combine in global policy advocacy coalitions or global policy networks to drive a particular global social policy.
- Some actors are more able than others to occupy the policy spaces that open up at an international level and hence have more influence on global social policy.
- The WB has been the most influential IO and has influenced social policy in a residual or market-orientated direction.
- Moves to strengthen the role of the UN continue but face large obstacles from several quarters.
- Regional associations of countries have also adopted supranational social policies and the strengthening of these is one possible reform direction.

Questions for discussion

- Why are the concepts of complex multilateralism, public–private partnerships, global policy advocacy coalitions and politics of scale useful in understanding global social governance?
- How does the contest over social policy ideas taking place between different international organisations manifest itself?
- How is it being proposed that the UN's role in global social governance be strengthened?
- What are the arguments for and against creating more global public–private partnerships to manage the world's social problems?
- Why might it be a good idea to strengthen the world-regional tier of supranational social governance?

Further suggested activities

- Review the Digest section of recent issues of *Global Social Policy: Journal of Public Policy and Social Development* to search for updates under the headings global social governance, global social policies and international actors and

social policy. (Electronic versions of the Digest can be found at www.gaspp. org. Follow links to Digest.)
- Search the WB, ILO, WHO, UNDESA, OECD and other IO websites for the latest publications and policy documents related to specific social policies.
- Search for examples of Southern Voices on global social policy issues from websites such as www.focusweb.org and www.tni.org.

Further reading

Deacon (2007) covers in much more detail all of the points made in this chapter. Held and McGrew (2002) deal more comprehensively with the issue of global governance, although their treatment of social policy is weak. Patomaki and Teivainen (2004) set out a radical global governance reform agenda aimed at the democratic transformation of global institutions and at increasing global taxes for global public goods. Finally, Munck (2005) emphasises the role of social movements 'from below' in influencing global social policy.

Electronic resources

www.ilo.org
www.oecd.org
www.worldbank.org
www.un.org (UNDESA section)
www.globalpolicy.org (UNREFORM section)
www.gaspp.org (GSP Digest section on global social governance and policy)

References

Armingeon, K. and Beyeler, M. (2004) *The OECD and European Welfare States*, Cheltenham: Edward Elgar.
Bello, W. (2000) *Why Reform of the WTO is the Wrong Agenda*, Bangkok: Focus on the Global South.
Bello, W. (2004) *Deglobalization: Ideas for a New World Economy*, London: Zed Books.
Boas, M. and McNeill, D. (2003) *Multilateral Institutions: A Critical Introduction*, London: Pluto Press.
Christian Aid (2003a) *Struggling to be Heard: Democratizing the World Bank and IMF*, London: Christian Aid.

Christian Aid (2003b) *Taking Liberties: Poor People, Free Trade and Trade Justice*, London: Christian Aid.

Cornia, A., Jolly, R. and Stewart, F. (eds) (1987) *Adjustment with a Human Face*, Oxford: Clarendon.

Deacon, B. (2007) *Global Social Policy and Governance*, London: Sage Publications.

Deacon, B. and Kaasch, A. (2008) 'Neo-liberal stalking horse or balancer of economic and social objectives', in R. Mahon and S. McBride (eds) (2008) *The OECD and Global Governance*, Vancouver: British Columbia Press.

Deacon, B., Ortiz, I. and Zelenev, S. (2008) *Regional Social Policy*, UNDESA Working Paper No 37. New York, NY: UNDESA.

Dean, H. (2008) 'Social policy and human rights: rethinking the engagement', *Social Policy and Society*, vol 7, no 1, pp 1-12.

Dervis, K. (2005) *A Better Globalization: Legitimacy, Governance, and Reform*, Washington, DC: Center for Global Development.

Esping-Andersen, G. (1990) *The Three Worlds of Welfare*, Cambridge: Polity Press.

Falk, R. (2002) 'The United Nations system: prospects for renewal', in D. Nayyar (ed) *Governing Globalization*, Oxford: Oxford University Press.

Gore, C. (2000) 'The rise and fall of the Washington Consensus as a paradigm for developing countries', *World Development*, vol 28, pp 789-804.

Gould, J. (2005) *The New Conditionality: The Politics of Poverty Reduction Strategies*, London: Zed Books.

Haq, M. (1998) 'The case for an Economic Security Council', in A.J. Paolini and A.P. Jarvis (eds) *Between Sovereignty and Global Governance*, Basingstoke: Macmillan.

Held, D. and McGrew, A. (2002) *Governing Globalization*, Cambridge: Polity Press.

Hines, C. (2000) *Localization: A Global Manifesto*, London: Earthscan.

ILO (International Labour Organization) (2004) *A Fair Globalization: Creating Opportunities for All. Report of the World Commission on the Social Dimension of Globalization*, Geneva: ILO.

Josselin, D. and Wallace, W. (2001) *Non-state Actors in World Politics*, Basingstoke: Palgrave Macmillan.

Kaul, I., Conceicao, P., Goulven, K. and Mendoza, R. (2003) *Providing Global Public Goods*, Oxford: Oxford University Press.

Khor, M. (2000) *Globalization and the South: Some Critical Issues*, Penang: Third World Network.

Khor, M. (2001) *Rethinking Globalization: Critical Issues and Policy Choices*, London: Zed Books.

Lendvai, N. and Stubbs, P. (2007) 'Policies as translation: situating transnational social policies', in S. Hodgson and Z. Irving (eds) (2007) *Policy Reconsidered*, Bristol: The Policy Press.

Mac Sheoin, T. and Yeates, N. (2007) 'Division and dissent in the anti-globalisation movement', in S. Dasgupta and R. Kiely (eds) *Globalisation and After*, New Delhi: Sage Publications, pp 360-91.

Martens, J. (2003) *The Future of Multilateralism after Monterrey and Johannesburg*, Berlin: Friedrich Ebert Stiftung.

Monbiot, G. (2003) *The Age of Consent: A Manifesto for a New World Order*, London: Flamingo.

Munck, R. (2005) *Globalization and Social Exclusion*, Bloomfield, CT: Kumarian Press.

Nayyar, D. (2002) *Governing Globalization: Issues and Institutions*, Oxford: Oxford University Press.

O'Brien, R., Goetz, A.M., Scholte, J. and Williams, M. (2000) *Contesting Global Governance: Multilateral Economic Institutions and Global Social Movements*, Cambridge: Cambridge University Press.

Ollila, E. (2003) 'Health-related public–private partnerships and the United Nations', in B. Deacon, E. Ollila, M. Koivusalo and P. Stubbs (eds) *Global Social Governance: Themes and Prospects*, Helsinki: Ministry for Foreign Affairs of Finland.

Ohmae, K. (1990) *The Borderless World*, London: Collins.

Orenstein, M. (2005) 'The new pension reform as global policy', *Global Social Policy*, vol 5, no 2, pp 175-202.

Ortiz, I. (2007) *Social Policy Guidance Notes*, New York, NY: UNDESA.

Patomaki, H. and Teivainen, T. (2004) *A Possible World: Democratic Transformation of Global Institutions*, London: Zed Books.

Richter, J. (2004) *Public–Private Partnerships and International Health Policy*, Helsinki: Ministry for Foreign Affairs of Finland.

Room, G. (2004) 'Multi-tiered international welfare systems', in I. Gough and G. Woods (eds) *Insecurity and Welfare Regimes in Asia, Africa and Latin America*, Cambridge: Cambridge University Press.

Scholvinck, J. (2004) 'Global governance: the World Commission on the Social Dimension of Globalisation', *Social Development Review*, vol 8, pp 8-11.

Social Watch (2007) *Social Watch Report 2007: In Dignity and Rights*, Montevideo: Social Watch

Soederberg, S. (2006) *Global Governance in Question*, London: Pluto Press.

Stone, D. and Maxwell, S. (2005) *Global Knowledge Networks and International Development*, London: Routledge.

Streck, C. (2002) 'Global public policy networks as coalitions for change', in D. Esty and M. Ivanova (eds) *Global Environmental Governance: Options and Opportunities*, New Haven, CT: Yale University Press.

UN (United Nations) (2005) *2005 World Summit Outcome A/60/L.1*, www.ony. unu.edu/seminars/2007/R2P/2005%20World%20Summit%20Outcome.pdf (accessed 17 September 2005).

UN Secretary General (2002) 'Strengthening the United Nations: An Agenda for Further Change (A/57/387), New York, NY: United Nations.

UN Secretary General (2005) 'In larger freedom: towards development and security and human rights for all', (A/59/(2005) New York, NY: United Nations, (www.un-ngls.org/UNreform/UBUNTU-1.pdf).

Wedel, J. (1998) *Collision and Collusion: The Strange Case of Western Aid to Eastern Europe*, New York, NY: St Martin's Press.

Woods, N. (2002) 'Global governance and the role of institutions', in D. Held and A, McGrew (eds) *Governiing Globalization*, Cambridge: Polity Press.

WB (World Bank) (2005) 'Global monitoring', www.worldbank.org/WBSITE/ EXTERNAL/TOPICS/GLOBALMONITORING .

WB (World Bank) (2006) *World Development Report 2006*, Washington DC: World Bank.

Yeates, N. (1999) 'Social politics and policy in an era of globalisation: critical reflections', *Social Policy and Administration*, vol 33, no 4, pp 372-93.

Yeates, N. (2005) *Globalization and Social Policy in a Development Context: Regional Responses*, Geneva: United Nations Research Institute for Social Development..

Yeates, N. (ed) (2007) 'The social policy dimensions of world-regionalism' *Global Social Policy*, vol 7, no 3.

Yeates, N. and Deacon, B. (2006) *Globalism, Regionalism and Social Policy: Framing the Debate*, United Nations University Centre for Comparative Regional Integration Studies (UNU-CRIS) Working Paper 0-2006/6, Bruges: UNU-CRIS.

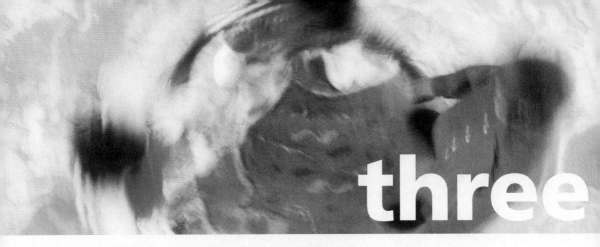

three

The global transfer of social policy

Rob Hulme and Moira Hulme

Overview

Social policies that feature similar language do not necessarily carry the same meaning or content in every context. Social scientists from a number of disciplines have developed concepts and metaphors in an attempt to characterise the international movement of policies. This chapter contrasts two of those conceptual frameworks, 'policy transfer' and 'travelling and embedded policy'. Policy transfer helps to explain the use of knowledge from elsewhere in decision-making processes. Travelling and embedded policy sheds light on the complex relationships between supranational, cross-national, regional and sectoral influences on policy making. Examples of education policy are used to illustrate the processes of global social policy making. In doing so, the chapter offers a particular focus on how global social policy agendas are mediated or negotiated by policy communities and networks in producing 'local' policy settlements.

Key concepts

Global social governance; policy learning; policy sociology; epistemic community; policy network

Introduction

A central component of global social policy formation involves the movement of ideas, structures and practices across national borders. The first two chapters in this volume have explored the means by which global networks of actors and global policy actors such as international organisations (IOs) are important in setting social policy agendas in the developed and the developing worlds. Chapter Two in particular addressed the global institutional architecture of social policy formation and referred to a system of 'emerging global governance' in which transnational corporations, international coalitions of policy advocates, policy experts and a variety of other policy actors interact through global networks and fora. This chapter examines in some detail the ways in which the making of social policy is said to be, and actually is, globalised. In particular, it focuses on how the knowledge that underpins policy (often carried by transnational organisations) is constructed and is expressed in diverse forms within national and sectoral contexts. In doing so, it addresses a different aspect of what Nicola Yeates in Chapter One refers to as the transnational processes of global social policy: the international movement of ideas and structures in policy making.

There is nothing new about policy forms moving around the globe. As Yeates observes in Chapter One, colonialism in the 19th century exported western forms of social and economic policy around the globe. The 20th century witnessed a tendency by developed western nations to 'borrow' policy structures from one another, sometimes over many years. Phillips and Ochs (2004) outline the incremental and ultimately unsuccessful attempt of the British government to borrow the German model of vocational education from the 1870s to the mid-20th century.

In recent years, the process of making social policy has become most visibly 'global' in that certain agendas such as human rights, public–private partnerships in welfare funding and delivery and the 'global knowledge economy' have 'travelled' around the globe. Depending on local political circumstances, the 'transfer' of 'generic' policy agendas such as these can either be a valuable instrument or an inevitable external intervention for policy makers within the new global governance.

Unlike other aspects of global social policy, the conceptual literatures on the international movement of policy reviewed here have primarily grown from Anglo-American models of policy analysis and reflect a 'technicist' focus on 'western' processes of government, emphasising stability and continuity. There is a need to 'globalise' this policy literature to address the scope of global policy change. Yet the narrower perspectives on transfer are still relevant to our purpose. We need both broad perspectives on the generic agendas promoted by global actors and a narrower focus on the processes of policy settlements (see **Box 3.1**). Global social policy analysis is founded on notions of growing 'interconnectedness' and, in keeping with other aspects of globalisation, it can be as illuminating to look for evidence of these processes in your 'back garden' as it is to look further afield. Hence our examples of 'travelling' policy highlight the way in generic global policy agendas can be contested and mediated within relatively small geographical areas (the nations of the UK) as well as on the wider global stage.

Two approaches to global policy studies are outlined to illustrate these broader debates: one uses a 'small lens' to focus on simple/linear transfers of ideas, the other a broader lens on the processes of mediation, contestation and deliberation of global discourses: the notion of 'travelling' and 'embedded policy' (Jones and Alexiadou, 2001; Ozga and Jones, 2006). Both perspectives help us to grasp the different ways in which social policy formation is said to have become globalised.

The chapter attends to the continued agency of 'local' policy actors in shaping global agendas, as well as the role of global actors in shaping local agendas. In this way, both the political nature of the making of social policy and the multi-directional nature of ideational influence among local, national and international 'levels' of policy making are emphasised. The chapter draws on education policy to illustrate how policies that employ similar language, and connect with common transnational agenda, produce different settlements.

What is policy transfer?

A substantial literature on the international movement of ideas and practices in social policy has developed over the past 15 years. In this section, we briefly outline the concepts of **policy transfer**, **policy diffusion**, **cross-national attraction**, **policy borrowing** and **policy convergence**, and we consider how **epistemic communities** (Haas, 1990) and advocacy coalitions (Sabatier and Jenkins-Smith, 1993) inform the development of **policy learning**.

Within the policy transfer literature, various frameworks have developed that seek to strengthen cross-national, international and historical analysis of social policies (Evans and Davies, 1999; Dolowitz and Marsh, 1996; Dolowitz et al, 2000; Wolman and Page, 2002). Dolowitz and colleagues (2000) offer a definition of policy transfer and the international movement of policy as:

> A process in which knowledge about policies, institutions and ideas developed in one time or place is used in the development of policies, institutions etc. in another time or place. (Dolowitz et al, 2000, p 3)

This framework is simple and uses a narrow lens, but it helps us to examine the origins of ideas about policy, who supplies this 'policy knowledge' and the political and practical purposes to which this knowledge is put. It is useful in explaining social policy formation at any level. The literature on 'diffusion' (Mintrom and Vergari, 1996) has a slightly broader focus on the international causes of policy 'adoption' of institutional forms within welfare systems, but again the focus is on structures and programmes. There has been a strong theme within the literature on policy transfer and diffusion on the influence of ideas and structures from the US on policy development in the UK (Dolowitz et al, 2000; *Global Social Policy* Volume 6, 2006). This work has highlighted examples ranging from the 'Americanisation' of British universities to the use of policies originating in the US, such as the Child Support Agency and electronic tagging of offenders. Transfer and diffusion here is seen to be driven by the close connections between US and UK policy elites and think tanks such the Institute for Economic Affairs as well as by the increasing linkages between welfare organisations and local and national policy communities in both countries.

The literature on 'lesson drawing' (Rose, 1991) is very close to the transfer framework and draws on a linear, rational understanding of the policy process, offering a focus on the tendency of policy elites to look for 'lessons' in how to deliver policy outcomes from other contexts, both domestic and abroad. These studies offer frameworks rather than complete theoretical perspectives and accordingly have been criticised as case studies in search of a global/international theory of policy change (Wolman and Page, 2002).

Box 3.1: Perspectives on the global movement of social policy

There are a number of theoretical perspectives and conceptual frameworks that help to characterise the global movement of social policy.

The broader perspectives used here tend to draw on sociological theories on globalisation, such as vernacular globalisation, policy sociology, and **travelling and embedded policy**.

Other 'broad brush' work includes **world society theory** (Meyer et al, 1997). This work starts from the premise of an already existing global society that transcends national boundaries. This operates through a series of global cultural associations, such as that established between groups of academic specialists in different countries, or through recognition of global norms and standards, such as universal human rights.

A 'narrower' perspective on the international movement of ideas is provided by a variety of conceptual frameworks that we have characterised as policy transfer, policy diffusion and **lesson drawing**. While each one has a slightly different scope and focus, all are essentially concerned with politics and decision making. Other frameworks include **cross-national attraction**, which examines the tendency for northern and western nations in particular to replicate structures evident in other similarly situated countries, and **policy borrowing**, which focuses primarily on the movement of policy between the US and the UK.

A model that tries to combine both broader and narrower perspectives is **policy convergence**. This examines global/international influence but emphasises the importance of the policy community and national cultural traditions in shaping the direction of domestic policy. The notion of international *influence* rather than top-down transfer of ideas into domestic social policy has been a key idea within the literature on globalisation and welfare states, and it remains central to the development of our perspective on how global social policy is made.

The literature on policy transfer offers a multi-level framework for exploring the movement of policy ideas and practices. For the purposes of global social policy, these transfer studies offer a simple lens for examining the increasing complexity of the 'global policy community' and the rise of generic agendas in education and other welfare policies.

Where generic agendas and policy platforms are *global* in reach – for example, contained within 'modernising' discourses supported by the global language of 'effectiveness', 'quality', 'diversity' and 'choice' – global and supranational agencies have an influence on the range of policy options that are available to domestic policy makers. However, as Yeates (2007a, 2007b) observes, the extent to which IOs have a significant influence on domestic policy making differs greatly depending on the organisation and policy areas concerned. Thus, the European Union (EU) has a strong influence over the domestic policy of its member states in matters of labour and social law, while the World Bank (WB) or Organisation for Economic Co-operation and Development (OECD) can be seen to have a more 'atmospheric' influence on the language and general direction and terms of policy debate across the range of social policy (see *Table 3.1*, page 54) . At the political level, it is increasingly argued that supranational institutions constrain divergence in national/state policy formation – but again, this is variable across the regions, nations and specific policy domains (Yeates, 2001, 2007a, 2007b). Despite these contingencies, IOs play a very significant role in policy making as the generators, purveyors and agents of knowledge about policy through which policy problems are defined and responses are

Table 3.1: *The global knowledge economy: competing discourses for education*

WB	OECD
Dominant discourse Neoliberal, market orientation	***Dominant discourse*** More socially oriented liberalism, humanistic
Policy agenda Skills for the global knowledge economy (WB, 2003)	***Policy agenda*** Education for human capital formation (OECD, 2001, 2000)
Curriculum form Individualised knowledge and skills: 'just for me, by me'	***Curriculum form*** School as 'learning organisation': mutual learning
Policy language *Choice* Educators (not necessarily teacher) guide towards *individualised learning plans* People learn in groups and from each other by 'doing' Strong focus on *information and communications technology and internet* (rather than teachers)	***Policy language*** *School improvement* Redesign schools as *'core social centre'* Develop schools into *'learning networks'* Growing need for a *'know why, know how' 'know who'* school curriculum, rather than 'know what' Need to *develop teachers*

Source: Adapted by author from Robinson (2005)

shaped. In finding and consuming research and policy analysis, they act as transnational knowledge networks (Stone, 2004).

At the level of domestic governance, policy ideas and practices are transferred 'indirectly' across sectors (private and public; and between sectors of domestic governance) and from previous governments or policy trajectories. For example, in the UK context, New Labour's education reforms ranging from higher education reform to the involvement of the private sector in school organisation have significant antecedents in previous Conservative government policy.

Policy transfer can also be seen to operate at inter-organisational level. Here, the movement of ideas and practices can be domestic or international, top-down or bottom-up and can bypass the central institutions of domestic governance. Local authorities seeking examples of urban renewal and various regional transport schemes such the Manchester metro link were based on direct contact with French and US city authorities. At another level, the International Labour Organization's (ILO) more recent position on pensions incorporates elements of the WB position that predates it (see Chapter Nine in this volume).

Depending on the context of the transferring agents, policy transfer can be voluntary or coercive (obligated transfer), direct or indirect. At all levels, the literature suggests that the transfer of ideas and institutions is a key instrument in the development of social policy programmes in response to emergent political, economic and social conditions.

The policy transfer literature has been enhanced by significant work that has examined the *processes* of learning. Haas (1990, 2004) highlights the role of epistemic communities or competing groups of policy specialists, often found in think tanks and research institutes (Stone 2001, 2004). Deacon (2007) offers an example of the way in which IOs such as the WB and international non-governmental organisations (INGOs), in this case international consulting companies such as the Soros Foundation, have acted in concert. This has often occurred through shared personnel to promote neoliberal, market-oriented packages of policy for welfare reform across the globe, from the 'reconstruction' of post-Soviet eastern Europe to welfare development in Africa and Latin America. Iterative policies promoting privatisation and private–public partnerships in public sector reform have ensued. In all contexts, the supply of expert knowledge by 'epistemics' involves the transfer of ideas developed in one context to other contexts – usually from other countries but occasionally through the recycling of policy ideas and structures from previous domestic policy.

For Haas (1990), the search for policy knowledge is what transnational policy making is all about. Changing policy is a dynamic process; it cannot take place without learning. He produces a knowledge-based definition of policies as packages of cause–effect prescriptions founded on 'scientific' or 'codified' knowledge. Such knowledge is (at the level of national central government institutions) based primarily on quantitative data supplied by professional organisations or policy specialists. Scientific knowledge is then moulded into 'consensual knowledge', or commonly accepted cause-and-effect propositions (for example, policy standards in education reflect the performance of teachers), which define the nature of policy problems and shape the responses available to government. Any departure from an existing policy requires learning on the part of policy makers or 'the penetration of political objectives and programmes by new knowledge' (Haas, 1990, p 316). Dolowitz and colleagues (2000) offer a view of the Americanisation of British higher education that reinforces this point. Here, transferring policy from the US is rational, since it is about making choices in policy development as well as about realising ideological goals. Thus, learning is primarily about the use of knowledge to define political interests and to refine the strategic direction of policy proposals.

Epistemic communities provide such knowledge, which acts as a 'trigger for learning' in helping to break policy makers' habits and their tendency to look for continuity and stability in policy. Haas (1990, p 41) defines them as groups of professionals 'usually recruited from several disciplines', linked by specialist knowledge and acting as a conduit for that knowledge in the service of policy makers. They may 'share a common causal model and set of beliefs' but are more like a community of scientists, 'like biologists', than groups bound together by ideological principles. If there is more than one epistemic community in a policy environment, they can be seen to behave like 'rival groups of scientists' (Haas, 1990, p 42) in that the ultimate test of their 'version of the truth' is the adoption of their prognoses by the users of knowledge.

Deacon (2007) provides a valuable focus on the global reach of epistemic communities and knowledge networks and the role they play in the global market for knowledge about policy. He argues that their role is crucial in determining that certain agendas for social policy 'travel' around the globe. Such networks of experts 'do not simply crystallise around different sites and forms of power ... the network is the site and form of power' (Deacon, 2007, p 17). Thus epistemic communities play a vital part in spreading a global contest between two policy platforms or 'the titanic struggle between the dominant neo-liberal tendency in the World Bank and the more social-solidarity tendency around the ILO and other UN agencies' (Deacon, 2007, p 90). The role of epistemic communities in this struggle, however, is not uni-dimensional, as our overview of the United Nations Educational, Scientific and Cultural Organization's (UNESCO) role in the making of global education policy (***Box 3.2***) demonstrates. Reiterating Deacon's point in Chapter Two of this volume, we need broader and more reflexive notions of the globalisation of policy formation. These global contests over ideas are examined in later chapters of this book in the context of health (Chapter Seven), housing and urban policy (Chapter Eight), pensions (Chapter Nine) and population (Chapter Eleven).

Box 3.2: UNESCO and the making of global education policy

Debates on global social policy tend to present UNESCO as a largely reformist, liberal influence within the transnational education policy networks (see Chapter Two in this volume). The emphasis is placed on human capital formation, providing, as former UNESCO Deputy Director General Colin Power (2006, p 3) has suggested, a 'strategic direction' for education that challenges the market ideology that has dominated social policy and practice since the 1980s. This position is often contrasted with the neoliberal, market-oriented, individualistic policy platforms of the WB.

Formed in 1945 as a key element in the post-war reconstruction of (particularly defeated) areas of Europe, UNESCO's policy goals have remained consistent with the original goals of its constitution to build a culture of peace and sustainable development. Power (2006, p 4) identifies four dominant themes as regards its education policy:

- promoting basic education for all (as a basic human right);
- improving the quality of education (for the fulfilment of human potential and respect for human rights);
- stimulating understanding and policy dialogue relating to global and regional challenges in education systems;
- assisting new and developing countries in the reconstruction and reform of their education systems.

UNESCO's current annual budget for education of around 100 million US dollars is divided roughly evenly between supporting global and regional programmes, including its six education institutes, and providing assistance to member states. Current policy priorities range from the promotion of inclusion, the promotion of early childhood care, gender parity in enrolments in Africa and South West Asia, encouraging adult literacy and promoting better quality teacher education.

Yet a brief examination of UNESCO's role highlights its complexity, and raises questions about the impact it has had in 'globalising' aspects of this essentially liberal agenda.

UNESCO has always provided an arena where the changing politics of global social policy is played out. From its early history in post-war reconstruction in the 1940s and 1950s, UNESCO's agenda for 'democratic education' became conflated with the cold war anti-Soviet position of the US. DeJong-Lambert (2006) and Dorn (2006) suggest that UNESCO's agenda was deliberately co-opted by the US government as a means to imposing conservative cold war propaganda. In the post-war period, 'though founded on the ideal of universal, common culture in education, capable of transcending national boundaries UNESCO ultimately became a place where divisions between East and West were accentuated' (DeJong-Lambert, 2006, p 92). During the 1970s and 1980s, the focus shifted to curriculum reform and the extension and promotion of networks, particularly in Africa.

'Literacy for All' or neo-colonialism?
One of UNESCO's core goals is the promotion of literacy in adults and children. The organisation has demonstrated a willingness to promote this agenda in opposition to market-oriented policy priorities of the WB (Lefrere, 2007). UNESCO points

to its role in raising the adult literacy rate in developing countries from 68% to 77% between the periods 1985-94 and 1995-2004 (UNESCO, 2008). However, critics suggest that however well intentioned this may be, the promotion of notions and forms of literacy derived from essentially English-speaking western nations amounts to a form of cultural neo-colonialism that assists the international movement of neoliberal policy structures (Wickens and Sandlin, 2007).

Travelling liberalism, embedding neoliberalism?

UNESCO's current role in the international movement of education policy is perceived to be increasingly complex. Growing world interconnectedness has ensured that UNESCO, along with the WB and OECD, is increasingly important in setting policy agendas for both developed and developing countries. Despite its role in diffusing the liberal language of inclusion and participation, and its long-standing criticism of the negative impact of market reform on literacy, some authors (for example, Rutkowski, 2007) suggest that it may be unintentionally undermining its core goals. UNESCO's key function within the structures of global social governance is as a multi-layered space for creating and exchanging ready-made packages of knowledge about policy. As such, it has a central role in spreading market-oriented responses such as public–private partnerships. In this sense, the travelling, 'atmospheric' influence of UNESCO's cultural globalisation is inseparably intertwined with the 'economic globalisation' discourses of the WB.

Global programme: local responses?

UNESCO's main influence within the national and global policy communities in recent years has been consistent with its original goals, the promotion of Education for All (EFA) or universal participation. UNESCO's EFA Global Monitoring Report for 2008 highlighted that between 1999 and 2005 with UNESCO funding, primary school enrolment had risen from 647 million to 688 million worldwide. This represented a 36% increase in sub-Saharan Africa and 22% in South and West Asia.

Recent reports reveal however, that member states are less keen to adopt UNESCO's broader objectives. In 2007, only five members had fully adopted these into national educational policy objectives, with 97% of member countries failing to do so. Only 35% acknowledge human rights as a significant objective within national education strategy (Toprakci, 2007)

Policy sociology: a global perspective

Policy sociology (Ozga, 1987; Ball, 1990, 1994; Whitty, 2002) has great utility for understanding global social policy, since it is concerned with *problematising* the policy process as complex and uncertain and looking at the 'bigger picture'. Central to this perspective is Ball's (1994, p 15) conceptualisation of '*policy as text*' and '*policy as discourse*'. Policy as *text* helps us to understand relative freedom of actors to be agents and influences, while policy as *discourse* recognises the existence of multiple constraints. Global social policy analysis is founded on the constraints of transnational discourse evident in social policy worldwide, but it highlights differences within regions and nations that retain the ability to interpret and mediate policy. It also serves to highlight that the making of global social policy involves the bottom-up 'refraction', 'filtering' and 'resistance' by local actors within global agendas. Yeates (2007b) has highlighted the complexity of global social policy. Policies are not simply handed down to national governments from international organisations. Rather:

> 'national' and 'supra-national' are better thought of as different elements of a multi-faceted governance structure whose different levels or 'tiers' are mutually constitutive and through which influence 'travels' multi-directionally. It is therefore as appropriate to ask questions about the ways in, and extent to, which actors located in domestic arenas influence the formation of supra-national policy as it is to ask questions about the ways in which supra-national agencies and actors shape the course of national social policy. (Yeates, 2007b, p 345)

Travelling and embedded policy

In approaching the globalisation of social policy making through a policy sociology perspective, the concepts of travelling and embedded policy are useful. Understanding global social policy requires close attention to processes of mediation and a recognition of complexity. Appadurai's (1996) notion of **vernacular globalisation** helps us with this in stressing the inherent complexity of global social policy. Lingard (2000) has used the term to describe the how local cultures and politics interact with the effects of globalisation to produce social policies that are different in each context.

The study of convergence and divergence in global policy has received a lot of attention in recent years (Burbules and Torres, 2000; Menter et al, 2006), with questions being centred on the extent to which the direction of national policies and their outcomes are influenced by globalisation processes.

Overly deterministic readings or 'strong versions' of globalisation (Yeates, 2001) have been challenged by various commentators who stress the continuing significance of the nation state and of national policy contexts in social policy formation (Lingard, 2000; Yeates, 2001, 2007a, 2007b; Maguire, 2006).

Evidence from international studies suggests that the political culture of the host country (or region) is significant in filtering, reforming and remodelling generic transnational policies, so much so that transfer has become culturally 'mediated' in their locality. Global social policy, then, is 'translated' and 'recontextualised' within local sites of influence – national, regional, institutional (Ball, 1998; Ozga and Jones, 2006). By way of illustrating this point, national governments across Europe are currently preparing for the implementation of the Bologna agreement in 2008, which seeks to standardise the structure of degree programmes in universities, with integrated progression routes in countries within and across Europe (Novoa and Lawn, 2002). There are radically different histories and traditions of higher education in each of the member states. These traditions will not be abandoned on Bologna's implementation; instead, they will be recontextualised to incorporate the 'generic' Anglo-American three-year degree structure.

Ozga (2005, p 207), drawing on the work of Jones and Alexiadou (2001), uses the notion of 'travelling policy' to refer to 'supra- and trans-national agency activity, as well as to common agendas' – for example, the reshaping of education throughout the sectors, from primary to higher, to develop human capital for the information age (see also *Table 3.1*). Such supranational themes include the pursuit of economic competitiveness, effectiveness and efficiency, quality assurance, public accountability and the construction of the 'lifelong learner' and 'knowledge worker' to meet the needs of a supposed 'knowledge-based economy'. Embedded policy is to be found in 'local' spaces (which may be national, regional or local) where global policy agendas come up against existing priorities and practices.

Possibilities for national differences are influenced by the particular social, political and cultural traditions and legacies of each nation state and further constrained by transnational organisations' influences towards 'harmonisation' or 'standardisation', in particular by national responses to the 'global knowledge economy'. Thus, the UK response to globalisation differs from that of certain East Asian countries, indicating that there is a regional dimension to these processes, as well as the evident differences within the 'core', and between 'core' and 'periphery'. Pressures for convergence in the field of education policy, for example, are evident in the creation of a common language of education, recognition of mutual qualifications, systems to regulate cross-border mobility of teachers, the search for comparability in the formation of international benchmarks/quantifiable performance indicators (PISA, International Association for the Evaluation of Educational Acheivements

(Novoa and Yariv–Mashal, 2003), and greater use of the private commercial sector in educational provision. However, the role of the policy community remains important in explaining the 'enactment' or 'realisation' of local policy forms and settlements.

> When we look more closely at how ideas get translated into policies and practices, the differences in national contexts loom larger than the similarities. In each setting general ideas must be turned into specific regulations and practices and at this level the pressure of local circumstances comes to the fore, so that what look like similar policies end up being quite different practices. (Levin, 1998, p 135)

The flexibility of travelling policy is valuable in advancing our understanding of complexity in the making of global social policy. The fact that policies travel does not mean that they are transferred without problems or major changes. There is always a local politics in adapting global agendas.

Policy communities and local policy settlements

If travelling or transferred policy is 'fundamentally about learning' (Wolman and Page, 2002, p 479), that learning takes place within policy networks or policy communities. Policy networks are groups of actors aligned by mutual interest and resource dependence (Marsh and Rhodes, 1993). Jordan (1990, p 317) defines a policy community as a 'special type of stable network which has advantages in encouraging bargaining in policy resolution.... [It] exists where there are effective shared "community" views on the problem'. Within stable policy communities, participants have a commitment to work together to achieve settlement.

How travelling or transferred policy becomes embedded within specific 'local' contexts is influenced by a number of factors: the composition of the policy community, the history and tradition of host countries and the local circumstances, such as the balance of power between national or regional government and donor agencies. It also reflects the relative influence of various actors within the policy and knowledge communities and their openness to learning. This is a political as well as a technical question. The policy transfer models referred to above assume that actors within policy communities are searching for 'evidence' to underpin policy. Both Deacon (2007) and Stone (2004) have acknowledged that global think tanks and epistemic communities have embedded themselves *within* national policy communities with a view to providing a body of 'evidence' for 'best practice' in the construction of social policy. Hulme (2006) highlighted the enduring influence of Anglo-American think tanks such as the Institute of Economic Affairs and the Social Market Foundation education and welfare policy development.

Those global agendas that have travelled most readily have strongly reflected the language of the movement for 'evidence-informed' policy and practice (Hulme, 2006). In one sense, this is because the evidence movement reflects a key aspect of the New Public Management agenda promoted by the WB. In particular, it has been used as a way of extending 'new managerialism' by regulating and codifying the work of teachers, health workers and other public service professionals through the promotion of an 'evidence-based' notion of good practice, often premised on the notion of 'what works'.

More importantly, the evidence-informed movement has provided critical insights into the globalisation of the social policy process, since it is all about the search for 'appropriate' knowledge to underpin policy. The following section explores the political nature of putting 'evidence' into policy. This is a key aspect of policy learning and therefore the global movement of policy ideas, structures and language. The UK government's 'evidence-based' movement is offered as an example of this global movement of policy development in the following discussion.

Evidence into policy: the political nature of decision making

The move towards evidence-based policy development in the UK, set out in the 1999 White Paper *Modernising Government* (Cabinet Office, 1999), was an integral aspect of New Labour's agenda for change. The White Paper emphasised that government departments 'must produce policies that really deal with problems, that are forward-looking and shaped by evidence rather than a response to short-term pressures; that tackle causes not symptoms' (Cabinet Office, 1999). Yet as Keynes famously said, ' there is nothing a government hates more than to be well informed; for it makes the process of arriving at decisions much more complicated and difficult' (cited in Solesbury, 2001, p 7). In reality, the search for evidence or knowledge about policy from all sources may be more of a 'game of truth'. McCormack (2006, p 89) suggests that 'some of these games are driven by governments under the guise of greater effectiveness, but in reality are more to do with efficiency, risk minimisation, control of the professions and centralisation of decision making'.

The evidence movement draws on the simple logic of rational decision making that underpins the most basic policy transfer models: namely that policy can be better made by seeking 'scientific' knowledge or evidence from expert organisations. Parsons (2002, p 43) explains that 'evidence is portrayed essentially as a problem of how knowledge can be utilised and managed'.

In contrast, our broader perspectives such as policy sociology draw attention to the strategic motivations of actors in the policy process. Senior decision makers in national governments deploy evidence as a commodity to give them greater leverage in realising political goals. Evidence is drawn from a variety of sources and research-based evidence forms one of many channels of information.

Decision making thus draws on multiple sources of evidence and is political because local resources and the balance of power come into play. Leicester (1999, p 5) reminds us that politics is the 'art of the possible' rather than 'what works'. The formation of social policy therefore depends on an array of influences, including how receptive national decision makers are to external evidence from transnational and other knowledge-based organisations. Decision makers can elect to ignore evidence and choose selectively from the array of evidence-informed positions available to them. The multiple demands on decision makers' time and the volume of information available to them can act as practical constraints on serious engagement with evidence. As Young et al (2002, p 218) observe, transnational and domestic 'think tanks and research institutes direct a stream of reports to government that largely remain unread'. Think tanks and specialist advisers are used as a resource or 'weaponry' in the competition to mould and shape policy and the take-up of research-based evidence is in proportion to its utility in this struggle (Solesbury, 2001). Armingeon and Beyeler's (2004) study of the 'ideational' impact of the OECD on member states points to a similar degree of selectivity on the part of national authorities when it comes to engaging with OECD policy advice.

Despite the fact that much commissioned university academic research is geared towards evaluation in social policy, not all evidence carries equal value. Hutchinson (2006, p 2) cites the comment from Phil Davies, Deputy Director of the UK Government Social Research Unit, that academic research is 'at the level of plankton in the evidence chain'. While the evidence-based movement has consistently promoted the importance of 'knowledge management' and 'knowledge utilisation' to support the 'emerging knowledge-based society' (OECD, 2000, p 3), the politics of decision making on social policy takes place within 'an economic innovation context' where different knowledges carry different value.

Transnational organisations can be seen to promote policy knowledge with particular flavours. Yeates has observed that the WB has presented itself as a 'knowledge bank' about development, and actively transfers or 'travels' readily-made, market-oriented packages of knowledge for policy formation, often involving public–private partnerships. The Global Development Network (GDN) was established with the intention of informing social policy development in developing counties. Stone (2004) highlights the political nature of some of the 'evidence' produced:

> The knowledge that is generated and transferred (by the GDN), research results, data, information about 'best practice' etc. is considered by some to be flavoured by the values of the Washington Consensus. The policy paradigm involves political choices in favour of certain policies such as privatisation, liberalisation, deregulation and public sector reform. (Stone, 2004, p 7)

Yet, as we have argued throughout, the history, politics and culture of local policy communities retains an influence on policy development and determines its character. Although the language and structure of policies for lifelong learning or the global knowledge economy seem to be repeated around the globe, the substance of social policy can still be determined in regions and localities.

In setting a policy agenda for the global knowledge economy and lifelong learning throughout the world, the WB and OECD have promoted subtly different agendas for changing schools and their curriculum (Robertson, 2005; see also *Table 3.1*). Yet national policy elites choose carefully which discourses to embed within policy documents. For example, while Canadian education policy makers prefer the OECD 'school as social centre' discourse, British policy makers have embedded the language of 'personalised' learning in their initiatives to promote the global knowledge economy through lifelong learning (Robertson, 2005).

We have argued that in studying the global movement of social policy, it is important to consider what has travelled, transferred or 'converged' (primarily policy discourse and language) and what have become embedded (the local 'interpretation') or divergent forms of policy. In the following section we examine in more detail the local interpretation of the generic notions of 'diversity' and 'choice' in education.

Making the global local: divergence within Britain

In recent years, the integration of services for young people in education, social work, health and the criminal justice system has become an increasingly important global agenda. Again, we find that notions of integrated 'educare' are legitimated by INGOs, with a familiar difference in emphasis between the WB and UNESCO/OECD. All are advocates of inter-agency working and use the notion of 'social capital' to encourage 'joined up' thinking by national governments. Robertson (2005) observes that the discourse of social capital for the WB is emphasised to support the almost universal notion in social policy of 'personalisation'. UNESCO, however, promotes the integration of 'education programmes with health, nutrition etc for the most disadvantaged children'. Here, the underpinning social capital discourse can be interpreted as the building of social capacity of 'bridging and bonding' and the development of human capital.

As with our other examples, this trajectory of policy has resonated with local communities in different ways. In developing countries, integrated service provision is nothing new: international agencies have developed such approaches as a means of building social capacity for many years. Robertson (2005) notes that ministers for education in African countries have rejected market models for the personalisation of services as undesirable. However, among western governments 'full service' schooling has developed from origins in the US (Dryfoos, 1994; Kronick, 2002) where the policy initiative No Child Left Behind was developed in 2000. The English policy response to this generic agenda has been through the development of a major reform of the children's workforce following *Every Child Matters* (HM Treasury, 2003). This was preceded by Scotland's New or Integrated Community Schools programme (*For Scotland's Children*, Scottish Executive, 2001). An analysis of the policy documentation in England and Scotland reveals different emphases, corresponding to the differing agendas of the IOs concerned. There is arguably a different politics of policy mediation in Scotland. Arnott and Menter (2007) argue that because Scotland has a longer established political culture with a very distinctive public sector ethos it was able to resist the market reforms favoured by New Labour south of the border. Implementation of the new community schools policy was very much tempered by *Count Us In: Achieving Inclusion in Scottish Schools* (HMIE, 2002). This document was produced by the schools inspectorate for Scotland and links the inclusion agenda firmly to the Scottish Executive's social justice agenda. This influential report recommended the development of shared aims and objectives and a clear understanding of the contribution that each agency could make towards the achievement of common goals. It emphasised the importance of partnership, in which all stakeholders are prepared to share decision making and the leadership of specific work in appropriate ways. In the US and English cases, the local policy settlement has embraced the WB's notions of 'personalisation' in which young people are constructed as economic contributors, an interpretation that connects with economistic readings of globalisation contained in the discourse of the 'knowledge society'

Conclusion

In this chapter, we have sought to problematise the notion of global social policy transfer. Specifically, we have sought to emphasise the complex interrelationship between supranational, cross-national, regional and sectoral influences on policy production. The multi-layered nature of policy making requires a less technicist conception that retains and emphasises local mediation. The examples used illustrate how local responses to travelling policies are put together or remodelled. National policy communities have negotiated policy settlements that reflect particular historical, cultural and political traditions. How responses are assembled reflects the complex interaction between transnational knowledge networks and local priorities and practices.

Summary

- Certain agendas in social policy have become global as the language and structure of policy has travelled or been transferred.
- For policy makers, the 'transfer' of knowledge about policies is a valuable instrument in the new 'global governance'.
- There is a large multidisciplinary literature on the international movement of policy ranging from transfer to diffusion, borrowing and lesson drawing. Policy transfer is a process in which knowledge about policies developed in one place or time is used in the development of policy in another place or time.
- Policy makers look for knowledge about policies in order to 'learn' how to realise their policy goals. This knowledge is often supplied by international communities of policy experts or epistemic communities. Epistemic communities can be linked to transnational governmental organisations such as the WB or UN, or they can be based in think tanks linked to national governments as well as IOs.
- Policy transfer is rarely direct, conclusive or successful. The concepts of travelling and embedded policy help us to see how policy is contested, interpreted and mediated in different national and regional contexts.
- While there is a common language to global agendas such as 'public accountability' and the 'knowledge-based economy', what emerges as policy in the 'local' context is influenced by the political, social and cultural legacies of the nation or region.
- Policy networks or communities determine which aspects of global travelling agendas become embedded within their contexts.
- There is a global agenda for evidence-based policy and practice in social policy. This is often presented as best practice for problem solving in health and education. But policy learning on the part of decision makers in social policy is about finding evidence to justify or reinforce their ideological positions and policy proposals.

Questions for discussion

- Compare the two models of policy within the chapter. How does the notion of policy within the transfer models compare with the notion of policy within the global policy sociology perspective?
- In what way does the notion of travelling and embedded policy contribute to our understanding of global social policy?
- Identify the supranational organisations that have contributed to the transfer or travelling of a particular policy. What are the relevant local influences on the same policy? You could draw on examples in this chapter or from another chapter in this volume.
- Why is it necessary to problematise and historicise the policy process in social policy?

Further reading

Dolowitz et al (2000) introduce the framework of policy transfer and offers a series of case studies from the Americanisation of higher education in the UK, through to the transfer of the Child Support Agency and electronic tagging for offenders in the early nineties.

Ozga and Jones (2006) introduce the perspective of travelling and embedded policy, which is key to understanding the movement of international agendas. It applies this to education policy and knowledge transfer.

It is vital that you understand not only the international movement of policies but who transfers them and why; a perspective is therefore needed on international networks and communities. Stone and Maxwell (2005) offer this and some very useful case-study material. Finally, you should aim to consult *Global Social Policy: Journal of Public Policy and Social Development*, which publishes a range of full-length and shorter articles on issues, debates and developments in global social policy as well as very good case-study material for policy transfer and globalisation.

Electronic resources

www.gassp.org offers papers that provide application of many of the issues raised in this chapter.

www.globalwelfare.net provides a range of teaching and learning material with very useful links to research, policy documents and statistics for case studies and examples of travelling or transferred policy.

References

Appadurai, A. (1996) *Modernity at Large: Cultural Dimensions of Globalisation*, Minneapolis, MN: University of Minneapolis Press.

Armingeon, K. and Beyeler, M. (eds) (2004) *The OECD and European Welfare States*, Cheletenham: Edward Elgar.

Arnot, M. and Menter, I. (2007) 'The same but different? Post-devolution regulation and control in education in Scotland and England', *European Education Research Journal*, vol 6, no 3, pp 250-65.

Ball, S.J. (1990) *Politics and Policy Making in Education: Explorations in Policy Sociology*, London: Routledge.

Ball, S.J. (1994) *Education Reform: A Critical and Post-Structural Approach*, Buckingham: Open University Press.

Ball, S.J. (1998) 'Big policies/small world: an introduction to international perspectives in education policy', *Comparative Education*, vol 34, no 2, pp 119-30.

Burbules, N.C. and Torres, C.A. (eds) (2000) *Globalisation and Education: Critical Perspectives*, London: Routledge.

Cabinet Office (1999) *Modernising Government*, Cm. 4310, London: The Stationery Office (www.archive.official-documents.co.uk/document/cm43/4310/4310-02.htm) (accessed 26 August 2007).

Deacon, B. (2007) *Global Social Policy and Governance*, London: Sage Publications.

DeJong-Lambert, W. (2006) 'UNESCO: bridging three world systems?', *European Education*, vol 38, no 3, pp 82-94.

Dolowitz, D. and Marsh, D. (1996) 'Who learns what from whom? A review of the policy transfer literature', *Political Studies*, vol 44, no 2, pp 343-57.

Dolowitz, D. with Hulme, R., Nellis, M. and O'Neal, F. (2000) *Policy Transfer and British Social Policy*, Buckingham: Open University Press.

Dorn, C. (2006) '"The world's schoolmaster":educational reconstruction, Grayson Kefauver and the founding of UNESCO 1942-46', *History of Education*, vol 35, no 3, pp 297-320.

Dryfoos, J. (1994) *Full-service Schools. A Revolution in Health and Social Services for Children, Youth and Families*, San Francisco, CA: Jossey-Bass.

Evans, M. and Davies, J. (1999) 'Understanding policy transfer: a multi-level, multi-disciplinary perspective', *Public Administration*, vol 77, no 2, pp 361-85.

Haas, E. (1990) *When Knowledge is Power: Three Models of Change in International Organisations*, Berkeley, CA: University of California Press.

Haas, P. (2004). 'When does power listen to truth? A constructivist approach to the policy process', *Journal of European Public Policy*, vol 11, no 4, pp 569-92.

HM Inspectorate of Education (2002) *Count Us In: Acheiving Inclusion in Scottish Schools*, Edinburgh: The Stationery Office.

HM Treasury (2003) *Every Child Matters*, London: The Stationery Office.

Hulme, R. (2006) 'The role of policy transfer in assessing the impact of American ideas on British social policy', *Global Social Policy*, vol 6, no 2, pp 175-97.

Hutchinson, B. (2006) 'Researchers' role in policy decision making: purveyors of evidence, purveyors of ideas?', *Healthcare Policy*, vol 1, no 2, pp 1-2.

Jones, K. and Alexiadou, N. (2001) 'Travelling policy: local spaces', Paper presented to '*The global and the national: reflections on the experience of three European states*' symposium at the European Conference on Educational Research, September, Lille.

Jordan, G. (1990) 'Bringing policy communities back in? A comment on Grant', *British Journal of Politics and International Relations*, vol 7, pp 317-21.

Kronick, R.F. (2002) *Full Service Schools: A Place for Our Children and Families to Learn and Be Healthy*, Springfield, IL:C.C. Thomas.

Lefrere, P. (2007) 'Competing higher education futures in a globalising world', *European Journal of Education*, vol 42, no 2, pp 201-12.

Leicester, G. (1999) 'The seven enemies of evidence-based policy', *Public Money & Management*, January-March, pp 5-7.

Levin, B. (1998) 'An epidemic of education policy: (what) can we learn from each other?', *Comparative Education*, vol 34, no 2, pp 131-41.

Lingard, B. (2000) 'It is and it isn't: vernacular globalisation, education policy and restructuring', in N. Burbules and C.A. Torres (eds) *Globalisation and Education: Critical Perspectives*, London: Routledge, pp 79-108.

Maguire, M. (2006) 'Globalisation, education policy and the teachers', in D. Hartley and M. Whitehead (eds) *Teacher Education: Major Themes in Education. Volume Five. Globalisation, Standards and Teacher Education*, London: Routledge: pp 39-58.

Marsh, D. and Rhodes, R.A.W. (1993) *Policy Networks in British Government*, Oxford: Clarendon.

McCormack, B. (2006) 'Evidence-based practice and the potential for transformation', *Journal of Research in Nursing*, vol 11, no 2, pp 89-94.

Menter, I.E. et al. (2006) *Convergence or Divergence? Initial Teacher Education in Scotland and England*, Edinburgh: Dunedin.

Meyer, J., Frank, D., Hironka, A. and Tuma, N. (1997) 'The structuring of a world environmental regime 1870-1970', *International Organisations*, vol 51, no 4, pp 623-51.

Mintrom, M. and Vergari, S. (1996) 'Advocacy coalitions, policy entrepreneurs and policy change', *Policy Studies Journal*, vol 24, no 3, pp 429-34.

Novoa, A and Lawn, M. (eds) (2002) *Fabricating Europe*, Dordtrecht: Kluwer Academic Publishers.

Novoa, A. and Yariv-Mashal, T. (2003) 'Comparative research in education: a mode of governance or a historical journey?', *Comparative Education*, vol 39, no 4, pp 423-38.

OECD (Organisation for Economic Co-operation and Development) (2000) *Schooling for Tomorrow*, Paris: OECD.

OECD (2001) *Knowledge Management in the Learning Society*, Paris: OECD.

Ozga, J. (1987) 'Studying educational policy through the lives of policy makers: an attempt to close the macro-micro gap', in S. Walker and L. Barton (eds) *Changing Policies, Changing Teachers*, Milton Keynes: Open University Press, pp 138-50.

Ozga, J. (2005) 'Modernising the education workforce: a perspective from Scotland', *Educational Review*, vol 57, no 2, pp 207-19.

Ozga, J. and Jones, R. (2006) 'Travelling and embedded policy: the case of knowledge transfer', *Journal of Education Policy*, vol 21, no 1, pp 1-17.

Parsons, W. (2002) 'From muddling through to muddling up: evidence-based policy making and the modernisation of British government', *Public Policy and Administration*, vol 17, no 3, pp 43-60.

Phillips, D. and Ochs, K. (eds) (2004) *Educational Policy Borrowing: Historical Perspectives*, Oxford: Symposium Books.

Power, C. (2006) 'Creating a literate and peaceful world: reflections on UNESCO's policies and programs at the end of the millennium', *Social Alternatives*, vol 25, no 4, pp 2-6.

Robertson, S. (2005) 'Re-imagining and rescripting the future of education: global knowledge economy discourses and the challenge to education systems', *Comparative Education*, vol 41, no 2, pp 151-70.

Rose, R. (1991) 'What is lesson drawing?', *Journal of Public Policy*, vol 11, no 1, pp 1-22.

Rutkowski, D. (2007) 'Converging us softly: how intergovernmental organisations promote neo-liberal education policy', *Critical Studies in Education*, vol 48, no 2, pp 229-47.

Sabatier, P. and Jenkins-Smith, H. (eds) (1993) *Policy Change and Learning: An Advocacy Coalitions Approach*, Boulder, CO: Westview Press.

Scottish Executive (2001) *For Scotland's Children: Better Integrated Children's Services*, Edinburgh: Scottish Executive.

Solesbury, W. (2001) Evidence-based policy: whence it come from and where it's going, London: ESRC UK Centre for Evidence Based Policy and Practice, pp 1-11.

Stone, D. (2001) 'Think tanks, global lesson drawing and networking social policy ideas', *Global Social Policy*, vol 1, no 3, pp 338-60.

Stone, D. (2004) 'Better knowledge, better policy, better world: the grand ambitions of a global research institution', *Global Social Policy*, vol 4, no 1, pp 5-8.

Stone, D. and Maxwell, M. (2005) *Global Knowledge Networks and International Development*, London: Routledge.

Toprakci, E. (2007) 'The rates of participation of the member countries in the institutional objectives of UNESCO', *International Journal of Progressive Education*, vol 3, no 1, pp 2-30.

UNESCO (United Nations Education, Scientific and Cultural Organisation) (2008) *Education for All: Global Monitoring Report*, New York, NY: UNESCO.

Wickens, C. and Sandlin, J. (2007) 'Literacy for what? Literacy for whom? The politics of literacy education and neocolonialism in UNESCO and World Bank sponsored literacy programs', *Adult Education Quarterly*, vol 57, no 4, pp 275-92.

Whitty, G. (2002) *Making Sense of Education Policy: Studies in the Sociology and Politics of Education*, London: Paul Chapman.

Wolman, H. and Page, E. (2002) 'Policy transfer among local governments: an information-theory approach', *Governance*, vol 15, no 4, pp 477-501.

WB (World Bank) (2003) *Lifelong Learning for a Global Knowledge Economy*, Washington, DC: WB.

Yeates, N. (2001) *Globalization and Social Policy*, London: Sage Publications.

Yeates, N. (2007a) 'Globalisation and social policy', in J. Baldock et al (eds) *Social Policy* (3rd edn), Oxford: Oxford University Press.

Yeates, N. (2007b) 'The global and supra-national dimensions of the welfare mix', in M. Powell (ed) *Understanding the Mixed Economy of Welfare*, Bristol: The Policy Press.

Young, K., Ashby, D., Boaz, A. and Grayson, L. (2002) 'Social science and the evidence-based policy movement', *Social Policy and Society*, vol 1, no 3, pp 215-24.

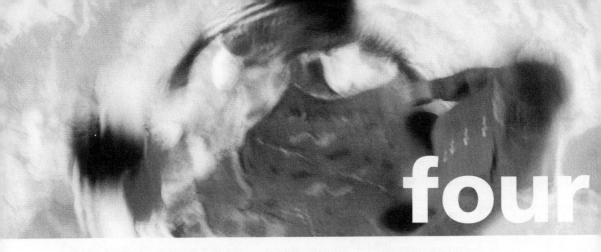

four

Business and global social policy formation

Kevin Farnsworth

Overview

The power of business to shape global policy agendas has increased substantially over the past two decades. Transnational corporations have greater opportunity to chase more profitable business locations and to forge more exploitative conditions for production and trade. The control and regulation of 'footloose' corporations is also more difficult. At the same time, global business interest associations, representing large individual firms and business organisations, enjoy an enhanced role global social policy making and governance. Global social policy discourse and initiatives reflect this enhanced power. This chapter examines some of the ways in which business might influence global social policy formation.

Key concepts

Business power and influence; global business interest association; corporate social responsibility; corporate codes of conduct; corporate-centred social policy

Introduction

Critics of neoliberal globalisation have been active in voicing their concern at the ways in which the distribution of power and authority has favoured the rich and powerful. One of the key beneficiaries of this in power relations under contemporary globalisation has been business; **global business** and **transnational corporations** (TNCs) in particular have been identified as a major political and economic force. However, corporate power is neither insurmountable nor constant, and, as subsequent sections illustrate, growing **business power** is not necessarily inconsistent with, nor does it rule out advances in, social policy.

This chapter examines some of the ways in which business is said to be entangled with, and influential in, global social policy formation. Three aspects of this are discussed. First, the chapter explores the growing influence of business interests in global social policy discourse and policy-making processes. Second, it examines some ways in which global business practices adversely affect – or cause harm to – workers, citizens and consumers. Third, the chapter outlines global policy responses to these challenges, discussing the contention that global social policy is corporate-centred. As we shall argue, social policy is the centrepiece of a global policy strategy to better govern globalisation processes. This strategy aims to simultaneously increase human welfare and both protect and promote business interests.

This chapter is concerned with organised business. *Box 4.1* defines what is meant by 'business' in the context of this chapter. Note that we confine ourselves to 'legitimate' legal business organisations and do not address the issue of transnational criminal organisations or global business actors and organisations operating in the **informal economy** or **shadow economy**.

Box 4.1: Distinguishing business and business organisations

The term business is used to denote a broad set of class interests that coalesce within and between private, for-profit business organisations. 'Business' refers to business people, firms and business interest associations (organisations that represent groups of business people or firms) operating on a for-profit basis.

Business organisations may take many forms. They include both individual firms and groups of individual firms, as well as clubs and associations of business people. Business organisations vary widely in terms of their size, and can range from small, family-run firms operating on a local basis to large global corporations. The majority are legitimate legal entities but do not always adhere to the law. Many exist and operate outside of the law, in the informal or shadow economy. Many operate within the private commercial sphere on a for-profit basis. Many have no direct contact with consumer markets, operating to furnish the requirements of government or to supply other firms.

For these reasons, while some common values and ideas are shared widely between business organisations, there is also a great deal of disagreement and, often, tensions between them. One of the key divisions is between those constituting or representing financial capital and those constituting or representing industrial capital. Although they often cooperate and even collude with each other to further their collective aims, they operate within environments that set them in competition with each other. Despite these diverse and often competing interests, there are a great many issues that unite business organisations, or at least the most powerful business organisations; in such instances, governments often find it difficult to act against such unity.

Globalisation and business power

Various commentators, from academia, **civil society**, the mass media and the business world, increasingly speak of the power and dominance of 'big business' over various aspects of our lives. But what does it mean to say that business is powerful? We have already come across this notion of influence in Chapter Three, which looked at it in the impact of global policy actors, such as international organisations (IOs), global networks and civil society in shaping global social policy. Here we are going to examine issues of power by referring to a distinction often made by sociologists and political scientists between two forms of power: structure and agency (*Box 4.2*). Both play out in different ways in different contexts, and both have helped to shape global social policy development.

Box 4.2: Business power: structure and agency

Structural theory argues that the primary source of business power within nation states is its monopoly control over existing and future private investments (Lindblom, 1977). These investment decisions have long-lasting and far-reaching consequences for governments and citizens, impacting as they do on future production, employment and consumption.

Agency perspectives stress the importance of direct political engagement to an understanding of business power. Business people may become politically active and seek election; others may be nominated to public decision-making bodies. Business organisations also use the media and other resources to win popular support and make direct representation to policy makers and decision makers through their lobbying activities.

Through structural power, business is able to command a great deal of influence over a vast array of policy agendas and across the policy-making process without having to resort to specific action or intervention at all. Influence in this instance is based on the fact that policy makers experience pressure to steer policy in a particular direction from the social and political structures within which they work to serve and protect the interests of business. Governments are dependent for their own revenue on existing or new business investments as well as taxes levied on profits, and their electability often closely mirrors the relative health of the economy. The electorate also depends on business – their employers – for their wages. Given their high level of dependence on continued business investment and profits, governments and employees have little choice but to create and sustain the conditions that do not damage these (Offe and Ronge, 1984). Once politicians and citizens accept this to be the case, business is said to assume a hegemonic position, meaning that business interests are legitimised as the 'common interest' (Lindblom, 1977).

International governmental organisations (IGOs) experience the structural power of business in similar ways to national governments. The World Bank (WB), International Monetary Fund (IMF), World Trade Organization (WTO) and United Nations (UN) were established during, or shortly after, the political and economic tumult of the Second World War in order to help coordinate economic cooperation, growth and stability. Business interests and priorities are therefore institutionally embedded within them. Pressure to prioritise business interests in IGOs' policies also comes from governments. Governments often lobby IGOs on behalf of the interests of businesses located in their territories, where these business interests are equated as being in the 'national interest'.

In terms of agency power, the opportunities for business to exert a tangible influence over global political and policy-making processes are substantial. Business has generally been very successful in organising and exploiting new openings arising from the creation of supranational institutions and global fora. Global business has been able to present a relatively united front and form linkages with globalising political and bureaucratic elites and other members of the transnational capitalist class (Sklair, 2001). Business agency has been boosted in global social policy making since the 1980s, by the increasing opportunities afforded to it for institutional engagement by IGOs. It has particularly benefited from the creation of new consultative mechanisms to enhance the role of civil society organisations in global agenda setting and policy making, since business organisations are defined as a civil society organisation for these purposes (Yeates, 2001). Whereas IGOs have gone out of their way to incorporate business voices within various committees and other decision-making bodies, labour and citizen groups have not been afforded the same advantages (Korten, 1997; Stiglitz, 2002, 2005; Tesner, 2000; O'Brien, 2002; Utting, 2006).

The creation of new channels and formalised linkages between IGOs and business organisations since the 1990s has further amplified the voices of **global business interest associations** (GBIAs). *Table 4.1* presents a summary overview of the different kinds of GBIAs and the mechanisms that facilitate their access to various IGOs. The Organisation for Economic Co-operation and Development (OECD), European Commission (EC) and UN have all developed formal institutional linkages with key global business organisations, both in an attempt to be better informed of the views and wishes of business and to actively engage with business actors to steer them towards particular objectives (Ollila, 2003). Other chapters in this volume highlight some other ways in which these institutional linkages have been forged: Chapter Seven, for example, discusses how business actors have been drawn into global health policy as institutional partners in the Global Fund. Business dominance has been further aided by the historical dominance of individuals with business backgrounds in senior positions within IGOs. National finance ministers and central bankers, many of whom – it is safe to say – are likely to have clear business sympathies, also play key roles in setting the agendas and policies of the international financial institutions (IFIs) in particular. As a former 'insider' in the WB, Joseph Stiglitz (2002) notes that this revolving door between business, the WB and IMF places senior business people at the heart of both of these IFIs so that they 'naturally see the world through the eyes of the financial community' (p 21).

Despite these advances made by business, its power should be viewed as variable. Different states have in place different institutional arrangements and traditions that reduce or amplify the power of business to influence policy making. Power also varies over time. During the 1980s in particular, business power was largely structural, but global business lacked institutional access. Thus, global policy tended to promote what was 'assumed' to be in the interests of business, and, as a general rule, it tended to favour those parts of business that stood to gain most from the expansion of the global economy, namely large transnational corporations (TNCs) keen to take advantage of cheaper and more docile labour or new market opportunities. As noted earlier, agency power of business gained in importance from the early 1990s with the creation of new institutional channels into global social policy making. The success of business

Table 4.1: *Global business interest associations and their links with IGOs*

Global business interest association	Membership	Key institutional links
Business and Industry Advisory Committee to the OECD (BIAC)	The largest business organisation representing business interests within the OECD countries.	Consulted on major OECD policies. Its main role is to put business arguments to OECD committees and member states.
International Chambers of Commerce (ICC)	Drawn from various trade organisations and companies from all sectors in over 130 countries throughout the world.	Has direct access to the most important political and economic institutions, including the OECD, WB, IMF and UN, where it promotes 'open international trade and investment ... and the market economy'. Has a particularly close relationship with the UN.
European Round Table (ERT)	Represents CEOs from around 45 leading EU companies. Membership is by invitation, and only the most powerful and largest corporations are allowed to join. As a result, it commands a huge amount of attention from Europe's decision makers.	Consulted regularly by institutions within the EU. It often coordinates its lobbying efforts with UNICE.
Union of Industrial and Employers' Confederations of Europe (UNICE)	Membership consists of 33 employers' federations from 25 European countries.	The official voice of industry in the EU and partner in the EU's Social Dialogue. It commonly attempts to influence policy at the EU level, but also acts to provide a steer to national employers' federations within member states. Often coordinates its efforts with the ERT.
European Association of Craft, Small and Medium-Sized Enterprises (UEAPME)	Represents the interests of small and medium-sized employers within the EU. It has a relatively small membership drawn from SME trade associations from each of the EU member states.	Lobbies on a range of issues that directly impact on SMEs within the EU. Sits alongside UNICE within the EU's Social Dialogue.

power in global social policy making is evidenced by global regulations: it was able to lever its power to shape global rules dealing with access to markets and investment, ownership, the right to free movement of capital and certain aspects of tax policy, for example with regards to **double taxation** arrangements, all of which developed rapidly from the early 1980s, while initiatives to regulate corporate behaviour were fewer in number and far weaker in substance. We return to these global social regulatory mechanisms later in the chapter, after examining the wider context in which they have emerged.

The globalisation of corporate harm

© www.CartoonStock.com

Corporations squeeze the world dry

Growing business power and the emergence of 'free' market globalisation, combined with relatively weak international regulations, have given rise to concerns about corporate harm. The concept of corporate harm has developed furthest within parts of the criminology literature where it refers to a range of activities that are detrimental to human welfare but not necessarily illegal (Hillyard et al, 2004; Fooks, forthcoming). The development of this concept was in part a reaction to the focus of criminologists on the crimes of the poor to the neglect of the crimes of the rich and powerful. The concept of harm distinguishes between the following:

• physical harm, such as that caused by exposure to environmental pollutants or by unsafe working conditions;
• financial/economic harm, such as poverty wages and financial losses that are the result of fraud or price fixing;
• emotional and psychological harm, such as anomie and depression resulting from poor working environments,

In this context, corporations and business practices are identified as a major cause of harm. Some critics argue that their basic rationale – of exploitation of populations and the environment, and profit-seeking motives – is inherently harmful, and that in so far as **neoliberal globalisation** processes have been largely about extending the profit-seeking opportunities for corporations so one can make a link between globalisation and the proliferation of harm worldwide. Corporate harm is also a result of regulatory deficits: it occurs where regulations fail to keep up with new risks presented by changes in commodity or labour markets or where these regulations are not implemented. One of the major concerns here is that the rapid growth of international markets since the early 1980s has outstripped regulatory reach. In other words, the international political community has failed to put in place an enforceable international 'social' floor below which national standards should not fall. While there have been attempts to do so, they have failed. The campaign to set such a floor is dealt with in Chapter Five in relation to the governance of international trade and in Chapter Six in the context of global labour policy.

This lack of concerted political will by the international community as a whole to act together can in many ways be understood in the context of the pressures that states are under to be internationally competitive. One of the major features of policy development in recent years is the way in which states have relaxed social, health and environmental regulations on firms in a bid to attract overseas investment and prevent capital flight (see Chapter One). Corporations have attempted to reduce production costs (for example, by cutting health and safety corners or shedding staff) and secure more favourable production conditions (for instance, by exerting greater control over staff or through sub-contracting processes), and this has been done through a combination of lobbying government and relocating part of the production base abroad, often to developing or peripheral countries (Yeates, 2001). This in turn has imposed structural pressures that, for reasons already outlined above, pressurise governments into policy reform to maintain a 'competitive investment climate'; these pressures have resulted in fears of a dynamic decline in social and labour standards – such fears being encapsulated in the terms **race**

to the bottom or **slide to the bottom** welfare scenarios (see also Chapter Five). In sum, there is a tension between the very real benefits brought to a country or region by inward investment – increased employment, incomes, tax revenues and improvements to infrastructure – and the subsequent risks this investment and production present to domestic economies and social institutions, especially where regulatory measures prove to be inadequate. The overall result of all this has been an increase in the level, and forms, of corporate harm committed by business and TNCs in particular. Some main elements of this are summarised in *Table 4.2* (see also Chapter Six of this volume, which provides further details of the harms experienced by labour worldwide).

The emergence of corporate-centred global social policy

Much of IGO policy has been oriented to increasing incentives for corporations to prioritise profits above all else, but more recent global policy initiatives have begun to redress the balance. The same advances in travel and communications technology that strengthened the power of global business interests have also helped to boost alternative and rival voices, most notably the anti-capitalist, anti-globalisation and other popular civil society movements, often acting in **transnational advocacy networks** to pressure corporations and policy makers to address various social and environmental corporate harms (Farnsworth, 2004b; see also Chapter One of this volume). These networks, together with influential epistemic communities (Chapters Two and Three of this volume), have employed a wide range of strategies and tactics to pressure governments, IGOs and businesses into taking remedial and precautionary measures to mitigate the worst effects of corporate practices. This struggle has also occurred from 'within' IGOs, whose staff and departments have attempted, with some success, to place welfare issues on global policy agendas. The result is that opposition to **neoliberal** modes of globalisation, together with the increasingly apparent systemic instability and unsustainability of this mode of 'development', has steadily grown so that, since the late 1980s, it has become impossible to ignore in the west.

Two further developments have also encouraged IGOs to revise their approach to corporate harm and human welfare. First, the rapid economic growth and concomitant growing political power of China, India and South Africa, coupled with opposition from some left-leaning governments in Latin America, notably Brazil and Venezuela, have directly challenged the ideas, authority and legitimacy of IGOs, especially the WB and IMF. Other countries have also turned their back on WB funding, unwilling to sign up to the prescriptive **liberalisation** strategies that accompany IFI loans, preferring instead to raise finance from private markets (Masson, 2007). Second, IGOs

Table 4.2: Globalisation and corporate harm

Example of corporate harm	Case studies/further reading
TNCs accused of exploiting weak labour regulations, especially in developing countries, paying poverty wages and exploiting employees, including young women and children. Existing social protection and revenues are placed under pressure from outward investment.	The apparel industry has been most strongly criticised here. NoSweat (www. nosweat.org.uk) alleges widespread exploitation within factories making clothing for Nike, Gap and Walmart. Actionaid recently carried out a detailed investigation of the practices of the four largest British supermarkets (Tesco, Asda, Sainsbury's and Safeway/Morrisons) and accused them of using their increasing purchasing power to drive down the price of goods sourced from developing countries, which in turn has driven down wages and conditions of work within those countries (www.actionaid.org.uk).
TNCs accused of investing in and/or colluding with undemocratic regimes that systematically torture and kill opposition groups, including trade unionists.	Columbia: Amnesty International reported death threats and assassinations of trade unionists in various industries, including eight trade union leaders from four separate Coca Cola bottling sites in Columbia between 1994 and 2002.* Nigeria: opponents to land-grabs and environmental destruction by government officials and the oil industry were executed in 1995. Led to a long-running campaign to boycott Shell Oil, one of the major oil companies operating in that region.

continued…

Table 4.2: *Globalisation and corporate harm continued*

Example of corporate harm	Case studies/further reading
Corporations accused of the inappropriate or illegal pursuit of new markets, including: • bribing government officials in order to gain access to markets; • selling inappropriate products, or marketing them in inappropriate ways, to the detriment of human health and welfare; • denying access to essential commodities for the poorest and most vulnerable. Water privatisation has led to large price increases and cuts in supply to the poor. Pharmaceutical companies are accused of denying access to essential drugs to those within developing countries. Agribusiness is accused of continuing to market pesticides in some states that have been banned over safety concerns in other countries and of using international patents and GM technologies to assert greater control over crop production.	Defence industry: BAE Systems was accused in 2007 of giving multi-million pound bribes to the Saudi Arabian government in order to secure major arms deals ('BAE accused of secretly paying £1bn to Saudi Prince', *The Guardian*, 7 June 2007). Baby milk formula: a lack of access to clean water directly contributes to the deaths of some 105 million babies each year, according to UNICEF (2001) (see also www.babymilkaction.org). Nestlé has been accused of consistently flouting global regulations on the marketing of baby milk formula, and this has led to one of the longest corporate boycotts against a single company in history (Richter, 2001). Bolivia: water prices increased by 200-300% following a WB-sanctioned water privatisation programme and water supplies were cut to those who could not or would not pay. Popular protest eventually brought a government about-turn and a renationalisation of the water supply.

continued...

Table 4.2: *Globalisation and corporate harm continued*

Example of corporate harm	Case studies/further reading
Corporations accused of profiteering and risk taking at the expense of human life and physical environments.	2007: fractured oil pipeline in Alaska and an explosion at an oil plant in Texas City that killed 15 people; both were owned by BP. According to investigations by the Congressional Committee on Energy and Commerce, and the Chemical Safety Board, both accidents were caused by cost-cutting measures ('US safety report slams BP over Texas City disaster', *The Guardian*, 20 March 2007).
	, India, 1983: four separate safety devices in a factory producing pesticides failed because of negligence resulting in a major gas explosion. According to official estimates, some 2,000 people died immediately, but others suggest that a death toll of around 7,000 is more accurate, with a further 20,000 people dying later from exposure. Many babies have subsequently been born with birth defects. A Greenpeace study conducted in 2004 found that soil and water supplies in Bhopal remain heavily contaminated. Union Carbide, the American firm that owned the plant, had neglected to properly maintain it in anticipation of selling it, and was ordered by a local court to pay $470m in compensation to the victims, an inadequate amount that, in any case, failed to find its way to most of the victims. The CEO of the company was arrested and charged with manslaughter, although he fled to the US and has never faced trial. In 2001, Union Carbide was taken over by Dow Chemicals, the largest chemical company in the world, which denies it has any outstanding liabilities in Bhopal.

Note: * http://us.oneworld.net/external/?url=http%3A%2F%2Fnews.amnesty.org%2F2Findex%2FENGAMR230172007 have moved towards more actively engaging with global business actors as a way of locating solutions to the systemic problems of neoliberal globalisation. The emergence of the **Post-Washington Consensus** in particular heralded a shift in thinking about global social policy so that it not only responds to some of the more powerful critiques of past policies but also provides a better fit with global business opinion. IGOs sought to harness the fact that global business is, by and large, less opposed to the development of global social policy than the supporters of neoliberal ideas, including some sectoral business interests.

These various pressures and constraints have led IGOs to reconsider past policy recommendations and seek out global social policy solutions that simultaneously reduce corporate harm and promote human welfare, but do so in a way that complements investment, competitiveness and corporate profits. The following two sections illustrate how these policies have evolved, starting with corporate social responsibility (CSR) and codes of conduct.

Corporate social responsibility and corporate codes of conduct

The result of the various pressures and influences outlined above has been growing interest in the concept of **corporate social responsibility**. Broadly defined, CSR describes a range of business initiatives and policies that contribute positively to the welfare of a company's stakeholders, whether employees, consumers or their communities, while maintaining the interests of another set of corporate stakeholders – its shareholders. As Robert O'Brien points out in Chapter Six of this volume, CSR garners support, albeit in varying degrees, from a range of business actors, IGOs, national governments and parts of civil society, but it also attracts a strong degree of scepticism for being little more than a corporate public relations stunt.

Today the majority of the world's largest companies audit and actively publicise a range of 'positive' activities that they engage in. Such activities are often distinct from their main production or sales activities. Many have whole departments dedicated to engaging in and promoting their positive and responsible engagement with various stakeholders. Many corporations have also established **corporate codes of conduct**, both as a response to negative publicity and the fear of the imposition of mandatory regulations being introduced (Haufler, 2000). GBIAs have encouraged companies to promote themselves as socially responsible organisations in order to foster 'peaceful conditions, legal certainty and good human relations' (ICC, 2002, p 10) and 'credibility and trust amongst stakeholders' (ERT, 2001, p 16).

However, moves towards anything resembling tighter global regulations on firms have been firmly resisted by international business (see, for example, ERT, 2001; UNICE, 2001; ICC, 2002). For global business, enforceable regulations fail to adequately take into account 'the vast differences in circumstances, objectives, operating methods and resources of individual companies' (ICC, 2002, p 16). They would also, according to the Union of Industrial and Employers' Confederations of Europe (UNICE), distract companies from their core task of 'creating prosperity' (UNICE, 2001). Moreover, the ERT argues, basic standards should remain the responsibility of individual governments, and if they fall short, governments, not corporations, are to be blamed (ERT, 2001).

In the face of a growing **global social justice movement** combined with powerful opposition to mandatory regulation from business interests and governments, a number of global voluntary or self-regulatory initiatives that lay down minimum standards for corporations to voluntarily sign up to have emerged. The UN's Global Compact is an example of one such initiative (**Box 4.3**). Although it is relatively comprehensive (see **Table 4.3**), it has won support from companies precisely because it is voluntary and it provides good opportunities for corporations to associate themselves, or their products, with the UN's positive 'brand'. For this reason, the Global Compact has grown rapidly since its establishment in 1999 to include around 3,000 firms (UN, 2007), despite criticisms of its lack of 'teeth' and its reliance on consumers and non-governmental organisations (NGOs) to monitor, highlight and respond to abuses (see Chapter Six for further discussion).

Box 4.3: Aim of the UN Global Compact

The stated aim of the Global Compact is to 'advance responsible corporate citizenship so that business can be part of the solution to the challenges of globalisation. In this way, the private sector – in partnership with other social actors – can help realize the Secretary-General's vision: a more sustainable and inclusive global economy' (UN, 2007).

Other IGOs have also entered the field of global corporate regulation. The OECD has drawn up a set of guidelines for multinationals (summarised in **Table 4.3**), and the EC has published a Green Paper on CSR (EC, 2001) for corporations operating within, and beyond, the European Union (EU). All of these, however, are merely recommendations – they have no legal basis – and all the major developments until now have repeatedly stressed their voluntary basis. This is partly because of the resistance of governments for reasons of national sovereignty, but it is also because governments have been heavily

Table 4.3: *OECD guidelines for multinational enterprises and the UN Global Compact*

OECD guidelines for multinational enterprises	UN Global Compact
The common aim of the governments adhering to the guidelines is to encourage the positive contributions that multinational enterprises can make to economic, environmental and social progress and to minimise the difficulties to which their various operations may give rise.	Principle 1: Businesses should support and respect the protection of internationally proclaimed human rights; and
Two key principles underpin the guidelines: they are voluntary but apply worldwide.	Principle 2: make sure that they are not complicit in human rights abuses.
The guidelines:	Principle 3: Businesses should uphold the freedom of association and the effective recognition of the right to collective bargaining;
• call on enterprises to take full account of established policies in the countries in which they operate;	Principle 4: the elimination of all forms of forced and compulsory labour;
• recommend disclosure on all matters regarding the enterprise such as its performance and ownership, and encourages communication in areas where reporting standards are still emerging, such as social, environmental and risk reporting;	Principle 5: the effective abolition of child labour; and
	Principle 6: the elimination of discrimination in respect of employment and occupation.
	Principle 7: Businesses should support a precautionary approach to environmental challenges;
• rule out child and forced labour, discrimination and encourage employee representation and constructive negotiations;	Principle 8: undertake initiatives to promote greater environmental responsibility; and
• encourage enterprises to raise their performance in protecting the environment;	Principle 9: encourage the development and diffusion of environmentally friendly technologies.
• stress the importance of combating bribery;	Principle 10: Businesses should work against corruption in all its forms, including extortion and bribery.

continued . . .

Table 4.3: *OECD guidelines for multinational enterprises and the UN Global Compact continued*

OECD guidelines for multinational enterprises	UN Global Compact
• recommend that enterprises, when dealing with consumers, act in accordance with fair business, marketing and advertising practices, respect consumer privacy, and take all reasonable steps to ensure the safety and quality of goods or services provided; • promote the diffusion by multinational enterprises of the fruits of research and development activities among the countries where they operate, thereby contributing to the innovative capacities of host countries; • emphasise the importance of an open and competitive business climate; • call on enterprises to respect both the letter and spirit of tax laws and to cooperate with tax authorities.	

Sources: OECD (2000, 2008)

lobbied by corporations keen to resist global regulation and eager to preserve their competitive advantage.

Given these limitations, the potential for voluntary agreements positively to influence corporate behaviour is likely to depend primarily on firms themselves. While some commentators argue that corporations are inherently harmful (Bakan, 2004), others take a more 'moderate' position, arguing that the extent to which business organisations are harmful depends on a number of variables: the regulatory regime in which they operate; the ownership of the firm (whether it is a publicly floated company and faces shareholder pressure to boost sales and profits or whether it is a private business following its own internal logic); prevailing sector standards and practices; the national regulations imposed by the host country; the relative strength of trade unions and other activist groups; and the extent of public scrutiny. A firm's options are also shaped by its brands and the particular niche they occupy within given markets. Certain brands, such as The Body Shop and Green & Black's chocolate, trade as 'ethical' labels with a commitment to higher environmental standards and socially responsible production methods. Moreover, some companies and 'philanthropists' (most notably, the Bill & Melinda Gates Foundation, Warren Buffet and George Soros), have established multi-million pound trusts to fund various 'good' causes of their choice and some (such as the Bill & MelindaGates Foundation) are involved in global welfare provision (the Global Fund – see Chapter Seven). Although the rise of **global philanthropy** has to be viewed alongside the growth in the number of super-rich business elites and the fact that charitable giving in many nations reduces overall corporate and personal tax liabilities, since the 1990s there has been a clear trend towards the establishment of more globally minded foundations and their involvement in global social policy formation and provision.

The limitations of these initiatives are strikingly apparent. Socially irresponsible corporate behaviour affects sales in only a small number of cases. To translate into consumer boycotts, the exposure and publicity of corporate harm needs to be widespread and reach groups of consumers that are knowledgeable, motivated and/or able to change their consumer behaviour. In many instances, corporations do not sell directly to the public and many target consumers that are invariably more interested in price than corporate behaviour. As a result, the potential impact of consumer boycotts is often weak. In other instances, consumers face limited alternative options in highly concentrated and ethically suspect markets. The oil industry, for instance, is dominated by a handful of companies and around 40% of world oil production comes from countries that fail to either recognise or protect basic human rights (Mitchell, 1998).

Even where corporations do assert their ethical credentials, they are rather selective in their choice of 'good' causes. Company policies on the environment and instances of company giving tend to be highlighted most enthusiastically; in contrast, the employment conditions of those that help to make or sell their products are seldom discussed. Moreover, firms have located ways of dealing with the ethical concerns of certain consumers without necessarily changing their behaviour. Rather than impose similarly high standards on their complete product range, some larger corporations have introduced new product ranges, or have bought out successful 'ethical' brands, which they sell alongside existing less 'ethical' lines. Cadbury, for instance, took over Green & Black's organic and fairly traded chocolate brand in 2005 and The Body Shop, which had been established as an ethical brand critical of testing perfumes on animals, was taken over by L'Oréal, in 2006, a global cosmetic company heavily criticised by animal rights activists.

Global business interest associations and social policy

For reasons explained earlier, IGOs have been drawn towards social policies that offer social protection while protecting the interests of business. It is important to note that the *general* views of global business may be quite different from the *specific* views of diverse business sectors. But as many (Holden, 2003, 2005; Lethbridge, 2005) have demonstrated, companies and organisations from the service sector have cooperated to force open international markets in health, education, social care and pensions (see Chapter Five). Although sectoral interests have played a key role in the formation of **global policy** on the liberalisation of services and other issues, their voice is limited to a relatively narrow range of issues and their presence on the international stage tends to be less formalised than the position occupied by GBIAs, which represent the collective voice of business at the international level. The membership of GBIAs is made up of firms and national business organisations from all sectors. Because they purport to speak for general business interests, GBIAs, rather than specialised or narrow sectoral interests, tend to have better access to IGOs, are better funded and are a more consistent presence in international policy debate.

The position of GBIAs can be summarised thus: social policy justified only if it contributes in some way to economic stability and growth, or at least does not undermine it, and affordable only if it exists in an environment populated by profitable and successful firms (see Farnsworth, 2005). To this end, a key priority has been to place pressure on governments to reduce expenditure and taxation (especially on corporations) and to utilise social provision to reduce disincentives to work, halt the propensity towards early retirement and increase the productivity of workers.

GBIAs have also lobbied hard to ensure that governments pay particular attention to the needs and concerns of employers in formulating social policy, especially regarding skills, flexibility and adaptability within the labour force (BIAC, 2002). Human capital formation policies, such as education and training provision, have therefore been prioritised and vigorously defended as key strategies to improving competitiveness, and benefit systems that increase employability, wage affordability and personal responsibility have been promoted. Although social protection benefits have been defended in instances where they might function to smooth out employment markets, they are considered to be viable only in certain circumstances (BIAC, 1998b). High social security costs and accompanying administrative burdens, business argues, undermine profitability and increase unemployment (BIAC, 1998b); hence strict qualifying conditions, time limitations, the retention of work incentives and conditionality based on the acceptance of employment are all viewed as essential. Similarly, sufficiently wide gaps between benefits and the lowest pay rates in order to maintain work incentives are considered to be crucial (OECD, 1981, p 87). Such basic principles are important, according to the Business and Industry Advisory Committee to the OECD (BIAC), if social protection systems are to remain viable (BIAC, 1998b). In the case of pensions, business has advocated greater private provision and argued for more flexibility in the age of retirement (BIAC, 1998b; see also Chapter Nine on global pensions policy). Whether in pensions or other forms of social protection, the key for business is that employers should be able to shed surplus labour with relative ease, but retain workers as economic conditions dictate.

With regard to the provision of services, the state is viewed by business as an important guarantor of certain minimum social conditions, and, in some instances, funding, but, with the exception of schooling, greater private involvement has been actively encouraged (BIAC, 1996). Each of the major global business organisations considers state-funded and state-regulated, but not necessarily state-provided, schooling to be essential. The approach of GBIAs to education varies by the level of learning, however. A far greater role for the state is envisaged for lower-level schooling than for the further and higher education sectors, within which an expanded role for the private sector is encouraged.

More generally, on the question of provision, GBIAs tends to favour **targeted provision** funded and delivered by a combination of efforts, both public and private. In those areas dominated by the state and with strong public support, for instance healthcare, an expansion of private insurance is advocated. In pensions, GBIAs has defended state provision, provided it is supported with robust occupational and private provision (BIAC, 1998b). In both instances, a mixed-economy approach is favoured. On the question of the method and impact of funding, GBIAS generally favour provision that is funded by employees or consumers and pays little attention to social equity issues. Redistribution, where it occurs, should be horizontal, across lifetimes, rather than vertical, from rich to poor.

What emerges from this analysis of GBIAs' social policy discourse is a remarkably clear and coherent position on social policy even over time. The basic assertions of GBIAs on social policy hardly shifted between the early 1980s and mid-1990s (Farnsworth, 2005). Moreover, the views of certain IGOs have shifted closer towards business in recent years, as our review of the EU, OECD and WB shows.

At world-regional level, the EU, historically a defender of more comprehensive social policies, has undergone a decisive shift towards a business agenda. For example, the Lisbon Agenda has, since 2000, pushed member states towards making improvements to education and training provision, cutting regulations and red tape on corporations, increasing work incentives, cutting non-wage labour costs and completing the internal market in services, with the aim of making Europe 'the most competitive and dynamic knowledge-based economy in the world' by 2010 (EC, 2004, p 1). In order to help increase competitiveness in services, the EU has also pushed member states to privatise telecoms, energy, rail transport, waste and postal services. More recently, it has tried to add public services, including education and healthcare, to the list of liberalised services in the Bolkestein directive. Opposition has ensured that most social policies have been excluded from the directive, although it is not clear whether education is excluded or not (Andruccioli, 2007).

The OECD has also changed its approach to social policy since the early 1990s. In 1994, its presented an archetypal Washington Consensus-style solution to unemployment: tackle inflation, increase wage and employee flexibility, eliminate 'impediments to the creation and expansion of enterprises', relax regulations on employment, increase employee skills and reform social protection systems to ensure that they do not impinge on labour markets (OECD, 1994). By 1999, however, the OECD was promoting an altogether more interventionist and positive model of social policy, which 'can ensure that those who lose their jobs are insured against loss of all their income during the period while they search for a new job' and can 'assist displaced workers to readjust to the new labour market opportunities' (OECD, 1999, p 77). However, it went on to argue that 'well administered' social provision can 'reduce resistance to change and new working practices' and enhance 'the attractiveness of the country concerned as a business location' (OECD, 1999, p 77). Although it concluded that 'one effect of globalisation could be to increase the demand for social protection', it went on to suggest that governments, under financial pressures, should make 'more effective use of the networks and skills of non-government organisations' including 'outsourcing some activities ... to the private and not-for-profit sector' in order to 'benefit from cost-efficiencies and competitive tendering' (OECD, 1999, p 126). By 2005, the OECD was acknowledging that 'however essential economic growth is to improving people's lives, it has not been sufficient to solve all social problems' and that 'despite greater prosperity, a substantial portion of the population in every OECD country continues to face ... risks of disadvantage in childhood, of exclusion from work in prime age, of isolation and limited self-sufficiency in old age' (OECD, 2005a).

In order to address these problems, the report recommended the pursuit of 'active social policies that seek to change the conditions in which individuals develop, rather than limiting themselves to ameliorating the distress these conditions cause' (OECD, 2005a, p 6). It goes on to argue against vertical redistributive taxation because 'better-off voters may reject continuing tax increases and climbing tax rates may deter investment and work effort' (p 6), favouring instead horizontal redistribution over the course the lifetime. In this way, active social policies 'hold the promise of reducing the negative effects of social protection systems on economic growth that have long dominated public discussions about the welfare state' (OECD, 2005a, p 13). The private financing of social policy, meanwhile, is defended because it 'may help individuals face the true price of social protection, and thereby reduce the risk of excess provision' (OECD, 2005a, p 43). This view was mirrored by social policy ministers meeting at the OECD in 2005, the substance of whose Final Communiqué restated the primacy of economic growth as a de facto social policy (OECD, 2005 b).

WB discourse on social policy has also changed since the 1990s, becoming more positive about the impact of social provision and embracing the need for state intervention in social welfare provided it results in more positive investment climates and returns for business. However, a powerful contingent of the WB continues to promote market liberalisation with particular effectiveness through its private sector development strategies. Its private finance arms – the International Finance Corporation and its Multilateral Investment Guarantee Agency – promote private sector financing and involvement in education and healthcare. Despite the change in terminology and structures, the WB's Poverty Reduction Strategy Papers are as prescriptive in terms of opening up markets and forcing privatisation deals as were the previous structural adjustment programmes (Mehrotra and Delamonica, 2005).

Conclusion

The global social policy 'story' involving global business is a complex one. A key development highlighted in the chapter is a global social policy that is as corporate-centred in its protection of business interests as it ever was, despite various global attempts to regulate corporations in the wider public interest.

Deacon (2005; see also Chapter Two) characterises this transformation in global social policy as a move from **neoliberalism** towards a more socially responsible – social democratic – globalisation. However, while there have undoubtedly been changes in discourse, it is not yet clear whether global social policy has already, or will in the future, gravitate towards social democracy. Social democratic welfare systems have certain ideals, including financial and social inclusion, greater equality of outcomes and positive freedom (Esping-Andersen, 1990), even if they have not always been successfully implemented. Where they have succeeded, social democratic governments have effectively challenged and contained business power and sought to establish consensus between various class interests in order to establish a firm base for inclusive social policy (Esping-Andersen, 1990; Swenson, 2002). Global social policy as a political practice, in contrast, remains corporate-centred: instead of being kept at arm's length, business has been increasingly integrated into global social policy making, and economic priorities are as deeply embedded in global social policy discourse as they were two decades ago (see also Utting, 2006).

While the more active engagement of GBIAS in policy discourse has revealed a more sympathetic line on social policy than that afforded by neoliberalism, a truly progressive future for global social policy may be limited by moves to engage more closely with business. The kind of voluntary agreements that are supported by GBIAs and IGOs are unlikely to resolve the gaps in corporate regulation that would help to protect citizens and their environments. It is also unlikely that they will be able to proceed much further while still retaining the support of business. It is possible, of course, for IGOs to go beyond business wishes, but this would require engagement with more powerful rival interests and the support of national governments. Unless IGOs help to boost the power of rival groups, including global civic actors and social movements, by affording them access to global social policy making on an equal footing with business, corporate values and interests rather than social democratic ones are likely to remain at the heart of global social policy.

Summary

- The power of corporations has increased in the contemporary period of globalisation. Structural power has increased as a result of greater investment options combined with the institutionally embedded economic growth priorities of IGOs. Agency power has grown as a result of the increased political opportunities offered for business organisation and mobilisation at global level.
- This greater corporate power has resulted in a range of harms on populations and the environment. Concerned citizens have mobilised nationally and

transnationally to increase knowledge and awareness of corporate harms and hold corporations to account.

- IGOs have come under pressure from an increasingly powerful global corporate lobby as well as from civic associations, NGOs and social movements to alleviate adverse social impacts of corporate investment, production and sales strategies. The promulgation of global social regulatory initiatives is a key means by which IGOs have responded to these pressures.
- Corporate interests are represented in global business interest associations at the global level. These have lobbied for social policies to be steered towards their needs and interests. Economic priorities continue to dominate global policy decisions.
- Global social policy has shifted closer towards business interests over the past two decades.

Questions for discussion

- What dangers do the globalisation of production and/or sales present for citizens and their environments?
- What are the limitations of current global initiatives to ensure that corporations behave more responsibly?
- What evidence is there for the development of a corporate-centred global social policy?

Further suggested activities

- Research an example of alleged corporate harm (such as those outlined in **Table 4.2**, for example, Bhopal or baby milk formula). Examine the allegations made against the TNCs involved and how they have responded to them. Investigate how successful opposition groups have been in forcing policy changes and/or how successful the companies involved have been in dealing with allegations against them.
- Compare the CSR policies of a selection of the largest global companies listed in *Fortune 500*. Investigate the similarities and differences in strategy and approach to CSR within various companies. What might account for these different strategies/approaches?

Further reading

Bakan's (2004) *The Corporation* accompanies the documentary by the same name. It is one of the most engaging and comprehensive books on the evolution and power of the corporation in the US. Balanya et al (2000) is (to date) the most thorough and well-referenced of research studies into the power and organisation of business interests within the EU. It is indispensible for those interested in how corporations became a powerful voice on the European stage. Tesner (2000) is an interesting study of the evolving relationship between global business and the UN since its establishment. It argues that both interests increasingly depend on each other and documents how the two have become closer since the 1990s.

Electronic resources

www.business-humanrights.org Business and Human Rights Resource Centre ('tracks the positive and negative impact of over 4000 companies worldwide').
www.corporatewatch.org Corporate Watch (documents alleged corporate abuses).
www.corporateeurope.org Corporate European Observatory (publishers of Europe Inc.)
www.biac.org Business Industry Advisory Committee to the OECD (one of the most important international business organisations).
www.multinationalmonitor.org Multinational Monitor (publishes research into the harmful activities of global corporations).

References

Andruccioli, P. (2007) 'Public Services in Europe: from privatisation to participation', www.tni.org/detail_page.phtml?&act_id=16816, accessed July.
Bakan, J. (2004) *The Corporation*, New York, NY: Free Press.
Balanya, B. et al (2000) *Europe Inc: Regional and Global Restructuring and the Rise of Corporate Power*, London: Pluto Press.
BIAC (Business and Industry Advisory Committee to the OECD) (1996) *Discussion Paper by A. Sommer: Productivity to the Rescue of Social Protection*, Paris: BIAC.
BIAC (1998a) *BIAC Views on Lifelong Learning (based on comments made by members of the BIAC Expert Group on Education at the OECD Seminar on Lifelong Learning, 18 November 1998)*, Paris: BIAC.

BIAC (1998b) *Meeting of the Employment, Labour and Social Affairs Committee at Ministerial Level on Social Policy*, Paris: BIAC.

BIAC (2002) *Employment and Learning Challenges for the 21st Century*, Paris: BIAC.

Deacon, B. (2005) 'From 'safety nets' back to 'universal social provision'. Is the global tide turning?', *Global Social Policy*, vol 5, no 1, pp 19-28.

EC (European Commission) (2001) *Promoting a European Framework for Corporate Social Responsibility*, Luxembourg: Office for Official Publications of the European Communities.

EC (2003) *Jobs, Jobs, Jobs: Creating More Employment in Europe*, Brussels: EC.

EC (2004) *Facing the Challenge: The Lisbon Strategy for Growth and Employment*, Brussels: EC.

ERT (European Round Table) (2001) *ERT Position on Corporate Social Responsibility and Response to Commission Green Paper 'Promoting a European Framework for Corporate Social Responsibility'*, Brussels: European Round Table of Industrialists.

Esping-Andersen, G. (1990) *The Three Worlds of Welfare Capitalism*, Cambridge: Polity Press.

Farnsworth, K. (2004a) 'Anti globalisation, anti capitalism and the democratic state', in G. Taylor and M. Todd (eds) *Democracy and Participation: Popular Protest and New Social Movements*, London: Merlin Press, pp 55-77.

Farnsworth, K. (2004b) *Corporate Power and Social Policy in Global Context: British Welfare Under the Influence?*, Bristol: The Policy Press.

Farnsworth, K. (2005) 'International class conflict and social policy', *Social Policy and Society*, vol 4, no 2, pp 217-26.

Fooks, G. (forthcoming) *Corporate Crime*, London: Sage Publications.

Haufler, V. (2000) 'Private sector international regimes', in R.A. Higgott, G.R.D. Underhill and A. Bieler (eds) *Non-state Actors and Authority in the Global System*, London: Routledge, pp 121-37.

Hillyard, P., Pantazis, C., Tombs, S. and Gordon, D. (2004) *Beyond Criminology: Taking Harm Seriously*, London: Pluto Press.

Holden, C. (2003) 'Actors and motives in the internationalization of health businesses', *Business and Politics*, vol 5, no 3, pp 287-302.

Holden, C. (2005) 'The internationalization of corporate healthcare: extent and emerging trends', *Competition & Change*, vol 9, no 2, pp 185-203.

ICC (International Chambers of Commerce) (2002) 'Business in society: making a positive and responsible contribution', www.iccwbo.org/uploadedFiles/ICC/static/B_in_Society_Booklet.pdf, accessed 25 May 2008.

Korten, D. (1997) 'The United Nations and the corporate agenda', www.globalpolicy.org/reform/korten.htm, accessed 25 May 2008.

Lethbridge, J. (2005) 'The promotion of investment alliances by the World Bank: implications for national health policy', *Global Social Policy*, vol 5, no 2, pp 203-25.

Lindblom, C.E. (1977) *Politics and Markets*, New York, NY: Basic Books.

Masson, P.R. (2007) *The IMF: Victim of Its Own Success or Institutional Failure?*, York, Canada: Centre for International Governance Innovation.

Mehrotra, S. and Delamonica, E. (2005) 'The private sector and privatization in social services: is the Washington Consensus "dead"?', *Global Social Policy*, vol 5, no 2, pp 141-74.

Mitchell, A. (1998) 'Human rights: one more challenge for the petroleum industry', in A. Mitchell (ed) *Companies in a World of Conflict: NGOs, Sanctions and Corporate Responsibility*, London: Earthscan, pp 227-52.

O'Brien, R. (2002) 'Organizational politics, multilateral economic organizations and social policy', *Global Social Policy*, vol 2, no 2, pp 141-61.

OECD (Organisation for Economic Co-operation and Development) (1981) *The Welfare State in Crisis: An Account of the Conference on Social Policies in the 1980s*, Paris: OECD.

OECD (1994) *Jobs Study: Facts, Analysis, Strategies*, Paris: OECD.

OECD (1999) *A Caring World: A New Social Policy Agenda*, Paris: OECD.

OECD (2000) *The OECD Guidelines for Multinational Enterprises*, Paris: OECD, www.oecd.org/dataoecd/56/36/1922428.pdf, accessed 25 May 2008.

OECD (2005a) *Extending Opportunities: How Active Social Policy Can Benefit Us All*, Paris: OECD.

OECD (2005b) *Meeting of OECD Social Affairs Ministers, 2005. Extending Opportunities: How active social policy can benefit us all. Final Communique*, Paris: OECD.

Offe, C. and Ronge, V. (1984) 'Theses on the theory of the state', in C. Offe (ed) *Contradictions of the Welfare State*, London: Hutchinson, pp 119-29.

Ollila, E. (2003) 'Health-related public–private partnerships and the United Nations', in B. Deacon, E. Ollila, K. Koivusalo and P. Stubbs (eds) *Global Social Governance*, Helsinki: Globalisation and Social Policy Programme, pp 36-76.

Richter, J. (2001) *Holding Corporations Accountable: Corporate Conduct, International Codes and Citizen Action*, London: Zed Books.

Sklair, L. (2001) *The Transnational Capitalist Class*, Oxford: Blackwell.

Stiglitz, J. (2002) *Globalization and its Discontents*, London: Norton House.

Stiglitz, J. (2005) 'More instruments and broader goals: moving towards the post-Washington Consensus', in UN University-World Institute for Development Economics Research (ed) *WIDER Perspectives on Global Development*, Houndsmill: Palgrave Macmillan, pp 16-48.

Swenson, P. (2002) *Capitalists Against Markets: The Making of Labor Markets and the Welfare States in the United States and Sweden*, Oxford: Oxford University Press.

Tesner, S. (2000) *The United Nations and Business: A Partnership Recovered*, London: Macmillan.

UN (United Nations) (2007) 'United Nations Global Compact', www.unglobalcompact.org/ParticipantsAndStakeholders/index.html, accessed 1 May 2007.

UN (2008) *The Ten Principles of the UN Global Compact*, www.unglobalcompact.org/AboutTheGC/TheTenPrinciples/index.html, accessed 25 May 2008.

UNICE (2001) *Corporate Social Responsibility: UNICE Position*, Brussels: UNICE.

UNICEF (2001) *The State of the World's Children*, Paris: UN.

Utting, P. (ed) (2006) *Reclaiming Development Agendas: Knowledge, Power and International Policy Making*, Basingstoke: Palgrave.

Yeates, N. (2001) *Globalization and Social Policy*, London: Sage Publications.

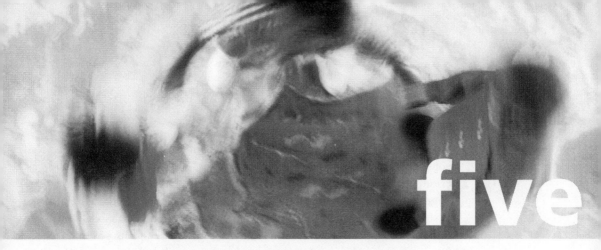

five

International trade and welfare

Chris Holden

Overview

International trade is a core element of economic 'globalisation' and its regulation in the interests of social welfare is a central concern of global social policy. This chapter examines a number of key perspectives and debates about the relationship between international trade and welfare from a global perspective. While economists generally favour 'free' trade, in practice international trade has been characterised by bargaining between states of varying degrees of power. Despite fears of a 'race to the bottom' in welfare provision engendered by economic competition, welfare states provide a key mechanism by which the risks and gains from trade can be more evenly distributed and inequalities reduced. Nevertheless, the emergence of international trade in welfare services has important implications for social policy and has emerged as a key issue in global social policy debates.

Key concepts

Trade negotiations; protection; liberalisation; displacement; global standards

Introduction

Trade is the earliest and most basic form of economic relationship between people of different communities and countries. International trade in the period after the Second World War laid the basis for the kind of economic integration we now associate with 'globalisation'. This chapter aims to explain the significance of international trade to current debates within global social policy. It reviews how the international trading system and its governance have developed in the post-war period, what forms trade policy making takes, and how trade relates to the welfare state, welfare services and 'welfare' more generally. It begins with a discussion of the different ways that economists and social policy analysts think about welfare, and why trade is important for social policy. It then explains how the trading system has developed in the post-war period, before looking in detail at policy-making processes and institutions. The role of the World Trade Organization (WTO) and the centrality of bargaining between states are explained. The final two sections examine in detail the social policy implications of international trade. While the penultimate section discusses the relationship of the welfare state to international trade in general, the final section looks at the development of such trade in welfare services themselves. As we shall see, the relationship between international trade and welfare can be a complex one.

Economics, trade and welfare

The development of capitalism as an economic system has been intimately entwined with the development of national states. States have played a crucial role in facilitating the development of capitalism through providing a system of law and contract that guarantees the rights of property owners and sets a framework within which exchange can take place, as well as legitimising and regulating a common currency. Of course, trade across the borders created by these states has taken place as long as those borders have been in place, but the existence of national institutions, governments and currencies has meant that such trade is necessarily *inter*national, that is, it takes place between countries as well as between specific individuals or firms. Governments have therefore usually tried to regulate this international trade to some extent, from the mercantilism of early capitalism (when the goal was seen as making the nation rich by accumulating as large a trade surplus as possible), to the trade barriers (and negotiations aimed at reducing them) still prevalent today. However, ever since the 19th century the most orthodox economists have operated on the premise that 'free trade' is good and therefore desirable and the **protection** of domestic industries against foreign competition (often referred to as 'protectionism') is bad and to be discouraged (see *Box 5.1*).

Box 5.1: Trade protection

Trade 'protection' entails the use of certain mechanisms such as tariffs and quotas in order to protect the interests of owners and workers in domestic industries from foreign competition. Tariffs are taxes that are levied on goods entering a country. Since the cost of these has to be passed on to consumers, the foreign goods end up being more expensive than would otherwise be the case. Quotas are restrictions on the amount of a given category of foreign goods that is permitted to be imported, thus limiting competition with domestically produced goods of the same type. Governments have also developed other more sophisticated forms of protection, such as 'voluntary export restraint', where one government agrees to 'voluntarily' limit its exports to another country, often as a result of political pressure placed on it by the government of that country. More recently, various forms of government intervention in the domestic economy, such as subsidies and regulatory mechanisms, have been identified as sometimes offering 'unfair' advantages to domestic firms. Including such domestic intervention in trade talks has proved particularly controversial, as it may have implications for the way welfare services are provided, since these are usually government-funded and/or regulated. For some, 'fair trade' and other initiatives to socially regulate the terms of trade also fall under the rubric of protectionism.

This commitment to free trade is based on the idea that if 'artificial' barriers to trade were removed, this would ensure that countries could import those goods made more cheaply elsewhere, leading to the optimum utilisation of the world's resources, in much the same way that markets were seen to produce the most efficient allocation of resources within countries. This idea is allied to the idea of **comparative advantage**, that is, that every country should specialise in those industries in which it has a comparative cost advantage over other countries. Although trade theory has subsequently been modified significantly, including through the development of the concept of **competitive advantage** (which recognises that the competitive position of specific industries in different countries is affected by historical, cultural and even political factors, as well as purely economic ones), this basic premise still informs the thinking of most economists (see Gilpin, 2001, pp 196–233, for a concise overview of these theoretical developments). Although economists often speak of free trade maximising the economic 'welfare' of societies, what they are usually referring to is economic growth rather than the broader and deeper concepts of welfare favoured by social policy analysts.

Economists therefore expect free trade to lead to greater efficiency and therefore greater wealth for society than protection. While this is clearly an important goal, from the point of view of social policy analysts, there are two problems with this approach. The first is that, although free trade may lead to society as a whole becoming richer over time, this tells us nothing about the distribution of that wealth. Social policy is centrally concerned with questions of income and wealth distribution, and the intervention of the government may be required to bring about more equal outcomes. The second related problem is that there are both 'winners' and 'losers' from the play of market forces. While the benefits of more open trade policy may be distributed quite widely across society, the 'losers' are sometimes highly concentrated and visible. What happens to these people is also the remit of social policy. Given that in the current period of economic 'globalisation' the losers may not just vary between economic sectors within a country but also between countries, affecting millions of people in both rich and poor countries, international trade is a key issue for global social policy.

This is exemplified by recent research undertaken by the United Nations Development Programme (UNDP, 2006), which showed that although East Asian economies have grown dramatically as a result of **export–oriented** economic policies, inequality has also grown substantially in these societies. Those in favour of free trade usually point to the gains provided by economic growth, and the UNDP report shows that absolute poverty has declined drastically in these countries, with the number of people living on less than $1 a day falling by nearly a quarter of a billion between 1990 and 2001. Yet at the same time, inequality has increased as some people have got richer much more quickly than others, with young people and women much more likely to be unemployed. As is often the case, much of this increase in unemployment relates to the shift to more high-tech and capital-intensive industries, which require fewer workers. However, according to the UNDP, the vast foreign exchange reserves accumulated by these countries have not been sufficiently invested in health and education, or used to redistribute income to compensate the poor.

These problems are brought into particularly sharp relief because, in common with many areas of economic and social policy, the free trade agenda at the global level has been driven by a strongly **neoliberal** ideology since the 1980s. The contours of this ideology are well known, and involve a belief that markets are nearly always better than state intervention and that (sometimes extreme) inequalities are an acceptable outcome of increased capitalist growth. In the domestic arena, this approach favours the privatisation of state-owned industries and a minimalist approach to welfare, where the welfare state is seen as at best a necessary evil that distorts economies, damages incentives and imposes costs on otherwise efficient businesses. In the global arena, the neoliberal approach assumes that **liberalisation** of trade and a minimisation of the regulatory functions of the state will usually be positive, regardless of the short or long-term social costs.

In contrast to this 'free trade' approach, proponents of 'fair trade' focus on the inequalities and exploitative relationships that are often produced by the trading system, arguing that trade should take whatever form most benefits the poorest and least developed countries. Fair trade initiatives sometimes take the form of consumer campaigns, whereby consumers are encouraged to buy goods from accredited suppliers that have ensured adequate working conditions and pay rates for workers, or to boycott companies that have been identified as engaging in particularly exploitative practices (see Chapter Six). Supporters of fair trade and 'trade justice' also run political campaigns aimed at exposing the way the system seems to be stacked in favour of the richest and most powerful countries, and point to the ways in which trade relationships in practice often fall short of free trade ideology. As we shall see in the next section, the reality of the modern trading system is a far cry from neoliberal prescriptions, and is characterised by extensive protection and bargaining between states.

The development of the trading system

The world economy has only rarely been characterised by anything close to free trade. The development of international trade between emerging capitalist economies first took the form of 'mercantalism', whereby governments tried to get rich by selling more of their country's goods abroad than they imported. However, in keeping with the free trade views of the classical economists, in which foreign exchange reserves are regarded as merely a means to pay for imports, the second half of the 19th century was characterised by a more 'hands-off' or 'laissez-faire' approach. Yet by the end of the century, protectionism had begun to increase again. In the period between the two world wars of the 20th century, governments resorted to 'beggar-thy-neighbour' policies of protection in a cycle that both responded to and deepened the economic depression of that time. The political and economic settlement that followed the Second World War was thus based partly on the recognition that protectionism in the inter-war period had damaged growth for all countries, and partly on the need to bind the capitalist economies of the west together in the face of economic and military competition from the expanded Soviet bloc. In Western Europe, the desire to avoid another European war and cohere the capitalist countries against the perceived threat from the east led to the creation of the European Economic Community in 1957 (which formed the basis for what we now call the European Union (EU)).

While the post-war settlement led to the creation of the International Monetary Fund (IMF) and the World Bank (WB) in the financial sphere, the allied countries were unable to agree on the creation of an international trade organisation until the World Trade Organization (WTO) was set up in 1995. The WTO is based on the system of negotiated trade agreements that formed the basis for the lowering of trade barriers up until that time, known as the General Agreement on Tarrifs and Trade (GATT). The GATT and other subsequent trade agreements, such as the General Agreement on Trade in Services (GATS) discussed below, are now administered through the WTO, but continue to be negotiated in a similar way. GATT and other agreements work on the basis of 'negotiating rounds', that is, a series of protracted negotiations between governments, the aim of which is to progressively lower trade barriers between countries. These rounds are based on 'reciprocity', that is, a quid pro quo process in which governments agree to concessions to each other that lead to an incremental reduction in protection. Since the WTO has 151 members and the aim is a general reduction in protection, agreements are facilitated by the principle of 'non-discrimination', which has two components, the 'most favoured nation' (MFN) rule and the 'national treatment' rule (Hoekman and Kostecki, 2001, p 29). The MFN rule requires that a product made in one member country be treated no less favourably than a like good made in any other country. Thus by immediately treating all member nations in the same manner as the country afforded best treatment relating to a specific product, the gains of tariff reduction are generalised to all member countries. The national treatment rule requires that foreign goods, once they have satisfied whatever border measures are applied, be treated no less favourably than like or directly competitive goods produced domestically in terms of internal taxes or regulations.

On this basis, barriers to trade in goods were significantly lowered as the result of a series of negotiating rounds, each of which usually took years to accomplish. The last of these prior to the current Doha round of negotiations, the Uruguay round, was held between 1986 and 1993. The most significant outcomes of the Uruguay round were the agreement to create the WTO and the agreement of two further treaties in addition to the GATT, the GATS and the Agreement on Trade-Related Intellectual Property Rights (TRIPS). These new agreements substantially expand the scope of **trade negotiations** so that they now cover services as well as manufactured goods, and incorporate issues relating to intellectual property rights, investment and domestic regulation as well as tariffs and quotas. Both GATS and TRIPS have extremely important implications for social policy, particularly for healthcare and education. TRIPS is discussed further in Chapter Seven in the context of global health policy, while GATS is discussed in more detail in the final section of this chapter.

One of the key outcomes of this process of relative trade liberalisation in the post-war period has been a substantial growth in trade as a proportion of world output. Thus for most countries, and for the world economy as a whole, trade has grown at a faster rate than gross domestic product. This means that trade has been one of the most important engines of the increasing integration of national economies, what has come to be known as economic 'globalisation'.

However, it is difficult to entirely separate trade from other aspects of economic integration. Economic globalisation is typically thought of as encompassing two other key aspects, **foreign direct investment** (FDI) and the globalisation of financial markets. Trade is integrated with financial markets because most countries still have their own national currencies (the obvious exception being the Euro countries), which must be exchanged with each other for trade to take place. Since the collapse of the post-war **Bretton Woods** monetary system in the 1970s, which was based on a fixed **exchange rate system** overseen by the IMF, most countries have been subject to floating exchange rates, which has rendered their currencies a prime object of financial speculation. Similarly, since the 1980s FDI has been growing at an even faster rate than trade. This means that more and more firms are becoming multinational corporations (MNCs) and choosing to invest in other countries, rather than simply producing their goods at home and exporting them to other countries. So dominant have MNCs become in the world economy that intrafirm trade (trade between different national branches of the same MNC) now accounts for between a quarter and a third of all trade (Held et al, 1999, p 175). This intrafirm trade has important implications for social policy and power in the world economy, since it allows firms to, for example, minimise the taxes they pay to governments by manipulating the prices of goods traded within the firm so that they can declare their profits where taxes are lowest.

Global institutions and policy processes

The creation of the WTO formalised and extended the structure of the global trading system that had been developed over a period of 50 years (Hoekman and Kostecki, 2001, pp 49-53). The organisation now has 151 members. It facilitates the implementation and operation of the multilateral trade agreements, provides a forum for government negotiations, administers a dispute settlement mechanism, provides surveillance of national and regional trade policies and cooperates with the WB and the IMF with a view to achieving greater coherence in global economic policy making. It is headed by a Ministerial Conference of all members that meets at least once every two years, but between these meetings it is run by a General Council of Officials that meets about 12 times a year. Three subsidiary councils deal with trade in goods, trade in services and intellectual property rights, and it has a number of other committees and working parties.

Although the trading system remains one characterised principally by bargaining between states, the primary function of the WTO is to facilitate the creation of a *rules-based* international trading system. The organisation's reliance on its member states means that its secretariat is relatively small, with only about 500 staff. However, the secretariat stands at the centre of a network of perhaps

5,000 people who work on trade matters in its member governments' trade and other ministries, central banks, and so on. Developing countries therefore find themselves at a particular disadvantage when it comes to participating fully in WTO activities, since they often do not have the resources to devote to these matters that developed countries do. Many developing countries do not have officials based permanently at the WTO in Geneva, and when they do, they might have only one or two people to cover all the activities of the WTO as well as of the other international organisations based in Geneva (Hoekman and Kostecki, 2001, pp 54-5, 396).

Trade negotiations take the form of bargaining between formally independent and equal states, based on the principle of 'one member, one vote', yet it is clear that the economic, political and military power of these states varies considerably, and that this disparity is the key factor in influencing the outcomes of trade negotiations. The WTO attempts to work by 'consensus', but consensus is usually arrived at in informal meetings in the so-called 'Green Room', which are dominated by 'the Quad' of the US, EU, Japan and Canada (Woods and Narlikar, 2001, pp 573). Developed countries also have access to a far higher level of technical advice in what are highly complicated negotiations, and sometimes bring various forms of informal pressure to bear on developing countries (Jawara et al, 2004). This differential power usually translates into differential outcomes from the negotiations, and it was to deal with the perception that previous trade rounds had served the interests of developed countries more than developing ones that the Doha round was declared the 'development round'. The Doha round, which at the time of writing had not reached a successful conclusion, began in 2001 following the failure of an earlier attempt to develop a new round in Seattle in 1999. This earlier round had failed as a result of a combination of domestic US politics, the failure of the negotiators to reach agreement on agricultural issues and the opposition of a broad coalition of civil society groups (Yeates, 2001, pp 150-1).

The main negotiating difficulty in the Doha round related to agricultural protection by the US and the EU, which for many years has prevented a number of developing countries from realising their comparative advantage in food production by, for example, subsiding American and European farmers. Such government subsidies allow farmers from the US and the EU to sell their goods at a lower price than would otherwise be possible, and therefore compete more effectively with farmers in developing countries who produce food more cheaply (partly as a result of lower wage costs). Agreement on terms deleterious to the interests of developing countries was prevented in the Doha round by the creation of the G20, a negotiating bloc led by China, India and Brazil, which has demonstrated an unprecedented level of cohesiveness (Narlikar and Tussie, 2004). Successful negotiation in trade rounds often depends on a group of countries being able to form a coalition of this kind, but developing countries have in the past often had trouble in sustaining them. Nevertheless, the developed countries signalled that they were only likely to give way if they achieved significant concessions allowing them to gain greater access to the manufacturing and service industries of developing countries, and have pressed for the removal of regulations that restrict investment by western corporations in those countries. The difficulties in concluding the round have tended to lead to more **bilateralism** on the part of the US and the EU, allowing them to negotiate favourable agreements with developing countries directly.

Civil society organisations (CSOs) and social movements have made key interventions in the political process surrounding global trade talks. CSOs have vigorously campaigned on a national and transnational basis against the perceived negative effects of WTO agreements, including both the health issues related to TRIPS and GATS and the wider issues of development and inequality related to trade more generally. They form an important **transnational advocacy coalition** seeking to promote fairer terms of international trade, and, to the extent that they have been able to shape the process, they are to be regarded as key players in the global governance of trade. WTO negotiations have often become the focus of 'anti' or 'alter' globalisation protests, most famously at Seattle in 1999 where the anti-globalisation movement won an important victory, but at other sites and locations since then (Mac Sheoin and Yeates, 2007). Trade justice campaigners who form a key part of this movement often argue, with substantial justification, that the now developed countries invariably used selective trade barriers when they were building their own industries, to protect them from competition until they were established, but want to deprive developing countries of the same mechanisms. The WTO has also suffered from a lack of transparency, and campaigners question the way that social policies made at the national level sometimes seem to be undermined by trade agreements made at the international level (see, for example, the discussion in the final section concerning GATS). The WTO has attempted to respond to this attention from social movements by developing a more transparent and consultative approach (O'Brien et al, 2000; Woods and Narlikar, 2001), although many of its critics argue that it has not yet gone far enough.

Although we have focused on the WTO in this chapter, world-regional trade agreements and formations, such as the EU and the North American Free Trade Agreement (NAFTA), have also come to be important in the world economy and its governance (see also Chapters Two and Six). The EU is the most developed regional initiative of this type; starting as a customs union (in which members eliminate all trade restrictions against each other and adopt a common external tariff), its goal is now full economic union (in which labour and capital as well as goods and services are free to move and there is a common monetary policy with a single currency), and it has its own supranational political institutions in the form of the European Commission and Parliament. Most other regions of the world have some form of regional trade agreement, some of which are developing social policies, although none of them is as advanced as the EU, which also aims at a degree of harmonisation of social policies (Yeates and Deacon, 2006). The level of economic and political integration brought about by the EU means that, in contrast to other regional trade organisations, the EU negotiates within the WTO on behalf of its member countries. One implication of efforts to reform global social governance in the direction of strengthened world-regional formations (Chapter Two) is that these formations may also in future come to negotiate directly within the WTO on behalf of member states.

Before we examine the implications of the growth of trade in welfare services themselves, we consider in some depth the relationship between the welfare state and trade more generally.

The welfare state and trade

The relationship between the welfare state and international trade (and the global economy more widely) is not a straightforward one. It has often been argued that economic globalisation is undermining the welfare state, since the competition it creates between countries leads to a **race to the bottom** in welfare provision, as governments pare back the costs imposed on businesses to the minimum (see also Chapter One). Trade openness is seen as one element in this process, since if labour and other production costs are cheaper elsewhere, businesses will choose to locate in those areas and export their goods from there. The relatively well-paid workers of advanced nations may then experience both downward pressure on their wages and unemployment as whole sectors of business become uncompetitive (see Chapters Four and Six). While this may present an opportunity for developing countries to grow their own businesses, these are often (initially at least) confined to particular, low-skilled, sectors of the economy. The disadvantages that developing countries experience in a whole range of business sectors, including lack of access to capital, technology and skills, may mean that trade openness is perceived as acting in the interests of those countries that are already rich, whatever the fate of particular groups of workers in those countries. Where production does shift to developing countries, the owners are often MNCs based in the developed countries that take advantage of lower wages while retaining control over technical knowledge and capital. Those developing countries that have moved from predominantly low-skilled production to more skilled capital-intensive production, such as in East Asia, have often done so by using selective trade barriers alongside an aggressive export-oriented industrial policy.

Furthermore, it is often argued that in order to remain competitive, developing countries need to continue to suppress wages and other conditions for their own workers, with the result that trade openness not only damages jobs in the advanced economies, but legitimises poor working conditions and even child labour in developing countries. One response to this is for trade unions and others in the advanced countries to try to tie labour standards to trade agreements, so that developing countries competing with advanced countries are forced to agree to certain minimum standards. Indeed, attempts have been made to try to pursue such labour standards agreements through the WTO itself. These have failed for various reasons, including the perception by developing country governments that this is a form of 'back door' protectionism by rich countries (see also Chapter Six in this volume).

There is in fact a range of factors in addition to trade (and other aspects of economic globalisation) that have been identified as contributing to unemployment in the advanced capitalist countries, the foremost of which is technological advance (Gilpin, 2001, p 204). Both technological advances and greater trade openness have a particular impact on low-skilled, low-waged workers. Trade-displaced workers in developed countries have tended to be older and less educated than typical workers, to have worked in only one industry, to take longer than average to find a new job, and to be paid less in their new job than in the one they held previously (*The Economist*, 2006). This has led to the widespread realisation on the part of governments in these countries that they cannot compete in the world economy on the basis of low wages, but only on the basis of high skills. A highly skilled workforce is likely to attract investment in industries that pay high wages, thus maintaining prosperity. Education and training have thus become a central plank of social policy in countries like Britain under New Labour, as well as in East Asia. Unlike some parts of the welfare state, such as social security, education is seen as a productive investment in competitiveness rather than a drain on resources, as well as a way of enhancing social inclusion and social mobility (Holden, 1999). However, the high level of mobility of both data and people facilitated by technological development means that even the highly skilled will be competing in a global labour market. The rapidity of technological and economic change has led governments to emphasise 'lifelong learning' rather than see education as a 'one-off' event taking place early in life.

However, the relationship between trade openness and the welfare state, and 'welfare' more generally, is by no means a straightforward or obvious one. While increased trade often leads to the **displacement** of particular industries and groups of workers, its effect on overall growth is often a positive one. Jobs may not be so much destroyed, as moved from one sector of the economy to another, while the result for consumers is usually that the goods and services they buy are cheaper than they otherwise would be. This may seem like scant consolation for those whose lives are disrupted, and it is often the case that those who lose out have difficulty in finding jobs elsewhere because, for example, their skills are redundant. It is commonly accepted that while the benefits of more open trade are widely diffused, the costs may be very concentrated, making it a difficult and highly contested political issue. Yet the consequences of protectionism may be that citizens pay to maintain inefficient producers.

The role of the welfare state in all this is crucial. Welfare states have played a key role in capitalist economies ever since they were created in *facilitating* economic change. It is in the nature of capitalist economies, even conceived of as bounded national entities (which they rarely ever have been), that readjustments constantly take place between and within businesses and industrial sectors. These adjustments are usually the outcome of the play of market forces rather than the decisions of governments. The welfare state has played a key role in allowing these adjustments to take place without the disastrous impact on workers that they would otherwise have. While unemployment benefits and other forms of income maintenance have provided an income for workers that substitutes for their wages while they are unemployed, education, retraining and job search services have facilitated their return to work. A number of authors have argued that welfare states have played the same role for workers within the world economy, providing protection from the potential impact of more openness to international trade.

An early example of this work is that by Cameron (1978), which showed that the size of the public sector tends to be positively correlated with a country's openness to trade. A number of smaller European countries in particular have had both greater exposure to the world economy, as a result of the limited size of their domestic economies, and more extensive welfare states. Welfare benefits, active labour market policies and public sector employment have all, therefore, compensated workers for the actual or potential losses from international competition and provided a form of 'insurance' against their greater vulnerability to external economic shocks (see Katzenstein, 1985; Rodrik, 1997, 1998; Garrett, 1998). Iversen (2001) has disputed this correlation between open economies and the growth of the welfare state, arguing instead that it is insecurities produced by 'deindustrialisation' that explains this welfare state growth. Whatever the causal relationship between trade openness and the growth of welfare states, however, it is clear that welfare states can play a key role in allowing economic adjustments to take place while protecting workers from at least some of the associated costs.

Rieger and Liebfried (2003) draw an explicit inverse link between trade protection and the welfare state, arguing that the welfare state has facilitated open trade by substituting for protectionism. The US, for example, has relied on protectionism as a means of shielding certain industries (and therefore workers) from foreign competition, but has a much less developed welfare state than most other economically advanced countries. Given the weaker welfare state in the US, some benefits have even been tied explicitly to trade. Trade

Adjustment Assistance (TAA) was introduced by President Kennedy in 1962 to build support for tariff cuts, and was expanded as part of the NAFTA in 1993 and again in 2002 when President Bush asked Congress for special negotiating authority on trade (*The Economist*, 2006). For those who successfully apply to be recognised as having lost their jobs as a result of trade competition, TAA provides up to two years of unemployment benefits while workers retrain (four times longer than for ordinary workers), temporary subsidies to help pay for medical insurance and, for those over 50, a temporary wage subsidy for those who get a new job that pays less than their previous one. However, while gains from trade for the US economy as a whole have been estimated at $1 trillion a year, the country spends only $1 billion a year on support for trade-displaced workers (*The Economist*, 2006).

Nevertheless, there are problems with targeting benefits specifically at those displaced by international trade. Given that the (positive and negative) effects of trade are often diffuse, it is not always easy to identify who has been affected, or whether trade is the cause of any particular outcome. The US targets benefits in this way because its welfare state is less developed than those in Europe, and because its political system encourages bargaining on policy choices in order to get specific measures, such as trade liberalisation, passed. Although the EU has created a Globalisation Adjustment Fund as 'a sign of solidarity from those who benefit from openness to the few who face the sudden shock of losing their job' (EC, 2008), European welfare states have tended to be more extensive and less based on targeting than in the US. This more institutionalised and comprehensive form of welfare support makes more sense in a (global) market economy where the gains from growth are diffuse and, even though the losses may be more concentrated, the risks are shared.

Such arguments demonstrate the key role that the welfare state has played in allowing capitalist economies to operate effectively while shielding workers from the worst risks of markets and redistributing the gains from growth. They provide a sound justification for the maintenance and strengthening of welfare states within the context of the current world economy, and a corrective to claims that welfare states are incompatible with globalised markets and must 'inevitably' whither away in the face of global economic forces. However, while this is fine for the developed countries, what of developing countries where welfare states have not yet been built but where the desire and potential for economic growth are great? These countries often have a clear comparative advantage in low-skilled, low-waged, labour-intensive production. Such countries have often resisted agreements on labour standards, such as the insertion of a social clause into WTO trade agreements, fearing they that they may lose one of their few main advantages.

Developments in China and elsewhere indicate that welfare provision tends to grow as economies grow, and despite the findings of the UNDP discussed above, a number of newly industrialised East Asian countries have begun to develop extensive welfare states. Welfare development in East Asia actually speeded up *after* the financial crisis of 1997, indicating once again the role that welfare states can play in both protecting people from the worst effects of economic crises and facilitating economic adjustment. Yet reasons of cost, the influence of the international financial institutions, and the desire for economic growth among governments may all militate against more than minimal welfare development in the poorest countries with the worst labour conditions. For governments in the developed countries, the more their competitors in developing countries seem to undercut their own working conditions and welfare provisions, the more they may feel the pressure to scale these back.

Mishra (1999) has suggested one way of addressing this (although he overstates the current slide to the bottom in welfare provision). This would involve the agreement at the international level of social standards that are related to the level of economic development of each country, so that those with the most developed economies would have the most developed welfare states. According to Mishra (1999, p 119), this link with economic development 'would provide an automatic "social escalator", in that as societies develop economically, their social standard of living rises in tandem', making for 'an upward harmonization in social standards'. Echoing the emphasis the WTO places on a rules-based global economy, Mishra (1999, p122) concludes that these social standards 'must not be allowed to become a part of the competitive game but must form a part of the *rules* of the game' (emphasis in original). Allied with greater global redistribution to help fund welfare provision in developing countries, an agreement on this basis could properly integrate social concerns into the almost exclusively economic (and neoliberal) concerns of the WTO as it is currently constituted. This would not only provide a **multilateral** basis for extending the welfare achievements of the advanced capitalist countries to developing countries, but would also in itself help to overcome the suspicion of and resistance to international trade present in both developed and developing countries, by recognising the social costs of economic adjustment and allowing for the social redistribution of the gains from economic growth (both nationally and globally). However, such a system would have to set a 'floor' of minimum standards, rather than a 'ceiling' of maximum standards, in order to avoid the institutionalisation of differentiated (that is, unequal) social standards to the detriment of those living in developing countries, which would undermine the principle of equality and human dignity irrespective of where one happens to live in the world.

Trade in welfare services

As the world economy has become more integrated, international trade in services has grown alongside international trade in goods. And as governments have increasingly contracted out many welfare services to the private (commercial) sector instead of providing them directly through state agencies, trade in welfare services such as health and education has also grown. What constitutes 'trade' in services is less straightforward than that in goods, since while goods can be produced in one country and then exported to be consumed in another, services usually have to be consumed as they are produced. It is therefore difficult to separate 'trade' in services from FDI, for example, or from the migration of professionals. The most significant WTO agreement relating to welfare services is the GATS, which identifies four 'modes of supply' in services (see *Box 5.2*).

Box 5.2: Services: 'modes of supply'

The WTO's GATS agreement identifies four modes of supply for services, all of which apply to welfare services. *Cross-border trade* takes place where services are traded across borders without the need for the movement of people. This may take the form of the shipment of laboratory samples for healthcare diagnosis, for example, or clinical consultation done via traditional mail channels, but it is advances in communications technologies that have led to a significant increase in this form of trade. The internet enables providers of diagnostic health services or education services, for example, to reside in one country while the consumers reside in another. *Consumption abroad* refers to the movement of the consumer of a service to another country where the service is provided, such as when patients travel abroad to have an operation in another country or students travel abroad to study. *Commercial presence* involves foreign direct investment in the establishment of business outlets such as hospitals, schools or universities. *Movement of natural persons* refers to the movement abroad of practitioners such as healthcare workers or teachers. It may arise from labour demand and supply imbalances between countries, or from the search by practitioners for better wages or working conditions.

Where services are included in the GATS, governments must adhere to the non-discriminatory principles of MFN and national treatment discussed above. This has raised a number of concerns about the extent to which welfare services such as health and education may be affected by the GATS, since it suggests that where governments allow foreign private providers to operate in their country they cannot discriminate between them and must treat them in the same way as domestic ones. However, governments must agree to include specific services in the GATS before they are required to meet the full obligations of the agreement, a process known as 'scheduling'. Few commitments on welfare services have so far been scheduled (Adlung and Carzaniga, 2002; Yeates, 2005), but since such commitments are made as a result of negotiations, the fear is that the specific concerns of social policy may be subordinated to wider trade goals, leading to welfare services being inappropriately included as a result of a 'trade-off' by trade negotiators designed to secure an overall agreement.

Article I.3 of the GATS exempts those services that are 'supplied in the exercise of governmental authority' and that are 'supplied neither on a commercial basis, nor in competition with one or more service sectors'. However, critics have pointed to the manner in which domestic reform processes that encourage private provision and competition, such as those in the UK National Health Service, may render even publicly provided welfare services vulnerable to the claim that they *are* supplied on a commercial basis and in competition with other providers (Price et al, 1999; Holden, 2003). Once commitments have been made under the GATS, they are extremely difficult to reverse, and therefore lock governments into decisions and tend to consolidate market-based public service reforms already made at national level.

Concerns have also been expressed about the rights of member states to regulate their welfare services under GATS in the manner of their choosing in order to pursue social policy goals. While a number of the provisions of the GATS appear to protect the right of member states to regulate services as they wish, closer inspection reveals a series of ambiguities and causes for concern. The GATS involves requirements related to regulation that could be interpreted as being 'top down', that is, as applying to *all* services regardless of whether they have been scheduled (Sexton, 2001, p 8). Developments in the WTO have tended to take the view that domestic regulations should take the form that is 'least burdensome' to trade (Pollock and Price, 2000), which may not necessarily be the form that governments decide best allows them to meet their social policy goals. Furthermore, where international trade does take place in welfare services, it raises a range of new regulatory issues that can only effectively be addressed through international agreements focused on the goals of social policy, rather than simply the goal of increasing trade (Holden, forthcoming).

One of the difficulties of these discussions about the impact of GATS on welfare services is that, while such impacts may come to be quite profound, there is little evidence of them having any direct effect so far. This combination of the potentially significant effects GATS may have on welfare services in the future and a context where these effects have not yet become evident has often led discussion of them to be speculative and highly contested. Two important observations can be made in this regard. First, the very ambiguity of some of the GATS provisions is in itself problematic. What these provisions will come to mean in practice for welfare services is dependent partly on negotiations that have not yet taken place or reached agreement and partly on future case law that will be decided through the WTO's disputes settlement mechanism, where trade officials rather than social policy experts take the decisions. Second, concrete examples relating to the other WTO agreements can be given that demonstrate the capacity for trade agreements to have an important impact on social policy, particularly in health. One such example is the ruling of the GATT dispute panel on Thailand's tobacco control policies in 1990. At the time, Thailand operated a domestic monopoly in tobacco products and an import ban on foreign tobacco goods. When the US trade representative, under pressure from American transnational tobacco corporations (TTCs), referred the Thai government to the disputes process under the GATT rules, the dispute panel ruled that Thailand must lift its restrictions on imported tobacco products. The Thai government was permitted to pursue tobacco control policies such as tax rises and advertising restrictions that were non-discriminatory, but it had to allow the TTCs to operate in its country, which then entered into aggressive marketing practices to increase the sales of cigarettes. Similarly, the TRIPS agreement is having a profound effect on access to medicines in developing countries, as discussed in Chapter Seven.

Furthermore, while we have focused on global trade agreements administered by the WTO in this chapter, agreements at the regional level may have a more profound effect on welfare services in the short term than GATS. For example, both NAFTA and ASEAN's Framework Agreement on Services contain similar provisions to the GATS. Meanwhile, policy developments in the EU resulting from decisions of the European Court of Justice make it likely that the EU will soon adopt measures to make trade in health services, particularly the movement of patients, much easier and more common.

Conclusion

International trade has played a key role in the development of economic 'globalisation', laying the basis for the economic integration that also includes extensive FDI and global financial flows. Yet we have seen that trade has rarely been genuinely 'free', and that governments use various forms of economic protection to pursue domestic political, social and economic goals. Despite the increasing importance of the WTO, the world trade system is therefore characterised by bargaining between states that have varying levels of power and influence. While international trade and economic globalisation more generally may exert pressure on them, welfare states have played a crucial role in allowing market economies to adjust. Strong welfare states have the potential to coexist with international trade in a way that allows economies to grow, while sharing both the risks and the gains of trade in a fairer way. International trade provides a means by which, in the right circumstances, developing economies can grow, but the outcomes both domestically and globally can involve huge inequalities. There is an extremely strong case, therefore, for trade negotiations to be conducted in a way that genuinely serves the needs of the poorest and least developed countries. International agreement could also lay the basis for the development of welfare states in developing countries that would match the development of their economies, avoiding any slide to the bottom in welfare provision and labour conditions. However, given the emergence of international markets in welfare services themselves, we need to clarify when such services should be exempt from trade negotiations and agreements, and allow national governments and their citizens adequate scope to determine the goals of their social policies and the manner in which they are to be pursued.

Summary

- Economists generally support free trade as leading to an increase in wealth production, while social policy analysts are also concerned with the inequality of outcomes and the distribution of risks.
- The modern world trading system is overseen by the WTO, whose job is to facilitate a rules-based system. However, outcomes are still largely the result of bargaining between states that have varying levels of power and influence.
- Trade agreements within the WTO and at the regional level increasingly have a direct impact on welfare provision. These international trade agreements have been criticised as subordinating wider social goals to narrow trade ones.
- Welfare states play a crucial role in allowing economic adjustment to take place in capitalist economies. International agreement could provide the basis for social welfare provision to be written into the 'rules' governing trade at the global level.
- The growth of international markets in welfare services has important implications for the way in which those services are provided and regulated.
- Civil society is increasingly engaged with the trade agenda. Improvements could be made to the transparency and accountability of international institutions such as the WTO. At the same time, the limits of WTO influence over governments' social policies need to be clarified.

Questions for discussion

- Why does genuinely 'free' trade very rarely exist?
- Why do economic considerations seem to dominate over social ones in organisations like the WTO?
- What are the challenges for social policy of the development of international markets in welfare services?

Further suggested activities

- Take the interactive training modules on the WTO website under the 'resources for students' heading.
- Using the websites listed below, compare the different ways that trade issues are presented by the WTO and the Trade Justice Movement (TJM). What kinds of activities are organised by the TJM and its member organisations?

Further reading

Gilpin (2001) and Held et al (1999) both provide good detailed introductions to the global economy, including trade issues. Yeates (2001) and Mishra (1999) provide good introductions to social policy and globalisation that complement this volume, and pay particular attention to trade issues. Drager and Vieira (2002) provide detailed chapters on trade in health services as an example of how welfare services can be traded across borders, including attention to the crucial issue of GATS. For a discussion of how GATS relates to social security, see Yeates (2005).

Electronic resources

www.wto.org World Trade Organization
www.unctad.org United Nations Conference on Trade and Development
www.tjm.org.uk Trade Justice Movement

References

Adlung, R. and Carzaniga, A. (2002) 'Health services under the General Agreement on Trade in Services', in N. Drager and C. Vieira (eds) *Trade in Health Services: Global, Regional and Country Perspectives*, Washington, DC: Pan American Health Organization and World Health Organization, pp 13-33.

Cameron, D.R. (1978) 'The expansion of the public economy: a comparative analysis', *American Political Science Review*, vol 72, no 4, pp 1243-61.

Drager, N. and Vieira, C. (eds) (2002) *Trade in Health Services: Global, Regional and Country Perspectives*, Washington, DC: Pan American Health Organization and World Health Organization.

EC (European Commission) (2008) 'The European globalisation adjustment fund', http://ec.europa.eu/employment_social/egf/index_en.html, accessed 21 January 2008.

Garrett, G. (1998) *Partisan Politics in the Global Economy*, Cambridge: Cambridge University Press.

Gilpin, R. (2001) *Global Political Economy: Understanding the International Economic Order*, Princeton, NJ: Princeton University Press.

Held, D., McGrew, A., Goldblatt, D. and Perraton, J. (1999) *Global Transformations: Politics, Economics and Culture*, Cambridge: Polity Press.

Hoekman, B.M. and Kostecki, M.M. (2001) *The Political Economy of the World Trading System: The WTO and Beyond*, Oxford: Oxford University Press.

Holden, C. (1999) 'Globalization, social exclusion and Labour's new work ethic', *Critical Social Policy*, vol 19, no 4, pp 529-38.

Holden, C. (2003) 'Actors and motives in the internationalization of health businesses', *Business and Politics*, vol 5, no 3, pp 287-301.

Holden, C. (forthcoming) 'Regulation, accountability and trade in health services', in E. Mordini and G. Permanand (eds) *Bioethics and Globalisation*, Rome: CIC International Publishing.

Iversen, T. (2001) 'The dynamics of welfare state expansion: trade openness, de-industrialization, and partisan politics', in P. Pierson (ed) *The New Politics of the Welfare State*, Oxford: Oxford University Press.

Jawara, F., Kwa, A. and Sharma, S. (2004) *Behind the Scenes at the WTO: The Real World of International Trade Negotiations /Lessons of Cancun*, London: Zed Books.

Katzenstein, P.J. (1985) *Small States in World Markets*, Ithaca, NY: Cornell University Press.

Mac Sheoin, T. and Yeates, N. (2007) 'Division and dissent in the anti-globalisation movement', in S. Dasgupta and R. Kiely (eds) *Globalisation and After*, New Delhi: Sage Publications, pp 360-91.

Mishra, R. (1999) *Globalization and the Welfare State*, Cheltenham: Edward Elgar.

Narlikar, A. and Tussie, D. (2004) 'The G20 at the Cancun ministerial: developing countries and their evolving coalitions in the WTO', *The World Economy*, vol 27, no 7, pp 947-66.

O'Brien, R., Goetz, A.M., Scholte, J.A. and Williams, M. (2000) *Contesting Global Governance: Multilateral Economic Institutions and Global Social Movements*, Cambridge: Cambridge University Press.

Pollock, A. and Price, D. (2000) 'Rewriting the regulations: how the World Trade Organization could accelerate privatization in healthcare systems', *The Lancet*, vol 356, pp 1995-2000.

Price, D., Pollock, A.M. and Shaoul, J. (1999) 'How the World Trade Organization is shaping domestic policies in health care', *The Lancet*, vol 354, pp 1889-91.

Rieger, E. and Leibfried, S. (2003) *Limits to Globalization*, Cambridge: Polity Press.

Rodrik, D. (1997) *Has Globalization Gone too Far?*, Washington, DC: Institute for International Economics.

Rodrik, D. (1998) 'Why do more open economies have larger governments?', *Journal of Political Economy*, vol 106, pp 997-1932.

Sexton, S. (2001) *Trading Health Care Away?: GATS, Public Services and Privatisation*, Briefing 23, Sturminster Newton: The Corner House.

The Economist (2006) 'In the shadow of prosperity. Briefing: trade's victims', *The Economist*, vol 382, no 8512, pp 28-30.

UNDP (United Nations Development Programme) (2006) *Trade on Human Terms: Transforming Trade for Human Development in Asia and the Pacific, Asia–Pacific Human Development Report 2006*, New Delhi: Macmillan and UNDP.

Woods, N. and Narlikar, A. (2001) 'Governance and the limits of accountability: the WTO, the IMF, and the World Bank', *International Social Science Journal*, vol 53, no 170, pp 569-83.

Yeates, N. (2001) *Globalization and Social Policy*, London: Sage Publications.

Yeates, N. (2005) 'The General Agreement on Trade in Services: what's in it for social security?', *International Social Security Review*, vol 58, no 1, pp 3-22.

Yeates, N. and Deacon, B. (2006) *Globalism, Regionalism and Social Policy: Framing the Debate*, United Nations University Centre for Comparative Regional Integration Studies (UNU-CRIS) Working Paper 0-2006/6, Bruges: UNU-CRIS.

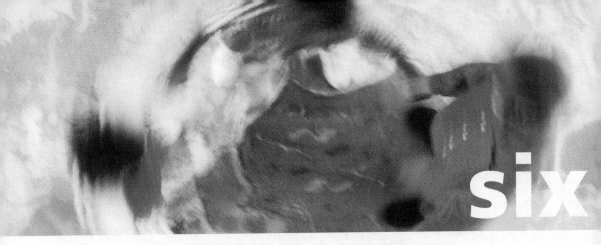

six

Global labour policy

Robert O'Brien

Overview

This chapter examines the collection of actors, ideologies and policies that compose global labour policy. Although international labour policy has been guided by the presence of a dedicated international organisation (the International Labour Organization), for over 90 years, this chapter argues that global labour policy is created by a much larger number of public and private authorities. Key public actors are states and international organisations, while private actors include civic associations and transnational corporations. The competition and struggle over global labour policy is illustrated in debates surrounding international enforcement of labour standards and corporate self-regulation. These debates pit a number of state and non-state actors against each other as they espouse a variety of ideological positions from neoliberalism to social democracy and from nationalism to cosmopolitanism. The United Nations-sponsored Global Compact is an example of how states, corporations and civic associations might come together to bolster global labour rights and standards. However, the potential effectiveness of that initiative is limited by its reliance on voluntarism.

Key concepts

Core labour standards; comparative advantage; self-regulation; cosmopolitanism; nationalism

Introduction

The inhabitants of western countries happily consume products from around the world. They drink coffee from Ethiopia, eat bananas from Columbia, use computers from China, wear clothes from Cambodia, walk on carpets from Pakistan, talk to customer service representatives in India, display flowers from Kenya and show off diamonds from Africa. These patterns of trade and consumption influence working conditions in both importing and exporting countries. When western industries need cheap labour for domestic production and service provision, they often turn from importing products to importing people. Examples include the UK importing health workers from Africa, the US relying on Mexican labour for agricultural and service work, Canada's importation of Filipinas to work as nannies, Arab Gulf states importing Indian construction workers, western Europe importing East European women to work in the sex trade. This movement of workers also affects labour conditions in both the importing and exporting countries.

As products and services move across borders, labour issues and policies increasingly have transnational impact. New patterns of consumption, production and movement have internationalised labour policy. Whereas domestic regulation of working conditions was seen to be sufficient in an era when most production and consumption was nationally based, increasing global exchanges reduce the influence of such regulation. Because of the globalisation of communication, the conditions of work generated by global production and exchange have also appeared in public debate and generated political pressure for action. Thus, stories of child labour in the carpet industry, forced labour in the West African diamond industry, sweatshop labour in China, dangerous and exploitative working conditions for migrants and undocumented workers in western countries have generated demands for new forms of regulation of working conditions on a transnational basis. The demand is that rules ensuring basic rights should reach across national boundaries to include workers around the world.

This chapter unfolds in four sections. The first section provides a brief overview of global working conditions so that readers get a sense of the challenges in this field. The second section examines the key actors in global labour policy: civic actors, states, international organisations (IOs) and transnational corporations (TNCs). In the third section two policy issues are investigated: enforcement of core labour standards and corporate self-regulation. The competing perspectives on enforceable labour standards are highlighted and the promise and perils of self-regulation are considered. The fourth section examines one particular policy arrangement – the Global Compact – as an example of the problems of dealing with global labour standards. The chapter concludes by arguing that the debate around securing labour standards and decent working conditions is likely to continue well into the future. While the issue of migrant labour makes an appearance in this chapter, the phenomenon of **international migration** is dealt with more fully in Chapter Ten by Nicola Yeates.

Global labour conditions

The world faces immense challenges in the field of employment and labour rights. For example, there are approximately:

- 15,000 people punished for legitimate trade union activity each year (ranging from dismissal to murder) (ITUC, 2007);
- 2 million people who die each year from accidents at work or occupational diseases (ILO, 2007b);
- 12.3 million people trapped in forced labour (ILO, 2005b);
- 195.2 million unemployed people (ILO, 2007a);
- 246 million child labourers (ILO, 2005a);
- 1.37 billion people living on $2 a day (ILO, 2007a);
- 80% of the world's population lacking access to formal social security programmes (ILO, 2006).

In addition to these startling figures, the past two decades have witnessed a decrease in secure employment and the growth of insecure and informal forms of employment (ILO, 2002a). The term 'informal sector' was coined in the 1970s to refer to that sector of the economy where workers are highly vulnerable to exploitation because they are not protected or recognised under legal regulatory frameworks. Examples of sectors that make wide use of informal workers are: street vendors, garbage and rag pickers, domestic workers, home workers, sex and entertainment workers and agricultural workers. Most new work in many developing countries is in the informal sector, while many jobs in the developed world are also being made more flexible, insecure and precarious. The problem with the growth of such employment is that the workers in these jobs are usually denied workers' rights and access to social security benefits, pensions and healthcare.

With the advent of global information technologies the poor state of working conditions around the world is increasingly apparent, moving the issue of global labour policy higher up the international agenda.

Actors in global labour policy

Labour policy that crosses international borders differs from national labour policy because it attempts to regulate relations between sovereign national political communities. This adds an extra layer of complexity to labour policy that tends to be highly charged even in the domestic context. Labour policy is often a source of intense conflict because its content can influence the profit levels of corporations and the wage levels of individuals. This section examines the activities of key actors engaged in influencing global labour policy: civic associations, IOs, states and transnational corporations. Key policy issues will be highlighted in the following section.

Civic actors

The demand for transnational or global labour policies comes in the first place from workers themselves. A wide range of workers, from unionised workers in developed states to informal sectors in developing countries, have mobilised on a national and transnational basis to oppose economic exploitation and demand improvements to their working conditions and their lives. These mobilisations, whether or not explicitly invoking or opposing 'globalisation', are a classic example of processes of 'globalisation from below' and of a transnational advocacy coalition (see Chapters One and Two of this volume).

Unionised workers are represented at the international level by their own associations. The most prominent union association is the International Trade Union Confederation (ITUC, formerly the International Confederation of Free Trade Unions (ICFTU) and the World Confederation of Labour). While the old ICFTU was subject to withering criticism for its conservatism (Greenfield, 1998), recent changes suggest a more progressive agenda that moves beyond male unionists in developed states to include women and people in developing countries (O'Brien, 2000). In 2007, the ITUC ran campaigns promoting decent work, the ethical production of sporting goods for the 2008 Olympics, the achievement of the **Millennium Development Goals**, AIDS prevention, the banning of child labour and the advancement of worker rights in the activity of the World Trade Organization (WTO), International Monetary Fund (IMF) and World Bank (WB) (www.ituc-csi.org).

In addition to the ITUC, workers in unions in particular industries have their own sector representatives called Global Union Federations (GUFs). For example, automobile unions are affiliated to the International Metalworkers' Federation, public servant unions can be members of Public Service International, and miners can belong to the International Federation of Chemical, Energy, Mine and General Workers' Unions. Some of these GUFs have negotiated global framework agreements with TNCs. The framework agreements set out the basic union rights and health and safety principles and conditions that will apply in TNCs all over the world. They also provide for a review mechanism to monitor the company's implementation of the principles. While global framework agreements advance workers' rights, only a small number of TNCs are covered.

Most of the world's workers do not have unions or political parties to take care of their interests. Although these 'unprotected' workers (Harrod, 1987) face more obstacles than their protected counterparts, they still attempt to influence global labour policy. For example, small farmers and peasants from many parts of the world have coalesced around the group Via Campesina. Via Campesina describes itself as 'an international movement which coordinates peasant organisations of small and middle-scale producers, agricultural workers, rural women, and indigenous communities from Asia, Africa, America, and Europe' (www.viacampesina.org). It advances farmers' interests by advocating for landless populations and small farmers while resisting the spread of **free trade agreements**, genetically modified organisms and national and transnational agribusinesses that undermine peasant incomes. Via Campesina has been active in the World Social Forums and has engaged institutions such as the WTO, WB and the Food and Agriculture Organization as well as regional integration projects. The goal is to create space in the global political economy for small-scale farmers to pursue their livelihoods free from the threat of economic and social extinction that is posed by large agricultural businesses.

In many developing countries, the vast majority of the population works as unprotected workers in the informal sector. Transnational cooperation between such groups is very difficult, since they often lack the resources to form even local or national institutions. However, there are instances of informal sector workers whose organisations become stable enough that they can develop an international presence and serve as an example to workers in other countries. One of the most prominent of these is the Self Employed Women's Association (SEWA) in India (www.sewa.org). In addition to affiliating with the established international union association ITUC, SEWA is building its own international networks. For example, in 2003 it hosted an international conference on organising in the informal economy that drew participants from 47 organisations in 23 countries.

One significant way in which unprotected workers have been making transnational contacts and advances has been with the cooperation of consumer groups. The movement for ethical trade links consumers in advanced industrialised countries with workers and farmers in developing countries. In its broadest sense, ethical trade encompasses two elements (Blowfield, 1999). The first element is a concern with how companies make their product. This involves pressuring companies to ensure that the production process respects key human rights and environmental standards. Examples include companies

Doonesbury's view of global labour politics

that adopt codes of conduct guaranteeing respect for workers' rights or banning child labour. The second element is the fair trade movement, which seeks to increase the financial return to poor producers as a method of improving sustainable development (see Chapter Five). Major fair trade initiatives have taken place with products such as coffee and chocolate. Both of these initiatives are designed to give workers in developing countries more autonomy in their working lives by supporting human rights or transferring wealth. This requires the formation of new transnational communities joining Southern producers with Northern consumers.

States in the global division of labour

The first stop for workers seeking protection in the global economy is their national state. However, states are differentially located in the **global division of labour**. As a result, they define their interests in different ways and take varying approaches to global labour policies (see *Table 6.1*). One crucial difference is between states with advanced industrialised economies and developing countries that are trying to industrialise. Advanced industrialised economies such as those in western Europe, Japan, the US, Canada and Australia share a number of characteristics. They are relatively wealthy states, they are home to a majority of the world's transnational corporations, they produce many high-value-added products, wages are relatively high, they have advanced service, manufacturing and agricultural industries and they have ageing populations. In contrast, many developing countries are struggling to industrialise, have large informal sectors, relatively low wages, widespread poverty and young and growing populations, and they are very dependent on investment from TNCs and overseas investors for economic growth.

States are locked into global competition with one another for investment and economic growth. However, they engage in different competitive strategies

Table 6.1: Divergent state interests

Type of state	Population	Wealth, wages, skill levels	Economic strategies	Labour policies
Advanced industrialised (EU, US, Canada)	Ageing and shrinking	High	Take migrant labour; high-value services and products	Control labour mobility; support international standards
Developing (China, India, Africa, Latin America)	Young and growing	Low	Send migrant labour; export processing zones; compete for labour-intensive investment	Promote mobility; resist restrictive standards

(Palan and Abbott, 2000). Relatively wealthy countries with high education levels can afford to pay relatively high wages to retain skilled workers because the value of their products produces large profits. Poorer countries may pursue other routes to maintain economic activity. Some countries will send their citizens abroad to find work that can support families at home. Other countries may create **export processing zones** to attract foreign investment. These zones often suspend features of domestic regulation such as labour standards and taxation as incentives to lure foreign TNCs to set up shop. The lack of labour standards in these zones can lead to very poor and dangerous working conditions. Some states may rely on exporting their natural resources to generate wealth. These resources can range from those highly prized in the international market, such as oil, to those that attract paltry returns, such as coffee or bananas.

The differences in resources and intense competition for economic growth encourage states to have differing interests with regards to global labour policies. The poorest countries, most desperate for investment, will be most likely to curb labour protection in order to attract investment. Since labour is inexpensive in these countries, there will be an effort to attract investment into industries that use a large amount of labour. A classic example is the textile industry. In order to keep that investment, countries may be reluctant to do anything that increases the cost of labour. In contrast, wealthier countries have industries where labour costs are a smaller percentage of the total cost of production. This means they are better able to afford the costs of labour standards. Poorer countries will also press for labour mobility so that their citizens can work abroad. They will also have an interest in trying to protect their citizens when they are working abroad. In contrast, wealthier countries will want to be more selective about allowing labour to move between states and may not be as concerned about the fate of migrant workers. Thus, we can hypothesise that wealthier countries will be more interested in global labour standards and poorer countries more interested in labour mobility and access to developed states markets. Both sets of countries will use the doctrine of state sovereignty as a justification for resisting compulsory labour regulations.

These general divisions are complicated by the fact that even advanced states are in global competition and limited as to the amount of labour protection they deliver. Advanced industrialised countries also point to the need to deregulate labour markets and have more flexible forms of labour available for their industries (McBride and Williams, 2001). The threat of TNCs moving production to lower wage jurisdictions threatens workers with unemployment. Competition from low-wage producers limits the wages that corporations from wealthy country will be willing to give their workers. The movement of migrant labour also serves to check the wage demands and puts pressure on working conditions in developed states.

Thus states find themselves in a balancing act. They must position themselves in the global competition for development and economic growth, but they must also respond to domestic and international pressure by workers for safe working conditions and fair remuneration.

International organisations

A number of IOs have become involved in the effort to create global labour policy. They can be divided into three groups: those whose primary concern is labour issues; those primarily concerned with freeing the movement of trade and services; those primarily focused on finance. Although each of these groups of institutions is engaged in labour issues, they have had a limited impact on advancing labour protection in the global economy.

The first category of institutions, those primarily focused on labour issues, is dominated by the International Labour Organization (ILO). The ILO is the oldest arm of the United Nations (UN) system, originating in the Treaty of Versailles (1919), which led to the creation of the League of Nations. The ILO promotes labour standards in its member states through its Conventions and Recommendations. Conventions are statements of principle that member states are asked to ratify, while Recommendations outline administrative matters that carry less weight. The ILO has no coercive power and relies on the power of its argument to influence state behaviour. The ILO also provides technical support to governments, employers and worker organisations that wish to improve working conditions. The organisation's primary task is to improve the living and working conditions of the world's population.

By the mid-1990s, advocates of international labour standards, such as trade unions and social democratic parties, had become discouraged about the possibility of ILO being an institution that could bring significant improvement. The problem lay with the inability of the ILO to ensure enforcement of its Conventions. Labour rights advocates shifted their attention to having labour standards written into trade agreements and institutions such as the newly formed WTO. The ILO's response to this marginalisation was to focus attention on its role in defending labour rights through the creation of a new political instrument. In 1998, the ILO adopted the Declaration on Fundamental Principles and Rights at Work. It committed all member states to respect and promote ILO Conventions in four key areas: freedom of association and collective bargaining; the elimination of forced or compulsory labour; the abolition of child labour; and the elimination of discrimination in employment. Whether countries had ratified particular ILO Conventions or not, they became bound by this Declaration.

A second component of the ILO's attempt to come to grips with globalisation was a recognition of the diversity of work relationships in the global economy. This involved a shift away from focusing on the standard employment relationship of a male unionised worker in a factory to considering the variety of employment patterns in the economy, which included precarious employment such as casual labour, work in the informal sector, various types of home work and contract work. The method for making this shift was twofold. One involved the introduction of a new theme and work programme – decent work (ILO, 2002a). The other was the introduction of new conventions such as the Homeworking Convention. The shift to a rhetoric of 'decent work' was designed to take account of the large range of labour-related issues beyond the employer–trade union relationship. Decent work covers issues such as fair incomes, employment security, social protection, social integration, freedom to express views and organise, and equality of opportunity and treatment for all women and men. It allows the ILO to address issues of informal employment as well as broad policy debates around social security and public policy.

A third initiative is the ILO's attempt to reinsert itself into debates about the impact and future of globalisation. The primary tool for accomplishing this objective was the 2002 creation of the World Commission on the Social Dimension of Globalisation. The Commission was composed of 26 high-profile people from different parts of the world involved in government, business, labour and academic fields. The Commission published its report, entitled *A Fair Globalisation: Creating Opportunities For All*, in 2004. While not challenging the general trend of existing globalisation, the report highlighted problems in current global economic governance and called for changes to ensure more equitable development (ILO, 2004). From a political point of view, the Commission's goal was to raise issues of equity and fairness in the global governance agenda. Similar to the UN's Millennium Development Goals, the ILO Commission was an effort to shift the economic agenda and focus attention on poverty and development.

A fourth area of activity is the ILO's attempt to regain a prominent role in the architecture of IOs. The ILO, similar to other IOs working in the social field, has been greatly overshadowed by international financial and trade organisations such as the IMF, WB and WTO. Even though these were all taking initiatives that had a direct impact on labour markets, the ILO was not a player in the formulation or implementation of those institutions' policies. In response to this lack of communication and feeling pressure from civil society groups, the ILO established formal inter-institutional channels of communication with the financial institutions and attempts to participate in their activities. In terms of policy, the ILO is attempting to influence other organisations' views on labour-related subjects. For example, it has tried to influence the content of **Poverty Reduction Strategy Papers** (PRSPs), which are used by the IMF and WB to demonstrate that their lending goes through a process of consultation with recipients.

Ideologically, the ILO challenges the international financial institutions (IFIs) because it suggests that macroeconomic stabilisation plans undertaken in the absence of proper labour market institutions risk failure (ILO, 2004). It also disagrees with IFI policies that blame labour rigidity for unemployment. The ILO argues that 'rather than create rigidities, the labour institutions that are built upon the realisation of these fundamental principles and rights at work can be key to negotiating flexibility' (ILO, 2000). The ILO review of early PRSP consultations also raised three concerns about the degree and significance of civil society participation in the 'pro-poor' policies of the IMF and WB (ILO, 2002b). First, insufficient attention was being given to equity issues. Second, trade unions, ministries of labour and even employers' organisations had difficulty participating in the process because it was dominated by trade and finance ministries. Third, labour market issues, social protection and other elements of decent work were often absent from poverty reduction policies.

Other institutions that influence labour conditions are those that focus on trade and services liberalisation, such as the WTO at the multilateral level and world-regional trade agreements (see also Chapters Two and Five). The establishment of the WTO in 1995 led workers rights activists to demand the inclusion of labour standards in its enforcement mandate. The WTO hosts a relatively robust legal structure that puts immense pressure on states to implement its decisions. Disillusionment with the weakness of the ILO led campaigners to lobby their states and the WTO to enforce labour standards. This campaign proved unsuccessful because of opposition from TNCs, neoliberal states in the developed world and many developing countries.

At the world-regional level, a new wave of expanded trade and investment agreements swept the world in the 1980s and continued into the 21st century. These agreements raised the issue of whether or not labour standards and broader social rights should be part of the economic packages. Chapter Two examines some of the responses by different regional associations of countries in terms of social policy generally. In terms of labour, the response varied greatly between regions, although the tendency was for labour standards to have a minor place. Indeed, one could build a regional integration typology based on provisions for labour rights and mobility. This would have the European Union (EU) with some common labour rights and representation at one end of the spectrum, the North American Free Trade Agreement simply urging states to enforce their own legislation in the middle and the Association of South East Asian Nations, with a tendency to deal with labour issues only under the heading of human resources, at the other end. Assessing the implications of world-regional economic agreements requires two steps. First, the provision or non-provision of labour issues within and around the agreements needs to be judged. Second, these provisions need to be compared with the institutional arrangements for other interests, such as investors. Labour groups continue to struggle to advance basic standards and rights, but the regional level, with the exception of the EU, has not proved to have been particularly fruitful (O'Brien, 2008).

IFIs are a third group of institutions having an impact on labour policy. IFIs disperse finance to countries either for the purpose of dealing with financial crisis or assisting with development. The two most prominent institutions are the IMF and the WB. These institutions become involved in labour policy because their loans come with conditions. In some cases, those conditions include restructuring domestic labour markets. A prominent strain of thought at the WB and IMF is that the competitiveness of developing countries would be increased if labour was more flexible and wages were lower. This view is sometimes articulated in the policy advice given to member states. For example, a WB-sponsored report on Mexico suggested that its labour laws be revised to increase flexibility because the labour code was 'at best, outdated (part of it dates back to 1917), at worst, an impediment rather than a tool for workers'(Oliver et al, 2001). A Letter of Intent between the IMF and Ecuador outlines how the government's 'economic transformation law' will facilitate the introduction of temporary contracts to increase labour market flexibility and boost employment (Ecuador, 2000). Trade unions are also unhappy with the lack of consultations under the IMF and WB's PRSP process. An August 2004 survey of trade unions in 23 developing countries showed that while labour groups were often included in discussion, this participation was seen to have no noticeable impact on policy (Egulu, 2004). Such examples confirm labour fears that the IFIs systematically work to weaken labour rights and wages as a development strategy.

In response to criticisms of the impact on labour, the IFIs have modified their procedures and policies. They have taken steps to regularise (but not formalise) their contact with trade unions at the international level. Every two years, leaders of the IMF and WB meet with those of the ITUC and GUFs, and smaller yearly thematic meetings are conducted. WB has indicated that it might support some movement on the issue of freedom of association and collective bargaining. Indeed, as WB pursues development strategies that touch on numerous domestic governance issues, it is difficult to argue that advocacy of core labour standards should be ignored. In September 2003, the WB's private sector lending arm, the IFC, announced that its loan recipients would soon have to abide by all the core labour standards. In January 2004, the IFC made approval of a loan to a free trade zone operator in Haiti conditional on the employer recognising its workers' rights to freedom of association and collective bargaining (ICFTU, 2004). The rhetoric around privatisation and pension reform has also changed, with IFIs claiming that they are not wedded to such policies if states propose alternatives.

Labour issues are a subject of considerable debate in a series of different international organisations. However, the struggle to forge a global labour policy that improves workers' conditions has not been very successful. This has caused some campaigners to turn their attention away from the state and inter-state organisations to the activity of corporations and the harms they cause (see *Box 6.1*).

Box 6.1: Deadly toys

On 10 May 1993, the worst-ever factory fire occurred in a toy plant just outside Bangkok in Thailand (ICFTU, 1994). Fatalities numbered 188. Of these deaths, 174 were women and girls, many of whom were as young as 13. Over 460 other people were injured in the fire. These injuries were due to people jumping from upper floors, being trampled in the panic or suffering from smoke inhalation or burns. The factory violated many basic health and safety standards: it lacked fire exits and sprinkler systems; hallways and stairwells were used to store flammable materials; and locked doors and barred windows made it impossible for some workers to escape. The mainly young female workforce had not been able to pressure the employer into providing a safe place to work.

The factory was owned by Kader Industrial Company based in Hong Kong. Among its many activities, Kadar manufactures toys for western companies such as Arco, Kenner, Gund, Hasbro, J.C. Penny, Toys-R-Us, Fischer-Price and Tyco. The responsibility for allowing the conditions that fuelled the fire begins with the company itself and reaches all the way to western consumers. The company failed in its duty to provide a safe working environment for its employees, the Thai government failed in its duty to enforce safety standards, western retailers failed in their duty to ensure that sub-contractors produced products in a safe environment, and western governments ignored the issue of safety in the production of imported products. Western consumers were indirectly implicated because their demand for ever-cheaper toy prices encourages producers to save costs by cutting back on expenses such as health and safety regulation.

Transnational corporations

The world's largest TNCs are larger and richer economic actors than many states. Because of this enormous economic influence, the decisions corporations make about where they will locate their production or the types of working practices they engage in have immense implications for global labour standards. Given the lack of success IOs have had in advancing labour rights, civic actors have increasingly targeted corporations to advance labour rights. The response by most corporate leaders to an upsurge in public interest in labour standards and labour rights has been to argue that such concerns are best addressed through self-regulation. The role of corporations will be addressed in more depth in the section on self-regulation below.

Policy issues in global labour policy

This section examines two linked policy issues in global labour policy. The first is whether there should be a common set of basic labour rights that covers all workers and is enforced worldwide through the activity of states and IOs. A second issue is whether international labour rights would be advanced by encouraging TNCs to engage in self-regulation.

International enforcement of core labour standards

One key policy issue is whether or not there should be international enforcement of core labour standards. There are a series of theoretical and practical arguments both for and against having states or IOs impose penalties on states that violate core labour standards.

The concept of core labour standards originates in a series of ILO Conventions (87, 98, 29, 105, 100, 111, 138). These were designed to protect the most important and basic of workers' rights: freedom of association, the right to collective bargaining, abolition of forced labour, prevention of discrimination in employment and a minimum age for employment. These rights are seen as enabling rights: the provision of these rights should enable workers to struggle for other rights. The core labour standards do not provide for specific wage levels or safety standards, but they do provide workers with the tools to organise and bargain over working conditions.

As mentioned above, all states are committed to core labour standards through the ILO's Fundamental Declaration. However, many states do not respect these standards. The question is whether some mechanism should be put in place to punish states that consistently violate labour rights. For example, the WTO could be used to sanction states that did not protect labour standards in the same way that it is used to enforce respect for intellectual property rights. Violating states could be hit with economic sanctions from other states.

The debate over global enforcement of core labour standards divides groups favouring rival economic programmes and having different views over the role of state sovereignty. Those against having an enforcement mechanism for core labour standards tend to take a neoliberal approach to labour conditions and often advocate state sovereignty over international regulation. The neoliberal ideology has guided much economic globalisation since the 1980s. In this view, labour is a commodity (something that is bought and sold), freedom of expression and association for workers is not essential or even desirable for economic growth, and poverty will be resolved by market rather than state mechanisms. The appropriate payment for work is determined by the market and the only real solution to poor working conditions is economic growth.

Neoliberals often point to the doctrine of comparative advantage (see also Chapter Five) to bolster their case against enforcement of labour standards. They argue that countries with a large pool of cheap labour should use that as an economic advantage and attract businesses that want to use such labour in their production. This allows poor countries to industrialise and begin the path to economic development. Thus, a difference in labour standards and working conditions between countries is seen to be both natural and beneficial. Opponents of labour standard enforcement also often cite the doctrine of **state sovereignty**. Under the doctrine of state sovereignty, governments only have a responsibility to their own citizens and are uninterested in the fate of people living in other countries. This suggests that states will engage in a variety of labour practices to advance national interests and that they will not be concerned about working conditions in other countries.

In contrast, those in favour of global enforcement of core labour standards tend to have a social democratic economic philosophy and a **cosmopolitan approach** to human rights. The social democratic approach to labour rights is captured in the core assumptions of the ILO's 1944 Declaration of Philadelphia. This Declaration declared that labour is not a commodity; freedom of expression and of association are essential to sustained progress; poverty anywhere constitutes a danger to prosperity everywhere; and the war against want must be vigorously pursued. In this view, labour is composed of human beings who deserve protection from economic exploitation. Failure to deliver this protection is not only immoral, but it will lead to political conflict and even warfare between states.

The doctrine of state sovereignty is challenged by the concept of **cosmopolitanism**. Cosmopolitanism posits that all people are part of a universal human community. Even through people are divided into national political communities by birth, they have moral obligations to all human beings by virtue of a common humanity. Ethical obligations transcend state borders. Thus economic activity and rule making must take into account their impact on foreigners as wells as national citizens. A cosmopolitan approach to global labour issues would stress two points. First, all people enjoy rights to basic labour standards. Second, people in wealthier countries have an obligation to ensure that their economic activity does not contribute to labour abuses in other countries.

The arena where the enforcement of core labour standards became most prominent in the 1990s was the negotiations surrounding the founding of the WTO and agenda setting in its early years. The establishment of the WTO in 1995 led workers' rights activists to demand the inclusion of labour standards in its enforcement mandate. This campaign proved unsuccessful due to the opposition of transnational corporations, neoliberal states in the developed world and many developing countries (O'Brien et al, 2000, pp 67-108). Developing countries feared that labour standards would be used as an excuse for protectionism in developed states. They were concerned that wealthier states would use labour standards to undermine their comparative advantage. While the effort to have the WTO deal with labour standards failed, it did result in the ILO refocusing its efforts (see above) and the initiation of new policies such as corporate codes of conduct and the Global Compact (see below).

State enforcement of core labour standards remains on the agenda. The negotiation of regional trade agreements usually features a debate about whether trade agreements should contain labour elements. Pressure for some enforcement of labour rights is generated by coverage of labour abuses and the influx of cheap consumer goods into industrialised states from countries that fail to respect core labour standards. Nevertheless, the failure to actually agree on a state-based enforcement mechanism has led to considerable discussion of corporate self-regulation as a method for improving global labour standards.

Self-regulation

Self-regulation is where corporations set and monitor their own rules. This can take place either through the actions of an individual corporation or through the activities of business associations in a particular sector. The concept and practice of corporate social responsibility (CSR) has been the primary rejoinder to those arguing for state-based international labour regulation (see also Chapter Four). The European Commission provides a useful definition of CSR as a concept 'whereby companies integrate social and environmental concerns in their business operations and in their interaction with stakeholders on a voluntary basis' (Greenwood, 2003, p 56). It has also come to be known as 'the triple bottom line' or 'corporate citizenship' signifying the responsibility of companies to create wealth, pursue sustainable development and enhance the lives of their employees and the communities in which they locate. As Chris Thomas, a corporate reputation consultant, writes, 'CSR is a prudent adaptation to changing circumstances: countering the increased ability of stakeholders to scrutinise corporate activities and motives with openness and complementary action' (Thomas, 2003). CSR policies have been put into practice by many firms, epically those caught in sweatshop scandals.

While TNCs and business organisations suggest that CSR will advance social rights, critics contend that CSR has been developed as a substitute and diversion for action (Justice, 2002). For example, one analyst argues that 'in plain terms, business "talks the talk" *so as not to* "walk the walk"' (Rowe, 2005, p 144) (emphasis in the original). In this view, CSR is a public relations ploy. The main targets are average consumers who may have encountered anti-corporate campaigns but are not particularly engaged with the issue and therefore largely ignorant of the ongoing situation on the company's factory floors. The goal is 'to solve guilty consumer consciousness' rather than to improve working conditions (Brooks, 2005, p 134).

In response to scepticism over in-house company codes of conduct, many TNCs have been forced to support a number of third party or joint corporate–non-governmental organisation (NGO) initiatives. In addition to numerous partnerships between firms and NGOs, the most prominent response has been the creation of a number of multi–stakeholder initiatives in the US and western Europe such as the Fair Labour Association (FLA) and the Ethical Trade Initiative (ETI), industry-based initiatives such as the Worldwide Responsible Apparel Production and the emergence of third-party certification providers such as Social Accountability International. All of these attempt to avoid traditional state-based regulation. For example, the FLA was created after sweatshop scandals in the US in the early 1990s raised industry fears that Congress would pass tougher regulation (Jenkins, 2002). Voluntary initiatives claim to support labour standards through a mix of cooperation between key actors, learning networks, 'enlightened company self-interest', benchmarking, internal and external monitoring and enforcement through market sanctions (O'Rourke, 2003).

Numerous organisations have sprung up to support the corporate response to labour and social issues. In Chapter Four, Kevin Farnsworth reviewed the ways in which global business interest associations, such as BIAC, ICC and ERT, have been involved in promoting corporate responses on these issues within global social policy making. In the UK, there are the following organisations: Business in the Community (the UK member of CSR Europe), Common Purpose, the Institute of Business Ethics, and the Prince of Wales International Business Leaders Forum (Greenwood, 2003). Most major TNCs belong to more than one such organisation in addition to having their own CSR committees. These initiatives are supported by academics within corporate-funded business schools who advocate CSR and carry out research to improve its practice and effectiveness. The vast majority of their focus is on how TNCs can use CSR to respond to anti-corporate activism, protect corporate reputations and brand names and encourage a 'business-friendly' regulatory environment.

In adopting CSR, corporations draw on both liberal economic and cultural/ nationalist arguments that suggest that movement to enforceable labour standards may hurt development. Many neoclassical economists argue that regulation and codes of conduct reduce wealth and harm the very workers labour activists are attempting to help. In 2000, a letter signed by over 250 economists was sent to US university presidents at a time when the FLA and the Worker Rights Consortium (WRC) were quickly gaining university memberships. According to these economists, the codes of conduct promoted by the FLA and WRC would cause employment in the developing world to shift away from the poorest workers. They also argued that regulation was unnecessary as TNCs already pay higher wages than the 'prevailing market wage' (Wells, 2004). The economists' intervention offered comfort to TNCs trying to avoid meaningful codes of conduct, much less effective regulation. Echoing arguments made by some developing country leaders (such as Mahathir Mohamad, the former Prime Minister of Malaysia), corporations have been able to argue that their hands-off approach to labour issues respects national sovereignty and cultural diversity. For example, some members of the Toy Manufacturers of America, when faced with demands to live up to the ILO's universal standards to avoid a repeat of the Kadar toy factory disaster (see **Box 6.1**, p 135), argued that they did not want to be seen as imposing 'western values' on non-western cultures (Justice, 2002).

A key element of CSR engagement is the emphasis on partnerships between firms and their NGO opponents. The concept of partnership has 'become an orthodox public affairs strategy' (Greenwood, 2003, p 54). From a public relations perspective, it is an attempt to protect brands plagued by mistrust by associating with NGOs that enjoy a higher level of trust (Hatcher, 2003). This strategy has come to be known as 'greenwashing' in relation to partnerships between environmental NGOs and TNCs. More recently, anti-corporate activists have coined the term 'bluewashing' to describe partnerships between TNCs and the UN, such as the Global Compact (see below). Some examples of partnerships between TNCs and/or employers' associations and NGOs linked to labour rights include: Gap and the National Labour Committee; the Fairtrade Foundation and Sainsbury's; the Co-operative Wholesale Society, World Federation of Sporting Goods Industry and Save the Children; and the FLA and the ETI.

Although there are literally hundreds of corporate codes of conduct in existence, there is increasing doubt about whether this will resolve the labour standards issue. Numerous studies have documented the serious weaknesses of these private regulatory approaches and it is increasingly apparent that they do not serve as an effective substitute for traditional labour regulation (Bruno and Karliner, 2002; Christian Aid, 2004; Rowe, 2005). Self- and voluntary regulation of labour standards is not successful in national markets and is even less likely to succeed transnationally. An extreme example of the divergence between intentions stated in codes of conduct and practices on the ground is provided in **Box 6.2**

Box 6.2: Codes versus practice

Statement from the Code of Conduct of Chiquita (famous for selling bananas):

Chiquita believes in doing business with suppliers and other business partners who demonstrate high standards of ethical business conduct. Our ultimate goal is to direct all of our business to suppliers that demonstrate their compliance with the social responsibilities included in our Code of Conduct and that operate in an ethical and lawful manner. (Chiquita, 2004)

Statement from lawyers suing Chiquita for activities in Columbia:

> Advocates for the families of 173 people murdered in the banana-growing regions of Colombia filed suit today against Chiquita Brands International, in Federal District Court in Washington, D.C. The families allege that Chiquita paid millions of dollars, and tried to ship thousands of machine guns to the Autodefensas Unidas de Colombia, or AUC. The AUC is a violent, right-wing terrorist organisation supported by the Colombian army, and was designated a 'terrorist organisation' in 2001 by the Bush Administration. Its units are often described as 'death squads'. (Iradvocates, 2007)

The Global Compact

The Global Compact is an example of an attempt to bring together states, civic associations and corporations to build better global labour policy. It was launched by the Secretary General of the UN and asks corporations to incorporate 10 principles drawn from the Universal Declaration of Human Rights, the ILO's Fundamental Principles on Rights at Work, the Rio Principles on Environment and Development, and the United Nations Convention against Corruption into their corporate practices. The Global Compact does not monitor corporate practice nor does it assess corporate performance. It is designed to identify and disseminate good practices. It asks leaders of some of the world's most prominent corporations to publicly commit themselves to good labour and environmental practices.

The Global Compact simultaneously addresses the concerns of some corporate, state and civic associations. From a developing country point of view, the initiative is tolerable because it is aimed at influencing the policy of TNCs rather than restricting state policy or punishing developing states for poor labour conditions. This is preferable to the WTO enforcing of standards because it removes the threat of northern protectionism. From the corporate viewpoint, it is tolerable because regulations are voluntary and allow continued expansion of the global economy and accumulation of profits. TNCs can claim to be good corporate citizens without being bound by compulsory regulation. For some civic actors, it represents a limited advance in enshrining some principles of social protection. It is a small step that might lead to more binding forms of regulation.

The Global Compact has severe shortcomings and many critics. Many of the companies participating in the venture are those that have been attacked as abusers of environmental and human rights or accused of engaging in the super-exploitation of workers. The list includes Shell, Nike, Disney and Rio Tinto. Each of these companies has been, or is subject to, boycotts or anti-corporate campaigns by civic associations. One can question the degree to which such companies will actually change their stripes. Domestically, reliance only on voluntary regulation of corporate behaviour is unacceptable. Why would such activity at the global level prove any more satisfying? The ILO has hundreds of conventions but sees many abused because of a lack of enforcement powers. How would this initiative be any different? Another problem is that the selection of participating civic associations in the Global Compact was very narrow and not reflective of the wider community. The UN selected civic groups based on its judgement of who would be the most likely to cooperate. Reaction from many other groups has been very critical. The initiative has been condemned because it threatens the integrity of the UN, as corporations attempt to 'bluewash' their record by association with the UN (TRAC, 2000). The Global Compact is accused of allowing corporations to claim higher ethical credentials while continuing to inflict serious harm on populations and environments, safe in the knowledge that such actions are likely to go unnoticed or unpunished (Actionaid, 2007).

This example of the Global Compact is informative for our efforts to understand global labour policy for three reasons. First, it illustrates that the concerns of civic actors about the damaging aspects of globalisation on labour are being taken seriously by other actors in the system. The UN is responding to public unease about the costs of globalisation. This initiative follows public demonstrations against institutions such as the WTO and the IMF. The UN Secretary General is trying to put a more humane face on globalisation so that the process will continue, but in a less brutal manner. The goal is to restrain competition that is based on the abuse of labour and environmental standards so that the public will not fight the liberal rules under which globalisation is taking place. Corporations are also being forced to respond to civic pressure by setting up codes of conduct and projecting the image of moral behaviour.

Second, it highlights the failure of existing global governance arrangements to deal adequately with global labour issues. We already have an institution that is designed to bolster labour standards – the ILO. However, the ineffectiveness of the ILO has forced labour activists to turn to the enforcement mechanisms found in the WTO to support labour standards. Many developing states oppose dealing with labour standards because they fear that developed states might increase their protectionism through the device of labour standards. Those groups in civil society trying to improve labour standards find themselves blocked at the WTO and faced with a weak ILO. Existing global governance mechanisms seem unable to improve social standards. Thus, new initiatives such as the Global Compact are being devised in an urgent attempt to resolve difficult dilemmas.

Finally, the Global Compact illustrates just how difficult it is to create global labour policy. The cost of freer markets is creating more public resistance, but many states and corporations resist instruments that would require better labour, environmental or social standards. Agreements that secure widespread corporate and state support are unlikely to satisfy the social interests that are pressing for protection. For the time being, social interests may have to accept incremental steps towards reforming institutions and policies at the global level.

Conclusion

The world faces several challenging issues in the field of global labour policy. Unemployment is widespread, poverty is extensive and basic labour rights are often lacking. One strategy to deal with these issues is to focus attention on core labour rights in the hope that securing these rights will allow workers to mobilise and attain other rights. However, states have pursued very different policies towards labour and have struggled to reach agreement in the international arena. The lack of state action to protect labour rights and improve working conditions has created a regulatory vacuum. Social groups such as labour unions and ethically motivated consumers continue to press for fair labour standards. Many TNCs have responded to these concerns by introducing codes of conduct and arguing that corporate self-regulation is the best path for improving labour conditions around the world. Critics doubt that self-regulation will improve standards.

The UN's Global Compact initiative is an example of an attempt by state, corporate and civic leaders to advance labour rights and standards by highlighting desirable labour practices. However, the voluntary nature of the Global Compact and many other international initiatives raises doubts about their effectiveness. With consumers demanding ever-cheaper products and corporations competing to supply mass consumer goods at low cost, it is likely that pressure on working conditions and wages will continue. It is also likely that workers and citizens will continue the struggle to advance a more humane global labour policy.

Summary

- The majority of the world's working population lacks the protection of core labour standards and access to social security.
- A wide range of actors, from civic associations to IOs and TNCs, attempt to influence global labour policy.
- State enforcement of labour standards at the global level remains a controversial topic.
- Increasing attention has been paid to corporate self-regulation to bolster labour standards, but there is considerable scepticism about whether it can deliver.
- The Global Compact is an example of a voluntary initiative supported by particular civic associations, corporations and states to improve global labour standards.

Questions for discussion

- What are the key challenges for workers in a global economy?
- Should core labour standards be enforced on a global basis?
- Why would some states oppose core labour standards?
- What are the opportunities and challenges posed by corporate self-regulation?

Further suggested activities

- Visit the No Sweat website (www.nosweatapparel.com) to see the marketing of clothes made by union-friendly producers in the developing world. Are you convinced by these producers' ethical pitch? Are their products reasonably priced? Are they fashionable?
- Examine the news stories from the LabourStart website (www.labourstart.org). Did you realise that all this activity was taking place? How many of these stories had you heard of in the papers you read or news that you watch?

Further reading

Dimitris and Boswell (2007) provide a recent overview of the impact of global governance mechanisms on labour and the attempt of labour unions to influence global governance.

Lipschutz and Rowe (2005) examine how more and more areas of global regulation are taking place outside of the reach of states and consider the political and policy implications of such regulation.

The World Commission on the Social Dimensions of Globalisation ILO (2004), examines how social standards could be improved and globalisation made into a fairer process.

Electronic resources

www.ilo.org International Labour Organization
www.unglobalcompact.org Global Compact
www.ituc-csi.org International Trade Union Confederation
www.studentsagainstsweatshops.org Students Against Sweatshops

References

Actionaid (2007) 'Critique of the Global Compact', www.actionaid.org/pages. aspx?PageID=34&ItemID=282, accessed 1 May 2007.

Blowfield, M. (1999) 'Ethical trade: a review of developments and issues', *Third World Quarterly*, vol 20, no 4, pp 753-70.

Brooks, E. (2005) 'Transnational campaigns against child labour', in J. Bandy and J. Smith (eds) *Coalitions across Borders: Transnational Protest and the Neoliberal Order*, Lanham, MD: Rowman & Littlefield, pp 212-39.

Bruno, K. and Karliner, J. (2002) *Earthsummit.biz: The Corporate Takeover of Sustainable Development*, Oakland, CA: Food First Books.

Chiquita (2004) Introduction to 'Code of conduct: living by our core values', available at www.chiquita.com, accessed 1 February 2008.

Christian Aid (2004) *Behind the Mask: The Real Face of Corporate Social Responsibility*, London: Christian Aid.

Dimitris, S. and Boswell, T. (2007) *Globalization and Labor: Democratizing Global Governance*, Lanham, MD: Rowman & Littlefield.

Ecuador, Government of (2000) *Memorandum of Economic Policies of the Government of Ecuador for 2000*, Ministry of Finance and Public Credit (ed), Washington, DC: International Monetary Fund.

Egulu, L. (2004) *Trade Union Participation in the PRSP Process*, Social Protection Discussion Paper Series no 0417, Washington: WB.

Greenfield, G. (1998) 'The ICFTU and the politics of compromise', in E. Wood (ed) *Rising from the Ashes: Labour in the Era of Global Capitalism*, New York, NY: Monthly Review, pp 180-9.

Greenwood, J. (2003) 'Trade associations, change and the new activism', in S. John and S. Thomson (eds) *New Activism and the Corporate Response*, New York, NY: Palgrave Macmillan.

Harrod, J. (1987) *Power, Production and the Unprotected Worker*, New York, NY: Columbia University Press.

Hatcher, M. (2003) 'Public affairs challenges for multinational corporations', in S. John and S. Thomson (eds) *New Activism and the Corporate Response*, New York: Palgrave.

ICFTU (International Confederation of Trade Unions) (1994) *From the Ashes: A Toy Factory Fire in Thailand*, Brussels: ICFTU.

ICFTU (2004) 'World Bank's IFC approves Haiti/Dominican Republic loan, with union rights conditions', Press Release, 20 January, Brussels: ICFTU.

ILO (International Labour Organization) (2000) *Organization, Bargaining and Dialogue for Development in a Globalizing World*, GB.279/WP/SDG/2, Working Party on Social Dimensions of Globalization, Geneva: ILO.

ILO (2002a) *Decent Work and the Informal Economy*, Geneva: ILO.

ILO (2002b) 'Poverty Reduction Strategy Papers (PRSPs): an assessment of the ILO's experience', Committee on Employment and Social Policy, Geneva: ILO.

ILO (2004) *A Fair Globalization: Creating Opportunities for All*, Geneva: ILO.

ILO (2005a) *Facts on Child Labour*, Geneva: ILO, available at www.ilo.org, accessed 3 October 2007.

ILO (2005b) *A Global Alliance Against Forced Labour*, Geneva: ILO.

ILO (2006) *Social Security for All*, Issues in Social Protection Discussion Paper 16, Geneva: ILO, available at www.ilo.org, accessed 3 October 2007.

ILO (2007a) *Global Employment Trends Brief*, 25 January, Geneva: ILO, available at www.ilo.org, accessed 3 October 3, 2007.

ILO (2007b) *Health and Safety at Work*, Geneva: ILO, available at www.ilo.org, accessed 3 October 2007.

Iradvocates (2007) Victims Advocates Sue Banana Giant, Press Release, 7 June, available at www.iradvocates.org, accessed 1 February 2008.

ITUC (International Trade Union Confederation) (2007) *Annual Survey of Violation of Trade Union Rights*, Brussels: ITUC, available at http://survey07.ituc-csi.org/, accessed 3 October 2007.

Jenkins, R. (2002) 'The political economy of codes of conduct', in R. Jenkins, R. Pearson and G. Seyfang (eds) *Corporate Responsibility and Labour Rights: Codes of Conduct in The Global Economy*, London: Earthscan.

Justice, D. (2002) 'The international trade union movement and the new codes of conduct', in R. Jenkins, R. Pearson and G. Seyfang (eds) *Corporate Responsibility and Labour Rights: Codes of Conduct in the Global Economy*, London: Earthscan.

Lipschutz, R. and Rowe, J.K. (eds) (2005) *Globalization, Governmentality and Global Politics: Regulation for the Rest of Us?*, London: Routledge.

McBride, S. and Williams, R. (2001) 'Globalization, the restructuring of labour markets and policy convergence,' *Global Social Policy*, vol 1, no 3, pp 281-309.

O'Brien, R. (2000) 'Workers and world order: the tentative transformation of the international union movement', *Review of International Studies*, vol 26, no 4, pp 533-55.

O'Brien, R. (2008) 'No safe havens: labour, regional integration and globalization', in A. Cooper, C. Hughes and P. Lombaerde (eds) *Regionalisation and Global Governance: The Taming of Globalisation?*, London: Routledge.

O'Brien, R., Goetz, A.M., Scholte, J.A. and Williams, M. (2000) *Contesting Global Governance: Multilateral Economic Institutions and Global Social Movements*, Cambridge: Cambridge University Press.

Oliver, L., Nguyen, V. and Giugale, M. (2001) *Mexico: A Comprehensive Development Agenda for the New Era*, Washington, DC: World Bank.

O'Rourke, D. (2003) 'Outsourcing regulation: analyzing nongovernmental systems of labor standards and monitoring', *Policy Studies Journal*, vol 31, no 1, pp 1-29.

Palan, R. and Abbott, J. (2000) *State Strategies in the Global Economy*, London: Continuum.

Rowe, J.K. (2005) 'Corporate social responsibility as business strategy', in R. Lipschutz and J.K. Rowe (eds) *Globalization, Governmentality and Global Politics: Regulation for the Rest of Us?*, London: Routledge.

Thomas, C. (2003) 'Cyberactivism and corporations: new strategies for new media', in S. John and S. Thomson (eds) *New Activism and the Corporate Response*, New York, NY: Palgrave Macmillan.

TRAC (2000) *Tangled up in Blue: Corporate Partnerships at the United Nations*, Oakland, CA: Transnational Resource and Action Center, available at www.corpwatch.org, accessed 1 February 2008.

Wells, D. (2004) 'How ethical are ethical purchasing policies?', *Journal of Academic Ethics*, vol 2, no 1, pp 119-40.

Global health policy

Meri Koivusalo and Eeva Ollila

Overview

This chapter examines actors, agendas, processes and challenges in the field of global health. After some initial general observations on the scope of health policy in a global context, the chapter turns to identifying key institutions of global health governance. It examines the role of different actors, agendas and influences in the emerging global health governance architecture. Three major global health policy agendas – Health for All, healthcare reform and access to pharmaceuticals – are reviewed and analysed in relation to the concepts of global regulation, rights and redistribution. The final section brings together and distils the main conclusions concerning actors, agendas and processes in the context of global health policy debates and global health governance priorities.

Key concepts

Health systems; public health; Health for All; healthcare reform; global health governance

Introduction

This chapter examines issues of global health governance and policy. Health has particular relevance to global social policy for three reasons. First, it is a universal human right and gross social inequalities in health undermine this right. Such inequalities can be addressed through various global measures, including overseas development aid, international programmes on HIV/AIDS and other neglected diseases, and through various regulatory measures to promote social equity in access to health services and medicines. Second, major issues of public health concern do not respect national borders; for example, the social risks of epidemics and contagious diseases are heightened by international travel. Coordinating action is therefore required at global level to mitigate or contain these public health risks. The health security threats of severe acute respiratory syndrome (SARS) and global pandemic influenza are good examples of this type of global health concern. Third, effective national policy measures affecting **health status** may require global frameworks: examples include the tobacco framework agreement at global level, measures to tackle obesity and alcohol consumption.

Our definition for global health policy is defined as policies and practices set by global actors, structures and measures that address health, as well as the ways in which national health policies are shaped by global actors and processes. Our focus on national health policy is set in the context of public policy, which may be implicit or explicit, but is based on the set of legal norms, guidance and institutions with responsibilities in the area of health. In the field of research and analysis, global health policy research includes analysis of the global aspects of health issues and transnational forms of collective action, as well as how these shape the development of health policy (Deacon et al, 1997; see also Chapter One).

While some measures of health policy directly address outcomes, others do not or are more geared towards the protection of health or addressing the financing of healthcare. The health status of individuals and populations is also influenced by factors other than those within the scope of health policy, for example, socioeconomic situation, diet, education and quality of sanitation and housing. These factors may in turn be determined at global, national, regional or local levels. Therefore it is important to recognise that neither health status nor health determinants are solely dependent on individual choice, but are influenced by policies and action in other sectors at different levels of governance. Thus health policies as a whole consist of:

- measures relating to health services provision;
- measures relating to the organisation and funding of healthcare;
- measures relating to health protection (for example, standard setting);
- measures influencing health status through prevention (for example, vaccinations), and promotion (for example, tobacco pricing); and
- measures relating to intersectoral policies, where the focus is on health in other policies (for example, the provision of healthier school meals) (Mackintosh and Koivusalo, 2005; Sihto et al, 2006).

Traditionally, global health agendas have focused on various infectious diseases and interventions to tackle them. While knowledge about health determinants outside the healthcare sector is long established (Rosen, 1993), the issue of social inequalities has recently re-emerged on the global health policy agenda in the context of the WHO Commission on the Social Determinants of Health (WHO, 2007a). Global health inequalities are a major indicator of wider global social inequalities. One such indicator is adult and child mortality rates (*Table 7.1*). It is worth noting here that despite the low child mortality rates in some countries, such as Russia and Ukraine, the adult mortality rate is high, and that some poorer 'developing countries', such as Cuba, Costa Rica and Chile, compare favourably relative to 'developed' or rich countries. High mortality rates are thus not the sole province of poor countries.

Global health governance

Responsibility for global health, health policy making and standard setting has traditionally been invested in the World Health Organization (WHO), a **United Nations** (UN) **specialised agency**. The WHO has a long history of international cooperation in the context of infectious diseases and global

Table 7.1: *International variations in child and adult mortality rates, 2005*

Country	Adult mortality[a]		Under-five mortality[b]
	Male	Female	
Sweden	78	50	4
Italy	89	46	4
Japan	92	45	4
Ireland	91	57	5
France	128	58	5
United Kingdom	101	62	6
Cuba	128	83	7
United States	137	81	8
Chile	128	64	10
Malaysia	199	107	12
Costa Rica	125	73	12
Sri Lanka	228	118	14
Russian Federation	470	173	14
Vietnam	195	88	15
Argentina	162	86	16

continued...

Table 7.1: *International variations in child and adult mortality rates, 2005 continued*

Country	Adult mortality[a]		Under-five mortality[b]
	Male	Female	
Ukraine	403	150	17
Mexico	162	94	27
China	155	98	27
Bolivia	245	180	65
Bangladesh	251	258	73
India	280	207	74
Kenya	464	483	120
Uganda	506	457	136
Mozambique	597	595	145
Zambia	702	666	182
Afghanistan	504	448	257
Sierra Leone	582	501	282

Notes: [a] Adult mortality is the probability of dying aged 15-60 (per 1,000 population); [b] Under-five mortality is the probability of dying before the age of five (per 1,000 population).
Source: WHO (2007b)

epidemics, which resulted in 1946 in the International Conference of Health and in 1948 in the first World Health Assembly.

The main mandate of the WHO is to operate as a global regulatory and normative health agency. A large share of its activity relates to technical standards and diagnostic criteria in health, and undertaking reference work. The WHO also issues 'soft' guidance and guidelines that provide a basis for benchmarking and the setting of national policy priorities.

The WHO's global role in the field of health regulation is a challenging one and is often opposed by those with conflicting interests. *Figure 7.1* captures a specific instance, which became more broadly known outside the WHO. The background to this cartoon concerns a draft version of the WHO's (2004) Global Strategy on Diet, Physical Activity and Health. This made several recommendations to governments on public policy measures to tackle obesity and nutritional problems and was to be approved by the Executive Board in January 2004 before going to the World Health Assembly. The US opposed this strategy and intervened on the matter, sending a letter to the WHO director, which was leaked to the press (Boseley, 2004). In the letter, William Steiger, Special Assistant to the Secretary for International Affairs at the US Department of Health, attacked the scientific credibility of an earlier

Figure 7.1: *US and war on the WHO*

Source: www.seppo.net

WHO and Food and Agriculture Organization (FAO) scientific document, stating that evidence was lacking on the role of fast-food marketing in child obesity, and the contribution of soft drinks and fruit juice to childhood health problems, and questioned whether increased fruit and vegetable consumption decreases the risk of obesity. The letter also reportedly placed responsibility for a healthy diet solely on individuals and their personal choices. In the WHO Executive Board, the US also delayed the adoption of the draft strategy for a month, which gave the US and several small sugar-producing countries more time for lobbying (Vastag, 2004). The similarity of the arguments presented by the US government and those of the food industry was striking (Brownell and Nestle, 2004; Vastag, 2004).

In the context of globalisation, global governance and global regulatory measures, three areas of the WHO's work deserve special mention: International Health Regulations, which govern how WHO member states address epidemics; the Tobacco Framework Convention, which governs issues relating to combating tobacco use, sale and marketing; and the Codex Alimentarius

Commission, co-hosted with the FAO, which provides a reference for international food-related standards.

In relation to health, the WHO's institutional linkages with representatives of ministries of health gives it a different type of mandate from the World Bank (WB), whose main accountability is to ministries of finance or international development agencies. It implies that the WHO is often distanced from development agencies and agendas – which, however, provide a larger share of financing to WHO work than do ministries of health. The WHO's regular budget comes from the assessed contributions of the member states' health ministries. However, additional resources mainly come from government development aid budgets and development-related sources. While the WHO's core funding has been in decline in real terms, extra-budgetary resources have increased sharply, from about 25% of total resources in the 1970s to 75% in 2006-07 (WHO, 2006a). This has meant that while voting lies with ministries of health, they have less power to control which WHO activities are funded through external funds.

WHO, infectious diseases and the global health security agenda

In the 1990s, the importance of HIV/AIDS, malaria and tuberculosis rose on two fronts in relation to global policy agendas. First, infectious diseases were identified as a security threat for industrialised countries (Ollila, 2005). Second, the existence (but non-accessibility) of HIV/AIDS drugs for the majority of the HIV-infected population made HIV/AIDS a human rights issue. The focus and increasing campaigning on HIV/AIDS, tuberculosis and malaria led to new initiatives for global health and access to medicines, including the establishment of the Global Fund. With the G8 increasingly taking up health issues, the fora for making key decisions also changed.

The WHO came into existence as a result of international cooperation over cholera epidemics and the International Sanitary Conferences. Thus, not surprisingly, its work started with disease-based **vertical** approaches to international health (Siddiqi, 1995; Koivusalo and Ollila, 1997). HIV/AIDS, malaria and tuberculosis continue to be recognised in the context of global health and development policies. However, the emergence of SARS may be seen as a trigger for change in global infectious disease governance and its emergence as a priority in global social policy making, as infectious diseases control now represents an important criterion of 'good governance' in world affairs (Fidler, 2004). The core of the WHO's historical mandate regarding global health policies to some extent lost importance in the early 1990s, when the emphasis was increasingly placed on development issues, but its mandate re-emerged in the context of growing concern over global epidemics – in particular the influenza pandemics and bird flu. This mandate was further enhanced by broader state security concerns following the attack on US financial and military targets in September 2001. The WHO's focus on epidemics has been strengthened by the substantial economic costs of them (*Table 7.2*).

Table 7.2: *WHO's estimates of the direct economic impact of selected infectious disease outbreaks between 1990-2003*

US	E.Coli 0157	US $1.6 billion	1991-99
UK	BSE	US $39 billion	1990-98
Peru	Cholera	US $770 milliom	1991
Asia	SARS	US $30 billion	2003
Tanzania	Cholera	US $36 million	1998
India	Plague	US $1.7 billion	1995
Malaysia	Nipah	US $625 million	1999

Source: WHO (2007c)

The importance of global epidemics in terms of security and the emergence of health as a trade issue have placed health higher up foreign policy agendas. Fears of international terrorism, in particular the use of biological weapons, are also reflected in the growing importance of health security and security-related health concerns. However, the securitisation of the global health agenda has been dominated by the countries belonging to the Organisation for Economic Co-operation and Development (OECD), although the WHO has recently also taken up this issue (WHO, 2007c).

Health, the UN and the human and social rights agenda

Various UN funds and programmes concern health issues, particularly in a development context, including the United Nations Children's Fund (UNICEF), United Nations Population Fund (UNPFA) and the Joint United Nations Programme on HIV/AIDS (UNAIDS). UNAIDS (founded in 1994) coordinates the UN's activities around HIV/AIDS and is co-sponsored by 10 UN agencies and the WB. Other UN agencies addressing health issues are the FAO (food standards and nutritional policies) and the ILO (occupational health standards, health–related social security issues and health insurance).

Health, and rights related to health, are part of the UN's broader human rights agenda and agreements (*Box 7.1*). The United Nations Commission on Human Rights (UNCHR) Special Rapporteur, Paul Hunt, has repeatedly emphasised health as being integral to economic, social and cultural rights, together with the right of everyone to the enjoyment of the highest attainable standard of physical and mental health (UNCHR, 2003, 2004, 2006). The interplay between global and national legislation is evident in a number of ways. For example, in the context of essential medicines, the extent to which the right to health is legally enforceable through court action (Hogerzeil et al, 2006), or the ways in which trade-related measures affect the right to health (Chapman, 2002; Petersmann, 2004).

Box 7.1: UN health-related human rights and social rights stipulations

- In terms of global governance, perhaps the most important stipulations in the context of the UN can be found in the United Nations Declaration of Human Rights. Health is most directly addressed in Article 25:
  1. *Everyone has the right to a standard of living adequate for the health and well-being of himself and of his family, including food, clothing, housing and medical care and necessary social services, and the right to social security in the event of unemployment, sickness, disability, widowhood, old age or other lack of livelihood in circumstances beyond his control.*
  2. Motherhood and childhood are entitled to special care and assistance. *All children, whether born in or out of wedlock, shall enjoy the same social protection.*

(emphasis added)

- Article 12 of the International Covenant on Economic, Social and Cultural Rights, adopted on 16 December 1966 and entered in force on 3 January 1976, sets out more detailed commitments on health and social rights:
  1. The State parties to the present Covenant recognise the right of everyone to the enjoyment of *the highest attainable standard of physical and mental health.*
  2. The steps to be taken by the States [sic] Parties to the present covenant to achieve the full realization of this right shall include those necessary for:
     a. *The provision for the reduction of the stillbirth-rate and of infant mortality and for the healthy development of the child;*
     b. *The improvement of all aspects of environmental and industrial hygiene;*
     c. *The prevention, treatment and control of epidemic, endemic, occupational and other diseases;*
     d. *The creation of conditions which would assure to [sic] all medical service and medical attention in the event of sickness.*

(emphasis added)

- The United Nations Economic and Social Council's Committee on Economic, Social and Cultural Rights provides guidance on the interpretation of substantive issues arising from the implementation of the International Covenant on Economic, Social and Cultural Rights, further elaborating the right to health:

In drafting article 12 of the Covenant, the Third Committee of the United Nations General Assembly did not adopt the definition of health contained in the preamble to the Constitution of the WHO, which conceptualizes health as 'a state of complete physical, mental and social well-being and not merely the absence of disease or infirmity'. However, the reference in article 12.1. of the Covenant to 'the highest attainable standard of physical and mental health' is not confined to the right to health care. On the contrary, the drafting history and the express wording [of] article 12.2. acknowledge that the **right to health embraces a wide range of socio-economic factors that promote conditions in which people can lead a healthy life, and extends to the underlying determinants of health, such as food and nutrition, housing, access to safe and potable water and adequate sanitation, safe and healthy working conditions, and a healthy environment.** (emphasis added)

- A further set of commitments can be found in the UN Convention on the Rights of the Child, which entered into force in September 1990. Specific health-related commitments are set out in Article 24:
  1. State Parties recognise **the right of the child to the enjoyment of the highest attainable standard of health and to facilities for the treatment of illness and rehabilitation of health.** States [sic] Parties shall strive to ensure that no child is deprived of his or her right of access to such health care services.
  2. States [sic] Parties shall pursue full implementation of this right and, in particular, shall take appropriate measures:
     a. **To diminish infant and child mortality;**
     b. **To ensure the provision of necessary medical assistance and health care to all children with emphasis on the development of primary health care;**
     c. **To combat disease and malnutrition, including within the framework of primary health care, through, inter alia, the application of readily available technology and through the provision of adequate nutritious foods and clean drinking water, taking into consideration the dangers and risks of environmental pollution;**

d. *To ensure appropriate pre-natal and post-natal health care for mothers;*

e. *To ensure that all segments of society, in particular parents and children, are informed, have access to education and are supported in the use of basic knowledge of child health and nutrition, the advantages of breastfeeding, hygiene and environmental sanitation and the prevention of accidents;*

f. *To develop preventive health care, guidance for parents and family planning education and services.*

3. State parties shall take all effective and appropriate measures with a view to *abolishing traditional practices prejudicial to the health of children.*

4. States [sic] parties undertake to promote and encourage international co-operation with a view to achieving progressively the full realization of the right recognized in the present article. In this regard, particular account shall be taken of the needs of developing countries.

(emphasis added)

Sources: UN (1948, 1966, 1989, 2000)

While in 1970s and 1980s the terrain of global health policies had been a domain of WHO – and a contested field between the WHO and UNICEF – in the 1990s the WB, International Monetary Fund (IMF) and OECD engaged more with health as a result of their involvement in public policy. The influence of the WB in global and national health policy occurs through its lending and health-related projects, research and policy analysis and the provision of guidance on health and public policies. Its guidance on macroeconomic policies, broader public sector reforms and poverty reduction strategy measures define the scope for national health policy options and available resources. The WB is also involved in health issues as part of the population, health and nutrition agenda, which initially began as a lending programme to fund population measures (Wolfson, 1983; WB, 2007; see also Chapter Eleven of this volume).

International financial institutions and trade agreements

Health concerns in the IMF are predominantly dealt with in the context of its mandate to ensure the stability of the international monetary system and its role in providing loans in times of economic crises. Health issues are therefore included in IMF policy advice to governments regarding economic reforms, terms of lending and debt repayment, and aid allocation. The capacity of governments to provide additional budgeting resources for health is influenced by IMF policy advice. Ensuring the capacity of governments to support health programmes has also become an issue of broader interest in the context of the Millennium Development Goals (MDGs) and increased spending needs for HIV/AIDS (Heller, 2006).

There has been major concern in recent years over the implications of international trade agreements for health policy (see also Chapter Four), and the interface between health and trade priorities has been the focus of substantial campaigning by national and international non-governmental organisations (INGOs) (Thomas, 2002; Sell, 2006). The General Agreement on Trade in Services (GATS) of the WTO, which focuses on liberalising services trade, has impacts on how ministries can regulate and finance healthcare or initiate health-related regulatory measures in other service sectors (Luff, 2003; Fidler, 2003; see also Chapter Four, this volume). In what follows, we look at the provisions of the Agreement on Trade-Related Aspects of Intellectual Property Rights (TRIPS) (see Matthews, 2002, for further discussion), which have become of particular importance for pharmaceutical policies.

The Doha Declaration (2001) was a major watershed in global health policy as it confirmed that the TRIPS should be applied in a way that supports public health priorities (see Yeates [2002] for further discussion). Since Doha, particular attention has been drawn to bilateral agreements, and in particular to the so-called TRIPS+ measures, which strengthen intellectual property protection beyond TRIPS requirements (see Correa, 2006, for further discussion). Intellectual property rights disputes focus in particular on new pharmaceuticals, since most essential drugs are no longer under patents. The issue therefore centres around new HIV/AIDS drugs and cancer drugs which have remained under patents.

TRIPS provides for product and process patents and in practice safeguards a time-limited monopoly for innovators (in this case, the pharmaceutical industry). This provision is considered important for industry to be able to recoup its investments in research and development. TRIPS allows some scope for governments to intervene. In this context, the focus of debate has been on what basis governments can issue compulsory licences or enhance competition to improve access to medicines – an issue somewhat clarified in the Doha WTO Ministerial Declaration (2001) on the TRIPS agreement and public health. Further challenges remain, however. Prices of medicines are known to fall substantially as result of competition, which results in strong incentives for the pharmaceutical industry to try to extend monopoly rights in order to maintain higher prices. This is a concern with respect to TRIPS+ measures and bilateral agreements. More recently, further attention has been drawn to the possibilities of directing research and development on the basis of health needs and priorities. These issues have been brought up in the context of the WHO Commission on Intellectual Property Rights, Innovation and Public Health and the intergovernmental working group on the issue to follow up the recommendations of the Commission for a global plan of action (WHO 2006c, 2006d).

OECD

Since the late 1980s, the OECD has become important in shaping the policy positions of OECD members through health policies and of public sector and regulatory reforms. Its ability to influence policy makers through policy networks has been of particular importance as, unlike the WB, it has no direct financial power or normative global mandate. The OECD's influence has been mediated through work on health as well as work in the context of the public sector and regulatory reforms. The OECD collection of comparative data on **health systems** and its work on health sector reforms (OECD, 1992, 1994) have been important in influencing not only OECD member states, but WB policies in the area as well (Moran and Wood, 1996; Koivusalo and Ollila, 1997). Another channel for OECD influence is the work of the Development Advisory Committee (DAC), which is important in the context of international development policies among aid agencies.

Global public–private partnerships and disease-specific vertical measures

New global actors, institutions and initiatives have emerged in global health policy since the late 1990s. The G8 began to engage with debates and policies concerning access to medicines and was important in shaping global public–private partnerships (G8, 2006, 2007; Labonte and Schrecker, 2007; UNITAID, 2006). The work of the G8 has taken place in the context of an increasing number of initiatives and new institutions, such as the Global Fund (Kirton and Mannell, 2005). The G8 Okinawa Summit initiated a commitment to a new global partnership for HIV/AIDS, malaria and tuberculosis, which was confirmed at the 2001 Genoa Summit. The emergence of new initiatives is thus associated with new global policy actors, such as G8. The G8 has for its part become a lobbying focus for a variety of civil society movements. The field of global health policies has thus not only become a terrain of other UN and intergovernmental agencies, but has become increasingly fragmented as different types of institutions, networks, partnerships and coalitions engage with global health issues (see Chapter Two).

Since the 1970s, collaboration between the public and private sectors in the international development system has grown in importance (Buse and Walt, 2000a, 2000b; Buse and Harmer, 2004). At the beginning of the 21st century, a new form of global health-related public–private partnership (GHPPP) emerged, with the formation of GHPPPs as independent legal entities outside the auspices of the UN. The first GHPPP to emerge was GAVI in 2000, which was used as a model in the formation of subsequent health partnerships, such as the Global Fund to Fight AIDS, Tuberculosis and Malaria ('Global Fund'). GHPPPs are by design issue-specific vertical programmes and have been criticised for not being coordinated with national health systems and wider international development policies. GHPPPs also suffer from the same criticisms as those directed at PPPs in the context of global social policy making, namely their conflicting aims, their bias against accountable public organisations and their diversion of limited public funds towards the corporate sector (Ollila, 2003; Richter, 2004; Beigbeder, 2005; Buse and Harmer, 2007).

It is also important to recognise that non-governmental organisations (NGOs), missionary organisations and other non-governmental actors have played an important role in global health policies and service provision in many countries over many centuries. NGOs have played an important role in emergency and humanitarian aid; the Red Cross and the Red Crescent, two major INGOs, are particularly crucial. While large service providers are not necessarily the most prominent in agenda setting at the global level, organisations such as Médecins Sans Frontières (MSF) are particularly notable for their active role in both agenda setting and service provision at local level. The People's Health Movement (PHM) is perhaps the main civil society *movement* engaged with health policies. Its major contribution is to compile the alternative World Health Report, which includes a focus on global health policy (PHM et al, 2005). Some consumer groups, such as Health Action International, have also been important in working with IOs. The International Baby Food Action Network contributed substantially to the development of global guidelines on the advertising of infant foods (Koivusalo and Ollila, 1997; Richter, 2004). The interface between health and trade priorities has been contested by substantial campaigning by NGOs (Thomas, 2002).

The role of HIV/AIDS-related organisations and action groups and MSF has been widely acknowledged in raising issues of HIV/AIDS and access to medicines on the global health policy agenda. It has even been argued that these organisations have replaced the WHO at the leading edge of policy development in the area (Horton, 2002a). While the role of churches and religious organisations has been pronounced in matters of sexual and reproductive health (see Chapter Eleven), it has been more limited in campaigns around broader health issues.

The global institutional architecture is markedly influenced by private sources of funds as well as public funds and international development aid. Private philanthropists have been a traditional source of funds, but whereas previously philanthropic funds did not come with conditions, the allocation of funds is now often tied to the requirement for seats on decision-making bodies or to the use of private sector management models such as performance targets and exit strategies (Richter, 2004). The global health programme of the Bill & Melinda Gates Foundation has become significant because of the volume of funds it raises and its influence on health policy options. Together with USAID and the World Bank International Development Association, it is currently among the three largest funders of global health programmes (Ollila, 2005).

Global NGOs also include representative associations for health professionals and health service-related industries, such as the International Federation of Pharmaceutical Manufacturers and Associations representing the pharmaceutical industry. Previous chapters (Chapters Four and Six) have discussed how influential corporations have been in shaping global social policy. Their role has been prominent on matters where there are large health-related industry interests (for example, pharmaceuticals) or where there are large health-related interests which would limit markets or marketing of products (for example, the tobacco, alcohol and infant food industries). The strong influence of the pharmaceutical industry, for example, has been clearly visible in intellectual property rights and access to medicines, and was apparent at the start of the WHO's essential drugs programme (Chetley, 1990). One of the biggest corporate battles to influence health policy took place over WHO initiatives to reduce tobacco consumption and advertising (Zeltner et al, 2000; Collin et al, 2002; Beigbeder, 2004) and corporations have been active in global policy debates on nutrition, infant foods and alcohol. The pharmaceutical industry has also influenced how and where pharmaceutical policy issues are dealt with. Drahos and Braithwaithe (2000) cite pharmaceutical policies as an example of governments utilising 'forum shifting' to relocate these issues from the WHO to other forums deemed more responsive to their interests. Particular attention has been drawn to the limits of, and the basis on which, the WHO engages with corporate actors with strong interests in influencing the process of standard setting (Ollila, 2003; Richter, 2004; Beigbeder, 2005).

Global health policy agendas

This section reviews three key global policy agendas and issues: the global health strategy Health for All and primary healthcare where the role of the WHO is central; and **healthcare reform**, where the role of the WB has been more prominent; and access to medicines, involving non-governmental organisations and the WTO.

Health for All: universal versus targeted approaches

By the late 1970s, a new philosophy had emerged in the WHO emphasising the role of national healthcare infrastructures, various societal sectors and multidisciplinary expertise in achieving improved public health. This new thinking was linked to failures in malaria eradication programmes (Siddiqi, 1995; Koivusalo and Ollila, 1997), and to scientific debates (McKeown, 1979; Rose, 1985; Milio, 1988). It also resulted from broader international policy developments during the 1960s and 1970s, which emphasised that primary healthcare should encompass not only survival needs (food and nutrition, drinking water, shelter, clothing, health, education and non-material needs), but also participation in those decisions tht affect people's daily lives and which are necessary for autonomy (Rifkin et al, 1988).

In 1978, the WHO and UNICEF organised an international conference on primary healthcare in Alma Ata in the Soviet Union (now, Kazakhstan) that resulted in the Declaration of Alma Ata (WHO and UNICEF, 1978). *Box 7.2* contains extracts from the Declaration (the full text is freely available from www.who.int/hpr/NPH/docs/declaration_almaata.pdf). There are several points worth noting here. First, the declaration reflects the ideals of justice and equality, taking as its point of departure that health is a fundamental human right. Second, it sets out a clear global agenda, not only on health but also on social justice and equality. While it points to global health inequalities, the underlying issue of global economic inequalities is not too far from the surface (indeed, elsewhere in the declaration it points to a new international economic order as necessary to address these health inequalities). The results of the conference were endorsed in 1979 by the World Health Assembly, and the strategy to achieve the principles set out in the declaration became known as 'Health for All by the Year 2000', or HfA.

Box 7.2: Declaration of Alma Ata

The Conference strongly reaffirms that health, which is a state of complete physical, mental and social wellbeing, and not merely the absence of disease or infirmity, is a fundamental human right and that the attainment of the highest possible level of health is a most important world-wide social goal whose realisation requires the action of many other social and economic sectors in addition to the health sector.

The existing gross inequality in the health status of the people particularly between developed and developing countries as well as within countries is politically, socially and economically unacceptable and, is therefore, of common concern to all countries.

Governments have a responsibility for the health of their people which can be fulfilled only by the provision of adequate health and social measures. A main social target of governments, international organizations and the whole world community in the coming decades should be the attainment by all peoples of the world by the year 2000 of a level of health that will permit them to lead a socially and economically productive life. Primary health care is the key to attaining this target as part of development in the spirit of social justice.

Sources: WHO and UNICEF (1978, points I, II and V)

The implementation of the strategy, however, has been less than rigorous. For example, international health-related development aid continued to be concentrated on targeted measures. Nevertheless, the declaration did prompt important policy debates, most particularly over the relative merits of targeted **selective healthcare** and more comprehensive approaches to global health (Walsh and Warren, 1979; Unger and Killingsworth, 1986). Here, the discrepancies between what the declaration and HfA were espousing and what the key IOs themselves were advocating were particularly apparent: despite being one of the architects of the Alma Ata conference, UNICEF advocated strongly in favour of a selectivist approach, in contrast to the more **comprehensive healthcare** approach advocated by the HfA (Koivusalo and Ollila, 1997). The main human resource and technical expertise of the WHO continued to be disease-related rather than focused on broader health policies and systems (Siddiqi, 1995; Ollila and Koivusalo, 2002). HfA continued to be part of the WHO's rhetoric until the election of Gro Harlem Bruntlandt as the Director General of the WHO in 1998, which may be considered a turning point in terms of ending advocacy for HfA. In the late 1990s and early 2000s, the WHO increasingly refocused its work on selected infectious diseases. However, the primary healthcare approach returned as a WHO strategy after the change of directorship in 2003 and seems to have re-emerged in the context of WHO work on primary healthcare and social determinants of health. The HfA has continued to be developed and implemented in the context of International Conferences on Health Promotion (Sihto et al, 2006).

Healthcare reforms

The launch of the *World Development Report* in 1993 (WB, 1993), combined with sharply increased lending for health from the late 1980s, indicated the growing dominance of the WB in shaping global health agendas during the 1990s. In many ways, the WB health reform agenda was an intellectual continuation of the earlier prioritisation of selective healthcare, but with additional emphasis on cost-effective health interventions targeted on the poorest, the introduction of user charges, and the promotion of non-governmental (including commercial sector) providers of healthcare services. The focus on healthcare reform became part of WB policies and measures to contain public sector costs in developing countries. Healthcare reforms have in general reflected broader policies and priorities set in the context of public sector reforms and structural adjustment policies (Koivusalo and Ollila, 1997).

The origins of healthcare reform proposals can be located in growing concerns by the OECD countries over healthcare costs and, consequently, seeking to implement healthcare reforms (OECD, 1992, 1994). While the OECD has no mechanism to force countries to change their systems and policies, the expansion of healthcare reforms has been referred to as 'globalisation of healthcare reforms' as a result of OECD influence (Moran and Wood, 1996). Epistemic communities (see Chapter Three) of UK and US research institutions and consultants and revolving doors between these institutions have been influential in this globalisation of healthcare reforms (Lee and Goodman, 2002).

In general, healthcare reforms involved an increased role for private healthcare provision, separation of the purchaser and provider of services, and renewed payment and revenue collections mechanisms, including incentives for providers as well as patients to change their patterns of health service usage and provision (Mills et al, 2001). At the global level, the WB's promotion of healthcare reforms has been criticised as representative of neoliberal policy influence in general, and biased towards the US's policy priorities and market-oriented healthcare in particular (Lloyd-Sherlock, 2004; Homedes and Ugalde, 2005; Lister, 2005).

Global healthcare governance has shifted from the WHO towards the WB in the area of healthcare financing. Under the leadership of Gro Harlem Bruntlandt, the WHO aligned itself with WB healthcare policies, while explicitly disengaging itself from HfA policies (WHO, 2000; Ollila and Koivusalo, 2002). The WHO also appointed a macroeconomics commission, strongly recommending a focus on selected health topics, most notably specific communicable diseases and interventions related to maternal and childcare (WHO, 2001).

In the 2000s, a second stage of healthcare reforms laid increased emphasis on targeting public services and provision for the poorest, increasing the scope for market involvement and contracting services to NGOs. This was reflected in the emphasis on 'pro-poor' health systems and services, as reflected in the *World Development Report* for 2001/2002, and in the OECD report on poverty and health (WB, 2001/2002; OECD DAC and WHO, 2003).

Tackling diseases, in particular HIV/AIDS, tuberculosis and malaria, has been the global focus of action. There has been a more general lack of global policy focus on health systems (both financing and operation) and common concerns with pharmaceutical policies across countries. However, more recently the ILO has promoted the universalisation of social insurance (in particular health insurance) as part of its focus on social security (ILO, 2007). While the WHO inclined in the 1990s more to the views of the WB, WB and OECD work on health sector reforms has recognised – and in some areas also shifted more towards – the traditional emphasis of the WHO on universal healthcare and a long-term focus to ensure the pooling of risks and resources within health systems as a means of ensuring solidarity and sustainable financing (Docteur and Oxley, 2003; Gottret and Schieber, 2007).

Access to medicines: universalism with selective focus

Access to and rational use of pharmaceuticals has been part of global health policy agendas for many decades. Rational drug use and purchasing were included in the NIEO initiative, and were one of eight basic elements of the HfA strategy. The underlying concerns have remained the same: financial and physical access to pharmaceuticals and proper quality, proper information, and proper use of the pharmaceuticals (Koivusalo and Ollila, 1997). The traditional emphasis on the rational use of pharmaceuticals changed towards an emphasis on access to medicines in the 1990s for two reasons: first, the concern over HIV/AIDS and the availability of new drugs for the treatment of HIV/AIDS for all, and second, the establishment of the WTO and increasing consideration of pharmaceuticals as a key trade-related issue both in the TRIPS agreement and bilateral trade negotiations.

While the issue of access and pricing of medicines is seen predominantly as a developing country concern, costs of medicines have risen all over the world. While the relative share of pharmaceuticals in health budgets remains lower in industrialised countries, the costs of pharmaceuticals have been rising faster than other healthcare costs in OECD countries (OECD, 2005), in particular due to costs of new drugs. There are also other broader health policy concerns in relation to intellectual property rights, such as incentives to research and development on new pharmaceuticals including, for example, concern over sufficient research and development on antimicrobials (Wenzel, 2004). While there have been hopes that developing countries would undertake research and development for diseases in developing countries, there is no reason to assume that the private sector in the developing countries will focus on diseases of the poor if greater profits can be achieved by addressing other diseases (Chaudhuri, 2005). A fundamental division on the matter thus exists between industrial policy and health policy priorities rather than between rich and poor countries.

The focus on access to medicines has clearly brought health higher on the global policy agenda, but in a rather limited form and focused on particular selective programmes addressing specific diseases. A further complication is concern over rational use of pharmaceuticals. The failing state of health systems in many countries has led to the criticism of 'medicines without doctors' because of a lack of health professionals and personnel in many countries (Ooms et al, 2007; see also Chapter Ten). The human resource crisis in many countries can be seen also as a global crisis caused by global *in*action (Mensah, 2005; WHO, 2006b). However, addressing particular diseases and their medication does not seem overall to sustain health systems and their financing. HIV/AIDS financing through specific vertical programmes can also dwarf all other spending on health and undermine local health services (Lewis, 2005).

Regulation, rights, redistribution and the politics of global health policy

As we have seen in this and other chapters, the politics of global social policy making and agenda setting is fraught with competing outlooks and interests. As regards global health policy, four broad currents can be identified:

- first, a tendency to define global health policy issues as development issues and to operationalise them as part of *international development policy* rather than *global health* policy;
- second, the inclusion of particular health issues on global foreign policy and security agendas, and global health policy being debated at summits such as G8;
- third, the weakening global basis for addressing crucial health systems issues, determinants of health, and regulatory needs in the context of global health policies and globalisation, including a weakening of the WHO's resource base, which affects its capacity to undertake public health and regulatory work; and
- fourth, the role of non-governmental organisations in agenda setting accompanied by the strengthening of commercial actors and their voices and fora as domains for global health policies.

Articulation of the right to access pharmaceuticals has brought a more universal rights-based discourse to global health policy and has questioned corporations' commercial rights. At the same time, however, this has shifted the focus of global health policy towards single-disease approaches, giving rights to access pharmaceuticals for some diseases and neglecting others. While focusing on the specific needs of developing countries is important for global social solidarity, it can also obscure the differences between corporate and public policy needs within countries and the common health policy interests across countries.

The impact of development policies and priorities on global health policies leads easily to a more selective focus in terms of diseases or countries, resulting in global health policy being conceptualised as dealing with only the least developing countries or the poorest populations. While MDGs are constructive in terms of some aspects of health, they were not designed as guiding principles for global health policies. Pressure towards further UN focus on MDGs is thus not always in the interest of global health policies. The UK has argued for refocusing the WHO's mandate and role on fulfilling the MDGs; this has been criticised as possibly leading to a dangerous reinterpretation of the WHO mandate (Horton, 2002b).

INGOs have played a crucial role in promoting health issues to the global agenda (in particular, HIV/AIDS and access to medicines). However, solutions to problems raised by NGOs may become colonised by approaches suitable for corporate actors and large foundations. While public–private partnerships have been seen as new mechanisms of global governance, they have also resulted in institutions, mainly financed by the public sector, where the private sector has a greater say in governance. This is reflected in the financing of the Global Fund, where the private sector's funding contribution is 5%, with the remaining funding coming from traditional development aid (Ollila, 2003; Kohlmorgen and Hein, 2008).

Conclusion

A global dimension to health policy is in many ways more explicit than in other areas of social policy. While health policies are grounded in cultural values and priorities, the biomedical and clinical aspects of health provide a more universal basis for common dialogue. A set of commonly agreed global commitments and a legal framework exists in health, even if it is in a rather limited form. The HfA strategy is an example of an intergovernmental strategy approved, although less than optimally implemented, by WHO member states. On the other hand, healthcare reforms represent a more technical and expert-driven agenda under the influence of international agencies that has not been formally agreed to or comprehensively debated in the context of global health policies and the WHO. The global health agenda on access to medicines is influenced not only by NGOs campaigning but also by trade and industrial policies and priorities at the global level. Another element is action and focus on selected diseases and access to their treatment through partnerships and networks outside UN agencies and decision-making structures.

Global health policies can result from conscious choices and efforts to tackle health problems through emphasis on determinants of health, as in the global framework agreement on tobacco. On the other hand, global health policies may respond to particular health crises and disease threats, such as HIV/AIDS or pandemics. Furthermore, global health priorities are not necessarily the same as national ones; for example, non-communicable diseases are a growing proportion of the **burden of disease** in developing countries, but these do not tend to be high on global agendas (Ollila, 2005). Even when priorities are compatible, lack of capacities, resources and implementation strategies, as well as other government priorities, may result in an acceptance of the rhetoric of global policies without implementing them – a criticism particularly levelled at the HfA policies.

A key challenge for global health governance and health policies is to ensure that health policy priorities – rather than trade, financial or industrial policy priorities – remain as priorities. An emphasis on rights, regulation and redistribution continues to be important. The need to engage with the underlying social determinants of health has been recognised in the context of health-related human rights. Globalisation requires that health policies incorporate normative and regulatory approaches to balance the process and consequences of economic integration. Finally, to address the social determinants of health and ensure access to healthcare for all, global health policies need to take account of the redistribution of resources, both between and within countries. However, like other policy areas, global health policy formation is not merely a matter of technical concern or biomedical facts, but is embedded in values, power relations, politics and institutional and cultural priorities.

Summary

- Over the past two decades, there has been a shift in the global health governance architecture. The importance of organisations and coalitions with mandates on economic, security, industry and trade policies has increased relative to the roles and activities of the UN agencies. This has been reflected in new entities formed around specific health issues and technologies.
- Global regulatory and standard-setting measures in health continue, with institutional responsibility for these resting with the WHO. However, the WHO's normative capacities have been hampered by insufficient human and financial resources. The WB, Global Fund and other non-governmental actors, such

as the Bill & Melinda Gates Foundation, have become increasingly important in global health agenda setting, although they do not have any normative mandate in global health.
- The role and influence of non-state actors in the making of global health policy varies across institutions and agendas. NGOs have been especially important in raising particular issues on the global agenda. Corporate and industrial interest groups have exerted a powerful influence on regulatory and standard-setting aspects of global health policy, especially in pharmaceuticals, tobacco, food and alcohol.
- Global health policy reflects the strengths and weaknesses of national health policies and policy priorities.

Questions for discussion

- How are global health policies both different from and similar to other areas of global social policy?
- What are the key principles and values underlying the WHO's Health for All strategy?
- How do the health agendas and priorities of different IOs compare with one another?

Further suggested activities

- Investigate the ways in which healthcare reforms (or health policy formation) in a country of your choice follow or depart from the principles of the Alma Ata and/or the WHO's HfA strategy. Think about which other global policy actors and principles have a tangible bearing on healthcare reform/health policy formation in the country you have chosen.
- Referring to the issues raised in this chapter, in Chapter Four on global business, and in Chapter Five on international trade, as well as to the 'Further reading' and 'Further resources' sections, examine further the different ways in which global trade and industry actors are involved in shaping global policies affecting healthcare. Among the issues you could focus on are access to medicines or plans to tackle obesity, malnutrition and hunger.
- Consult the websites of national or international NGOs involved in trade, environmental and social justice campaigns. To what extent do they raise health as an issue of global concern rather than one of national or local concern? If they do highlight health as a global concern, what are the global policies, measures and practices they particularly highlight that need to be changed?

Further reading

For further information and discussion about global health policy and governance, see Beigbeder (2004). The focus of this book is broader than its title suggests, and covers in particular discussion of the WHO's regulatory role and issues relating to global measures regarding tobacco, essential medicines and infant feeding as well as public–private partnerships.

Ollila (2005) is an essay about the ways in which global health priorities have shifted and provides a useful lead into current global health debates, and Koivusalo and Ollila (1997) introduce main global institutional actors and agendas in the 1990s with a focus on global actors and agendas.

Two volumes dealing with issues of globalisation, health and healthcare more generally are Lee et al (2002) and Mackintosh and Koivusalo (2005). The first of these is an edited volume dealing with a wide range of issues in relation to globalisation and health policy making, while the second has a detailed focus on issues arising from and case studies about globalisation and commercialisation in healthcare.

Finally, the following journals regularly carry articles and features on global health policy: *Bulletin of the World Health Organization* (www.who.int/bulletin/en/index.html); *Globalization and Health* (www.globalizationandhealth.com; some materials are open access); *Global Social Policy* (a pre-published version of this journal's Digest section is available from www.gaspp.org); and *Global Public Health*.

Electronic resources

Additional information can be found on the websites of international organisations and national development agencies. NGOs and foundations active at the global level have easily accessible websites. Websites with global NGO movement material include:
www.phmovement.org People's Health Movement
www.ghwatch.org Global Health Watch

www.gapminder.org provides analysis of income and life expectancy ratios and trends across countries for those interested in global inequalities and statistics. Global health statistics are also easily available from the WHO and the UN websites, annual flagship reports of UN organisations and the World Health Statistics report.

www.gaspp.org the Globalism and Social Policy Programme website maintains materials on global social and health policy, including a longer web version of the *Global Social Policy Digest*, which tracks developments in global social policy and also covers global health policy.

www.un.org UN website that provides human rights-related materials; materials and information on human rights and health can also be found on: **www2.essex.ac.uk/human_rights_centre/rth/** website of the Right to Health Unit in the Human Rights Centre at the University of Essex.

www.tarsc.org/WHOCSI/globalhealth.php a useful annotated bibliography on this subject is available from TARSC if you are particularly interested in following up the role of civil society in global health policy making.

www.medact.org website on global health issues from the perspective of health professionals.

References

Beigbeder, Y. (2004) *International Public Health. Patients' Rights vs the Protection of Patents*, Burlington, VT: Ashgate.

Boseley, S. (2004) 'US accused of sabotaging obesity strategy', *The Guardian*, 16 January, available at www.guardian.co.uk/food/Story/0,2763,1124467,00.html, accessed 18 January 2008.

Brownell, K.D. and Nestle, M. (2004) 'The sweet and lowdown of sugar', *New York Times*, 26 January, www.foodpolitics.com/pdf/sweetlowdown.pdf, accessed 18 January 2008.

Buse, K. and Harmer, A. (2004) 'Power to the partners ? The politics of public–private partnerships', *Development, vol* 47, no 2, pp 49-56.

Buse, K. and Harmer, A. (2007) 'Seven habits of highly effective global public–private partnerships: practice and potential', *Social Science and Medicine*, vol 64, no 2, pp 259-71.

Buse, K. and Walt, G. (2000a) 'Global public–private partnerships for health: part I – a new development in health', *Bulletin of the World Health Organization – The International Journal of Public Health*, vol 78, no 4, pp 549-61.

Buse, K. and Walt, G. (2000b) 'Global public–private partnerships for health: part 2 – what are the health issues for global governance?', *Bulletin of the World Health Organization – The International Journal of Public Health*, vol 78, no 5, pp 699-709.

Chapman, A.R. (2002) 'The human rights implications of intellectual property protections', *Journal of International Economic Law*, vol 5, no 4, pp 861-82.

Chaudhuri, S. (2005) 'Indian pharmaceutical companies and accessibility of drugs under TRIPS', in M. Mackintosh and M. Koivusalo (eds) *Commercialisation of Health Care. Global and Local Dynamics and Policy Responses*, Basingstoke: Palgrave Macmillan, pp 155-69.

Chetley, A. (1990) *A Healthy Business. World Health and Pharmaceutical Industry*, London: Zed Books.

Collin, J., Lee, K., and Bissell, K. (2002) 'The framework convention on tobacco control: the politics of global health governance', *Third World Quarterly*, vol 23, no 2, pp 265-82.

Correa, C.M. (2006) 'Implications of bilateral free trade agreements on access to medicines', *World Health Bulletin*, vol 84, no 5, pp 399-404.

Deacon, B., Stubbs, P. and Hulse, M. (1997) *International Organisations and the Future of Social Welfare*, London: Sage Publications.

Docteur, E. and Oxley, H. (2003) *Health Care Systems. Lessons from the Reform Experience*, OECD/ELSA/WD/HEA, OECD Health Working Paper no 9, Paris: OECD.

Doha WTO Ministerial Declaration (2001) *Declaration on the TRIPS Agreement and Public Health*, WT/MIN(01)/DEC/2, www.wto.org/english/thewto_e/minist_e/min01_e/mindecl_trips_e.htm

Drahos, P. and Braithwaite, J. (2000) *Global business regulation*, Cambridge: Cambridge University Press, pp 39-87.

Fidler, D. (2003) *Legal Review of the General Agreement on Trade in Services (GATS) from a Health Policy Perspective*, Geneva: WHO.

Fidler, D.P. (2004) 'Germs, governance, and global public health in the wake of SARS', *Journal of Clinical Investigation*, vol 113, no 6, pp 799-804.

G8 (2006) *G8 Meeting in Russia*, http://en.g8russia.ru/

G8 (2007) *G8 Meeting in Germany*, http://www.g-8.de/Webs/G8/EN/Homepage/home.html

Gottret, B. and Schieber, G. (2007) *Health Financing Revisited. A Practitioner's Guide*, Washington, DC: World Bank, http://siteresources.worldbank.org/INTHSD/Resources/topics/Health-Financing/HFRFull.pdf

Heller, P.S. (2006) 'The prospects of creating "fiscal space" for the health sector', *Health Policy and Planning*, vol 21, no 2, pp 75-9.

Hogerzeil, H., Samson, M., Casasnovas, J.V. and Rahmani-Ocora, L. (2006) 'Is access to essential medicines as part of the fulfilment of the right to health enforceable through the courts?', *The Lancet*, vol 368, issue 9532, pp 305-11.

Homedes, N. and Ugalde, A. (2005) 'Why neoliberal reforms have failed in Latin America', *Health Policy*, vol 71, no 1, pp 83-96.

Horton, R. (2002a) 'WHO's mandate: a damaging interpretation is taking place', *The Lancet*, vol 360, issue 9338, pp 960-1.

Horton, R. (2002b) 'WHO: the casualties and compromises of renewal', *The Lancet*, vol 359, issue 9338, pp 1605-11.

ILO (International Labour Organization) (2007) *Social Health Protection. An ILO Strategy Towards Universal Access to Health Care*, Issues in Social Protection. Discussion Paper 19. Geneva: ILO.

Kirton, J. and Mannell, J. (2005) 'The G8 and global governance', Paper presented at conference on Global Health Governance: 'Past practice – Future innovation', 11 November, Ottawa and Waterloo, Canada.

Kohlmorgen, L. and Hein, J. (2008) 'Global health governance. Conflicts on global social rights', *Global Social Policy* (in print).

Koivusalo, M. and Ollila, E. (1997) *Making a Healthy World. Agencies, Actors and Policies in International Health*, London: Zed Books.

Labonte, R. and Schrecker, T. (2007) 'Foreign policy matters: a normative view of the G8 and population health', *Bulletin of the World Health Organization*, vol 85, no 3, pp 185-91.

Lee, K. and Goodman, H. (2002) 'Global policy networks: the propagation of health care financing reform since 1980', in K. Lee, K. Buse and S. Fustukian (eds) *Health Policy in a Globalising World*, Cambridge: Cambridge University Press.

Lee, K., Buse, K., Fustukian, S. (eds) (2002) *Health Policy in a Globalising World*, Cambridge: Cambridge University Press.

Lewis, M. (2005) *Addressing the Challenge of HIV/AIDS: Macroeconomic, Fiscal and Institutional Issues*, Center for Global Development Working Paper 58, Washington DC: Center for Global Development.

Lister, J. (2005) *Health Policy Reform: Driving the Wrong Way?*, London: Middlesex University Press.

Lloyd-Sherlock, P. (2004) 'Health sector reform in Argentina: a cautionary tale', *Social Science and Medicine*, vol 60, no 8, pp 1893-903.

Luff, D. (2003) 'Regulation of health services and international trade law', in A. Mattoo and P. Sauve (eds) *Domestic Regulation and Service Trade Liberalisation*, New York, NY: World Bank and Oxford University Press, pp 191-220.

Mackintosh, M. and Koivusalo, M. (2005) (eds) *Commercialisation of Health Care. Global and Local Dynamics and Policy Responses*, Basingstoke: Palgrave Macmillan.

Matthews, D. (2002) *Globalising Intellectual Property: The TRIPS Agreement*, Oxford: Routledge.

McKeown, T. (1979) *The Role of Medicine: Dream, Mirage or Nemesis*, Oxford: Blackwell.

Mensah, K. (2005) 'International migration of health care staff: extent and policy responses, with illustrations from Ghana', in M. Mackintosh and M. Koivusalo (eds) *Commercialisation of Health Care. Global and Local Dynamics and Policy Responses*, Basingstoke: Palgrave Macmillan, pp 188-201.

Milio, N. (1988) 'Making healthy public policy; developing the science of art: an ecological framework for policy studies', *Health Promotion*, vol 2, no 3, pp 236-74.

Mills, A., Bennett, S. and Russell, S. (2001) *The Challenge of Health Sector Reform: What Must Governments Do?*, New York, NY: Palgrave Macmillan.

Moran, M. and Wood, B. (1996) 'The globalisation of health care policy?', in P. Gummet (ed) *Globalisation and Public Policy*, Cheltenham: Edward Elgar, pp 125-41.

OECD (Organization for Economic Co-operation and Development) (1992) *The Reform of Health Care. Comparative Analysis of Seven OECD Countries*, Paris: OECD.

OECD (1994) *The Reform of Health Care Systems. A Review of Seventeen OECD Countries*, OECD Health Policy Studies, Paris: OECD.

OECD (2005) *OECD Health Data,* Paris: OECD.

Ollila, E. (2003) 'Health-related public–private partnerships and the United Nations', in *Global Social Governance. Themes and prospects*, Elements for Discussion, Helsinki: Ministry for Foreign Affairs of Finland, available at www.gaspp.org

Ollila, E. (2005) 'Global health priorities – priorities of the wealthy?', *Globalization and Health*, vol 1, no 1, p 6, available at www.globalizationandhealth.com/content/1/1/6.

Ollila, E. and Koivusalo, M. (2002) 'The World Health Report 2000: World Health Organization health policy steering off course – changed values, poor evidence, and lack of accountability', *International Journal of Health Services*, vol 32, no 3, pp 503-14.

Ooms, G., van Damme, W. and Temmerman, M. (2007) 'Medicines without doctors. Why the global fund must fund salaries of health workers to expand AIDS treatment', *PLOSmedicine*, vol 4, no 4, pp 0605-8.

Petersmann, E.-U. (2004) 'The human rights approach advocated by the UN High Commissioner for Human Rights and by the International Labour Organization', *Journal of International Economic Law*, vol 7, no 3, pp 605-27.

PHM (People's Health Movement) et al (2005) *Global Health Watch 2005-2006*, London: Zed Books.

Richter, J. (2004) *Public–private Partnerships and International Health Policy-making. How can Public Interests be Safeguarded?*, Helsinki: Ministry for Foreign Affairs of Finland, shortened version in the form of a policy brief www.gaspp.org

Rifkin, S.B., Muller, F. and Bichmann, W. (1988) 'Primary health care: on measuring participation', *Social Science and Medicine*, vol 26, no 9, pp 931-40.

Rose, G. (1985) 'Sick individuals and sick populations', *International Journal of Epidemiology*, vol 14, no 1, pp 32-8.

Rosen, G. (1993) *A History of Public Health* (expanded edition), Baltimore: John Hopkins University Press.

Sell, S. (2006) 'Books, drugs and seeds: the politics of access', Paper presented in the Transatlantic Consumer Dialogue, 20-21 March, Brussels, www.tacd. org/events/intellectual-property/s_sell.doc

Siddiqi, J. (1995) *World Health and World Politics*, London: C. Hurst & Co.

Sihto, M., Ollila, E. and Koivusalo, M. (2006) 'Principles and challenges of health in all policies', in T. Stahl, M. Wismar, E. Ollila, E. Lahtinen and K. Leppo (eds) *Health in all Policies. Prospects and Potentials*, Helsinki: Ministry for Social Affairs and Health.

Thomas, C. (2002) 'Trade policy and the politics of access to drugs', *Third World Quarterly*, 23, vol no 2, pp 251-64.

UN (United Nations) (1948) *Universal Declaration of Human Rights*, New York, NY: UN, www.un.org/Overview/rights.html

UN (1966) *International Covenant on Economic, Social and Cultural Rights*, New York, NY: UN.

UN (1989) *Convention of the Rights of the Child*, New York, NY: UN, www2. ohchr.org/english/law/crc.htm

UN (2000) *The Right to the Highest Attainable Standard of Health, 11 August, United Nations Economic and Social Council*, E/C12/2000/4. New York, NY: UN.

UNCHR (United Nations Commission on Human Rights) (2003) *Report of the Special Rapporteur on the Right to Everyone to the Enjoyment of the Highest Attainable Standard of Physical and Mental Health*, E/CN.4/2003/58, 13 February, New York, NY: UN.

UNCHR (2004) *Report of the Special Rapporteur on the Right to Everyone to the Enjoyment of the Highest Attainable Standard of Physical and Mental Health*, E/CN.4/2004/49/add.1, 1 March, New York, NY: UN.

UNCHR (2006) *Report of the Special Rapporteur on the Right to Everyone to the Enjoyment of the Highest Attainable Standard of Physical and Mental Health*, E/CN.4/2006/48 3 March 2006, New York, NY: UN.

Unger, J.-P. and Killingsworth, J.R. (1986) 'Selective primary health care: a critical review of methods and results', *Social Science and Medicine*, vol 22, no 10, pp 1001-13.

UNITAID (2006) 'UNITAID Constitution', 30 November, www.unitaid.org

Vastag, B. (2004) 'Obesity is now on everyone's plate', *Journal of American Medical Association*, vol 29, no 10, pp 1186-8.

Walsh, J.A. and Warren, K.S. (1979) 'Selective primary health care. An interim strategy for disease control in developing countries', *New England Journal of Medicine*, vol 301, no 18, pp 967-74.

WB (World Bank) (1993) *World Development Report*, Washington, DC: WB.

WB (2001/2002) *World Development Report*, Washington, DC: WB.

WB (2007) *Healthy Development. The World Bank Strategy for Health, Nutrition and Population Results*, Washington, DC: WB.

Wenzel, R. (2004) 'The antibiotic pipeline – challenges, costs and values', *New England Journal of Medicine*, vol 351, no 6, pp 523-6.

WHO (World Health Organization) (2000) *World Health Report*, Geneva: WHO.

WHO (2001) *Report of the Commission on Macroeconomics and Health*, WHO: Geneva, available from http://whqlibdoc.who.int/publications/2001/924154550X.pdf

WHO (2004) *Global Strategy on Diet, Physical Activity and Health*, WHO: Geneva.

WHO (2005) *World Health Report*, Geneva: WHO.

WHO (2006a) *Programme Budget 2006-2007 Update*, 7 December, WHO EBPBAC5/5, Geneva: WHO.

WHO (2006b) *World Health Report*, Geneva: WHO.

WHO (2006c) *Public Health, Innovation and Intellectual Property Rights. Commission on Intellectual Property Rights, Innovation and Public Health*, Final report, Geneva: WHO, www.who.int/intellectualproperty/en/

WHO (2006d) *Public health, innovation, essential health research and intellectual property rights: Towards a global strategy and plan of action*, World Health Assembly Resolution 59.24, Geneva: WHO.

WHO (2007a) *Commission on Social Determinants of Health*, Geneva: WHO, www.who.int/social_determinants/en

WHO (2007b) *World Health Report*, Geneva: WHO.

WHO Observatory on Health Systems and Policies (2007c) *Glossary*, www.euro.who.int/observatory/Glossary/TopPage?phrase=A, accessed 18 January 2008.

WHO/UNICEF (1978) *Declaration of Alma Ata*, Geneva: WHO, www.who.int/hpr/NPH/docs/declaration_almaata.pdf

Wolfson, M. (1983) *Profiles in Population Assistance. A Comparative Review of the Principal Donor Agencies*, Development Centre Studies, Paris: OECD.

Yeates , N. (2002) 'The "anti-globalisation" movement and its implications for social policy', in R. Sykes, N. Ellison and C. Bochel (eds) *Social Policy Review 14*, Bristol: The Policy Press, pp127-50.

Zeltner, T., Kessler, D.A., Martiny, A. and Randera, F. (2000) *Tobacco Companies' Strategies to Undermine Tobacco Control Activities at the World Health Organization*,Geneva: WHO.

eight

Global housing and urban policy

Sunil Kumar

Overview

This chapter explores the involvement of global actors in housing and urban policy in developing countries from the 1970s to the present day. Three key policy shifts over this time are identified: first, from government as provider to government as enabler of housing; second, from housing to urban services and then urban development; and third, the emergence of alliances between international institutions and governments on the one hand and people's organisations and their representatives on the other. A number of issues are discussed: the mismatch between national capacity and increasing policy complexity; the difficulty in scaling up interventions, given the nature of the challenges involved and the limitations of non-state actors; deficits in the political will of governments; and a reluctance of international and donor organisations to engage with the politics of housing and urban inequalities.

Key concepts

Urbanisation; slums; squatter settlements; slum upgrading; sites and services; enabling housing strategies; urban development

Introduction

With more than half of humanity living in urban areas, it is difficult to ignore the challenge of housing and urban development. This chapter focuses on the role of global actors in shaping **housing policy** and **urban policy** in response to the challenges of an urbanising world characterised by entrenched social inequalities and poverty (*Box 8.1*).

> **Box 8.1: Poverty in an urbanising world**
>
> ... urban poverty and inequality will characterise many cities in the developing world, and urban growth will become virtually synonymous with **slum** formation in some regions. (UN-HABITAT, 2006b, p viii)

As *Box 8.2* effectively highlights, the range of issues that urbanisation (and the associated growth of slums) raises is wide-ranging, going beyond the immediate need to provide adequate housing for resident populations to address issues of wider social welfare, amenities and employment, land use and distribution, and economic investment. It also demonstrates that urbanisation raises important governance issues, in the context of both the relationship between neighbourhood, city, regional and national authorities and the relationship between the state, private commercial and community sectors. For the purposes of this chapter, we are particularly concerned with the global dimensions of housing and urban policy and its governance. We situate housing need as a social phenomenon – indeed crisis – of global proportions, requiring effective and coordinated responses from a range of organisations. We focus on the role of Northern international agencies in particular, both **bilateral actors** and **multilateral actors**, and the kinds of ideas they advance and prescribe to developing countries.

> **Box 8.2: The challenges of an urbanising world**
>
> 1. Slum upgrading: physical upgrading of housing, infrastructure, environment; social upgrading through improved education, health and secure tenure; governance upgrading through participatory processes, community leadership and empowerment;
> 2. Urban development: stimulation of job creation through city wide advance land use planning, development and management of the revenue base, infrastructure improvement, amenities provision, city management and urban governance practices, community empowerment, vulnerability reduction and better security;

3. Regional development: maximising the positive impact of urbanisation and reducing its negative impacts (regional disparity, rural–urban disparity, excessive pressure on natural endowments etc) through appropriate national and regional investment policies, decentralisation of authority to undertake local development, creating a broad based system of urban centres for the efficient distribution of development services, and promoting reciprocal urban–rural relationships.

Source: UN-HABITAT (2005, p 8)

One of the themes of the chapter is the international origins and global transfer of ideas (see also Chapter Three) in the context of the urban developing world in Africa, Asia and Latin America, where the influences of 'global' ideas on policy and provision have been most apparent. The chapter identifies four key global ideas to have informed housing and urban policy over the past half century: **modernisation theory** (1950s and 1960s), **dependency theory** (1970s), the neoliberal **Washington Consensus** (1980s and 1990s); and the **Post-Washington Consensus** (late 1990s and 2000s). Expanded reference to these global policy ideas and wider development discourse shifts over time and across different world-regions is made in the context of the discussion of changes in housing policy and urban policy later in the chapter.

Beginning with an overview of global urban poverty and housing challenges, the chapter proceeds to discuss global housing and urban development policy shifts from the mid-1970s onwards. We see how these policy shifts reflect the level of economic and social development of individual countries; the historical relationships between them and international organisations; and the varied development and strength of non-state actors within and across them. The chapter examines the role of a range of global policy actors: multilateral governmental organisations – notably the World Bank (WB), the United Nations Human Settlements Programme (UN-HABITAT) and the United Nations Development Programme (UNDP) – national governments acting on a bilateral basis – the United States Agency for International Development (USAID), the Department for International Development (DfID) and the Swedish International Development Agency (SIDA) – non-governmental organisations, and poor people's collectives and their representatives.

Poverty and housing in an urbanising world

Urbanisation (*Box 8.3*) is by no means a new phenomenon but its increased pace and scale are a central feature of contemporary globalisation processes. It was predicted that by 2008, more than 3.3 billion of the world's population would be living in urban areas. This is forecast to rise to 5 billion by 2030.

> **Box 8.3:** Urbanisation
>
> **Urbanisation as population distribution**
>
> The process of transition from a rural to a more urban society. Statistically, urbanisation reflects an increasing proportion of the population living in settlements defined as urban, primarily through net rural to urban migration. The *level* of urbanisation is the percentage of the total population living in towns and cities while the rate of urbanisation is the rate at which it grows. (UNFPA, 2007, p 6, emphasis in original)
>
> **Urbanisation as a social process**
>
> Urbanisation, and more particularly the urbanisation process, ... refers to much more than simple population growth and involves an analysis of the related economic, social and political transformations. However, the dimensions of urban population growth do form an essential background to the distribution and extent of the urbanisation process. (Drakakis-Smith, 1987, p 1)

Most of this growth will be in developing countries (UNFPA, 2007), rendering poverty and housing not only a predominantly urban issue but also one that affects the South in particular ways. As Breman (2006) notes, up to the mid-20th century, rural migrants to cities in the North were, in a relatively short space of time, accommodated in regularised employment. But it is a different matter for the South: 'the notion of industrialisation as the handmaiden of urbanisation is no longer tenable. This goes a long way to explain why huge numbers of the new arrivals to the city are slum-dwellers, and are likely to remain so throughout their lives' (Breman, 2006, p 142). The challenge for the South is also one of scale: 'the total population of cities in developing regions of the world already exceeds that of cities in all of the developed regions (by 1.3 billion people)' (UN-HABITAT, 2006b, p 4).

As more and more people live in urban areas, the locus of poverty will become urban. Although the majority of the world's poor, on average, now live in rural areas, this will no longer be true by 2035 (Ravallion, 2001) as the poor are 'urbanising more rapidly than the population as a whole' (Ravallion et al, 2007, p 1). Even now, in some parts of the world, urban poverty has already overtaken rural poverty (Haddad et al, 1999). For example, in 1999, 77 million of Latin America's poor lived in rural areas compared with 134 million in urban areas (UN-HABITAT, 2006b).

Although the world has witnessed improvements in relation to average life expectancy at birth (48 years in 1955, rising to 65 years in 1995 (WHO, 2007)) and infant mortality rates (a decline from 148 per 1,000 live births in 1955 to 59 in 1995, with a projected fall further to 29 in 2025), no such improvements in housing conditions are evident (*Table 8.1*). As this table shows, while the proportion of the urban population living in slums has remained constant, an additional 283 million people have become slum dwellers in a 15-year period between 1990 and 2005. At a disaggregated level, these increases, particularly in sub-Saharan Africa, East Asia and South Asia, and to a lesser extent in Latin America and the Caribbean, bring into perspective the challenges of the financial and institutional constraints facing urban governments.

The relationship between housing, urbanisation and poverty is complex. At one level, there is a strong association between housing disadvantage and urban dwelling. Noting that '**shelter** *is at the core of urban poverty...*', the United Nations Population Fund (UNFPA) (2007, p 38, emphasis in original) goes on to say that:

> ...overcrowding, inadequate infrastructure and services, insecurity of tenure, risks from natural and human-made hazards, exclusion from the exercise of citizenship and distance from employment and income-earning opportunities are all linked together.

At another level, though, not all slum dwellers are poor. The concept of **shelter deprivation** enables us to gain a clearer sense of the relationship between slum dwelling and housing poverty. In 2001, it was estimated that more than 1 billion individuals (one in three city dwellers) in the South were deprived of one or more of the following: durable housing; sufficient living area; access to improved water; and access to improved sanitation. *Table 8.2* shows that shelter deprivation is most acute in South Asia followed by sub-Saharan Africa and South-East Asia. Unfortunately, comparable figures for developed regions of the world are not available.

The enormity of the challenges presented by the scale of shelter deprivation in the world is reflected in Target 11 of Millennium Development Goal 7 (ensuring environmental sustainability), which aims to improve the lives of 100 million slum dwellers by 2020. Should that target not be met, the total number of slum dwellers is predicted to rise to 1.4 billion by that year. The context is now set for an examination of the changing involvement of global actors (multilateral and bilateral governmental organisations) and non-state actors in shaping housing and urban policy.

Global actors and housing policy change

Overall responsibility for the formulation of housing policy, and the regulation and provision of housing itself lies primarily with national and sub-national government. However, from the immediate aftermath of the Second World War, there has been a distinctly transnational dimension to housing and urban

Table 8.1: *Population of slum areas at mid-year by region: 1990-2005 and annual slum growth rate*

	% slum* 1990	Slum population (000s) 1990	% slum** 2005**	Slum population (000s) 2005**	Slum annual growth rate (%)
World	31.3	714,972	31.2	997,767	2.22
Developed regions	6.0	41,750	6.0	46,511	0.72
EURASIA (countries in Commonwealth of Independent States)	10.3	18,929	10.3	18,637	−0.10
European countries in Commonwealth of Independent States	6.0	9,208	6.0	8,761	−0.33
Asian countries in Commonwealth of Independent States	30.3	9,721	29.0	9,879	0.11
Developing regions	46.5	654,294	41.4	933,376	2.37
North Africa	37.7	21,719	25.4	21,224	−0.15
Sub-Saharan Africa	72.3	100,973	71.8	199,231	4.53
Latin America and the Caribbean	35.4	110,837	30.8	134,257	1.28
East Asia	41.1	150,761	34.8	212,368	2.28
East Asia, excluding China	25.3	12,831	25.4	16,702	1.76
South Asia	63.7	198,663	57.4	276,432	2.20
South-East Asia	36.8	48,986	25.3	59,913	1.34
West Asia	26.4	22,006	25.5	33,057	2.71
Oceania	24.5	350	24.0	568	3.24

Notes: * % slum indicates the proportion of the urban population living in slums; ** 2005 figures are projections.

Source: Adapted from UN-HABITAT (2006b, p 16)

Table 8.2: *Proportions of slum dwellers by shelter deprivation in developing country regions, 2003*

Region	Shelter deprivations (%)			
	Durability	Overcrowding	Water	Sanitation
North Africa	1.0	1.9	2.4	1.5
Sub-Saharan Africa	20.6	16.8	27.6	20.1
Latin America and the Caribbean	5.7	12.2	12.3	11.8
East Asia	7.0	11.9	25.9	30.8
South Asia	51.4	39.1	15.5	26.4
South-East Asia	11.0	15.3	12.6	8.2
West Asia	3.4	2.8	3.7	1.1

Source: UN-HABITAT (2006b)

policy formulation in developing countries. This section reviews the nature of this transnationalism, showing how the nature of international housing aid and the aims of policies have developed over time and how these changes have been informed by global ideas and ideological positions.

Conventional housing policy: government as provider (1960s)

Conventional housing policies refer to models of housing provision adopted from those practised in the UK from the 1950s to the 1970s. These involved slum clearance and the construction, by local authorities, of rental housing units. By 1970, local authorities were the biggest landlord, owning 30% of the national housing stock (Balchin, 1995). This model involving the **government as provider** was adopted by governments in the South, for whom the existence of slums was antithetical to the modernisation project (Hardoy and Satterthwaite, 1989). Until the late 1960s, lending for housing by international organisations such as the USAID (beginning in 1949), the UNDP (1960s) and the Inter-American Development Bank (IDB, 1960s) was for conventional housing policies (WB, 1975). For example, of the US $1.9 billion (1961-69) lent by the IDB, 97% was spent on conventional housing with the remaining 3% spent on neighbourhood improvement.

By the mid-1960s, urban housing research posited that western models of housing provision were not meeting the needs and priorities of the poor in developing countries (Abrams, 1964; Mangin, 1967). John Turner (1968, 1972, 1976, 1978) articulated these concerns most explicitly: in developing countries with nascent urbanisation trends, housing was inextricably linked to the household lifecycle. Thus, a newly arrived migrant ('bridge-header') sought cheap rented space close to employment opportunities. Only when households were economically more stable did they seek tenure ('consolidators') and later higher levels of services ('status-seekers') (Turner, 1968). Affordability constraints resulted in the poor squatting on land and incrementally building their dwellings through self-help. Turner was in essence highlighting that housing was a 'verb' (a doing thing) and not a 'noun' (an object) as in the counting of completed housing units (Turner, 1972). This argument suggested that informal urban settlements were not a problem but a solution and that a more appropriate role for government was one of enabling the poor to meet their housing needs.

Aided self-help was heavily criticised by those adhering to dependency theory, notably Rod Burgess (Burgess, 1977, 1978, 1985). According to Burgess (1985), housing has three characteristics: it is a necessary good (for the reproduction of labour); it is a fixed good (enshrined in legal rights to property); and it has both use value and exchange value (that is, it is useful to the person living in it as well as having market value). Burgess thus argued that by solely focusing on the use value of housing (what it did for people), Turner had failed to place the persistence of poor housing conditions within the wider structural relations of capitalist development. Burgess argued that the state was complicit in failing to address poor housing conditions in order to suppress demands for increased wages, which in turn would ensure the competitiveness of capitalist production. Thus, the promotion of the idea of self-help was not only an unpaid extension of the working day of the poor; in addition, the resulting upgrading and sites-and-services projects increased opportunity for the penetration of industrial capital (in various elements of housing) and thus gave housing an exchange value. Analytically, this argument powerfully demonstrated the link between the causes of poverty and the persistence of informal settlements. However, Burgess did not offer alternative housing policy options, since the main cause of the housing problem was seen to lie outside the housing arena.

The lack of an alternative to the policy solutions proposed by Turner left the way clear for his ideas to influence the thinking of multilateral institutions, namely the WB and IDB and some bilaterals, notably DfID and USAID. In many ways, the idea of self-help housing sat comfortably with existing ones: it was already in use in the 1940s and 1950s and was articulated by the Housing and Home Finance Agency in Washington DC (Harris, 1998). The policy applications of the idea of self-help housing were manifested in 'enabling' housing policy. This policy would discourage governments from constructing completed dwelling units, focusing instead on tasks beyond the ability of individual households: namely, ensuring access to land that is serviced with water, sanitation and roads, and making credit and building materials available. It was proposed that this be achieved through the use of **slum improvement** and **site-and-service** housing layouts (***Box 8.4***). Responsibility for the construction and/or management of house building was to be left to the poor themselves so that they could emulate the process found in informal settlements – in sum, 'aided self-help'.

Box 8.4: Slum improvement, sites and services

Slum improvement

Slum improvement or slum upgrading was originally envisaged with environmental improvement objectives. Whenever possible, infrastructure such as water, sanitation, electricity and roads would be provided to those 'slum' or **squatter settlements** not deemed to occupy sites of public interest or located in areas deemed hazardous. At times this may involve the reallocation of plots in a planned manner to make service provision easier. Of significance is the fact that slum improvement does not add to the housing stock.

Sites and services

Unlike slum improvement, site-and-service projects add to the housing stock. It involves the government making new serviced land available for beneficiaries to manage and or construct their dwellings.

Government as enabler (1970s)

USAID and the WB were some of the first international organisations to articulate their new **government as enabler** housing policy positions. The following quote from the WB indicates the extent of the policy shift that this new donor position represented, as well as the resistance to it by developing country governments:

> The approach ... represented an important shift with which many borrowers did not initially agree. Education, demonstration and dissemination, therefore, became important. (World Bank, 1983, p 6)

This enabling approach, set out in *Housing: Sector Policy Paper* (WB, 1975), was based on three principles: the notion of affordability (by reducing standards); cost recovery (achieved affordability); and replicability (recovered costs for reinvestment) (Pugh, 1995). Between 1972 and 1981, the WB had lent US $2.02 billion (44% of project costs) for urban development to countries in Africa, Asia and Latin America and the Caribbean. Lending for shelter and **integrated projects** accounted for 47% and 22% respectively (WB, 1983).

The 1970s also witnessed the emergence of a wider global – specifically the United Nations (UN) – interest in human settlements. The first global conference on human settlements (Habitat I) was held in Vancouver, Canada, in 1976. Habitat I was an assessment of global human settlement conditions and an attempt to define a set of common goals that national governments would address. It led to the setting up of the United Nations Centre for Human Settlements (UNCHS (Habitat)) in Nairobi in 1978. This was an intergovernmental body responsible for coordinating human settlement activities within the UN system. In 2001, UNCHS (Habitat) became a fully-fledged UN programme (similar to UNDP) and was relabelled UN–HABITAT with its own core funding. While core funding potentially increased its ability to influence policy, UN–HABITAT – like other UN agencies – does not have the financial or legal powers necessary to influence national government policy beyond securing the assurances of member governments. For example, the WB has been able to use its lending policies to influence the direction of housing policy and has paved the way for other international lenders to follow suit.

The key point to note here for this period is the direct engagement of international actors as well as city governments in attempting to ameliorate shelter deprivation. Policy was focused and, by and large, matched the institutional, technical and financial capacity of public authorities.

From shelter to housing finance and policy (1980s)

By the 1980s, the WB had recognised the limited impact of upgrading and sites and services at the city and neighbourhood levels. The problem areas identified were 'the institutional framework of the project, land acquisition and tenure, cost recovery, shifts on standards, project management, and experience with special components' (WB, 1983, p 24). Three areas of future lending were identified: first, the 'importance of housing markets' – the need for a greater involvement of the private sector in recognition of the limited impact of public sector involvement; second, the role of 'institutional finance' – especially the setting up and strengthening of local financial institutions; and third, 'urban management and productivity' – to deal with city-wide projects (WB, 1983). The latter two areas were also adopted by the IDB across South America, whose spending on upgrading and municipal development between 1980 and 1989 indicates a 20% and 80% split respectively (IDB, 2004).

This change in direction of housing policy in the 1980s reflected the adoption of structural adjustment policies under the auspices of the neoliberal Washington Consensus. While these most directly affected developing countries, the ideological position they represented was evident in parts of the North. In both the UK and North America, the market was favoured over other mechanisms of ensuring access to housing (UNCHS (Habitat), 1996, section 10.2). In the

South, the WB was able successfully to use its financial leverage to bring about changes in housing policy across a number of countries to which it had made loans. The clearest example of this is the Indian Madras Urban Development Projects 1 and II, which experimented, on a large scale, with site-and-service and settlement upgrading (see, for example, Pugh, 1990). The emphasis was on the further reduction of subsidies and the ushering in of reforms in housing finance and policy. The WB was not, however, always successful in levering policy changes – some countries, such as Thailand, were able to resist such policy prescriptions until the 1990s (see, for example, Giles, 2003).

This shift from a direct to an indirect involvement in housing and basic services provision was supported by arguments favouring '*assistance to cities ...* [having] ... *other, broader, and deeper justifications than simply providing basic services to slum dwellers*' (Cohen, 2004, p 2, emphasis in original). This was reflected in the restructuring of spending on urban housing, which saw a decline in moneys spent by both the WB and UNDP on shelter and an increase in housing finance (see *Figures 8.1* and *8.2*). In this context, many were justifiably concerned that shelter would slip off the lending agenda of international organisations, especially in the rapidly urbanising and poor countries of sub-Saharan Africa (see, for instance, Buckley and Kalarickal, 2006). DfID was an exception to this trend and, until 1991, DfID India was involved in slum improvement (Barrett and Beardmore, 2000), filling a gap in shelter lending. Today, however, there is little sign of direct housing support from DfID – the priority has become municipal development and services (water and sanitation).

Figure 8.1: *Proportion of WB spending on urban housing, 1972-86 and 1987-2005*

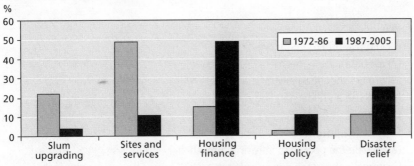

Notes: Housing finance is support for setting up national housing finance institutions. Housing policy refers to support for national housing policy development.

Source: WB (2007)

Figure 8.2: *Proportion of IDB urban spending, 1970-2003*

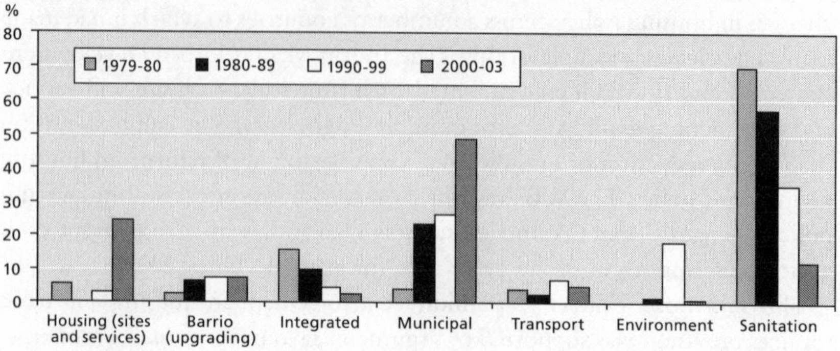

%

Legend: □ 1979-80 ■ 1980-89 □ 1990-99 ■ 2000-03

Categories: Housing (sites and services), Barrio (upgrading), Integrated, Municipal, Transport, Environment, Sanitation

Source: IDB (2004)

Housing markets and city development (1990s)

Despite the differing pace of change in the policy stances of different international agencies, the scene had been set for a change in policy direction in the 1990s, with the priority lying with the development of housing markets, cities and economic development. This shift took place in both the WB and the UN. ***Box 8.5*** sets out the main elements of these organisations' policy papers: *Urban Policy and Economic Development: An Agenda for the 1990s* (WB, 1991) and *Cities, People and Poverty: Urban Development Cooperation for the 1990s* (UNDP, 1991). Note the similarity between the policy stances of these two international organisations.

On the housing front, the shift was signalled by the policy paper *Housing: Enabling Markets to Work* (WB, 1993), which emphasised links to the wider

---

Box 8.5: The WB and UNDP urban policy papers compared

WB

(1) Improve urban productivity;

(2) alleviate urban poverty;

(3) protect the urban environment; and

(4) increase an understanding of urban issues.

UNDP

(1) Alleviate poverty;

(2) provide the poor with infrastructure, shelter and services;

(3) improve the urban environment;

(4) strengthen local government; and

(5) promote the private sector and non-governmental organisations.

Sources: WB (1991); UNDP (1991)

---

city and national economy and the need to treat housing as a *sector* (***Box 8.6***). It also set out priorities for lending to the housing sector, focusing on policy reform in: property rights development; enhancement of housing finance; rationalisation of subsidies; infrastructure for residential land development; enhancing the efficiency of the building industry; regulatory reform; and institutional reform. The emphasis on a role for government – which until then the WB had eschewed – was a partial attempt to address the mounting criticisms of the structural adjustment policies that favoured a withdrawal of the state, a reduction in subsidies for social development and privatisation (see, for instance, Cornia et al, 1987). The role of the market and private sector, however, was as central as ever to this policy vision.

Box 8.6: WB housing policy of the 1990s: enabling markets to work

Objective of housing policy

'... a *well functioning housing sector* that serves the needs of consumers, producers, financiers, and the local and central governments; and that enhances economic development, alleviates poverty, and supports a sustainable environment'

Role of government

'... adoption by government agencies with policy making, coordination and regulatory responsibilities of an *enabling role* to facilitate the provision of land and housing by the private sector; improved **coordination** of sector and macro-economic policy'

Policy and lending instruments

'... *integrated array* of policy and lending instruments to *stimulate demand* (property rights development, housing finance, and targeted subsidies); *facilitate supply* (infrastructure provision, regulatory reform, and building industry organization); and *manage the housing sector as a whole* (institutional reform and coordination with macro-economic policy.' (WB, 1993, pp 52-3, emphasis in original)

The WB is the only organisation so far to have explicitly articulated a comprehensive housing policy. Since no developing country has the institutional capacity or the political will to implement such a policy in full, it is not surprising that only selective parts of this policy have been adopted. Favoured elements are reform of the urban land market, not by redistribution but in the form of land titling (Peru) (Cantuarias, 2004); the involvement of the private sector in housing (India) (Mukhija, 2004); and the one-off provision of housing grants and the use of the private sector to develop housing units for the poor (South Africa) (Huchzermeyer, 2001). The rather selective take-up of WB policy is also attributable to its failure to provide a 'route map' for policy makers as to how to develop policy: simply setting out a comprehensive housing policy stance and a list of housing policy dos and don'ts has proved insufficient (Jones and Datta, 2000, p 410).

In comparison, other international organisations have adopted a broader policy stance within the rubric of urban poverty (DfID, 2000) or social development (IDB, 2003). In doing so, they are following a more 'process'-oriented approach that allows for policies to be tailored to the local context (see, for example, Brinkerhoff and Ingle, 1989). DfID (2000) – in contrast to the WB – has adopted a more informal and progressive urban policy development approach. This approach, termed the 'urban ladder' (***Box 8.7***), shows how DfID's engagement in housing and urban policy has gradually moved from a focus at the micro level (slum improvement and urban services at the settlement level) to urban governance and urban development at the city and regional levels. Although DfID claims to continue to focus on all rungs of the ladder, the principal emphasis is currently on urban basic services (for example, water and sanitation) at the city level and with much less attention to activities at the higher end of the urban ladder (DfID, 2001).

The international flow of policy ideas is by no means a one-way street from Northern global actors to Southern national governments. For example, some argue that recommendations for housing policy change in South Africa and Colombia, especially the rationalisation of subsidies, was an attempt to replicate the Chilean government's neoliberal reforms in this area of housing. Of course, replication has its problems – and as Gilbert (2004, p 19) notes, 'perhaps the principal challenge to governments in the housing field is how to bridge the gap between the substantial demand for housing and the rather limited resources available to satisfy that demand. No housing policy, the capital subsidy approach included, can get round that problem'.

Although housing policy solutions within this enabling housing policy framework have been broadened, a number of limitations are evident. First, the predominant goal still remains a property-owning democracy (Daunton, 1987). Although there is plenty of evidence to show that rental housing can play an important role in enabling the poor to access housing and providing a route for residential mobility (Gilbert, 1983, 1991, 1999; Kumar, 1989), international actors have remained silent on issues of tenure. The exception to this is UN-HABITAT, which is supportive of rental housing but does not have the ability to influence government policy. Second, increasing support for upgrading rather than sites and services has sidelined issues of land distribution. A slum

Box 8.7: The urban ladder

Intervention	Emphasis	Poverty angle
Urbanisation	Rural–urban links District/state-level planning	Considers all poor Addresses poverty at source
Urban development	Investment Employment Economic growth	Good labour markets Well-regulated employment opportunities
Urban governance	Municipal reform Pro-poor policies Decentralisation	Responsible and accountable elected representatives From patronage to civic rights
Urban management	City planning Municipal finance Capacity building	Poor 'planned' into city Sustainability of services Formal/informal sector partnerships
Urban services	City systems Stakeholder participation Vulnerable groups	Poor included in the city Stakeholder choice Non-slum poor included
Slum improvement	Physical improvements Area-specific Community initiatives	Improved environmental conditions within recognised slums Improved 'quality of life' for the better-off poor Skills upgrading

Source: Adapted from DfID (2000, p 11)

household in India occupies, on average, 20 square metres, while sites and services had an element of redistribution, providing sites of 30 square metres. Third, although poverty is a key determinant of poor housing conditions, there is no political will to consider how housing could be used as a means of generating household income. This could be done by encouraging the renting of rooms

(Kumar, 1996a, 1996b, 2001) or supporting the development of home-based enterprises (Tipple, 2005, 2006). Doing so would, however, bring issues of land redistribution to the fore, since existing plot sizes are a key constraining factor. Relatedly, there is little attention to the links between housing and the labour market, with a failure to address the preponderance of informal, low-paid, intermittent and unprotected work (Harris et al, 1996). Although the International Labour Organization (ILO) has been actively advocating the notion of 'decent work' (ILO, 2002a) (see Chapter Six), governments in Africa, Asia, Latin America and the Caribbean have been slow to engage with this agenda. The WB has also been show to address the links between labour market and housing conditions.

Housing and urban development in the 21st century

Several key elements are evident in global urban and housing policy at the beginning of the 21st century. First, is the welcome recognition of the importance of cities and urban centres in economic and social development (WB, 2000b, 2003; UNFPA, 2007). Specifically for urban policy, this is clearly set out in *Cities in Transition: World Bank Urban and Local Government Strategy* (**Box 8.8**).

Box 8.8: Cities in transition

The WB's *Cities in Transition* strategy paper argues for the need to 'recognise cities and towns as a dynamic development arena where the convergence of sectoral activities, and collaboration among communities, levels of government, and other private and public sector institutions can create a microcosm of sustainable development for the country' (2000a, p 9) and that 'if cities and towns are to promote the welfare of their residents and of the nation's citizens, they must be sustainable and functional in four respects. First and foremost, they must be liveable – ensuring a decent quality of life and equitable opportunity for all residents, including the poorest. To achieve that goal, they must also be competitive, well governed and managed, and financially sustainable, or bankable' (WB, 2000a, pp 11-12).

Second, there is a realisation that cooperation between international organisations (IOs) can substantially enhance the outcome of urban interventions. This need for inter-organisational cooperation and coordination – obvious as it may seem – was noted by UNCHS (Habitat) in its *A New Agenda for Human Settlements* 20 years ago:

... the first step to addressing human settlements issues must be to develop a partnership approach – to work together to reach consensus on specific policy objectives and strategies which are consistent with national development objectives ... the absences of consensus on policy objectives and strategies is, at least in part, due to the fact that each aid agency employs a variety of its own analytical tools and techniques of appraisal in support of programme objectives ... projects have often seemed sensible individually but have not added up to a well balanced whole. (UNCHS (Habitat), 1988, p 24)

Third, national and global federations of non-governmental and poor people's organisations have succeeded in enhancing their collective voice, making it increasingly difficult to ignore their demands. Partnerships between organisations of the urban poor, national and international non-governmental organisations, municipal and state governments, and international organisations in areas of housing finance and sanitation are now being developed.

Before exploring the latter two issues further, it is important to note that these policy changes took place within a wider context of changes in the economic and social policy approaches of IOs and Northern governments. First, a series of UN Conferences in the 1990s – environment and development (1992); human rights (1993); population (1994); social development (1995); women (1995) and human settlements (1996) – highlighted the need for equal importance to be given to the 'social' and the 'economic' in development. A growing discontent with WB's economic policies, which were seen to 'impose upon' and 'ignore local context', also led to the WB being forced to rethink its policy stance to develop what has become known as the Post-Washington Consensus (PWC). PWC saw the rejection of the 'old' structural adjustment policies and their replacement by **Poverty Reduction Strategy Papers** (PRSPs), based on five principles. These were that policies would be country-driven (ushering in a sense of ownership through the broad-based participation of civil society and the state); results-oriented (ensuring that outcomes benefited the poor); comprehensive (addressing the multi-dimensional nature of poverty); partnership-oriented (involving bilateral, multilateral and non-governmental organisations); and policy reform-oriented (focused on long-term poverty reduction). The application of these principles also led to support for isolated projects being replaced by **Sector Wide Approaches** (SWAps), with **Poverty Reduction Budget Support** for sectors identified in the country PRSP. Housing and urban policy reflects this shift in policy stance. For example, a DfID grant and a WB credit and loan to the Indian state of Andhra Pradesh for 'budget support' is juxtaposed with the Andhra Pradesh Urban Basic Services for the Poor programme, thus attempting to ensure the financial and long-term sustainability of services.

Alliances and partnerships between cities and international organisations

One of the key developments in global housing policy in recent years has been the increase in partnerships between multilateral and bilateral organisations. The second global conference on human settlements held in Istanbul in 1996, produced the Habitat Agenda (UN–HABITAT, 1996), which was adopted by 171 countries and contained over 100 commitments and 600 recommendations for national governments to undertake. The two main thrusts of Habitat II were 'adequate shelter for all' and 'sustainable urbanisation'. UN–HABITAT has also, in partnership with the WB, created the **Cities Alliance** to meet Target 11 of Millennium Development Goal 7. Launched in May 1999, the cities alliance is a 'multi-donor coalition of cities and their development partners':

> [it] has been conceived to improve the efficiency and impact of urban development cooperation in two key areas: (a) making unprecedented improvements in the living conditions of the urban poor by developing citywide and nationwide slum-upgrading programs; and (b) supporting city-based consensus-building processes by which local stakeholders define their vision for their city and establish city development strategies with clear priorities for action and investments. (Cities Alliance, 2006)

The UN–HABITAT campaigns for 'good governance' and 'secure tenure', launched in 1999 and 2000 respectively, are also related to MDG Target 11. The good governance campaign focuses on the role that governance can play in addressing urban poverty and sustainable urbanisation, while the secure tenure campaign focuses on the rights of the poor to the city. Both 'good governance' and a rights-based approach to development are part of the wider PWC agenda. Although UN–HABITAT has been able to get national governments to commit to a plan of action, it does not have the power to hold them to account for not achieving these commitments. Both the campaigns for good governance and secure tenure are, at best, simply a plea to governments. The WB is in a comparatively stronger position as it can use its financial packages to leverage policy change.

New partnerships: the state, international organisations and non-state actors

In the early days of the implementation of non-conventional housing policy (the 1970s and much of the 1980s), community participation mostly involved beneficiaries as a way of reducing project costs (by contributing labour) and achieving project sustainability (involvement in maintenance). This efficiency-effectiveness principle behind participation became an 'end' in itself rather than a 'means' to an end, namely, empowering the poor by involving them in decisions that affected their lives (Moser, 1989).

Despite facing an uphill struggle, national and transnational alliances of the poor and their civil society representatives are slowly finding 'ways to have their voices heard and to influence the decisions and practices of larger institutions that affect their lives' (Gaventa, 2001, p 275; see also, Mayo, 2005). In relation to housing, India has been in the forefront of alliances between poor peoples' organisations and NGOs. In Mumbai, the Indian Alliance of the National Slum Dwellers Federation (NSDF), Mahila Milan[1] (a women's savings and credit group) and the Society for the Promotion of Area Resource Centres (SPARC)[2] has been able to convince the provincial government of the state of Maharashtra to adopt a policy of community-provided and managed sanitation that it pioneered. The 1990s and since has seen the activity of these groups, through the auspices of the South African-based Shack/Slum Dwellers Federation (SDI), expand to incorporate national and transnational alliances, in a number of countries across Africa, Asia and Latin America[3]. The aim of these transnational alliances is not only to provide support and share ideas, but more importantly to amplify their voices with a view to influencing the policies of international actors and national governments, a process termed 'deep democracy' (Appadurai, 2001).

Some success is evident on this front – examples include a partnering of the Indian Alliance, the Mumbai city government and the WB for the provision of community-built and managed toilets as part of the Mumbai sanitation project (Sarkar and Moulik, 2006); a partnership between the Thai government, the Community Organisation Development Institute and organisations of the poor, which has given rise to a city-wide upgrading programme in Bangkok that is set to improve the lives of some 300,000 people in 2,000 slum communities[4]; and the Community Led Infrastructure Financing Facility (CLIFF) in Mumbai[5], an initiative based on the recognition that the poor's lack of collateral (either in the form of regular income or land and other physical assets) puts institutional finance out of their reach. However, what the poor have demonstrated is the ability to save: the local revolving fund owned by SPARC and Nirman (National Slum Dwellers Federation, India and Mahila Milan) is worth approximately £1.2 million. CLIFF is designed to fill this collateral void by providing guarantees to the banking sector through Homeless

International, a UK shelter INGO. Institutional credit is thus made available to federations of the urban poor for investment in housing and sanitation. CLIFF now operates in two other countries, Kenya and the Philippines. DfID and SIDA have so far committed £8.34 million to the venture (Homeless International, n.d.). More recently, SDI, UN-HABITAT and the WB have secured funding from the Cities Alliance to enable slum dwellers in India, the Philippines and South Africa to record their experiences with slum upgrading (UN-HABITAT, 2006a).

Notwithstanding the successes that alliances of the poor and non-state actors have achieved in terms of settlement relocation (through a process of dialogue rather than assuming confrontational stances in relation to forced evictions), housing finance (through partnership that provides financial guarantees) and sanitation (through processes of community-designed and managed toilets), a number of questions remain. First is whether social movements have the ability to move from just filling gaps in housing and service provision to a role that aims to influence and change housing and urban policy – thereby building in equity for all the poor. For instance, partnerships between the alliances of the poor on the one hand and international actors, the state and the private sector on the other, have in practice been limited to a few privileged non-state representatives that by no means represent all the urban poor. As a result, most policy changes (for example, in settlement relocation and sanitation) are selectively negotiated and targeted at the membership of participating alliances. Second is the question of scale. Although these new movements of the urban poor comprise disenfranchised groups, they remain only a tiny proportion of those that are disenfranchised. Thus, even though they may make gains in influencing policy, the inability of other similar groups in being able to voice their claims remains. Third, success in influencing policy change has depended on 'windows of opportunity'. The policy direction provided by such windows of opportunity can lead to compromises being made that may then become **institutionalised**. For example, opportunities to develop a policy on community sanitation in Mumbai have overshadowed questions of the inequitable distribution of land in the city that is integral to solving the city's housing crisis (O'Hare et al, 1998).

It is clear that the housing challenge in the urban developing world cannot be overcome by governments or international actors alone and that a certain degree of civic and civil society engagement is called for. However, the extent to which the involvement of non-state actors can help **scale up** solutions to housing and urban problems remains questionable.

Conclusion

This chapter has reviewed the changing role of international actors in housing and urban policy in developing countries. It has identified different policy stances, ranging from the explicit economic approaches of the WB on housing and urban policy and governance to the more diffused social development approaches of DfID and IDB that are framed within urban poverty and the Millennium Development Goals. The ensuing policy shifts of governments, fostered by global policy actors, now incorporate the involvement of the private sector, organisations of the poor and other non-state actors in policy making. The chapter has also considered how the direction of housing and urban policy change has been influenced by wider global shifts in economic and development policy ideas. While the direction of this change is broadly welcome, key concerns still remain. These are the mismatch between institutional capacity of city governments and the increasingly complex policy stances being recommended; the failure of the housing and urban development solutions being pursued to link up with other policy arenas, notably labour markets; the challenge of scaling up and institutionalising innovative practices; and the ability and unwillingness of policy actors to address issues of equity in the distribution of assets and claims.

At a broader level, there is also the question about the role global policy actors should play in bringing about changes to the practices of national, regional and city governments. For example, by bringing about change from conventional to non-conventional housing policies and linking urban poverty to urbanisation, the international community has certainly brought about institutional change. However, certain key issues have been studiously avoided in global housing and urban policy, with inequalities in land distribution being one spectacular example. This is true of all IOs, even the UN-HABITAT campaigns for secure tenure. As Strassmann notes, Habitat II was unable to settle differences between the European Commission on the one hand and the US and Latin American countries on the other hand on whether there was a 'separate and distinct human right to housing' or simply 'a right to an adequate standard of living' with housing a derivate right along with food and clothing (Strassmann, 1997, p 1729).

Notes
[1] www.iisd.org/50comm/commdb/list/c16.htm
[2] www.sparcindia.org
[3] See www.sdinet.org/rituals/ritual1.htm for more detail
[4] www.codi.or.th/index.php?option=com_content&task=category&sectionid=9&id=136&Itemid=52
[5] www.homeless-international.org/standard_1.aspx?id=0:27820&id=0:27813

Summary

- Housing need is a major global social policy issue and is set to become even more significant in the context of current and projected urbanisation trends.
- There has been a transnational element to housing and urban policy since the Second World War, in particular from the 1960s with various multilateral agencies (WN, UN, IDB) and bilateral agencies (DfID, USAID, SIDA) involved in housing and urban policy formation in developing countries across Africa, Latin America and Asia.
- The UN has been less effective in levering its desired policy changes than multilateral and bilateral donor organisations. National authorities have often taken up global actors' policy prescriptions selectively.
- The aims and approaches of global housing and urban policy have changed over time. The shift from conventional housing policies to non-conventional housing policies is a welcome change in direction, but this has been accompanied by a decline in efforts to ameliorate housing deprivations.
- Global housing policy privileges housing ownership at the expense of rental accommodation and the involvement of other non-state actors in housing provision. However, comprehensive solutions to housing deprivation cannot be found in housing alone; there is an urgent need to link to other policy arenas, most notably labour markets, especially in urban areas, and to address issues of land distribution.
- The poor and their representatives have demonstrated an ability to make innovative and meaningful contributions to housing policy. However, there is some concern that current structures may hinder the realisation of equitable outcomes.

Questions for discussion

- Are housing problems merely the result of financial and technical resource shortages or are they the outcome of wider structural inequalities in society?
- Should non-governmental not-for-profit organisations seek to influence the housing policy agendas of governments or act to make up for the failure of governments to ensure access to decent housing for the poor?
- Should international organisations refocus their attention on housing issues or is the attention to wider urban issues the way forward?

Further suggested activities

- Get a group of people together to watch the film *City of God*, directed by Fernando Meirelles. Discuss the extent to which housing and labour market constraints give rise to the problems depicted.
- Discuss the housing challenges facing poor communities where you live. What are the root causes of these challenges and how are they being addressed, by whom, if at all?

Further reading

Buckley, R.M. and Kalarickal, J. (2005) 'Housing policy in developing countries: conjectures and refutations', *The World Bank Research Observer*, vol 20, no 2, pp 233-57.

Harris, R. (2003) 'Learning from the past: international housing policy since 1945 – an introduction', *Habitat International*, vol 27, no 2, pp 163-6.

Pugh, C. (1994) 'Housing policy development in developing countries: the World Bank and internationalization, 1972-93', *Cities*, vol 11, no 3, pp 159-80.

Electronic resources

www.adb.org/urbandev/default.asp Asian Development Bank (urban development).

www.iadb.org/topics/subtopics.cfm?subtopicID=VIV&topicID=DU &language=English Inter-American Development Bank (neighbourhood upgrading);

www.iadb.org/topics/subtopics.cfm?subtopicID=HIP&language=Englis h&topicID=DU&parid=2&item1id=3# (housing and mortgage finance);

www.iadb.org//sds/SOC/site_15_e.htm (urban development).

http://go.worldbank.org/OTO3F852E0 WB (housing and land).

References

Abrams, C. (1964) *Housing in the Modern World: Man's Struggle for Shelter in an Urbanising World*, London: Faber & Faber.

Appadurai, A. (2001) 'Deep democracy: urban governability and the horizon of politics', *Environment and Urbanization*, vol 13, no 2, pp 23-43.

Balchin, P.N. (1995) *Housing Policy: An Introduction*, London: Routledge.

Barrett, A.J. and Beardmore, R.M. (2000) 'India's urban poverty agenda: understanding the poor in cities and formulating appropriate anti-poverty actions', Discussion Paper for South Asia Urban and City Management Course, Goa, January 9-21.

Breman, J. (2006) 'Slumlands', *New Left Review*, vol 40, no July-August, pp 141-8.

Brinkerhoff, D.W. and Ingle, M.D. (1989) 'Integrating blueprint and process: a structured flexibility approach to development management', *Public Administration and Development*, vol 9, no 5, pp 487-503.

Buckley, R.M. and Kalarickal, J. (2006) *Thirty Years of World Bank Shelter Lending: What Have we Learned?*, Washington, DC: World Bank.

Burgess, R. (1977) 'Self-help housing: a new imperialist strategy? A critique of the Turner school', *Antipode*, vol 9, no 2, pp 50-9.

Burgess, R. (1978) 'Petty commodity housing or dweller control? A critique of John Turner's views on housing policy', *World Development*, vol 9, no 9/10, pp 1105-33.

Burgess, R. (1985) 'The limits of state self-help housing programmes', *Development and Change*, vol 16, no 2, pp 271-312.

Cantuarias, F. (2004) 'Peru's urban land titling project', Paper presented at the Global Conference on Scaling up Poverty Reduction, Shanghai, 25-27 May.

Cities Alliance (2006) 'Charter', www.citiesalliance.org/about-ca/charter-english.html#objectives, accessed 6 August 2007.

Cohen, M.A. (2004) *Reframing Urban Assistance: Scale, Ambition and Possibility*, Washington DC: Woodrow Wilson International Center for Scholars.

Cornia, G.A., Jolly, R. and Stewart, F. (1987) *Adjustment with a Human Face: Protecting the Vulnerable and Promoting Growth (Volume 1)*, Oxford: Clarendon.

Daunton, M.J. (1987) *A Property-owning Democracy?: Housing in Britain*, London: Faber & Faber.

DfID (Department for International Development) (2000) *Reducing Urban Poverty in India: The Evolution of DfID India's Urban Poverty Reduction Programme*, London: DfID.

DfID (2001) *Meeting the Challenge of Urban Poverty*, London: DfID.

Drakakis-Smith, D.W. (1987) *The Third World City*, London: Methuen.

Gaventa, J. (2001) 'Global citizen action: lessons and challenges', in M. Edwards and J. Gaventa (eds) *Global Citizen Action*, London: Earthscan, pp 275-87.

Gilbert, A. (1983) 'The tenants of self-help housing: choice and constraint in the housing markets of less developed countries', *Development and Change*, vol 14, no 3, pp 449-77.

Gilbert, A. (1991) 'Renting and the transition to owner occupation in Latin American cities', *Habitat International*, vol 15, no 1/2, pp 87-99.

Gilbert, A. (1999) 'A home is for ever? Residential mobility and homeownership in self-help settlements', *Environment and Planning A*, vol 31, no 6, pp 1073-91.

Gilbert, A. (2004) 'Helping the poor through housing subsidies: lessons from Chile, Colombia and South Africa', *Habitat International*, vol 28, no 1, pp 13-40.

Giles, C. (2003) 'The autonomy of Thai housing policy, 1945-1996', *Habitat International*, vol 27, no 2, pp 227-44.

Haddad, L., Ruel, M.T. and Garnett, J.L. (1999) 'Are urban poverty and undernutrition growing? Some newly assembled evidence', *World Development*, vol 27, no 11, pp 1891-1904.

Hardoy, J.E. and Satterthwaite, D. (1989) *Squatter Citizen: Life in the Urban Third World*, London: Earthscan.

Harris, N., Rosser, C. and Kumar, S. (1996) *Jobs for the Poor: A Case Study in Cuttack*, London: UCL Press.

Harris, R. (1998) 'The silence of the experts: "aided self-help housing", 1939-1954', *Habitat International*, vol 22, no 2, pp 165-89.

Homeless International (n.d.) 'Community-led infrastructure finance facility', www.homeless-international.org/standard_1.aspx?id=0:27820&id=0:27813, accessed 9 August, 2007.

Huchzermeyer, M. (2001) 'Housing for the poor? Negotiated housing policy in South Africa', *Habitat International*, vol 25, no 3, pp 303-31.

IDB (Inter-American Development Bank) (2003) *Social Development: Strategy Document*, Washington, DC: IDB.

IDB (2004) *The Challenge of an Urban Continent,* Washington, DC: IDB.

ILO (International Labour Organization) (2002) *Decent Work and the Informal Economy*, Geneva: ILO.

Jones, G.A. and Datta, K. (2000) 'Enabling markets to work? Housing policy in the "new" South Africa', *International Planning Studies*, vol 5, no 3, pp 393-416.

Kumar, S. (1989) 'How poorer groups find accommodation in third world cities: a guide to the literature', *Environment and Urbanisation*, vol 1, no 2, pp 71-85.

Kumar, S. (1996a) 'Landlordism in third world urban low-income settlements: a case for further research', *Urban Studies*, vol 33, no 4/5, pp 753-82.

Kumar, S. (1996b) 'Subsistence and petty capitalist landlords: a theoretical framework for the analysis of landlordism in third world low income settlements', *International Journal of Urban and Regional Research*, vol 20, no 2, pp 317-29.

Kumar, S. (2001) *Social Relations, Rental Housing Markets and the Poor in Urban India*, London: Department of Social Policy, London School of Economics.

Mangin, W. (1967) 'Squatter settlements in Latin America: a problem or a solution', *Scientific American*, vol 217, no 4, pp 65-98.

Mayo, M. (2005) *Global Citizens: Social Movements and the Challenge of Globalization*, London/New York, NY: Zed Books.

Moser, C.O.N. (1989) 'Community participation in urban projects in the third world ', *Progress in Planning*, vol 32, no 2, pp 71-133.

Mukhija, V. (2004) 'The contradictions in enabling private developers of affordable housing: a cautionary case from Ahmedabad, India', *Urban Studies*, vol 41, no 11, pp 2231-44.

O'Hare, G., Abbott, D. and Barke, M. (1998) 'A review of slum housing policies in Mumbai', *Cities*, vol 15, no 4, pp 269-83.

Pugh, C. (1990) *Housing and Urbanisation: A Study of India*, New Delhi: Sage Publications.

Pugh, C. (1995) 'The role of the world bank in housing', in B.C. Aldrich and R.S. Sandhu (eds) *Housing the Urban Poor: Policy and Practice in Developing Countries*, London: Zed Books, pp 34-92.

Ravallion, M. (2001) *On the Urbanization of Poverty*, Washington, DC: World Bank.

Ravallion, M., Chen, S. and Sangraula, P. (2007) 'New evidence on the urbanization of global poverty', Policy Research Working Paper 4199, Washington, DC: World Bank.

Sarkar, S. and Moulik, S.G. (2006) *The Mumbai Slum Sanitation Program: Partnering with Slum Communities for Sustainable Sanitation in a Megalopolis*, Washington, DC: World Bank.

Strassmann, W.P. (1997) 'Avoiding conflict and bold inquiry – a recapitulation of Habitat II', *Urban Studies*, vol 34, no 10, pp 1729-38.

Tipple, G. (2005) 'The place of home-based enterprises in the informal sector: evidence from Cochabamba, New Delhi, Surabaya and Pretoria', *Urban Studies*, vol 42, no 4, pp 611-32.

Tipple, G. (2006) 'Employment and work conditions in home-based enterprises in four developing countries: do they constitute "decent work"?', *Work Employment and Society*, vol 20, no 1, pp 167-79.

Turner, J.F.C. (1968) 'Housing priorities, settlement patterns and urban development in modernising countries', *Journal of the American Institute of Planners*, vol 34, no 5, pp 354-63.

Turner, J.F.C. (1972) 'Housing as a verb', in J. F.C. Turner and R. Fitcher (eds) *Freedom to build*, New York, NY: Macmillan, pp 148-75.

Turner, J.F.C. (1976) *Housing by People*, London: Marion Boyars.

Turner, J.F.C. (1978) 'Housing in three dimensions: terms of reference for the housing question redefined', *World Development*, vol 6, no 9/10, pp 1135-45.

UN-HABITAT (United Nations Human Settlements Programme) (1996) 'The HABITAT agenda goals and principles, commitments and the global plan of action', www.unhabitat.org/downloads/docs/1176_6455_The_Habitat_Agenda.pdf, accessed 15 January 2007.

UN-HABITAT (2005) *Responding to the Challenges of an Urbanizing World – UN-HABITAT Annual Report 2005*, Nairobi: UN-HABITAT.

UN-HABITAT (2006a) *Analytical Perspective of Pro-poor Slum Upgrading Frameworks*, Nairobi: UN-HABITAT.

UN-HABITAT (2006b) *State of the World's Cities 2006-07 – The Millennium Development Goals and Urban Sustainability*, London: Earthscan.

UNCHS (Habitat) (United Nations Centre for Human Settlements) (1988) *A New Agenda for Human Settlements*, Nairobi: UNCHS (Habitat).

UNCHS (Habitat) (1996) *An Urbanising World: Global Report on Human Settlements*, Oxford: Oxford University Press.

UNDP (United Nations Development Programme) (1991) *Cities, People and Poverty: Urban Development Cooperation for the 1990s*, New York, NY: UNDP.

UNFPA (United Nations Population Fund) (2007) *State of World Population 2007: Unleashing the Potential of Urban Growth*, New York, NY: UNFPA.

WB (World Bank) (1975) *Housing: Sector Policy Paper*, Washington, DC: WB.

WB (1983) *Learning by Doing: World Bank Lending for Urban Development (1972-82)*, Washington, DC: WB.

WB (1991) *Urban Policy and Economic Development: An Agenda for the 1990s*, Washington, DC: WB.

WB (1993) *Housing: Enabling Markets to Work*, Washington, DC: WB.

WB (2000a) *Cities in Transition: World Bank Urban and Local Government Strategy*, Washington, DC: WB.

WB (2000b) *World Development Report 2000-2001: Attacking Poverty*, Oxford: Oxford University Press.

WB (2003) *World Development Report 2003 – Sustainable Development in a Dynamic World: Transforming Institutions, Growth, and Quality of Life*, Washington, DC: WB.

WB (2007) 'Housing and land', http://go.worldbank.org/OTO3F852E0, accessed 15 March 2007.

WHO (World Health Organization) (2007) *50 Facts: Global Health Situation and Trends 1955-2025*, www.who.int/whr/1998/media_centre/50facts/en, accessed 5 September 2007.

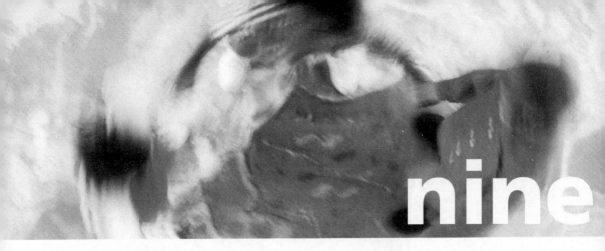

nine

Global pensions policy

Mitchell A. Orenstein

Overview

This chapter provides an overview of global pensions policy and shows that global policy actors have had an increasing influence on country reform decisions. Awareness of the impact of global pensions policy has grown with the rise of a transnational campaign for new pension reforms led by the World Bank since 1994. Through this campaign, the World Bank has successfully supplanted the International Labour Organization as the dominant force in global pensions policy. Case study evidence shows that a World Bank-led coalition of global policy actors has helped to launch and implement the new pension reforms in more than 30 countries worldwide.

Key concepts

Transnational policy campaign; global policy actors; new pension reforms; funded pension systems; pay-as-you-go pension systems; notional defined contribution pension systems

Introduction

As an experiment, ask a classmate, friend, family member, or colleague which organisations and institutions shape pensions policy in your country. You are likely to hear answers such as parliament, government ministers and domestic interest groups including pensioners' associations, trade unions and large employers. It is unlikely that your interviewee will respond with international organisations or other global policy actors. This is because, in the popular consciousness in most countries, pensions policy is a quintessentially national policy domain, influenced primarily by domestic considerations and actors. Yet global policy actors including international organisations, independent policy entrepreneurs, bilateral aid agencies, and the like have played an increasingly important role in shaping pensions policy in countries around the world in recent years.

This chapter provides an overview of **global pensions policy** and shows that it has become increasingly central to decision making in countries around the world. Whereas only a few years ago, social policy scholars would have regarded the idea of global pensions policy as a pipe dream, today it is a reality. Awareness of the impact of global pensions policy has grown with the rise of a transnational campaign for new pension reforms led by the World Bank (WB) since 1994. Through this campaign, the WB has successfully supplanted the International Labour Organization (ILO) as the dominant force in global pensions policy, a position held by the ILO since the end of the Second World War (Charlton and McKinnon, 2002, p 1178; Deacon, 1997). The success of this campaign demonstrates the emergence of a transnational social policy process in pensions, supporting the *cosmopolitan* perspective on global governance outlined by Deacon in Chapter Two of this volume. This chapter provides historical background on the ILO's global pensions policy and the rise of the transnational campaign for the new pension reforms. It demonstrates the extent to which key ideas about pension reform have 'travelled' or diffused internationally (Chapter Three). It shows that **global policy actors** have a major impact on pensions policies of countries in all regions of the world and provides several country examples. This chapter then looks to the future, to emerging debates about the new pension reform trend, and shows why, despite various criticisms and concerns, this trend is likely to continue to define global pensions policy over the next 10 to 20 years.

The new pension reform phenomenon

Awareness of global pensions policy has grown with the dramatic emergence of a transnational policy campaign for new pension reforms led by the WB. This campaign was launched in 1994 with the publication of a major WB report, *Averting the Old Age Crisis* (WB, 1994). This advocated new pension reforms worldwide to cope with an emerging demographic 'crisis' in developed and soon in many developing countries as well: population ageing (see also James, 1998; James and Brooks, 2001). Chapter Eleven in this volume takes up the issue of how population changes come to be constructed as a global social problem, but for the present purposes we just note the WB's use of it in the highly influential 1994 document. While most **pay-as-you-go** or **social security**-type pension systems were established under more favourable demographic conditions, economic development, improved medical care and falling birth rates have reduced the proportion of contributing workers to pension beneficiaries in many countries, particularly in Europe. Many developing countries, including China with its one-child policy, will face these issues in coming years. The pay-as-you-go pension systems common in most countries of the world use current revenues from current workers to pay current pension beneficiaries. As people live longer and have fewer children, pay-as-you-go pension systems suffer from growing fiscal pressure. To support a growing proportion of older persons living longer and longer in retirement, the WB report argues that either payroll tax rates must rise, pension ages increase or benefit levels fall. A fourth possibility introduced in the report is to fully or partially replace pay-as-you-go pension systems with ones based on private, individual, pension savings accounts. Pre-funding seeks to ameliorate the budget crisis of pay-as-you-go systems by providing benefits from an individual's own mandatory (and often state-subsidised or tax-preferred) savings. The new pension reforms are controversial because they revolutionise the structure of pension systems.

The reform model advocated by the WB recommends a 'multipillar' structure for pension provision that includes a redistributive state pension pillar comprising either a minimum flat or means-tested benefit or a reduced pay-as-you-go pension system, a second funded pillar based on privately managed pension savings accounts, and a third voluntary pillar of occupational pensions. In this model, pension systems have two sorts of objectives: to provide a safety net for most older persons and to provide an income-related benefit that enables people to maintain their standard of living in retirement. The WB report argued that private savings accounts are a superior method of providing income-related benefits, since private sector managers can achieve higher rates of return on investment than state social security administrations. Individual accounts, however, cannot provide the redistribution that is often achieved in state pay-as-you-go systems, so must be coupled with some other method to protect those with low earnings or short or interrupted working histories. In addition, the report argued that private pension funds provide an important source of capital for investment in emerging market economies. Creating such funds can spur economic growth and increase standards of living across the board. A further argument for the new pension reforms has been that handing the management of pension funds over to private sector companies relieves beneficiaries from reliance on inefficient and sometimes corrupt state administration. While pay-as-you-go pension systems have been well managed in most developed countries, some developing countries have faced significant problems with the administration of their state-managed systems.

Critics have easily disputed most claims made on behalf of the new pension reforms. First, they have argued that pension funds do not create new capital for investment, since savings in **individual pension funds** are likely to be offset by reductions in government and individual savings in other areas. Thus, the introduction of private, individual accounts merely reallocates savings (Barr and Diamond, 2006, p 30). Second, critics have questioned the high administrative fees typically charged on individual pension savings accounts, arguing that these often substantially reduce investment returns, making these programmes a boon for private investment companies rather than small investors (Minns, 2001; Gill et al, 2005). Third, critics have pointed out that reform of pay-as-you-go pension systems remains a more effective way of achieving the most important pension system objectives (Barr, 2005). Many of these critiques are rooted in the social democratic perspective underpinning the earlier pay-as-you-go model pension systems.

Debates have also focused attention on the roots of these new reforms, spread in part by a transnational coalition of global policy actors as part of a loosely coordinated campaign or what Tarrow (2005) calls a 'campaign coalition'. Scholars analysing the adoption of the new pension reforms in Latin America, central and eastern Europe and elsewhere have become more attuned to the role of global policy actors in social policy. Müller (2003) has argued that global policy actors are more influential in countries with high indebtedness, which makes them more exposed to global policy advice. Madrid (2003) shows that the presence of a WB pension advisory mission makes countries on average 20% more likely to adopt new pension reforms. Weyland (2004) assembled a team of experts to investigate the role of global policy actors in pension and health policy in Latin America, reaching a variety of conclusions (Brooks, 2004; Demarco, 2004; Nelson, 2004; Pinheiro, 2004). Brooks (2005) found little quantitative evidence of international influence on pension policies, but suggested that qualitative research may be better at isolating WB influence. Indeed, many country case studies show the influence of global policy actors in particular countries' pension reforms since the 1990s. In Brazil, global actors introduced notional defined contribution pensions, which introduce individual accounts to a pay-as-you-go system (Pinheiro, 2004). In central and eastern Europe, global policy actors were often the first to put new pension reforms on the policy agenda and spent years supporting policy implementation (Orenstein, 2000). A broad scholarly literature has thus emerged that suggests that global policy actors have taken a major role in pensions policy worldwide, particularly in middle-income developing countries.

Historical background: the ILO and post-war global pensions policy

While interest in global pensions policy has risen recently, the phenomenon is not new (Orenstein, 2003). An effort to create a global pensions policy began towards the end of the Second World War as allied leaders considered ways to better regulate the world economic system with a view towards preventing the outbreak of another war. Political leaders such as US Franklin Delano Roosevelt had become convinced that global depression, inflation and poverty were contributing factors to the rise of Nazism in Germany and other extremist political movements. In order to prevent the outbreak of war in the future, the allies established a set of international financial institutions to better regulate the world economy. A top-level conference in 1943 put the ILO in charge of developing a post-war social policy order. This new social policy encouraged all countries to implement state-administered pensions and unemployment insurance, public health systems and social assistance in the interest of social peace. The ILO's Declaration of Philadelphia became the blueprint for this new global social policy order. The ILO vigorously pursued this agenda worldwide by advising countries on social policy development, organising high-profile regional conferences and spreading this new vision of social policy, including state-managed, pay-as-you-go pension insurance. Prior to the Second World War, countries in Europe, North America and Latin America had already established national pension systems. These were revised according to the new ILO model. After the war, state-managed pay-as-you-go pension systems quickly became standard practice worldwide. ILO dominance of global pensions policy waned with the decline of trade unions in developed western countries and the rise of **neoliberal economic policy** in the 1980s. However, it took a number of years for a serious challenge to the ILO pensions agenda to arise.

The rise of the new pension reforms

The first neoliberal experiment in pensions policy took place in Chile in the early 1980s. Chile, under military dictator General Augusto Pinochet, undertook radical economic reforms led by the so-called 'Chicago boys', a group of young economists trained at leading US universities. The University of Chicago, in particular, had established a training programme for young Chilean economists in the 1950s with US government support that turned out a cadre of neoliberal economists who returned to work at the Catholic

University of Santiago (Valdes, 1995). Pinochet called on these economists to undertake various reforms in Chile, including a pension reform that replaced the previous pay-as-you-go pension system with one based on individual pension savings accounts. The Chilean model of pension reforms became celebrated in neoliberal economic circles. While the Chilean model of pension reforms excited much interest in other countries in Latin America (Brooks, 2004; Weyland, 2004), its association with the Pinochet regime tarnished its reputation in other countries, particularly among the political left.

After a period of poor economic performance in the mid-1980s, Chile's economy began to improve dramatically and other Latin American countries began seriously to consider the new pension reform model in Chile. At the same time, major international organisations like the WB, Inter-American Development Bank (De Oliveira, 1994), United Nations Economic Council for Latin America and others began to support these reforms (Müller, 2003). They were joined by Chilean reformers and **pension fund** managers, who organised international conferences to promote the Chilean reforms and acted as consultants throughout Latin America and beyond (Brooks, 2004). In 1994, the World Bank published *Averting*, signalling its full support for the new pension reform campaign and presenting a new, more flexible template for including private pension savings accounts as part of national pension systems.

Backed by comprehensive research and powerful figures in the international economics community, *Averting* quickly became a template for WB policy advice; its authorship team became the core of WB pension advisory efforts worldwide. *Averting* was commissioned by the then WB chief economist, Larry Summers, and placed under the control of research director Nancy Birdsall. The lead author was economist Estelle James. The WB successfully recruited other organisations as partners in its efforts. In particular, it enjoyed the support of regional development banks such as Inter-American Development Bank and Asian Development Bank. Second, WB developed a strong relationship with the United States Agency for International Development (USAID), the US bilateral aid agency that saw the new pension reforms as part of its fiscal sector reform strategy for central and eastern European transition states (Snelbecker, 2005). The Organisation for Economic Cooperation and Development (OECD) also supported efforts to promote the new pension reforms among and beyond its member states.

Starting in the early 1990s, new pension reforms inspired by the Chilean model and the WB's multipillar model spread to more than 30 countries around the world. Most of these countries have been concentrated in two regions of the world: Latin America and central and eastern Europe (CEE). In Africa, Nigeria became the first adopter in 2004; South Africa was in the process of considering these reforms in 2007 (Republic of South Africa National

Treasury, 2007). Taiwan's adoption of the new pension reforms in 2004 signalled increasing prevalence of these reforms in Asia as well.

Table 9.1 shows all countries worldwide that have adopted the new pension reforms by the end of 2006. It divides these countries' reforms into three categories: substitutive, mixed and parallel. **Substitutive reforms** are those that fully replace social security-type systems with ones based on individual, funded pension savings accounts. In substitutive reforms, the previous pay-as-you-go pension system is phased out; all new labour force entrants make **contributions** to individual pension savings accounts only; and those with accumulated credits under the old system may have the opportunity to switch to the new system and to have their previous contributions credited in some manner. Those nearest to retirement typically stay with the pay-as-you-go system, which is phased out over time. **Mixed reforms**, the most common type in CEE states, partially replace the former social security-type system with individual accounts. Under mixed systems, popular in CEE, participants contribute to both a scaled-down, pay-as-you-go pension system and to an individual account and gain benefits from both systems over time. **Parallel reforms** maintain both systems side by side and allow individuals a choice of which system to participate in. Participants may opt to stay with the pay-as-you-go system or choose to devote some portion of their contribution to an

Table 9.1: *New pension reforms worldwide by type*

Substitutive	Mixed	Parallel
Chile 1981	Sweden 1994	UK 1986
Bolivia 1997	China 1998	Peru 1993
Mexico 1997	Hungary 1998	Argentina 1994
El Salvador 1998	Poland 1999	Colombia 1994
Kazakhstan 1998	Costa Rica 2001	Uruguay 1996
Dominican Republic 2001	Latvia 2001	Estonia 2001
Nicaragua 2001	Bulgaria 2002	Lithuania 2002
Kosovo 2001	Croatia 2002	
Nigeria 2004	Macedonia 2002	
Taiwan 2004	Russia 2002	
	Slovakia 2003	
	Romania 2004	
	Uzbekistan 204	

Sources: Orenstein (2000), Madrid (2003), Müller (2003), Palacios (2003), Fultz (2004), Becker et al (2005), Holzmann and Hinz (2005), Orifowomo (2006) and WB, IDB and USAID websites.

individual pension savings account. Substitutive reforms are often the most radical, while parallel reforms are likely to result in smaller private pension systems.

The new pension reforms spread from Chile first to Latin America and then, with extensive support from global policy actors led by the WB and USAID, to CEE starting in 1998. Britain and Sweden implemented new pension reforms without substantial external policy advice. Many African, Asian and Middle Eastern countries began to seriously consider and adopt new pension reforms in the late 1990s and 2000s, facilitated by the World Bank Institute organising numerous seminars to promote new pension reform ideas (interview with Gustavo Demarco, World Bank Institute, 2004) in these regions. While the new pension reforms had initially been viewed as a regional trend affecting Latin America and CEE, it has recently become clear that this trend has global scope and implications.

Methods of policy diffusion

How have global policy actors helped to spread the new pension reforms to more than 30 countries worldwide? Global policy actors face substantial challenges in influencing state pensions policy, since they do not hold any formal veto power (Tsebelis, 2002) over domestic policy. Therefore, global policy actors are forced to use more indirect methods of influence. These are typically broken down into two broad categories: coercion and persuasion. Coercive methods include loan or membership **conditionalities** that enable global policy actors to create conditions under which a country may or may not gain access to certain resources or opportunities. For instance, international financial institutions often use conditions for the release of loans to influence domestic policy, including that on pensions. Persuasive methods include the exercise of ideational or normative influence by creating new problem definitions, new measures of pension system crisis and new policy solutions, and seek to convince domestic policy makers of the benefits of new ways of looking at things (Barnett and Finnemore, 2004). Persuasion may be particularly effective when global policy actors can rely on like-minded domestic partners (Chwieroth, 2007).

While scholars have debated the relative influence of coercion and persuasion (Kelley, 2004), both methods are often used in combination (Johnson, 2008) and often combine in ways that are difficult to disentangle (Epstein, 2008). This makes Jacoby's (2004) typology of global policy actor **influence mechanisms** particularly relevant (see also Tarrow, 2005). Jacoby finds that global policy actors tend to use four different mechanisms of influence. The first is 'inspiration', in which global policy actors seek to influence state bodies through the development and promotion of reform ideas. The second is 'subsidy', in which global policy actors offer support conditional on the enactment of reform. The third is 'partnership', in which global policy actors support the political fortunes of domestic political allies. The fourth is 'substitution', in which global policy actors seek to enforce their preferred solution without cooperation from domestic actors. Inspiration, subsidy and partnership are common means by which global policy actors have supported the new pension reforms.

Global pension policy advocates have typically used several methods to advance their pension reform agenda. First, they develop pension policy ideas, metrics, problem definitions and solutions. Second, they seek to spread these ideas through publications, conferences and seminars. Third, they identify local partners with whom they can work and provide resources to these actors to advance their agendas. Fourth, they fund government reform teams planning new pension reforms. Fifth, they provide technical assistance to government reform teams. Sixth, they provide long-term assistance with reform implementation. These mechanisms are illustrated in case studies of reform presented below.

Country examples

Kazakhstan exemplifies a case in which the WB and USAID helped to place the new pension reforms on the policy agenda through persuasion of governmental leaders, used loan conditionalities to keep reforms on track and later provided long-term assistance with reform implementation. Kazakhstan began to consider the new pension reforms in 1996, when Central Bank chief Grigori Marchenko attended a WB-sponsored seminar and heard a speech by José Piñera, the Chilean former labour minister and father of the Chilean reforms. Marchenko returned to Almaty resolved to cancel the reform programme he had already begun planning and implement the new pension reforms in Kazakhstan (interview with author, July 1998). He persuaded the President of Kazakhstan to create a reform team to plan the new pension reforms, which completed its work in 1997. With USAID and WB assistance, Kazakhstan prepared reform legislation and led a public relations campaign to sell these reforms to a population sceptical of privatisation and investment companies. The Kazakh parliament approved these reforms under threat of dissolution by the President in 1998. The WB ultimately lent $300 million to Kazakhstan to finance the transition to the new system, while USAID provided extensive technical assistance for the establishment of the pension system over a period of eight years (see Orenstein, 2000).

The case of Hungary also demonstrates the critical role the WB and USAID played in putting the new pension reforms on the agenda and pushing them through despite substantial domestic opposition. Hungary began to consider the new pension reforms in 1995, after socialist Lajos Bokros was appointed Finance Minister and began to pursue a controversial set of liberal economic reforms called the 'Bokros plan'. Bokros appointed a small working group on pension reform to begin work within the Ministry of Finance. This group received substantial financial and intellectual backing from the WB and USAID. It advanced a fully elaborated proposal for the new pension reforms in Hungary in 1996. After a deadlock between the Ministries of Finance and Labour was broken with the appointment of a new Finance Minister, Hungary decided to move ahead with a more limited version of the Ministry of Finance's new pension reform proposals. The WB and USAID again provided tremendous technical and financial support for this project. The WB took the unusual step of seconding two of its top pensions advisers to the inter-ministerial working group on pension reform in Hungary. These advisers engaged in day-to-day discussions about the planning of the new pension reforms with government officials and helped to design a comprehensive strategy for reform adoption in Hungary, including public opinion polls, public relations campaigns, access to top advisers worldwide and help in drafting reform legislation. After a variety of consultations and negotiations with domestic interest groups, the reform was passed in Hungary in 1998. USAID continued to provide support for pension fund regulators in Hungary for many years after the reform (Snelbecker, 2005).

China provides an additional example of the extent of the ideational influence of global policy actors. China reformed its pension system in 1997 under the influence of WB advice. Although the implementation of these reforms has been troubled, with some provincial administrations inadequately or not funding individual accounts (China Economic Research and Advisory Programme, 2005, p 1), China appears to be committed to continuing down the path of the new pension reforms. While China had been considering reforms to its pension system throughout the 1990s, its subsequent development was heavily influenced by a WB report conducted in 1995 and led by Ramgopal Agarwala (Piggott and Bei, 2007, p 15). This report, which advocated a multipillar pension system for China along the lines of *Averting*, was debated by top Chinese policy makers and then adopted in Circular No. 26 of 1997, which created a second, funded pension pillar in China (Piggott and Bei, 2007, p 19). While China has also taken advice from a variety of other global policy actors, including the ILO, the influence of the WB has been paramount. The Asian Development Bank has supported the development of a multipillar pension model in China by funding a pilot programme for funded pension systems in Liaoning in 2001 (Piggott and Bei, 2007, p 13). While China has clearly taken its own decisions on the future shape of social security, its thinking has been shaped by the WB. Progress on further reforms and reform implementation has occurred with the assistance of a variety of global policy actors working as part of a coordinated campaign.

Peru was the first Latin American country to follow Chile in adopting the new pension reforms. Peru's adoption of its reform decree in December 1992, prior to the publication of *Averting*, has sometimes been seen as evidence that the new pension reform trend took place without the assistance of global policy actors. However, Chilean economic advisers, particularly Chilean former labour minister José Piñera, were deeply influential in Peru. Piñera is credited with convincing Peruvian President Alberto Fujimori to adopt the new pension reform decree (Rofman, 2007, p 3). Because of the strong influence of the Chilean model, the Peruvian reforms were similar in many ways, although workers were allowed to continue to opt into the state system if they preferred. Peru's pension system suffers from a low rate of coverage, below 12% of the total labour force. The WB was not involved in the design of the pension system in Peru. However, it did help to support pension system work in Peru through a 1992 **Structural Adjustment Loan** and a 1992 **Financial Sector Adjustment Loan**. A 1996 Pension Reform Adjustment Loan was a vehicle for persuading Peru to adopt some important adjustments to its pension system, creating more monitoring, auditing and equal treatment of workers in both pension systems (Rofman, 2007, p 10). The Peruvian experience shows that even in the small number of developing countries in Latin America that considered reform prior to 1994, the WB played an important supporting role in reform implementation and redesign.

Limits of global pensions policy

While the preceding sections have argued that global policy actors have been highly influential in spreading the new pension reform trend to more than 30 countries worldwide, it is clear that this influence has its limits. This section considers three cases that demonstrate the limits of global policy actor influence and the continuing importance of domestic political factors in the design of pension systems.

Brazil has sometimes been used as an example of the limits of global policy actor influence on pension reforms (Weyland, 2005). Although it considered adopting the new pension reforms promoted by the WB, it decided instead to adopt a **notional defined contribution** (NDC) system that continues pay-as-you-go financing but accounts for benefits via 'notional' individual accounts. This innovation in pension system design was first adopted in Sweden in 1994. It has three functions: first, it links benefits closely to contributions; second, it provides transparency to beneficiaries, who can examine their individual accounts; and third, it discourages governments from over-promising future benefits. Individual accounts are generally paid an interest rate that corresponds to the overall growth in contributions and thus to average wages. Brazil had come under considerable pressure from the WB and other global policy actors to adopt the new pension reforms based on the multipillar system. The WB had started to work on pension reform in Brazil in 1997. By that time, the government was already immersed in a controversial debate over whether to change the pension system benefit formula contained in the Brazilian constitution (Pinheiro, 2004, p 128). In 1997, the Brazilian government set up a working group to discuss more radical pension reforms and considered the WB model. The international financial crisis of 1997-98 made it difficult for Brazil to finance the transition to a new pension reform system. The government concluded that private accounts would over-burden the country's finances and decided instead on an NDC reform in 1999, based on ideas 'disseminated in courses and seminars organised by the World Bank with the participation of Brazilian technical staff' (Pinheiro, 2004, p 135). This reform received the support of the IMF, WB and IDB (Melo, 2004).

The experience of Brazil shows that countries do not always adopt the preferred solutions advocated by the World Bank-led coalition of global policy actors. It also shows that global policy actors can be sensitive to country conditions and when it is not possible for them to achieve their first-choice option, they will consider other options. The WB considers NDC pension systems to be a step towards individual pension savings accounts, since NDC accounts establish the information systems for individual contributions and can be converted to funded accounts. Two other cases, however, show that the WB-led coalition for new pension reforms has experienced at least two outright failures to influence country pension policy: in Slovenia and Korea, high-level domestic political opposition succeeded in preventing the reforms. Another case not discussed here is Venezuela, which appears to have followed the same pattern. In all three cases, global policy actors organised powerful campaigns for the implementation of the new pension reforms that were successfully resisted by the domestic political leaders. This suggests that both global policy actors and willing domestic partners are necessary to the adoption of new pension reforms.

In Slovenia, the WB was deeply involved in reform discussions with the government, but failed to enact reforms, including individual private pension savings accounts. While Minister of Labour Tone Rop was initially highly committed to the new pension ideas (interview with Dusan Kidric, Slovenian Ministry of Economic Relations, 11 May 1998), the government ultimately stepped back from its plans to switch to a new pension reform system (Stanovnik, 2002, p 49). To some extent, this reflected opposing advice given by the global policy actors and to some extent the threat of domestic labour mobilisation and criticisms voiced by the Slovenian Ministry of Finance (Stanovnik 2002, p 57). In the mid-1990s, the WB was deeply involved in supporting Tone Rop in the development of a government White Paper that would outline a new pension reform system for Slovenia. The WB supported the new pension reforms in Slovenia in a number of ways. It provided funding for reform preparation and sponsored a major conference in Ljubljana in October 1997 to discuss the White Paper, published in November 1997. It also sent Slovenian members of parliament to Switzerland and the Netherlands to study private pension funds. Other global policy actors opposed the implementation of new pension reforms in Slovenia, especially a team of French consultants supported by EU PHARE, who represented more traditional continental European approaches to pension system design (Stanovnik, 2002, pp 42-5). Italian officials also warned against the new pension reforms for political reasons; Italy had experienced major protests that brought reforms to a halt a few years before. Opposition to the new pension reforms also came from leading Slovene pension experts, the Minister of Finance and the Free Trade Unions of Slovenia, which organised several demonstrations against the pension reform plans in early 1998 (Stanovnik, 2002, pp 48-9; interview with Dusan Semolic, Free Trade Unions of Slovenia, 13 May 1998). Ultimately, lead reformer Tone Rop dropped the idea of individual private accounts in response to this opposition.

Korea is another example of extensive global policy actor intervention but no reform. Yang (2004, pp 197-8) shows that new pension reform ideas were proposed by Korean government officials in 1995-96 under the government of Kim Young Sam and laid out in a Public Pension Development Plan published in 1996. The Public Pension Development Plan called for a low basic pension for the poor and a large funded system on the model of the UK. This plan was opposed by social policy bureaucrats from the Ministry of Health and Welfare and National Pension Corporation. The government attempted to mediate the dispute through the National Council for Social Security, chaired by the Prime Minister. The council ultimately backed the original Public Pension Development Plan. However, in 1997 Korea was in the throes of a major financial crisis and elections in December 1997 brought veteran democratic dissident Kim Dae Jung to the presidency. Kim Dae Jung opposed the new pension reforms (Yang, 2004, p 199). The WB intervened with a $2 billion structural adjustment loan and tried to influence the pension reform debate in Korea. It demanded that a government-wide task force draft a White Paper on pension reform that would include a basic and earnings-related component with a funded, privately managed component (Yang, 2004, p 201). The government created a Pension Reform Task Force in December 1998, but dragged its feet on the new pension reforms, which have yet to be implemented. The Korean case is interesting because it shows that domestic leaders have the power to resist the most extreme leverage applied by global policy actors (Yang, 2004, p 202). Pension reform debates continued in Korea in

2003-05, with different parties and the government offering different proposals for reform. The WB and OECD supported a **funded pension plan** system, while the ILO supported reform of the existing system. Mandatory, individual accounts (**mandatory personal pension plans**) still do not figure highly in the programmes of domestic political actors in Korea (Chong-Bum, 2005).

This section has shown that despite the tremendous leverage and authority exercised by global policy actors, domestic actors still retain a veto power over pension reform and can effectively resist reform pressures under certain circumstances. However, the relatively small number of cases where global policy actors have unleashed a major campaign for new pension reforms and failed to enact reform suggests that their influence is not often resisted.

Emerging debates in global pensions policy

While a WB-led coalition of global policy actors has supported the new pension reforms in countries around the world, it would be a mistake to emphasise cooperation and ignore the conflicts that can exist between global pensions policy actors. The World Bank-led coalition has continually faced confrontations with the ILO in transnational and national policy forums. While the WB has strongly advocated the new pension reforms, the ILO has continued to back reform of pay-as-you-go pension systems as the best way forward for most countries. In recent years, the ILO has been forced to accede that funded pension systems can be a legitimate part of country pension systems (Gillion et al, 2000). However, it has continued to criticise these reforms in most specific country circumstances. In 2004, the ILO's CEE office issued a report that stated that new pension funds in CEE countries were earning either negative rates of return or rates lower than those for simple bank deposits (Fultz, 2004).

Debates have also occurred within the WB. Chief Economist Joseph Stiglitz famously opposed the WB's work on pension reform and organised a conference in 1999 to present his paper on '10 myths' of pension system design (Orszag and Stiglitz, 2001). In 2005 and 2006, three books published by the WB took aim at aspects of the Bank's work on the new pension reforms. Gill et al (2005) criticised the high fees charged in Latin American pension savings accounts and questioned whether the new pension reforms had been adequately designed. Barr (2005) advocated reforms to pay-as-you-go pension systems rather than the introduction of funded individual accounts. The WB's Independent Evaluation Group (WB, 2006) also issued a report critical of the Bank's pension work, suggesting that it had foisted the new pension reforms on countries with insufficient financial and administrative preconditions, creating potential for disaster.

As a result, neither the WB nor other global policy actors should be regarded as monoliths connected with a stable, single-policy approach. Rather, global policy actors are sites of contestation between different contending approaches and often contain individuals with conflicting views (see also Chapter Two). These may be expressed simultaneously or the policies of organisations may change over time in response to external pressures and internal policy debates. Nonetheless, the WB has not substantially changed its approach to the new pension reforms as a result of these internal debates. Opponents of these reforms within the Bank have so far lost the political battles to control Bank policy. Holzmann and Hinz (2005) both refute and take on board some of the criticisms levelled at the WB's work, and argue for a more flexible strategy that nonetheless continues the main lines of the WB's previous approach and its strong advocacy of the new pension reforms.

A bottom-up perspective

Although the policy process for the diffusion of the new pension reforms has been mostly top-down, a bottom-up perspective helps to understand the formulation of global pensions policy. While social movements, non-governmental organisations and other social actors have been deeply involved in national pensions debates, they have been notably absent from cross-border discourse in this area. Since the impact of pension reforms is perceived to be national in scope, social actors have typically confined their activity to the national context. The only major exception is the role of individual experts and epistemic communities (see Chapters One and Three of this volume). New pension reform ideas were developed first by independent academics and expert communities before being exported to Chile and elsewhere in the world. Independent experts eventually won opportunities to work in pioneering reform countries and to help define the world of leading global policy actors such as the WB and ILO. This suggests that bottom-up influences can be important in setting global policy agendas (although the anti-land-mine campaign is perhaps a better example of this). But under what conditions can social movements define global actor policies? This constitutes an important topic for comparative policy research. The experience of global pensions policy suggests that such opportunities are available, but that only a small number of organisations have the resources and inclination to undertake global policy campaigns.

Conclusion

In Chapter Two of this volume, Deacon notes that the WB-led social agenda has faced growing attacks in recent years from what he calls the radical right, the radical left and the radical South. While observers have questioned the durability of the new pension reform trend in the face of emerging criticisms of the benefits of these policies in some of the countries where they have been implemented, this chapter ventures to predict that the trend towards the new pension reforms will continue to define global pensions policy in the next 10 to 20 years. First, the coalition campaign for the new pension reforms remains intact, despite internal and external debates. Second, in the past few years, the first African country (Nigeria) and another leading Asian economy (Taiwan) have adopted the new pension reforms. Since countries often learn from their neighbours through a process of social learning that may be facilitated by global policy actors, we can expect to see this reform trend spread in Africa, the Middle East and Asia in coming years. Third, developing countries have continued to explore the possibilities of implementing the new pension reforms. Fourth, while the new pension reforms were rejected in the US in 2005 and in several other developed OECD countries, they remain on the policy agenda and cannot be discounted. Should any additional developed countries adopt the new pension reforms, this will have a substantial influence on the rest of the world.

Summary

- Global policy actors have a renewed importance in setting pensions policy in countries around the world.
- The campaign for the new pension reforms is a good example of what authors such as Woods (2006) and Deacon (Chapter Two) call a global governance network or coalition.
- While global pensions policy originated with the ILO after the Second World War, the new pension reform campaign of the WB has replaced ILO dominance over global pensions policy and sparked a growing awareness of the international influences on pension system design.
- Evidence presented here has shown that global policy actors have exerted effective influence over country reform adoption in Europe, Asia and Latin America. The first cases in Africa are starting to appear.
- Global policy actors use a mix of influence mechanisms to achieve their goals, including norms creation, persuasion and economic incentives. While global policy actor influence has its limits and these reforms require willing domestic partners in order to proceed, global policy actors have been a determining factor in the spread of new pension reforms to more than 30 countries worldwide.
- While some analysts have questioned whether emerging debates about the costs and benefits of the new pension reforms will slow down or halt this reform trend, this chapter suggests that the new pension reform trend will continue to shape global pensions policy over the next 10 to 20 years. Seminars

and conferences have introduced policy makers from countries around the world to new pension reform ideas and the adoption of these reforms by influential model countries in Asia and Africa suggest that the reform trend will continue by mechanisms of social learning.

Questions for discussion

- What are the new pension reforms and how do they differ from pay-as-you-go pension systems?
- Are domestic politics and economics or global policy actor influence more important in explaining the adoption of the new pension reforms?
- Will concerns about the impacts of the new pension reforms be sufficient to stop the further spread of these reforms? Why or why not?

Further reading

Brooks (2005) and Müller (2003) are recommended if you wish to follow up the issues explored in this chapter. For further reading on the ways that policy ideas 'travel' around the world, see Weyland (2005).

Electronic resources

www.worldbank.org/pensions World Bank Pensions
www.oecd.org/department/0,2688,en_2649_34853_1_1_1_1_1,00.html
OECD Private Pensions
**www.ilo.org/public/english/protection/secsoc/areas/policy/pensions.
htm** ILO Social Security Department

References

Barnett, M. and Finnemore, M. (2004) *Rules for the World: International Organizations in Global Politics*, Ithaca, NY: Cornell University Press.

Barr, N. (ed) (2005) *Labor Markets and Social Policy in Central and Eastern Europe: The Accession and Beyond*, Washington, DC: World Bank.

Barr, N. and Diamond, P (2006) 'The economics of pensions', *Oxford Review of Economic Policy*, vol 22, no 1, pp 15-39.

Becker, C.M., Seitenova, A.-G.S., Urzhumova, D.S. (2005) *Pension Reform in Central Asia: An Overview*, PIE Discussion Paper Series, Tokyo: Hitotsubashi University.

Brooks, S.M. (2004) 'International financial institutions and the diffusion of foreign models for social security reform in Latin America', in K. Weyland (ed) *Learning from Foreign Models in Latin American Policy Reform*, Washington, DC and Baltimore, MD: Woodrow Wilson Center and Johns Hopkins University Press.

Brooks, S.M. (2005) 'Interdependent and domestic foundations of policy change: the diffusion of pension privatization around the world', *International Studies Quarterly*, vol 49, no 2, pp 273-94.

Charlton, R. and McKinnon, R. (2002) 'International organizations, pension system reform and alternative agendas: bringing older people back in?', *Journal of International Development*, vol 14, no 8, pp 1175-86.

China Economic Research and Advisory Programme (2005) 'Social security reform in China: issues and options', Unpublished manuscript, http://econ.lse.ac.uk/staff/nb/Barr_SocialSecurityStudy2005.pdf, accessed 29 May 2007.

Chong-Bum, A. (2005) 'Implications of efforts to reform the national pension system', *Korean Association of Applied Economics,* vol 7, no 2, www.koreafocus.or.kr/

Chwieroth, J. (2007) 'Neoliberal economists and capital account liberalization in emerging markets', *International Organization*, vol 61, no 2, pp 443-63.

De Oliveira, F. (ed) (1994) *Social Security Systems in Latin America*, Washington, DC: Inter-American Development Bank.

Deacon, B. 1(997) *Global Social Policy: International Organizations and the Future of Welfare*, London: Sage Publications.

Demarco, G. (2004) 'The Argentine pension system reform and international lessons', in Kurt Weyland (ed) *Learning from Foreign Models in Latin American Policy Reform*, Washington, DC and Baltimore, MD: Woodrow Wilson Center and Johns Hopkins University Press.

Epstein, R. (2008) 'Transnational actors and bank privatization', In M.A. Orenstein, S. Bloom and N. Lindstrom (eds) *Transnational Actors in Central and East European Transitions*, Pittsburgh, PA: University of Pittsburgh Press.

Fultz, E. (2004) 'Pension reform in the EU accession countries: challenges, achievements, and pitfalls', *International Social Security Review*, vol 57, no 2, pp 3-24.

Gill, I.S., Packard, T. and Yermo, J. (2005) *Keeping the Promise of Social Security in Latin America*, Washington, DC and Stanford, CA: World Bank and Stanford University Press.

Gillion, C., Turner, J., Bailey, C. and Latulippe, D. (eds) (2000) *Social Security Pensions: Development and Reform*, Geneva: International Labour Office.

Holzmann, R. and Hinz, R. (2005) *Old Age Income Support in the 21st Century: An International Perspective on Pension Systems and Reform*, Washington, DC: World Bank.

Jacoby, W. (2004) *The Enlargement of the European Union and NATO: Ordering from the Menu in Central Europe*, Cambridge: Cambridge University Press.

James, E. (1998) 'The political economy of social security reform: a cross-country review', *Annals of Public and Comparative Economics*, vol 69, no 4, pp 451-82.

James, E. and Brooks, S.M. (2001) 'The political economy of structural pension reform', in R. Holzmann and J.E. Stiglitz (eds) *New Ideas about Old Age Security: Toward Sustainable Pension Systems in the 21st Century*, Washington, DC: World Bank.

Johnson, J. (2008) *Two-track Diffusion and Central Bank Embeddedness: The Politics of Euro Adoption in Hungary and the Czech Republic*, in M.A. Orenstein, S. Bloom and N. Lindstrom (eds) *Transnational Actors in Central and East European Transitions*, Pittsburgh, PA: University of Pittsburgh Press.

Kelley, J. (2004) *Ethnic Politics in Europe: The Power of Norms and Incentives*, Princeton, NJ: Princeton University Press.

Madrid, R.L. (2003) *Retiring the State: The Politics of Pension Privatization in Latin America and Beyond*, Stanford, CA: Stanford University Press.

Melo, M.A. (2004) 'Institutional choice and the diffusion of policy paradigms: Brazil and the second wave of pension reform', *International Political Science Review*, vol 25, no 3, pp 320-41.

Minns, R. (2001) *The Cold War in Welfare: Stock Markets Versus Pensions*, London: Verso.

Müller, K. (2003) *Privatising Old-age Security: Latin America and Eastern Europe Compared*, Aldershot, UK: Edward Elgar.

Nelson, J.M. (2004) 'External models, international influence, and the politics of social sector reforms', in K. Weyland (ed) *Learning from Foreign Models in Latin American Policy Reform*, Washington, DC and Baltimore, MD: Woodrow Wilson Center and Johns Hopkins University Press.

Orenstein, M.A. (2000) *How Politics and Institutions Affect Pension Reform in Three Postcommunist Countries*, World Bank Policy Research Working Paper 2310, Washington, DC: World Bank.

Orenstein, M.A.(2003) 'Mapping the diffusion of pension innovation', in R. Holzmann, M. Orenstein and M. Rutkowski (eds) *Pension Reform in Europe: Process and Progress*, Washington, DC: World Bank.

Orifowomo, O.A. (2006) 'A critical appraisal of pension system reforms in Nigeria', *Gonzaga Journal of International Law*, vol 10, no 2, pp 164-201.

Orszag, P.R. and Stiglitz, J.E. (2001) 'Rethinking pension reform: ten myths about social security systems', in R. Holzmann and J.E. Stiglitz (eds) *New Ideas About Old Age Security: Toward Sustainable Pension Systems in the 21st Century*, Washington, DC: World Bank.

Palacios, R. (2003) *Pension Reform in the Dominican Republic*, Social Protection Discussion Paper 0326, Washington, DC: World Bank.

Piggott, J. and Bei, L. (2007) *Pension Reform and the Development of Pension Systems: An Evaluation of World Bank Assistance*, Background Paper: China Country Study, Washington, DC: Independent Evaluation Group, World Bank.

Pinheiro, V.C. (2004) 'The politics of social security reform in Brazil', in K. Weyland (ed) *Learning from Foreign Models in Latin American Policy Reform*, Washington, DC and Baltimore, MD: Woodrow Wilson Center and Johns Hopkins University Press.

Republic of South Africa National Treasury (2007) *South Security and Retirement Reform: Second Discussion Paper*, Pretoria: Republic of South Africa.

Rofman, R. (2007) *Pension Reform and the Development of Pension Systems: An Evaluation of World Bank Assistance*, Background Paper: Peru Country Study, Washington, DC: Independent Evaluation Group, World Bank.

Snelbecker, D. (2005) 'Pension reform in Eastern Europe and Eurasia: experiences and lessons learned', Paper prepared for USAID Workshop for Practitioners on Tax and Pension Reform, Washington, DC, June 27-29.

Stanovnik, T. (2002) 'The political economy of pension reform in Slovenia', in Elaine Fultz (ed) *Pension Reform in Central and Eastern Europe, vol 2*, Budapest: International Labour Office, Central and Eastern European Team, pp 19-73.

Tarrow, S. (2005) The New Transnational Activism. Cambridge: Cambridge University Press.

Tsebelis, G. (2002) *Veto Players: How Political Institutions Work*, New York, NY and Princeton, NJ: Russell Sage Foundation and Princeton University Press.

Valdes, J.G. (1995) *Pinochet's Economists: The Chicago School in Chile*, Cambridge: Cambridge University Press.

Weyland, K. (2004) 'Learning from foreign models in Latin American policy reform: an introduction', in K. Weyland (ed) *Learning from Foreign Models in Latin American Policy Reform*, Washington, DC and Baltimore, MD: Woodrow Wilson Center and Johns Hopkins University Press.

Weyland, K. (2005) 'Theories of policy diffusion: lessons from Latin American pension reform', *World Politics*, vol 57, no 2, pp 262-95.

Woods, N. (2006) *The Globalizers: The IMF, the World Bank and their Borrowers*, Ithaca, NY: Cornell University Press.

WB (World Bank) (1994) *Averting the Old Age Crisis: Policies to Protect the Old and Promote Growth*, Oxford: Oxford University Press.

WB (2006) *Pension Reform and the Development of Pension Systems: An Evaluation of World Bank Assistance*, Independent Evaluation Group Report, Washington, DC: WB.

Yang, J-j. (2004) 'Democratic governance and bureaucratic politics: a case of pension reform in Korea', *Policy & Politics, vol* 32, no 2, pp 193-206.

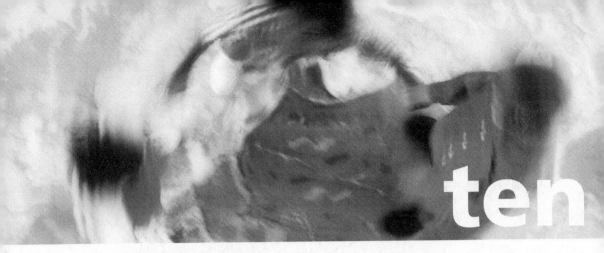

Global migration policy

Nicola Yeates

Overview

This chapter provides an overview of global migration policy debates and responses as they pertain to social policy and welfare provision. It argues that global migrations expand the realm of global social policy and analysis in several important ways: by introducing non-elitist and non-institutional realms in which global social transformations, global social policy formation and global actors operate; by attending to 'bottom-up' processes of globalisation by foregrounding migrants as global policy actors; and by highlighting the role of transnational advocacy networks in global social policy formation. The chapter relates international migration trends and policy responses to issues of citizenship, social equity and development on a global scale. It reviews the policy approaches of key international organisations to international migration issues and highlights concerns arising from attempts to construct a multilateral migration regime.

Key concepts

Cosmopolitan citizenship; household internationalisation strategies; transnational social welfare; global care chains; managed migration; multilateral migration regime

Introduction

The movement of peoples across state borders is one of the oldest forms of global flow, long pre-existing the kinds of processes and conditions often associated with 'globalisation'. To the extent that such movements are placed in an historical context, many western histories of international migration begin somewhere around the 19th century, but for as long as people have existed they have migrated, whether for personal safety, trade purposes, economic security, religious or political freedom – or simply a better climate. For most of history, this migration was unrestricted; it was only from the end of the 19th century that states imposed formal border controls, through the introduction of passports and visas that limited who was permitted to enter or leave national territories. These restrictions on international population movements were part of the process of nation and welfare state building.

Nationalist conceptions of citizenship were central to the making of national communities, with social, civil and political rights and entitlements forging a distinction between members (nationals) of the nation state and non-members (foreigners). In many respects, similar processes are reproduced on a transnational scale. In the creation of a European political community, not just a Social Europe but also a Fortress Europe has been constructed, with non-EU citizens from poorer countries in particular being restricted from entering its member states. Other regional concentrations of economic wealth – such as South-East Asia and North America – also maintain highly controlled access regimes for non-nationals. These continued delineations between peoples of particular national origin sit uneasily in the context of global human rights declarations that assert the right to human dignity and equality irrespective of national or social origin.

This chapter examines the global dimensions of migration together with the role of global actors and policies in shaping responses to it. It explores the different ways in which population movement relates to contemporary global dynamism and global social policy debates. It also examines social protection and welfare issues arising from the emerging global governance of migration and efforts to construct a coherent **global migration regime**.

In keeping with the tenets of **methodological transnationalism** (Chapter One), the focus of discussion lies with the relations between people and places around the world that are forged by international migration together with the processes and systems that both enable and result from these global social relations. It relates these processes to the concept of **global social reproduction**. A key element of this discussion involves the notion of **cosmopolitan citizenship** that does not limit social rights and entitlements only to those born or long-term resident in a particular country.

We begin by providing a brief overview of international migration to provide some overall context, before turning to explore how migration processes are embroiled in the globalisation of the economy and in the globalisation of social care and welfare provision. The chapter then moves on to address the policy agendas of different international organisations with regard to international migration and various attempts to construct a more coherent global regulatory and rights regime governing international migration. The focus of the chapter lies specifically with labour migration, both skilled and unskilled, and its entanglements with social policy and provision. Political migration – asylum seeking and refugees – lies outside the scope of this chapter.

Global migration flows

From the headlines and stories in the mainstream media and the seemingly endless flurry of policies and measures to better 'manage' migration and migrants, many would be forgiven for thinking that the volume of people moving from their country of birth to other countries to live, work or study is phenomenally high. In many respects, the figures are impressive. According to the International Organization on Migration (IOM, 2005):

- There were an estimated 191 million migrants worldwide in 2005, up from 175 million in 2000 and 76 million in 1960;
- The top three sending countries are Asian: China (estimated **diaspora** of 35 million people), India (20 million people) and the Philippines (7 million people);
- In 2005, there were roughly 30 to 40 million unauthorised migrants worldwide, comprising around 15% to 20% of the world's immigrant stock.

But we need to contextualise this apparent growth:

- **International migrants** comprise just 3% of the global population (IOM, 2005); thus, 97% of people stay in their country of birth. Of those who do emigrate, many international migrants stay within their 'home' region. For example, by the mid-1990s, some three million Asians were employed outside their own country but within the Asian region, while a further three million were working outside the Asian continent (Castles, 1998).
- No novelty can be claimed for international migration, a process as old as human history itself. As Cohen (1997) notes, 'the earliest diasporas precede the age of globalisation by 2,500 years' (p 175). Indeed, the current phase of migration is not that in which international migration has been highest: the levels of international migration had at the turn of the 21st century

reached those of the 1920s, but were still far below that recorded before the First World War (Hirst and Thompson, 1996).

• International migration is dwarfed by the scale of internal (rural to urban) migration prompted by agricultural restructuring, 'depeasantisation' and urbanisation resulting from ongoing transformations of national and global economies since the early 1970s (Araghi, 1995). Indeed, the greatest population movement currently under way is happening within the borders of one country, China, where recent calculations estimate that 140 million people are on the move, driven from the land by the market system and drawn to the cities by the prospect of work in world factories.

We also need to look at how these global flows of people are patterned. The traditional receiving countries are predominantly located in the west – Australia, Canada, the US and New Zealand – although these have more recently been joined by countries in western Europe, notably Ireland, Italy, Norway and Portugal. Virtually the entire growth in international migrant stocks during the 1990s was absorbed by 'developed' countries, in particular the US, Europe and Australia, and most regions of the world have experienced a decrease in their share of the global migrant stock (IOM, 2005). International migrants are therefore increasingly concentrated in a small number of countries (75% of all international migrants are in 12% of all countries). *Table 10.1* shows that Europe, Asia and North America have the most substantial populations of overseas migrants, although, as a proportion of the area's population, Oceania and North America have by far the most significant migrant populations (column 3). *Figures 10.1 and 10.2* visually portray the ways in which many richer parts of the world are experiencing **net immigration** and many poorer parts of it are experiencing **net emigration**. These maps adjust actual territory size according to the relative levels of net immigration and emigration in all territories.

Table 10.1: Migrant population, 2005

Geographic area	Migrants (millions)	Percentage of the area's population
Europe	64.1	8.8
Asia	53.3	1.4
North America	44.5	13.5
Africa	17.1	1.9
Latin America	6.7	1.2
Oceania	5.0	15.2

Source: IOM (2005)

Figure 10.1 Net immigration map

© SASI Group, University of Sheffield)/Mark Newman, University of Michigan (2006)
(www.worldmapper.org/)

Figure 10.2 Net emigration map

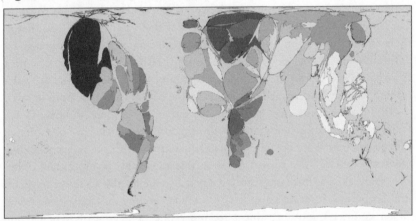

© SASI Group, University of Sheffield)/Mark Newman, University of Michigan (2006)
(www.worldmapper.org/)

There are many reasons for this apparent increase in international migration. One relates to the geo-political context: a large share of the increased migration from 1990 especially is attributed to changing state borders rather than greater movements of people. In particular, the disintegration of the Soviet Bloc has meant that people are now classified as international migrants whereas previously they would have been internal migrants. A further reason is the extent of conflict in the world, with millions of people being displaced by repression, war, and terror. A third factor propelling international migration is uneven development, inequality and poverty. The general direction of international migration is from poorer countries to richer countries, whether these be in the same region in which people already live, or further afield, to the west. Economic restructuring and the removal of a range of social protections leave many with little choice but to move from where they were born, often initially from rural to urban areas before moving abroad, in search of economic opportunity and security not otherwise (or no longer) available to them. A fourth reason is the emergence of cheaper and more accessible transport and communications technologies that enable people to travel further in shorter time periods and maintain contact with their 'home' country while living abroad.

It is clear that international migrants are part of global processes through their own strategies to relocate themselves geographically over long distances, often in response to wider global economic change. It is also clear that they are both advantaged and disadvantaged by the kinds of global changes taking place. On the one hand, changes in the global economy and the development of international labour markets create new possibilities for personal adventure, increased income, and educational, skills and career advancement. Those who are prepared to move overseas and have (or can access) the means to do so can take advantage of these opportunities for their own benefit and that of their families and communities. In this account, international migrants are entrepreneurs in the 'new' global economy, responding to opportunities, moving where labour is needed, and reaping the benefits from it. Such migrations may be regarded as a key example of 'globalisation from below'.

On the other hand, most people would rather stay in their country of birth and much international migration is involuntary – they may have been drawn into people trafficking operations, for example, be fleeing from political conflict (civil war and/or state terror) or be unable to survive economically unless they emigrate. Far from constituting a privileged elite able to freely travel on diplomatic or corporate 'passports', most face extreme difficulty in accessing richer countries and are subject to uncertainty and controls when living there. Many enter global circuits of 'invisible', precarious and hazardous work – whether in global factories, agriculture and mariculture, or servicing the personal and intimacy needs of the rich and other local populations. In many ways, international migration heralds the 'globalisation' of servitude (Sassen, 2000; Parreñas, 2001), with the denial of dignity and entitlements that many people take for granted.

Finally, migration can be seen as another form of international trade – a trade in human beings. It can be seen as another of the global flows associated with the growth in international trade and commerce, a global flow of people, which adds another aspect to concerns over the connections between international trade and welfare (see Chapter Five).

Transnational social welfare: cash and care

If a focus on international migration opens up the possibility of seeing migrants as global actors in a way that is often overlooked in global policy studies, household internationalisation strategies also reveal the globalisation of families, communities and the informal sector. The kinds of **household internationalisation strategy** associated with international migration result in **globalised families** or **transnational families**, whose members may reside in different countries but which sustain active, regular links and connections with one another, often across large geographical distances. These connections, assisted by travel and communications technologies (television, internet, radio, email, text messaging), reproduce the family bond and cultural contact despite the vast distances involved, forging and sustaining 'multi-stranded' social relations that link societies of origin and settlement (Basch et al, 1994). International migration has also given rise to transnational communities and global diasporas. Although less visible actors than transnational corporations, such communities are essential to understanding how the 'real' economy works. As Cohen notes:

> ... traders place orders with cousins, siblings and kin 'back home';
> nieces and nephews from 'the old country' stay with uncles and
> aunts while acquiring their education or vocational training; loans
> are advanced and credit is extended to trusted intimates; and jobs
> and economically advantageous marriages are found for family
> members ... [By] being attached to a strong and tightly integrated
> diaspora, family- and kin-based economic transactions are made
> easier and safer. (Cohen, 1997, p 160)

Migrant remittances illustrate particular aspects of these transnational social relations. Remittance flows are estimated to have exceeded US $276 billion worldwide in 2006, of which US $206 billion went to developing countries (IOM, 2005). The inclusion of informal or undeclared remittances increases this amount very substantially. Migrant remittances are a key financial flow, crucial to the maintenance of transnational familial and community relations and, moreover, constitute a source of international welfare financing. They are used to meet basic health and welfare needs (enabling the purchase of food and medicine, payment of school fees and house repairs) and support family businesses. Diasporic communities mobilise funds in support of the economic and social welfare of communities at home – be it through raising funds for community health, education and welfare projects, local enterprise initiatives or the purchasing of land for house building in the area. The Indian state of Kerala is internationally renowned for a relatively high quality of life, which is substantially attributed to the remittances sent back from generations of Keralese overseas contract workers. Disaporic communities are also important in raising funds at times of humanitarian disaster in the 'home' country, supplementing international relief efforts by non-governmental organisations (NGOs) and governments. Migrant remittances are a key source of external revenue for governments in the country of origin. In some cases, they may be one of the few sources of foreign currency for some countries, exceeding the value of exports and overseas development aid (Faini, 2002). Because of the remittances it generates, migrant labour is central to the international politics of debt.

In many ways, international migration and the global families it forges reveal the transnational dimensions to the social organisation and relations of cash and care, and represent one aspect of **global social reproduction**. Transnational welfare, like national forms of welfare, is strongly gendered, with feminist scholars pointing to the relationship between international migration, family care giving and the involvement of women. At one level, informal (familial) care giving constitutes one of the main means by which international migration is enabled and sustained. Migration decisions, processes and practices are ones in which female agency is generally attributed a decisive role. It is the 'motherly' care labour that women provide to children and elders in their capacity as family members, friends or neighbours that enables and sustains household internationalisation strategies (Kanaiaupuni, 2000). At another level, international migration transforms organisational arrangements, relations and practices of informal (family) care giving. In addition to financial support, emigrants provide care through the sending of 'care packages' and emotional support through the exchange of letters, photos, phone calls, text messages, email and videos(Parreñas, 2001, 2005).

While much research in this field centres on the ways in which emigrant parents – mothers in particular – provide care for their children 'left behind' in the home country, attention also focuses on such care-giving practices for other family members. In her study of care-giving practices of migrants for their elderly parents, Baldock (2000) argues that while migrants are not available to assist with daily care tasks and activities, they provide emotional and practical support from afar through the provision of health advice and assistance in the organisation of finances. They also remain involved in daily care activities (and major decisions about care) provided to the parent/relative in the home country. Return visits (during paid leave or holiday leave) are used to provide practical support to siblings by providing respite care. Whether the subject of care is young or elderly, emigration does not close down migrants' roles or identities as carers; instead, it transforms them into 'distant carers' who are incorporated into informal care provision that relies on family, neighbours and friends living in close vicinity to the elderly parent or child. The role of grandparents is also emphasised, with parents circulating between different adult children who have emigrated to different countries. Often staying with them for extended periods of time, they assist with childcare. In Spain, such people are known as 'swallow grandparents' (Escrivá, 2004, p 14).

Transnational families and care practices are not historically new phenomena. Historical research shows that the raising of emigrants' children has often been a collective endeavour involving extended family members and the wider community in a range of slave, colonial and settler societies. In the Caribbean, for example, contemporary familial practices of care for emigrants' children are consistent with culturally established roles of (maternal) grandmothers in family social reproduction (Plaza, 2000). Colonial elites sent their children abroad to boarding school, while some local families in colonies sent their children to be educated in colonising countries (Vuorela, 2003, p 79). There are many historical precedents of children raised by paid caregivers or by unpaid family members while their mother is abroad (see Hondagneu-Sotelo and Avila, 1997). Contemporary practices of globalised families are therefore best understood as current expressions of an age-old means of fulfilling care responsibilities for a variety of family members – from small children to the ailing aged – when for a range of reasons and circumstances parents (or children) were not able to be physically proximate.

These practices of cash and care provision not only demonstrate the substantial transnational and global dimensions of social welfare, but are also important expressions, or 'acts', of **cosmopolitan citizenship** that transcend national social and state borders. Such acts extend into the arena of formal social politics, policy and entitlements. For example, political activism by migrant workers has seen claims making not only for individual (labour and residency) rights but also for wider social rights, including family and citizenship rights. Thus, migrant workers, often constituted as second-class citizens in the 'host' country, may assert their right to be treated as first-class citizens, and constitute themselves as such, through their claims, demands and practices with regard to social rights and entitlements. In the European context, these rights have been won by European Union (EU) nationals living in other EU countries, but increasingly non-EU nationals migrating to EU countries are making similar demands on host countries. These claims take on significance when seen in the context of discussions about the need for a stronger 'social dimension' to world-regional formations to accompany trade and investment agreements (see Chapters Two and Five). Key to these demands for stronger transnational social policy are rights of family reunification for migrant workers, with various campaigns organised by transnational advocacy networks being supported by labour and social movement organisations within and across countries.

The migration of welfare workers and global care chains

Migrants not only play a key role in forging multi-stranded social relations across families and communities across the world and transnational social care and financial support systems, but they also link the formal welfare systems in the countries of origin and settlement.

One way in which this issue has been studied is through the **global care chain** (GCC) concept (**Box 10.1**) (Yeates, 2005). This concept emphasises how care resources are extracted from poor countries for use by rich ones, how the increased female labour force participation is often underpinned by the use of migrant female labour, and the costs of this migration on the populations in the sending country, especially its effects on the welfare of family members left behind.

> **Box 10.1:** Global care chains
>
> The term global care chain was coined by Hochschild (2000, p 131) to refer to 'a series of personal links between people across the globe based on the paid or unpaid work of caring'. Hochschild's focus lay with transnational transfers of 'motherly' labour, so she describes a GCC as typically entailing 'an older daughter from a poor family who cares for her siblings while her mother works as a nanny caring for the children of a migrating nanny who, in turn cares for the child of a family in a rich country' (2000, p131).

Yeates (2004, 2005, 2008) has expanded the GCC concept to examine how it operates across the spectrum of health, social and educational provision and how the functioning of advanced industrialised countries' welfare states depends on migrant labour forces – from surgeons, physicians, nurses and midwives, through dentists, physical therapists and child and elder-care workers, to social workers and teachers – together with the impacts on sending countries' populations. In 2005, for example, 46% of the dentists who began working for the British National Health Service qualified overseas (Branigan and Hall, 2006), while in Ireland, two thirds of newly registered nurses were trained in countries outside the EU, predominantly developing countries (Yeates, 2008). Indeed, many European welfare states are effectively dependent on professionally qualified migrant workers, as well as those prepared to take up unskilled or minimum wage jobs (Kofman, 2007). This phenomenon is not new or associated with the most recent phase of globalisation: Britain actively and extensively recruited skilled and unskilled care workers to provide health and social care services from its colonies throughout the 20th century (Doyal et al, 1981; Yeates, 2008).

The advantages for the recruiting country are obvious: it obtains cheaper and possibly more submissive labour without the costs involved in educating and training that labour, while importing labour from abroad helps keep wages from rising in a situation of scarce labour supply. In the sending country, the benefits to the state include the following: remittances raise the state's foreign exchange holdings and help pay off debt; the use of remittances to purchase commodities, build houses, invest in businesses and pay for training of further exportable labour helps invigorate the economy; and the production and supply of labour for export creates business and profits for trainers, educational institutes, recruiters and travel agents in the migration industry. In recent years, however, there is increasing concern at the costs of this 'trade' in welfare professionals (and other workers). Much of this debate has revolved around the notion of the 'brain drain' involved in the migration of skilled health workers.

The brain drain became a concern of the development studies literature for the first time in the 1970s when attention concentrated on the loss of scientific and technological labour power and its effects on economic development in developing countries, when scientific and technological labour was seen as a key ingredient in economic development. In this context, attention was also paid to the loss of highly skilled labour power involved in the emigration of medical labour power, primarily considered in terms of doctors/physicians (Meija et al, 1979). Attention to this loss of medical labour power returned with a vengeance during the 1990s. Contributing factors were the impact this trade would have on the implementation of the Millennium Development Goals and on the treatment of the AIDS epidemic in Africa. In particular, transfer of skilled healthcare labour can have devastating impacts on the country of origin. A World Health Organization (WHO) study of medical migration in six countries showed that:

> ... the emigration of skilled health personnel has important negative effects on the accessibility and equitable distribution of health care, for the departure of skilled health personnel has a direct effect on reducing the quality of health care in the institutions concerned. Marginal and disadvantaged areas such as rural areas have been worst effected [sic], as the skilled workers tend to shun such areas. (Awases et al, 2004, p 58)

These negative effects are regionally varied. In Africa, where Bretton Woods structural adjustment policies have taken a devastating toll over the past four decades (Aina et al, 2004), the effects of brain drain have exacerbated a worsening health sector human resources crisis. As an International Labour

Organization (ILO) study pointed out, '[t]his catastrophe is reflected in the extent to which the proportion of health workers to the population has stagnated or declined in nearly every African country since 1960' (Bach, 2006, p 6) and the worsening health status of populations. Other countries, such as the Philippines, a major producer of migrant nurses, also experience chronic health labour shortages. This global solution to core country problems essentially entails the export of staffing and training crises to poorer countries (Yeates, 2006) and has a regressive redistributive impact, since it entails a net flow of benefits from poor to rich countries' health services (Mensah et al, 2005). These global transfers in care are contributing to and exacerbating rising international inequity in healthcare and in many cases exceed international medical aid to developing countries.

These trends have given rise to concerns about the justice of this international trade, leading to debates about how to reconcile trade interests and social equity. There is a consensus now that '**managed migration**' is the most appropriate framework to achieve this. The premise of this policy approach is that since migration is inevitable and that any attempts to prevent it would infringe human rights, it should be managed in the best interests of both sending and receiving countries while respecting the individual migrant's right to choose their place of work and residence. The IOM accordingly encourages countries to examine 'schemes that aim at managing the movement of these professionals in a way that would benefit all partners, and would develop or strengthen capacity for provision of quality healthcare' (Grondin, 2005).

Managed migration raises the question, however, of whether and how the competing (and potentially conflicting) interests of state, commerce, professions, labour and households can be reconciled. How can the interests and needs of individuals and their families in low-income countries weigh against the need to fill vacancies in middle- and high-income countries? How can the need for nurses, for example, to take care of older people in developed countries be weighed against the need for nurses in developing countries to help care for people with AIDS? This goes to the heart of the problem: how far should international migration be regulated in the wider public interest? Are bilateral agreements sufficient to address the problem, or is a multilateral framework needed? Should government and private recruitment agency participation in it be voluntary or mandatory?

The limitations of both bilateral and voluntaristic approaches are suggested by the use of ethical codes of conduct. Supported by the World Health Assembly, ethical codes of conduct seek to regulate the trade in health workers. The UK's Department of Health was the first to adopt such a code in 1999 but various other countries and states have since also adopted ethical codes. The UK code prohibits government from actively recruiting nurses from developing countries suffering nurse shortages. Like all voluntary codes, this one is not without its limitations: it concerns only government recruitment and excludes private sector healthcare providers and agencies. It is of limited effectiveness when entrants come to the UK to study rather than to work (Deeming, 2004; Grondin, 2005). Indeed, despite the existence of this agreement, more than 5,000 South African nurses were registered in the UK between 2001 and 2004; this is more than twice the growth in the number of nurses registered in South Africa in the same period (Redfoot and Houser, 2005). In a review of eight international and national codes of conduct, Willetts and Martineau (2004) concluded that 'support systems, incentives and sanctions, and monitoring systems necessary for effective implementation and sustainability are currently weak or have not been planned' (p i).

Other policy approaches to address global health disparities entailed by health worker migration focus on changing its economics. Various African countries have put in place 'bonding schemes' that require health workers to spend a certain number of years working in their national health services or repay to the government the costs of training should they wish to emigrate (Padarath et al, n.d.). Others propose changing the economics of the trade to remove the cost advantage of recruiting foreign nurses. This could involve, for example, obliging the recruiting body to pay the full cost of educating and training nurses to the source country government or contributing to the general costs of running its healthcare service (Mensah et al, 2005). Even here, however, such proposals are ultimately limited unless they extend beyond bilateralism and voluntarism. The question therefore becomes how to develop a multilateral binding framework to govern (health labour) migration. As we will see in the next section, there are a great many political and policy issues involved in constructing such a framework.

Towards a global migration regime?

International migration takes place within a highly institutionalised context involving a matrix of state and non-state actors on national and transnational scales. Immigration regimes (IRs) determine which – if any – rights migrants will have in their host country and control their pathways to citizenship. Expressed bureaucratically through the issuing of visa and work permits and quantitative measures such as quota systems, IRs involve a wide variety of agents and agencies that act as 'gatekeepers to citizenship' in selecting, rejecting and/or restricting the conditions of entry to a country, including state policy makers and legislatures in both the source and receiving countries, government immigration personnel, and professional accreditation bodies and educational institutions. One essential distinction between IRs is the differences in their treatment of skilled and unskilled migrants. Core countries' need for skilled labour means they offer easier entry, the right to be accompanied by one's family and for family members to work, permanent residency status and eventually citizenship (Kofman, 2007). In comparison, unskilled migrants enter as contract labour, tied to employers by work permits that are issued to the employer, not the migrant, greatly increasing their vulnerability to abuse by restricting migrants' ability to leave their employment, arrangements that are close to 'bonded' labour.

IRs are primarily enacted on a unilateral basis, although bilateral and multilateral cooperation occurs. EU-wide agreements prohibit discrimination by member states against nationals of other member states in respect of rights of entry, stay, paid employment and some social entitlements. These rights are not extended to nationals from outside the EU, however, and the rights of those people in any given EU member state are determined by whatever intergovernmental (bilateral) agreement is in place with the source country's government. Increasingly, overseas development aid such as that of the EU to some African countries includes conditions that require recipient countries to put in place measures to prevent certain kinds of emigration, such as illegal emigration. Some other world-regional formations – such as the East African Community, the West African Community, Mercosur and the Association of South East Asian Nations (ASEAN) – have also enacted multilateral cooperation that lifts certain immigration controls for certain groups of economic migrants, while other regional formations, such as CARICOM, are considering putting in place structures that forge regional labour markets in an effort to keep skilled labour from emigrating to the Global North (Hosein and Thomas, 2007).

Alongside these immigration and welfare regimes (and forms of international cooperation among governments in the form of bilateral agreements), there is a range of global policy agencies and agendas dealing with international migration issues. The main focus of multilateral cooperation in the legal sphere takes place through the United Nations (UN) system, whose emphasis lies with upholding the human rights of everyone irrespective of whether or not they remain in their country of birth. Its various agencies have either a specialised remit in international migration issues (the Office of the UN High Commissioner for Refugees (UNHCR) is mandated to lead and coordinate international action to protect refugees) or a mandate that overlaps with them: the ILO has an interest as part of its remit to promote labour and social protection rights; the WHO has an interest from the point of view of migrating health workers' and migrants' access to healthcare services; UNICEF (United Nations Children's Fund) has an interest from the perspective of rights and services for migrant children; and the United Nations Educational, Social and Cultural Organization's (UNESCO) emphasis lies with promoting respect for the human rights of migrants and their peaceful social integration.

Alongside the UN system is a range of international governmental organisations whose remit draws them into international migration but whose primary concerns are not necessarily with promoting universal human rights or adequate social provision for all. The IOM, originally mandated to help European governments resettle refugees from the Second World War, has since broadened its scope to become what it calls *the* Migration Agency aiming to promote dialogue on humane and orderly migration. The World Trade Organization (WTO) deals with international migration by virtue of the provisions of the General Agreement on Trade in Services (GATS) (Chapter Five) in which international migration is addressed as an international trade in services. The World Bank is involved because international migration is a key development issue. Only the UN and WTO have the authority to pass international law relating to international migration: the former privileges the human rights of workers (***Box 10.2***), while the latter privileges trade-related aspects of migration (***Box 10.3***).

Box 10.2: The human rights of migrant workers and their families

- The right to work and receive wages that contribute to an adequate standard of living.
- The right to freedom from discrimination based on race, national or ethnic origin, sex, religion or any other status, in all aspects of work, including in hiring, working conditions and access to housing, healthcare and basic services.
- The right to equality before the law and equal protection of the law, particularly in regard to human rights and labour legislation, regardless of a migrant's legal status.

Box 10.3: Migration-related trade rights in the GATS

GATS prohibits discriminatory treatment by one member state of the foreign service providers of another. 'Mode 4' provisions prohibit discrimination against 'natural persons' moving to provide a service in another member state.

The Annex on the Movement of Natural Persons excludes from this all measures affecting access to the employment market of a member or to measures regarding citizenship, residence or employment on a permanent basis.

Alongside these organisations exists a range of global political groups (G7, G20, G77 and so on), global professional and labour bodies (international trade unions, professional associations) and quangos (Global Commissions) on whose policy agendas international migration appears either as one issue among many or the sole focus. To these can be added regional groupings of nations and world-regional formations (Chapter Two) such as the EU, and more recently Mercosur and ASEAN, all of which address issues of cross-border migration in the context of regional labour markets and the social entitlements that facilitate them.

There are various other multilateral initiatives. The 'Five plus Five' Dialogue holds annual ministerial meetings and focuses on migration in the western Mediterranean and links migrant sending countries in North Africa with receiving countries in southern Europe. The Berne Initiative convenes policy makers, NGOs and scholars from all regions to discuss migration issues and identify a common framework to facilitate cooperation between states and planning and managing the movement of people in a humane and orderly way. The institutional structures and mechanisms of the global governance of migration have been strengthened in recent years.

The ILO and Global Commission on International Migration (GCIM) are among the most significant attempts to develop a more robust global migration regime. At the 2004 ILO conference, governments, employers and labour representatives agreed to adopt a new action plan calling for the development of a non-binding multilateral framework for a rights-based approach to labour migration. They agreed also to establish an ILO dialogue on migration in partnership with other international and multilateral organisations. The GCIM (2002-05) complemented these efforts and is perhaps the most significant recent attempt to develop a 'coherent, comprehensive and global response to migration issues'. This is because it was the first time both the UN Secretary General and major industrialised countries took a lead in providing a multilateral forum on international migration (Oishi, 2005).

Despite a complex mix of international and national governmental and non-governmental actors, and a history of international cooperation on migration over the best part of the 20th century, 'there is no comprehensive international legal framework governing cross-border movement of people and related to this, no one single UN agency whose exclusive mandate is international migration' (Piper, 2007, pp 8-9). The UN General Assembly has adopted numerous legal and political instruments in the form of Conventions and Resolutions addressing different groups or aspects of migration. Beginning in 1949 with the ILO Migration for Employment Convention, the most recently passed Convention was in 1990 – the International Convention on the Protection of the Rights of all Migrant Workers and Members of their Families (known as the Migrant Workers' Convention). In 1992, it passed a resolution on violence (sexual and other forms of maltreatment) against female migrant workers – the first ever to specifically address international female migration. The General Assembly has adopted a resolution on migrant women almost every year since then. Between 1993 and 2002 the UNCHR issued 24 Resolutions on migrant workers as a whole, while the UN Economic and Social Council has issued seven Resolutions on migration-related issues since 1983 (Oishi, 2005).

Although there have been advances in international law to protect migrant workers, UN legal instruments have not been very effective for two main reasons. First, most states in major migrant-receiving countries have not signed or ratified them. In the case of the 1990 UN Convention, all ratifications came from migrant-sending states, while none of the major receiving states have ratified it. There is some reluctance to ratify Conventions because once they are ratified, domestic laws must be reformed to align with their provisions and states must provide reports on their implementation. Second, the Conventions lack substantial enforcement mechanisms. This is a general problem of UN law, although states have been especially forthright in claiming migration as a national sovereignty issue. Under current institutional arrangements, no international body can directly intervene in cases of violations of migrants' rights. The receiving state, being the body that has ratified it, is the only actor that can take action against the offending party (for example, an employer or recruitment agency).

As with other areas of human rights legislation, NGOs have been instrumental in ensuring that human rights instruments are developed and implemented (Yeates, 2001). Political campaigns have been key to developing this multilateral regime. One such campaign was the Global Campaign for the Ratification of the UN Migrant Workers' Convention. Between 1998 and 2004, ratifications of the Convention increased from nine to 27. While this may seem a modest achievement, it is an unprecedented success, given the slow progress made over the preceding eight years (Oishi, 2005). This last example shows how protecting international migrants not only depends on building robust supranational institutions, but also on coalition building and activism on the part of states, NGOs and social movements. An example from Asia usefully serves to illustrate this point. In 2003, the Philippines successfully led a coalition of six countries (Indonesia, Thailand, Vietnam, Myanmar and Sri Lanka) to pressure Hong Kong to withdraw its wage cuts for foreign workers (Oishi, 2005), while transnational advocacy networks filed a complaint to the ILO (Piper, 2007). Other examples of campaigns initiated by transnational advocacy networks include the placing of trafficking of women and children on the global policy agenda, campaigns for the regularisation of undocumented workers, such as the 'sans papiers' in France, and defence campaigns for domestic workers accused of crimes in countries such as Singapore and the Gulf states.

These 'bottom-up' global practices advance the claims of cosmopolitan citizenship on the national, regional and global agendas.

Conclusion

International migration is a key issue and area of concern in global social policy. This area exhibits a matrix of competing rights, claims and interests, illustrates the difficulties involved in balancing human rights, global social equity and justice, and reveals the limitations of contemporary global governance of migration. Migration can be seen as a form of 'globalisation from below' as well as a form of international trade in human beings. The case study of health worker migration raises basic issues for global social policy about welfare provision systems and global justice and equity, balancing the competing needs of social care and healthcare in the North and primary healthcare in the South. The care-giving practices and remittances of transnational families illustrated informal transnational welfare and care provision and financing, as well as their gender dimensions. The activities of these 'cosmopolitan citizens' challenge national citizenship and illustrate the need to move beyond the national sphere in analysing welfare and other claims. While attempts are being made to formulate a global regulatory regime, the limitations of existing international legal structures, especially the lack of enforcement mechanisms, means questions of global justice are not yet central to the governance of international migration. Finally, campaigns by transnational advocacy networks are an essential part of efforts to place the welfare of migrants at the centre of the global governance of international migration.

Summary

- International migration currently accounts for just 3% of the world's population but has become a high-profile area of global social policy. One suggested reason for its political topicality is that western countries currently attract more migrants than the rest of the world.
- The main flows of international migrants are from poorer to richer countries, but many migrants stay within their region rather than travel to the Global North. South–South migration is currently of major importance.
- International migration helps 'square the circle' of welfare finance and provision both in source and destination countries, and reveals the extent to which the social organisation and relations of welfare (cash and care) provision are transnationalised.
- International migration opens up questions of 'cosmopolitan citizenship', social equity and justice on a global scale.

- The prevailing global migration policy paradigm is that of 'managed migration', but this raises questions of how diverse interests and needs can be reconciled to the satisfaction of all concerned.
- Despite the existence of a multilateral legal regime, international migration-related human rights law is weakened by its lack of comprehensiveness, an emphasis on bilateralism and voluntarism, and the lack of 'teeth' on the part of the UN to force countries to ratify and implement legal provisions.
- Transnational coalition-based political activism has sometimes proved effective in pressuring governments to implement international conventions to protect the rights of migrant workers overseas.

Questions for discussion

- Is international migration an answer to the problems of welfare in (a) developed countries of the Global North and (b) 'developing' countries of the Global South? Discuss with reference to health workers or another occupational group of your choice.
- How does international migration enlarge our understanding of the global dimensions of social policy and welfare provision?
- What kinds of reform to global and national institutions and/or policies do you think are needed to ensure a truly 'cosmopolitan citizenship'?

Further suggested activities

- Think of your own experience of moving overseas to study, live or work. What kinds of issues about entry to and residence in the destination country did you face? Was it a straightforward matter, or did it involve lengthy, costly bureaucratic arrangements? If you needed to use that country's health, housing or education services while you were there, what kinds of entitlement and support – if any – could you call on? If you built up a record of social security and pension contributions in that country, did this actually entitle you to any support if you needed it while you were there or since returning? How were your experiences related to your national origin and citizenship status, or to the bilateral or multilateral arrangements your government has entered into with other countries? If you have never lived abroad, you may have friends or relatives who have done so and to whom you can pose these same questions.
- Now think about your own experiences of meeting international migrants in the country in which you currently live. What kinds of work are they doing, and under what conditions? If it is appropriate, discuss with them what

brought them to this country, what kinds of issues they faced in migrating, and what kinds of issues their home country faces in meeting the population's social needs. You could also discuss the kinds of issues they face in their working lives and in accessing welfare services, and what kinds of support they are providing for their relatives back home.

- Get involved with campaigns to advance the rights of international migrants (www.december18.net provides a list of campaigning organisations in different countries). What kinds of international and national policy reform would you recommend they advocate to bring about more humane and effective ways of addressing issues of international migration?

Further reading

For a comprehensive overview of key trends and issues in international migration, see IOM (2005) and the final report of the GCIM's *Migration in an Interconnected World: New Directions for Action* (2005).

For further information about the dynamics of international migration in the contemporary global economy, see Harris (1995). Given the tendency for orthodox policy literatures unquestioningly to accept the need to regulate or restrict migration and assume that this can be done humanely and effectively, it is important to be aware of arguments that take an opposite point of view. For this, you should consult Hayter's (2000) excellent *Open Borders: The Case Against Immigration Controls*, which makes the case for the abolition of immigration controls, and Cohen et al's (2002) *From Immigration Controls to Welfare Controls*, which looks at the implications of past and current UK government legislation for those subject to controls and those implementing controls. There is no dedicated journal that deals systematically with *global* policy issues in relation to international migration, but *International Migration* (a publication of the IOM), *Global Social Policy* and *Journal of Ethnic and Migration Studies* carry full-length and short articles on global migration policy.

Electronic resources

There is a wide range of resources (data, commissioned research studies, policy briefs) on different aspects of international migration, most of which can be downloaded for free. The following sites bring you to the main page for each organisation; use the search tool to look for more information on the agency's work on migration.

www.iom.int IOM
www.ohchr.org OHHCHR (Office of the High Commissioner for Human Rights)
www.unfpa.org UNFPA (United Nations Population Fund)
www.ilo.int ILO
www.who.int WHO
www.unesco.org UNESCO
www.worldbank.org World Bank

The UN has a designated site (**www.un.org/depts/dhl/events/migrants**) celebrating International Migrants' Day (18 December every year). It contains comprehensive information on the work of the UN around international migration and a list of international conventions and agreements. It also provides further resources you can follow up. The GCIM website (**www.gcim.org**) hosts a range of research and policy papers on the welfare dimensions and impacts of international migration that can be freely downloaded.

The Organisation for Economic Co-operation and Development's annual publication, *International Migration Outlook*, is worth consulting (**www.oecd. org/els/migration/imo**), but be aware that this covers just three dozen of the world's richest countries, and the publication is not downloadable for free.

The following independent websites on international migration are worth consulting: **www.december18.net**, a portal for the promotion and protection of the rights of migrants, provides comprehensive information and an excellent set of resources including international legal instruments and provisions for migrants, books and films about migrants, and information on migrant rights campaigns; the Migration Information Source (**www.migrationinformation. org**) offers useful tools, vital data and essential facts on the movement of people worldwide; Forced Migration Online (**www.forcedmigration.org**) deals with the situation of forced migrants worldwide; Human Rights Watch (**www.hrw. org/doc/?t=migrants** and **http://hrw.org/doc/?t=refugees&document_ limit=0,2**) is dedicated to protecting the human rights of people around the world, including those of migrants and refugees. Migration Dialogue (**http:// migration.ucdavis.edu/**) provides factual and non-partisan information and analysis of international migration issues.

References

Aina, T.A., Chachage, C.S.L. and Annan-Yao, E. (eds) (2004) *Globalisation and Social Policy in Africa*, Senegal: Council for the Development of Social Sciences Research in Africa.

Araghi, F.A. (1995) 'Global depeasantization, 1945-1990', *Sociological Quarterly*, vol 36, no 2, pp 337-68.

Awases, M., Gbary, A., Nyoni, J. and Chatora, R. (2004) *Migration of Health Professionals in Six countries: A Synthesis Report*, Brazzaville: World Health Organization, Regional Office for Africa, www.afro.who.int/dsd/migration6countriesfinal.pdf, accessed 19 November 2006.

Bach, S. (2006) *International Mobility of Health Professionals: Brain Drain or Brain Exchange?*, Research Paper No. 2006/82, Helsinki: United Nations University, www.wider.unu.edu/publications/rps/rps2006/rp2006-82.pdf, accessed 18 November 2006.

Baldock, C.V. (2000) 'Migrants and their parents: caregiving from a distance', *Journal of Family Issues*, vol 21, no 2, pp 205-24.

Basch, L.N., Schiller, G. and Blanc, C.S. (1994) *Nations Unbound: Transnational Projects, Postcolonial Predicaments and Deterritorialized Nation-states*, Langhorne, PA: Gordon & Breach.

Branigan, T. and Hall, S. (2006) 'Half of new dentists are migrants', *The Guardian*, 24 August.

Castles, S. (1998) 'New migrations in the Asia-Pacific region: a force for social and political change', *International Journal of Social Science*, no 156, pp 215-27.

Cohen R. (1997) *Global Diasporas: An Introduction*, London: UCL Press.

Cohen, S., Humphries, B. and Mynott, E. (eds) (2002) *From Immigration Controls to Welfare Controls*, London: Routledge.

Deeming, C. (2004) 'Policy targets and ethical tensions: UK nurse recruitment', *Social Policy and Administration*, vol 38, no 7, pp 775-92.

Doyal, L., Hunt, G. and Mellor, J. (1981) 'Your life in their hands: migrant workers in the National Health Service', *Critical Social Policy*, vol 1, no 2, pp 54-71.

Escrivá, A. (2004) *Securing Care and Welfare of Dependants Transnationally: Peruvians and Spaniards in Spain*, Working Paper No. WP404, Oxford: Oxford Institute of Ageing.

Faini, R. (2002) 'Migration, remittances and growth', www.wider.unu.edu/conference/conference-2002-3/conference%20papers/faini.pdf, accessed 28 August 2007.

GCIM (Global Commission on International Migration) (2005) *Migration in an Interconnected World: New Directions for Action*, Geneva: GCIM.

Grondin, D. (2005) *The Breakdown of Borders – Shaping the Delivery of Long-term Care*, www.aarp.org/ltcforum/dgrondin_keynote.html, accessed 11 November 2005.

Harris, N. (1995) *The New Untouchables*, London: Penguin.

Hayter, T. (2000) *Open Borders: The Case Against Immigration Controls*, London: Pluto Press.

Hirst, P. and Thompson, G. (1996) *Globalization in Question: The International Economy and the Possibilities of Governance*, Cambridge: Polity Press.

Hochschild, A.R. (2000) 'Global care chains and emotional surplus value', in W. Hutton and A. Giddens (eds) *On the Edge: Living with Global Capitalism*, London: Jonathan Cape, pp 130-46.

Hondagneu-Sotelo, P. and Avila, E. (1997) 'I'm here, but I'm there: the meanings of Latin transnational motherhood', *Gender and Society*, vol 11, no 5, pp 548-70.

Hosein, R. and Thomas, C. (2007) 'Caribbean single Market Economy (CSME) and the intra-regional migration of nurses: some proposed opportunities', *Global Social Policy*, vol 7, no 3, pp 316-38.

IOM (International Organization on Migration) (2005) *World Migration*, Geneva: IOM.

Kanaiaupuni, S.M. (2000) *Sustaining Families and Communities: Nonmigrant Women and Mexico-US Migration Processes*, Centre for Demography and Ecology Working Paper No 2000-13, Madison, WI: University of Wisconsin-Madison.

Kofman, E. (2007) 'Gendered migrations, livelihoods and entitlements in European welfare regimes', in N. Piper (ed) *New Perspectives on Gender and Migration: Livelihood, Rights and Entitlements*, London: Routledge, pp 59-100.

Meija, A., Pizurki, H. and Royston, E. (1979) *Physician and Nurse Migration: Analysis and Policy Implications: A Report of a WHO Study*, Geneva: World Health Organization.

Mensah, K., Mackintosh, M. and Henry, L. (2005) *The 'Skills Drain' of Health Professionals from the Developing World: A Framework for Policy Formation*, London: Medact, www.medact.org/content/Skills%20drain/Mensah%20et%20al.%202005.pdf, accessed 14 July 2006.

Oishi, N. (2005) *Women in Motion: Globalization, State Policies and Labor Migration in Asia*, Stanford, CA: Stanford University Press.

Padarath, A., Chamberlain, C., McCoy, D., Ntuli, A., Rowson, M. and Loewenson, R. (n.d.) *Health Personnel in South Africa: Confronting Maldistribution and Brain Drain*, Regional Network for Equity in Health in South Africa, Equinet Discussion Paper No 3, Harare: Equinet.

Parreñas, R.S. (2001) *Servants of Globalization*, Stanford, CA: Stanford University Press.

Parreñas, R. (2005) *Children of Global Migration: Transnational Families and Gendered Woes*, Stanford, CA: Stanford University Press.

Piper, N. (2007) *Governance of Migration and Transnationalisation of Migrants' Rights – An Organisational Perspective*, COMCAD Working Paper 22, Bielefeld: Centre on Migration, Citizenship and Development, Bielefeld University.

Plaza, D. (2000) 'Transnational grannies: the changing family responsibilities of elderly African Caribbean-born women resident in Britain', *Social Indicators Research*, no 51, pp 75-105.

Redfoot, D.L. and Houser, A.N. (2005) *'We Shall Travel On': Quality of Care, Economic Development, and the International Migration of Long-term Care Workers*, Washington, DC: AARP, www.mecf.org/articles/AARP_immigrant.pdf, accessed 9 November 2005.

Sassen S. (2000) 'Women's burden: counter-geographies of globalization and the feminisation of survival', *Journal of International Affairs*, vol 53, no 2, pp 503-24.

Vuorela, U. (2003) 'Transnational families: imagined and real communities', in D. Bryceson and U. Vuorela (eds) *The Transnational Family: New European Frontiers and Global Networks*, Oxford: Berg, pp 63-82.

Willetts, A. and Martineau, T. (2004) 'Ethical international recruitment of health professionals: will codes of practice protect developing country health systems?', www.liv.ac.uk/lstm/research/documents/codesofpracticereport.pdf

Yeates, N. (2001) *Globalization and Social Policy*, London: Sage Publications.

Yeates, N. (2004) 'A dialogue with "global care chain" analysis: nurse migration in the Irish context', *Feminist Review*, no 77, pp 79-95.

Yeates, N. (2005) *Global Care Chains: A Critical Introduction*, Global Migration Perspectives No 44, Geneva: Global Commission on International Migration.

Yeates, N. (2006) 'Changing places: Ireland in the international division of reproductive labour', *Translocations: The Irish Migration, Race and Social Transformation Review*, vol 1, no 1, pp 5-21.

Yeates, N. (2008) 'Here to stay? Migrant health workers in Ireland', in J. Connell (ed) *The International Migration of Health Workers*, London: Routledge, pp 62-76.

Yeates, N. (forthcoming) *Globalising Care Economies, Migrant Workers: An Exploration of Global Care Chains*, London: Palgrave.

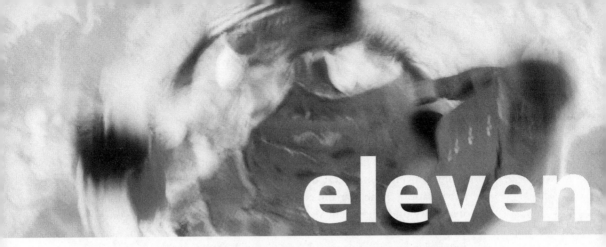

eleven

Global population policy

Sarah Sexton, Larry Lohmann and Nicholas Hildyard

Overview

Population policy is one of the earliest examples of global social policy and draws on population theory dating back over 200 years. This chapter[1] outlines and explains the significance of this theory, showing how it has informed various policies and practices from the 19th century to the present day. It discusses 19th-century restrictions on welfare and famine relief; early 20th-century attempts in the US and Europe to restrict reproduction of the 'feeble-minded'; and later 20th-century attempts to limit the number of children to which poor, black or 'Third World' women give birth. The chapter describes the rise in the 20th century of international organisations, both public and private, whose focus on overpopulation underpinned international development policies for several decades. In the 21st century, while international enthusiasm for anti-natalist population policies has waned since the end of the Cold War, population theory continues to inform policies and debates on national security, environmental degradation, ageing and immigration, undermining the rights and interests of a wide variety of social groups.

Key concepts

Population control; Malthusianism; neo-Malthusianism; overpopulation; scarcity; eugenics; security

Introduction

Population, or **overpopulation**, has been held to be the ultimate cause of many current global social and environmental problems: deforestation, pollution, environmental degradation, poverty, hunger, climate change, urbanisation, crime, war and conflict, social instability, slow economic growth, insecurity, unemployment and migration. Chapter Eight in this volume notes how population concerns – specifically an ageing population – have been invoked in levering new pension reforms, while Chapter Ten discusses how the control of international migration into rich Northern countries (sometimes attributed to overpopulation) is informing social policy reforms. Tackling all these problems directly is often considered futile without external (often technical) measures to control, slow and stabilise the growth in the number of the world's people and their distribution across different geographical locations. Another view, however, holds that claims of overpopulation cover up more immediate causes of the problems – and invariably victimise and scapegoat already vulnerable groups in the process. Ever since English economist Thomas Malthus wrote his first *Essay on the Principle of Population* in 1798, his theory and arguments have been refuted endlessly by practical instances indicating that any problem attributed to human numbers can just as easily have a different explanation, or that the statistical correlation is ambiguous.

Facts and figures have never had much effect on population debates or disagreements over policies. This is because, deep down, the disagreements are less about numbers than about ideology, values, power and economic interests, about rights, economic markets and welfare. They are political and cultural disagreements, not mathematical ones. Overpopulation arguments and the policies based on them tend to persist, not because of their intrinsic merit, but because of the ideological advantages they offer to powerful political and economic interests. In this sense, **population policy** could be considered as one that aims to minimise redistribution and restrict social rights.

This chapter looks at the reasons why the argument that there are 'too many' people in the world continues to manifest itself in a range of contexts. It first outlines the context in which Malthus was writing in the late 18th and early 19th centuries, and the uses to which his theory were put in the 19th century. Here we point to population policy as an 'early' example of global social policy, highlighting transnational ideational and policy transfers associated with the British empire. The chapter then gives some examples from across the 20th century of how **eugenics** used population theory and influenced global policy actors. We show how the US deployed Malthusian arguments in the 1950s as a justification to contain communism in other countries and to pursue various development policies. We describe how international organisations (IOs), both public and private, have been instrumental in the transfer of overpopulation theory and in claiming the urgency of tackling **population growth** and **population decline**. The chapter concludes with a round-up of how population arguments are being deployed in the 21st century, particularly in global debates on security, conflict and environmental degradation.

The origins of population control thinking

Underpinning many an overpopulation argument is the work of English economist Thomas Malthus, who is best remembered for the 'law of nature' he first set out in his 1798 *Essay on the Principle of Population* (***Box 11.1***). This was written against a background of major social and economic transformations in England, which led to an era of immense suffering. For example, large amounts of common pasture and forest land, over which an entire community had rights of use, were being fenced off for private use. The enclosure of common woodland alone amounted to shredding what was known throughout Europe as 'the poor's overcoat'. Denied access to common land on which their livelihoods depended, many of the dispossessed could not find secure employment or alternative livelihoods either in the countryside or in the towns, and so had to depend on poor relief from local parishes, the closest thing to social welfare at the time.

> **Box 11.1: Thomas Malthus's theory of population**
>
> Thomas Malthus's theory maintains that population increases will eventually lead to starvation. Malthus claimed that food production increases at an arithmetic rate (1, 2, 3, 4, 5 and so on), but the number of people doubles every 25 years because it grows at a geometric rate (1, 2, 4, 8, 16 and so on) – unless people delay and check their childbearing through later marriage and self-discipline. If they do not keep their numbers in check, warfare, epidemic disease and starvation will do so – and because Malthus believed that poorer people found self-restraint or self-discipline difficult, disease and starvation were not only inevitable but also 'natural': he originally presented his theory as a 'law of nature'. Malthus subsequently admitted that his mathematical and geometric series of increases in food and humans were not observable in any society and that his famous 'power of number' was only an image, admissions that demographers have since confirmed.

A variety of explanations and proposals for action were advanced in response to this mass poverty, of which Malthus's *Essay* was one. Market forces and market reasoning, Malthus argued, bring discipline into the chaos that is Nature. Private property brings prudence, and prudence separates the deserving from the undeserving. Without private property and with unchecked population growth, the world is catapulted headlong into **scarcity**. Scarcity did not result from periodic natural disasters: the *Essay* declared that it was a permanent feature of nature, always impinging disproportionately on the poor. Scarcity, poverty, private property, inequality, food and labour markets, and unequal marriage were inevitable given any starting point whatsoever, Malthus argued. By suggesting that the poor's fertility was the main source of their poverty – rather than the fencing off of common lands, chronic or periodic unemployment, or high food prices – Malthus's theory served the interests of property-owning classes. The solution to poverty, it was maintained, was a matter of individual responsibility: it had nothing to do with wider institutional structures and contexts. These classes argued that any form of social welfare, therefore, was little more than a subsidy for the fertility of the poor and brought about further misery. Malthus insisted that anything that humans might do to redress inequalities or to mitigate suffering would be counterproductive because it would only increase population and therefore place more pressure on productive resources. Private property, not the poor laws and not the commons, would provide the best possible deal for the poor, he maintained (Lohmann, 2003).

Within a generation, Malthus's population theory enabled English elites to argue that the underlying cause of distress among the poor was overpopulation. The 1834 Poor Law Amendment Act instituted a system of workhouses in which conditions were deliberately made as prison-like as possible so that people would choose to take the poorest-paid work rather than enter them. The Malthusian spectre of overpopulation was of central intellectual and political significance in shaping this law, which was, arguably, the first time a 'population policy' was introduced.

The global ramifications of this theory were almost immediately evident. A few years later, Malthusian thinking was exported to Ireland and India, two of Britain's overseas colonies, experiencing famines – with disastrous consequences (***Box 11.2***).

Box 11.2: Global policy transfer: the export of Malthusianism to British colonies

A decade after the 1834 Poor Law Amendment, overpopulation was invoked by the British government as an explanation of famine and death, and as a rationale for policy (in)action, in Ireland. In 1845, a fungus ruined the potato harvest, the staple food crop that most peasants grew on the poor-quality land allotted them by landlords. Instead of attributing the resulting starvation to the peasants' lack of access to land or lack of access to food other than potatoes – during these famine years, Irish exports of wheat and cattle to England and its Caribbean plantations increased – the colonial British government, dominated by absentee landlords, maintained that too many peasants had caused the famine. Applying the tenets of **Malthusianism**, they argued that it was futile and counterproductive to intervene by allowing the peasants access to other food or land or by reducing their taxes so they could buy food; this would simply delay and exacerbate the impending crash when the number of people outstripped the amount of food available. As a result of the Great Famine, some one million people died while another million emigrated within five years (Ross, 2000, p 4).

Thirty years later, Malthusian principles were again invoked to legitimise British policies in India, turning a drought into a famine. From 1876 to 1879, India experienced a devastatingly destructive drought when the monsoon rains failed. Yet although crop failures and water shortages were the worst in centuries, there were grain surpluses that could have rescued drought victims. As in Ireland, however, much of India's surplus rice and wheat production had been exported to England. Besides bad weather, many policy makers ascribed the famine to Malthusian pressures – too many people, too little land, too little food. Britain's Viceroy argued in 1877 that the Indian population 'has a tendency to increase more rapidly than the food it raises from the soil' (Davis, 2002, p 8).

As in Ireland, those with the power to relieve famine convinced themselves that exertions against implacable natural laws, whether of market prices or population growth, were worse than no effort at all. 'The staggering death toll – 5.5 million to 12 million died in India despite modern railways and millions of tons of grain in commercial circulation – was the foreseeable and avoidable result of deliberate policy choices.... Malthusian explanations were not only wrong-headed at the time: they were also contributory causes of the deaths that occurred' (Davis, 2002, pp 3, 1).

Administrators in the Indian Civil Service after independence from Britain in 1947 often had quite consciously Malthusian attitudes that can be traced back to the 19th century. The 1943-44 Bengal famine, in which at least 1.5 million people died, not least because of British policies, contributed to India's 1951 decision to opt for a family planning programme, one of the first countries in the world to do so (Rao, 2004).

Malthusian transformation: eugenics

From Malthus's time onwards, the implied 'over' in population has invariably referred to poorer people, people from black and disadvantaged ethnic groups or people from the colonies or countries of the South – or a combination of all three. In practice, the 'too many' are never the speaker, they are always the 'other'. It is not surprising, therefore, that Malthusianism found an intellectual ally in the late 19th century and early 20th century in eugenics:

> Malthus's theory had always presumed that the poor were not the equals of the more privileged – that one of the reasons they had 'too many' children was that they lacked the middle-class virtues of 'moral restraint' such as prudence, foresight, self-discipline and the capacity to manage their affairs in a rational manner. In the second half of the 19th century, eugenics took this thinking a step further by arguing that the overpopulous poor's moral deficiencies were innate. (Ross, 2000, p 5)

Francis Galton coined the term 'eugenics' in 1883 to denote the means by which the physical and moral attributes of a population might be improved by 'selective breeding'. Such breeding would favour the increased genetic representation of those who had more 'natural ability' or 'civic worth' – and less of those who did not.

In the US and UK, middle-class intellectuals and eugenic reformers proposed at first that birth control, including sterilisation, be used to prevent certain categories of the ill or disabled from polluting the 'national gene pool'. But it rapidly came to be viewed as a way of dealing with a broader spectrum of social ills. By the turn of the 20th century, control of the population of the 'feeble-minded' (a term first used in 1876 in the UK) was seen as a remedy for a wide variety of social problems, including prostitution, vagrancy and petty crime. Inspired by eugenic and Malthusian thinking, policy makers increasingly believed that science had demonstrated that poverty, too, was primarily the result of innate physical and moral debility.

Most eugenic-inspired policies focused on restricting births of certain groups. Although eugenicists recognised birth control as an important instrument of social policy, they were ambivalent about it because it was used primarily by the middle and upper classes whose fertility they did not want to limit. Stopping some people from reproducing altogether seemed more effective. By 1920, when much of the medical profession had absorbed eugenic and racialist ideas, 25 states in the US had enacted laws for the compulsory sterilisation of the criminally insane and other groups (Lifton, 1986, p 22). Drawing on British and US eugenic thinking, Germany introduced a sterilisation policy in 1933.

This soon evolved into a programme of euthanasia of 'valueless life' and a pilot 'medical killing' scheme for the Holocaust, which transformed 'state remedies' for curbing fertility into systematic mass murder on an unprecedented scale (Ross, 1998, p 72). Sweden began forcibly sterilising people from minority ethnic groups and those with mental health conditions just before the Second World War, and did not abandon its policies until 1975.

Eugenic ideas went underground after the end of the Second World War following revelations about the Holocaust. Nonetheless, some countries and many US states kept their sterilisation policies for several decades, and eugenic ideas are still common today even though the policies and laws have been repealed. In the 21st century, some key arenas in which eugenic assumptions continue to circulate include debates about environmental degradation and immigration; biological determinism; rebiologising and geneticising 'race'; the use of reproductive technologies such as prenatal screening and prenatal genetic diagnosis; fears of future scarcities; national security; and ageing and **population decline** (Minns, 2006). These issues are selectively taken up later in this chapter; for further details, see Hartmann and Oliver (2007) and the further resources section at the end of this chapter.

Population policies in the 20th century

The rise of population institutions

After the Second World War, the 'population issue' was raised by a variety of government, military and corporate interests, particularly in the US. In the ensuing decades, they disseminated the 'overpopulation' discourse across the countries of the Third World, particularly in Asia, directly and indirectly as they supported the development of key IOs.

The principal vehicle for Malthusian fears became the threat of communism, and Malthusian and eugenic thinking quickly became enshrined in Cold War 'containment' policies from the late 1940s onwards. Population growth, rather than global social injustice or inequalities in resource distribution, was seen as the ultimate source of the conditions that attracted peasants to communism, particularly across Asia. **Population control** thus became part of national security planning, particularly in the US, then emerging as the dominant power in international politics. By the 1940s, US government bodies were recommending government financing of population research as part of security planning (Ross, 2000, p 9).

Population control was adopted as a major international development strategy in the 1950s. By the end of the 1960s, it had become pivotal to development strategies designed to address poverty, hunger and low wages. Since official international population assistance began in the mid-1960s, the

US has been the acknowledged leader in the field. It has consistently been the largest donor (until recently), provided much of the intellectual leadership linking fertility reduction with economic development, and been the pillar of multilateral efforts through the United Nations (UN) system, the World Bank (WB) and organisations such as the International Planned Parenthood Federation (IPPF).

The Population Council was established in 1952 out of concern for the potential impact of population growth in developing countries. It wanted to opt for qualitative controls because of its eugenic sympathies, but called instead only for quantitative ones because of the supposed urgency of tackling the 'population explosion' in the Third World. The Population Council has since played a critical role in theoretical research on 'population questions' and in the development of contraceptive techniques. The UN organised the first world population conference in 1954, which focused on demography.

The WB, UN Population Fund, World Health Organization (WHO) and United Nations Children's Fund (UNICEF) entered the family planning area in the 1960s, when governments of many recipient countries became increasingly tolerant of efforts to create or strengthen international population assistance. In 1967, with financial support coming from the US, the UN established its Population Trust Fund, reorganised in 1969 as the United Nations Fund for Population Activities (UNFPA), later renamed the United Nations Population Fund. By 1968, curbing population growth had become central to WB development policy, and has remained so ever since.

The United States Agency for International Development (USAID) established an office of population in 1964 and began funding direct family planning activities in 1967. In 1969, the chair of the Population Crisis Committee, another privately funded, population-focused institution, stated that 'unless and until the population explosion now erupting in Asia, Africa and Latin America is brought under control, our entire aid program is doomed to failure' (Ross, p 10). The US Foreign Assistance Act quickly earmarked $35 million for population programmes. By 1971, USAID's annual allocation for population had risen to $100 million, far more than was allocated for healthcare. Much of the population budget was channelled through the IPPF. USAID has continuously emphasised the role of the private sector in population programmes. One analysis of USAID funding for population activities in 114 countries over 20 years concluded that adopting a population policy increased the likelihood of a country receiving international aid and the amount received (Nair et al, 2004). Although international donors financed many family planning programmes, some Third World governments, particularly those in Asia, gradually began to provide an increasing proportion of the funding themselves. In many Latin American countries, however, both church and state opposed modern contraceptives.

The issue of population growth was first addressed in an international forum at the 1974 World Population Conference. Northern countries wanted to implement population control policies in the south; southern countries shifted the debate to development issues, arguing that 'development is the best contraceptive'. By the 1984 International Conference on Population in Mexico City, however, there was more consensus among Southern countries, donors and non-governmental organisations (NGOs) about the need to limit population growth. Many southern economies had deteriorated and their dependence on western aid had increased. By 1991, 69 countries had officially endorsed, comprehensive population policies (Nair et al, 2004).

'Feminist' population policy: reform or business as usual?

In theory, population policies should address all attributes of a population – age structure, geographical distribution and total size. After all, the study of 'population' – demography – looks at trends in ageing and dying, and where people are living, encompassing rural–urban, regional and international migration. But from its earliest days, demography has problematised 'overpopulation' largely as a question of women's fertility. In practice, most population policies address a population's growth and size only, focusing more on births and fertility levels than mortality and migration.

Thus unlike almost all other development, economic, environment or social policies devised by think tanks, implemented by governments and funded by multilateral agencies, population policies tended to focus primarily on women from the outset. For some 50 years or more, many countries have implemented policies explicitly aimed at reducing their populations by reducing the number of children to whom women give birth, either directly by increasing the numbers of women who use modern contraceptives or are sterilised, or indirectly through women's education, employment and empowerment. The idea that for policy makers women are the 'key' to overpopulation is illustrated by a statement from Dr Hugh Gorwill, who in 1992 said: 'We know more about what makes females work than what makes males work. That's only because females create population problems....The common pathway to turn off having people is females' (Burfoot, 1992, p 11).

While many countries responded by providing contraception, others went further, introducing quantitative targets for the numbers of women to be sterilised or fitted with intra-uterine devices (IUDs). Some brought in financial incentives or disincentives for family planning providers and potential contraceptive users, while others employed outright coercion. The latter took various forms around the world: forced vasectomies in India in the 1970s (one of the few programmes focusing on men); a one-child policy in China introduced from the 1980s onwards that forced women to have late-term abortions; and implantation of women in Indonesia with five-year contraceptive doses in 'safaris' organised by the military forces were some of the more extreme measures that resulted.

Many women's health groups supported contraception that contributed to human health, welfare and self-determination by enabling women and men to have greater influence over the timing and spacing of births, but opposed contraception that harmed women's health and welfare. In this respect, population policy has largely been a global social policy contested by national and transnational social movements rather than supported by them; it has been a top-down global policy that has often encountered bottom-up global resistance. In the early 1990s, however, some large 'multinational' women's health groups believed that cooperating with governments, international donor agencies or UNFPA might ensure better reproductive health and counter abuses in population policies. They targeted the UN's 1994 International Conference on Population and Development (ICPD), aiming to have women's **reproductive rights** and gender equity accepted as vital aspects of population policies. They made concerted efforts to draw support from population organisations, some of which had also begun to acknowledge that coercion, mistreatment and poor services were driving women away from family planning clinics. The result was that many (but not all) population groups saw the advantage of abandoning demographic targets for national population policies (although not of dropping the goal of reducing women's overall fertility). They accepted that until women's status improved, population reduction was unlikely, and agreed that gender equity and education strategies could 'stabilise' population levels, and family planning activities should be supplemented with reproductive health ones.

The ICPD, the largest and costliest of all the UN conferences on population, was marked by the unprecedented involvement of NGOs and women's organisations (Koivusalo and Ollila, 1997). Its Programme of Action, heralded as a paradigm shift in the discourse about population and development and endorsed by 179 countries, was intended to establish international and national population policy for the following two decades. The programme's main recommendation – that population programmes provide reproductive health services rather than just family planning – assumes that women's fertility will not drop until children survive beyond infancy and young childhood, until men also take responsibility for contraception, and until women have the right to control their fertility and enough political power to secure that right. It expressly rejected the use of incentives and targets in family planning services. Women's reproductive rights and health activists used the internationally agreed Programme of Action's guidelines and human rights framework to lobby for better quality and access to services in their home countries, particularly where church or state institutions limited women's self-determination, such as in some Latin American countries (Nair et al, 2004, p 7).

In general, governments increasingly talk about 'reproductive rights', 'women's empowerment' and 'women's rights', instead of 'couple protection rates', 'family planning methods' or 'mother and child programmes'. International development organisations, meanwhile, reframed family planning programmes as reproductive health programmes, and population control programmes as gender equity programmes. The Indian government, for instance, changed the title of its population programme from 'Family Welfare' to 'Reproductive and Child Health', and declared that it had abandoned the use of targets. But India's national population policy for the year 2000 still aims for 'replacement level fertility rates' by the year 2010 and a 'stable population' by 2045, while the change in language has not changed the programme's approach substantially (*Box 11.3*).

Box 11.3: India's population policies since 1994: the resurgence of neoliberal coercive population control

After the 1994 ICPD, and under both internal and donor pressure, India attempted to move away from an approach stressing 'target' numbers of women sterilised or IUDs inserted. Instead, the policy was to emphasise gender-sensitive quality of care. Since then, population control in the country has moved away from a tightly connected system of policies imposed by the central government mainly to pressure the poor to be sterilised by specified methods. Instead, individual states, along with NGOs, corporations and micro-credit lenders, devise their own schemes, incentives and disincentives to 'persuade' people to use contraception or sterilisation. The idea is to instil a two-child norm.

In four states – Uttar Pradesh, Madhya Pradesh, Rajasthan and Maharashtra – anyone married before the legal age is banned from holding a government job; state financial assistance to *panchayats* (local governing bodies) is linked to family planning performance; and medical officers and other health staff are assessed according to their performance in the family planning programme. The Madhya Pradesh policy links rural development schemes, income-generating schemes for women and poverty alleviation programmes as a whole to family planning. Both Rajasthan and Maharashtra make 'adherence to a two-child norm' a service condition for state government employees. The Andhra Pradesh policy links funding for construction of schools and other public works, as well as rural development schemes generally, to family planning. Allotment of surplus agricultural land, housing schemes and a variety of social programmes are also tied to acceptance of sterilisation.

Moreover, problematic practices with potentially harmful substances continue, including moves to bring injectable contraceptives into state programmes and illegal NGO sterilisation programmes using untested drugs. Thus family planning policies and practices have increased socioeconomic and political disparities. Critics stress that 'the accomplishment of the Cairo declaration with its gender-progressive content seems to have blinded many to the continuing reality of population control abuses' (Bhatia, 2005, p 3).

Institutions such as USAID, UNFPA and the WB now use language that does not explicitly imply population control and that advocates women's reproductive health and rights and an integrated approach to health services. Supporters of women's rights working within population and aid institutions, moreover, have been able to push a reproductive rights agenda within their agencies. For example, UNFPA and IPPF now prioritise working with adolescents in their HIV/AIDS and 'unwanted pregnancy' programmes, even though adolescent sexuality and abortion programmes remain controversial and funding-constrained.

But policies inspired by population thinking have not become a thing of the past. Neo-Malthusian thinking is still found in the words and actions of the WB, USAID and UNFPA. The UNFPA, for example, still links poverty with 'too many people', contending that 'poverty, poor health and fertility remain highest in the least developed countries where population has tripled since 1955 and is expected nearly to triple again over the next 50 years' and concluding that 'promoting reproductive health and rights is indispensable for economic growth and poverty reduction' (UNFPA, 2002). WB has introduced a new concept, 'demographic dividend', but its arguments are more or less the same as before. It maintains, for example, that:

> ... lower fertility and slower population growth, in combination with decreasing mortality ... increases the proportion of productive individuals relative to dependents. This change creates a 'window of opportunity' conducive to economic growth. Countries that exploit this 'demographic dividend' ... can experience economic growth and reduction in poverty. (WB, 2004, p 3)

In similar vein, USAID has most recently contended that:

> ... the health of the planet and its inhabitants depends on the reproductive choices that people make. For countries already struggling to provide adequate food, water, shelter, and jobs, rapid

population growth can further reduce the possibilities of improving
the lives of the poor. (USAID, 2008, p 1)

In sum, even if IOs seldom market population policies in explicitly demographic
terms these days, they have not necessarily dropped or modified their goals
of reducing fertility.

Population policies in the 21st century

In the early 21st century, population policies and rationales changed once
again. As religious fundamentalist interests became more dominant in the
US, US government support for the ICPD waned. In what can be seen as a
backlash against the ICPD's framework and its human rights approach, for
instance, the UN, in consultation with the International Monetary Fund, WB
and Organisation for Economic Co-operation and Development (but not
'civil society'), ignored the Programme of Action's goal of reproductive health
services being accessible to all women who need them by the year 2015 when
it drew up its eight Millennium Development Goals in September 2001.

In the US, President George W. Bush's first official presidential act in 2001
was to reimpose the 'global gag rule', a measure first introduced in 1984 but
suspended in 1993 by President Clinton, which prohibits any NGO overseas
from receiving US government aid if it provides or makes referrals for abortions,
actively promotes abortion, or lobbies for reform of its country's abortion
laws. In 2002, the US administration refused to pay its approved $34 million
contribution to UNFPA, and called for all language referring to reproductive
health services, reproductive rights and sexual health in the Programme of
Action to be removed.

Changes in donor funding

In addition, funding for population programmes has not been forthcoming.
The Programme of Action estimated the annual costs of meeting basic
reproductive health needs in developing countries and countries in transition
(such as those of the former Soviet Union) at US $17 billion by the year
2000 and US $21.7 billion by 2015. In contrast, an estimated US $5 billion
was spent on family planning in the Third World in 1995: US $3 billion by
Third World governments; more than US $1 billion by developed countries,
multilateral institutions and private western population agencies; and the rest
by individual contraceptive users.

By July 1999, however, just $10.9 billion of the $17 billion estimate had been
committed, $2.6 billion by the international donor community (less than one
quarter of the total expenditure and less than half their commitment) and $8.3

billion by developing countries, particularly China, India and Indonesia (about three quarters of their commitment). The Japanese government agreed in 1994 to contribute US $3 billion for global population and AIDS issues, and is now the leading country aid donor for overseas population activities.

Of the $2.6 billion from donors, $1.6 billion was bilateral assistance, with the US contributing the largest proportion (43%). Development banks accounted for $600 million in loans, the majority of which came from the WB. (In 1999, in contrast, the WB gave loans of $12.8 billion to private sector development.) Private foundations and NGOs contributed some $260 million. The top private funders have been the Gates, Ford, Packard, MacArthur and Rockefeller Foundations.

In 2000, sub-Saharan Africa was the largest recipient of population assistance (43%), followed by Asia and the Pacific (31%). Other regions received much less: Latin America and the Caribbean (13%); western Asia and North Africa (9%) and eastern and southern Europe (3.5%). Some 33% went to global and inter-regional activities (Nair et al, 2004, p 22).

Over the past decade, about half of all aid for population programmes has been channelled through NGOs, such as the IPPF and the Population Council, and a quarter through bilateral and multilateral programmes. In Egypt, NGOs have become essential conduits through which the internationally sponsored family planning programme establishes itself outside the realm of government control. As a result, many NGOs have become more accountable to foreign donors than to the people they are meant to serve (Asdar Ali, 2003).

Health and gender impacts

The primary focus of current international population policy tends to be on the countries of sub-Saharan Africa with high fertility rates – even though these countries account for just 10% of world population. But the emphasis on contraceptive delivery in population policies is undermining efforts to address AIDS in Africa, which is home to 60% of all people in the world living with HIV. In Tanzania, for example, AIDS and reproductive health programmes are still thought of and implemented through separate channels to the detriment of both (Richey, 2003, p 32).

The focus on women's childbearing to the detriment of their underlying health can often cause more deaths than childbearing itself. A large proportion of maternal and infant deaths in India, for instance, are attributable to under-nutrition, anaemia and communicable diseases stemming from lack of food, poverty and social inequity. Diseases that are predominantly infectious cause some two thirds of women's deaths in India. Most women's deaths occur before they give birth; nearly 30% of women's deaths are of girls under the age of 15. Of women of reproductive age, nearly 30% of deaths are caused by major infectious diseases, while about 12.5% are due to childbirth and conditions associated with it. Indian public health activist and academic Mohan Rao argues that 'given the overall health situation among women, dominated by communicable diseases, anaemia and under-nutrition, to concentrate on reproductive health is to utterly miss the wood for the trees' (Rao, 2004, p 195).

Population policies seeking to enforce a one- or two-child norm have reinforced existing gender biases against women. China, for instance, introduced its one-child policy in 1979-80 in response to a 1972 report, *Limits to Growth* (Meadows et al, 1972), which modelled the consequences of a growing world population on industrialisation, pollution, food production and resource depletion. The leaders of the People's Republic of China defined the country's population problem as too many people of too backward a type. In China's son-loving culture, struggles over the number of children soon became contests over the sex of those offspring. Because of the patriarchal, patrilineal and patrilocal nature of the Chinese family, boys were the children who counted. Only a son could carry on the male-centred family line; sons would remain with their parents after marriage and look after them. Fierce resistance forced the authorities to revise the one-child policy in the late 1980s, allowing parents with a daughter to have one more child even if it too was a girl.

From the early 1980s, peasant couples had reluctantly begun disposing of their daughters in a desperate attempt to get a son. Outright infanticide seems to have declined in the 1980s, but infant abandonment persisted. From the mid-1980s, the spread of ultrasound machines into every corner of rural China pushed the state gender norm back into the period before birth. Prenatal sex determination followed by sex-selective abortion became an attractive, high-tech alternative to disposing of already living infants. Today, the practice of prenatal sex selection followed by sex-selective abortion is the single greatest contributor to a growing dearth of girls. By the turn of the millennium, the abortion of female foetuses had become a thoroughly normalised practice in the villages, and the sex ratio at birth had soared to 120 boys per 100 girls – the highest in Asia and globally (the biologically normal ratio is 105-106 boys for every 100 girls) (Greenhalgh and Winckler, 2005).

Population control as counter-insurgency

In the 21st century, connections continue to be made between population control and national security, but with varying targets. Since the 1950s, Malthusian fears had been expressed in terms of environmental catastrophe, climaxing in the 1968 publication of Paul Ehrlich's *The Population Bomb*, which presented overpopulation as the greatest threat to global ecological survival (Ehrlich, 1968). By 1978, an eminent biologist and ecologist, Paul Colinvaux, was claiming that 'ecology's first social law should be written: "All poverty is caused by the continued growth of population"' (Ross, 2000, p 8).

Today, the prevalent nexus of neoliberalism, fundamentalism and militarism holds that regional conflicts arise chiefly from environmental crises in which Malthusian pressures play a paramount role. For instance, a 2003 report from Population Action International suggests that civil conflict is generated in large part by demographic factors (Cincotta et al, 2003).

One architect of prevailing ideas about environmental conflict in the mid-1990s was political scientist Thomas Homer-Dixon, who argued that scarcities of renewable resources such as cropland, fresh water and forests, induced in large part by population pressure, contribute to migration and violent intrastate conflict in many parts of the developing world. This conflict, he said, could in turn potentially disrupt international security as states fragment or become more authoritarian (Hartmann, 2006, pp 196-7).

Writing in the journal of the Population Council, Homer-Dixon represented the growing scarcity of natural resources as principally the product of local or regional population growth. Ignoring the historical roots of resource depletion and the way structural adjustment and neoliberal trade policies result in pressures on resources, he suggested that southern countries will suffer 'a downward and self-reinforcing spiral of crisis and decay' due to their 'underdeveloped economic institutions', 'social friction' or lack of capital investment in research (Homer-Dixon, 1995, pp 605, 598).

The threat of future crises resulting from overpopulation is also frequently raised in relation to food, water and climate change. A prediction of millions of yet unborn 'extra mouths to feed,' (primarily dark-skinned ones) is used to justify genetically modified crops as a 'partial solution' to world hunger, just as Green Revolution agriculture was marketed in the 1960s and 1970s (*Box 11.4*).

Box 11.4: Green Revolution agriculture

'Overpopulation' was used to justify one of the most influential western development and agricultural strategies of the post-war period: the 'Green Revolution'. Development planners maintained that the only solution to the Malthusian spectre of famine was enhancing output through technological means – irrigation, chemical fertilisers and pesticides, and high-yielding seeds. Peasant agriculture was subordinated to or replaced by a more commercial and capital-intensive mode of production geared towards agricultural exports. Western multinationals, such as fertiliser and chemical manufacturers, profited as suppliers of agricultural inputs.

Local food production in developing countries was reduced and the US became the principal source of food grains for the Third World. In the end, the Green Revolution turned out to be less about producing more food for the needy and improving the food security of the poor in developing countries than about securing the economic interests of western multinationals. The Green Revolution denied the yield-raising potential of land redistribution and reoriented production to world markets rather than to local subsistence needs.

Despite the Green Revolution's failure to solve the problem of world hunger, the growing nutritional crisis in the Third World is still attributed to 'overpopulation' or 'environmental stress'. Leading agricultural research organisations claim that ultimately the only solution is the curbing of world population growth and an extension of the Green Revolution through genetically modified crops and privatised water supplies (Ross, 2000, pp 12-17).

The **World Commission on Water for the 21st Century** has argued that the 'gloomy arithmetic' of future thirsty slum dwellers will lead to generalised water scarcity and water wars unless water use is privatised through water pricing (World Commission on Water for the 21st Century, 2000, pp 15, 35). But if over one billion people do not have access to safe drinking water, it is not because the water is lacking: there is more than enough water available, even in water-stressed areas, to provide sufficient water for basic household needs (40 litres per capita per day) to all those classified as 'unserved' today – and the extra two billion expected by 2025. To understand why people go short of water – or any other resource – it is necessary to look at the complex interplay between various actors, global, national and local, and the imbalances of power between them. The reality is – and has always been – that water (like food) flows to those with most bargaining power: industry and bigger farmers first, richer consumers second, and the poor last. In the process, the water supplies that the poor rely on are polluted by industrial effluent, exported in foodstuffs or poured down the drain through wasteful consumption.

Even global warming – principally a result of digging up fossil fuels to drive a century and a half of Northern industrialisation – is used to argue for population control in the developing world through the suggestion that future teeming numbers of Chinese and Indians will cause whole cities to be lost to flooding through their greenhouse gas emissions. This is despite the fact that per capita greenhouse gas emissions from rich countries are far higher than those from poor countries.

Malthus justified the privatisation of communal land through predictions of population-induced scarcity. The privatisation of seeds, water and air are being promoted through a similar scarcity discourse. Of all the rationales for adjusting human numbers, the belief that 'overpopulation' is a primary cause of resource scarcity is one of the most popular and pervasive. Yet differentiating between absolute scarcity – no food or water at all – and socially generated or manufactured scarcity – not enough food or water in some places for some people because others have the power to deny them access – is essential for any sensible discussion of the causes of food insecurity, lack of access to potable water, and 'overpopulation'.

'War on terror'

Security and population issues have also become entwined through the discipline of 'strategic demography', which uses population characteristics such as age, ethnicity, geographic location and numbers to target 'terrorist' or criminal threats. This discipline, adopted by many western demographers and military analysts, cites a 'youth bulge' in the proportion of the world's population aged 27 and under, the majority of whom live in the south, as a 'political hazard' and a threat to social and economic stability and security. Developed in 1985 by a visiting scholar, geographer Gary Fuller, at the US Central Intelligence Agency, 'youth bulge' theory aimed to provide a tool to predict unrest and uncover potential national security threats. Claiming that a proportion of over 20% of young people in a population signals the possibility of political rebellion and unrest (as against the current world total of 50%), it equates large percentages of young men with an increased possibility of violence. This theory is embodied in a twinned set of images: angry young men of colour on the one hand, and veiled young women as victims of repressive regimes on the other. The implied dual threat – of explosive violence and explosive fertility – provides an apparently seamless racially- and gender-based rationale for continued US military intervention and US-promoted population control initiatives in other countries, particularly in the south (Hendrixson, 2004).

Similar arguments claim that sex-selection practices in Asian countries – aborting female foetuses or abandoning girl children – lead to 'surplus sons and missing daughters', resulting in male aggression from lack of sexual partners, lack of employment and lack of education. The solution to this problem is blatantly expressed: 'There is only one short-term strategy for dealing with [this] problem: Reduce their numbers....There are several traditional ways to do so: Fight them, encourage their self-destruction, or export them' (Hudson and Den Boer, 2002, p 26).

The gender stereotyping of 'veiled young women' sees the young women of the 'youth bulge' mainly as potential mothers, reinforcing the notion that young southern women's fertility is responsible for population growth, including the rise in numbers of young male terrorists, and justifying the curtailment of Southern birth rates through population programmes focusing on women. Lobby group Population Action International proposes that the US military team up with international aid agencies to further Southern women's education, family planning services and economic opportunity to ensure both US national security and the well-being of Southern countries themselves (Hendrixson, 2004, p 11).

The prison industrial complex as population control

The youth bulge theory also influenced US domestic policy when a rise in the proportion of young (black and Latino) men was correlated with a rise in the numbers of criminal young men. A lethal stereotype of ruthless young black male criminals increasingly influenced US government policy regarding crime and imprisonment. 'Americans are sitting atop a demographic crime bomb', proclaimed the Princeton professor who in 1995 first made the assertion (Hendrixson, 2004, p 3). Today, over 6.9 million people in the US are behind bars, on parole or probation, or otherwise under supervision by the criminal justice system. In absolute numbers of those in jail and per capita incarceration rates, the US leads the world. Longer and tougher sentencing has contributed to these unprecedented rates.

Two thirds of US prisoners are black or Latino – groups that comprise just over a fifth of the population as a whole, and almost half of Americans living in poverty. In addition, between 1986 and 1991 the number of women in prison increased eight-fold. Just as Malthus left key political and economic processes out of his theory, so too, the image of 'demographic time bombs' and the 'young black criminal' theory behind it are selective. Most of those locked up have committed non-violent crimes out of economic need. During the past two decades, welfare services have been cut, while capital has fled in search of cheaper labour markets, resulting in plant closures and job losses in urban centres that have disproportionately affected African-Americans and semi-skilled workers. With one of the few remaining means of surviving financially being the narcotic drug economy, the country's 'War on Drugs' has resulted in drug offenders comprising the bulk of those either in jail or on parole or probation. Prison population growth in the US can thus be linked not to serious crime rates – which have dropped since 1991 – but to economic stagnation, unemployment and the consequences of structural adjustment at home. The 'War on Drugs', meanwhile, has not stopped drug use but has taken thousands of unemployed (and potentially angry and rebellious) young men and women off the streets.

This 'superpredator' image depicting young men of colour in the inner city as potential criminals is correlated with another gendered, racialised and age-based image: the teen mother 'welfare queen', who is depicted as producing *subsequent* generations of menacing males. There were renewed government efforts in the 1990s to reduce teen birth rates by denying welfare recipients cash benefits as well as through abstinence and contraception education initiatives and welfare-to-work measures. The imprisoning of black men (and women) and the coerced sterilisation and contraception of young black women can be viewed as a US domestic population policy (Hendrixson, 2004).

Conclusion

This chapter has traced the entanglements of population theory and global policy formation over the past two centuries, showing that population policy is one of the earliest forms of global social policy. Here we see how one theory, developed in a particular historical period in a particular part of the world, was quickly adopted and transferred to a range of countries and contexts by state and non-state global policy actors.

From the theoretical work of Malthus in the 19th century to contemporary claims that overpopulation presents a fundamental threat to human security, population policy has mainly been directed at controlling women's fertility, especially that of women in 'developing' countries. While the policy applications of this theory and set of underlying assumptions and concerns may have changed, the thinking has remained constant. We have traced the changes in policy emphasis from population control in the 1950s to reproductive health in the 1990s, noting that over this time, US state and non-state transnational actors have remained prime movers behind the perpetuation of the overpopulation discourse and its influence on global policies. Indeed, despite persistent refutations of the theory and its assumptions, and various concerted social movement and NGO campaigns against it, neither population policies nor Malthusian thinking show signs of dying out: the targets of both policies and thinking continue to shift, reflecting changing demographic, economic and political realities, but also remain much the same. Throughout, the chapter has emphasised the ideological use of population theory, whether Malthusian, eugenic or neo-Malthusian, to advance and legitimise various political and economic interests. In the words of Hartmann and Oliver (2007, p 4), this demonstrates:

> ... the need to remain vigilant about the construction, circulation and deployment of ideas about population. Ideas matter. They are not innocent or neutral. Ideas and theories about population have informed and shaped harmful policies and practices in the past as well as the present, and have the power to do so in the future.

Note

[1] The authors of the chapter are all members of The Corner House, a UK-based research and solidarity group focusing on social and environmental justice issues. They have been trying to understand and to help challenge new manifestations of population thinking and practices when they undermine the rights and welfare of vulnerable groups, weaken grassroots democracy, and limit genuine reproductive choice. The work and thinking of several other scholar activists were indispensable to this collaborative research project, and thus to this chapter: Mohan Rao, Betsy Hartmann, Anne Hendrixson, Sumati Nair, Eric Ross and Mike Davis.

Summary

- Population policy is a long-standing concern of global social policy and an early example of how ideas and policies are transferred across national borders; it predates the emergence of IOs in the 20th century.
- Global policy actors – IOs, private institutions and global sources of finance such as northern donor funds – constitute key channels through which population policy is promoted, even as it is enacted through recipient governments and NGOs.
- Population control policy has usually been directed at women's fertility and has involved the use of quantitative and qualitative targets, and voluntary and coercive techniques.
- Women's and public health movements have primarily opposed global population policies and practices, but in recent years some have attempted to use them to help achieve their own goals.
- The theory of overpopulation is currently finding new outlets, and is applied to issues of international security and conflict.
- Discourses on 'overpopulation' invariably obscure the real roots of poverty, inequality and environmental degradation and overwhelm other explanations of poverty.

Further reading

Hartmann (1995) traces the history of population thinking and population control; describes the development, implementation and consequences of contraceptive technologies; and examines the political, economic and social contexts in which policies are deployed – and their impacts, especially on women in 'developing' countries.

Lugton with McKinney (2004) challenges readers to think critically about national and international population issues. It addresses the complexity of population, environment and development with ideas, analysis and exercises. It contains background readings, up-to-date facts and figures, reasoned arguments, quotes, poems, cartoons, and a comprehensive resource list.

Richey (2008) examines the interactions between global population discourse and local family planning practices across Africa (Tanzania in particular) against a backdrop of neoliberal models of development, and the dominant focus on HIV/AIDS.

Maternowska (2006) queries why so few poor people in Haiti attend health and family planning clinics run by foreign aid organisations despite wanting fewer children. It highlights the range of political dynamics that shape people's decisions about family planning, illustrating the complex interplay between global and local politics.

Krause (2005) traces fears about the potential societal consequences attributed to low birth rates, ageing and immigration to demographic reports that present their opinions about society, women and cultural identity as scientific truth.

Rao and Sexton (forthcoming) present a collection of essays, each focusing on different parts of the globe, critically assessing the 1994 United Nations ICPD and population policies since then. The essays raise issues of politics, economics and ethics, all enmeshed with health and gender concerns.

Halfon (2006) explores how population policies during the 1990s gradually changed from focusing on 'population control' to advocating women's empowerment, and how an international consensus was built up around this transition.

Finally, Connelly (2008) presents a new global history on the global population control movement, highlighting how it has been supported by affluent countries, foundations and NGOs.

Electronic resources

www.thecornerhouse.org.uk/subject/overpopulation The Corner House, UK

http://popdev.hampshire.edu/projects/dt/ Population and Development Program at Hampshire College, US

www.cwpe.org Committee on Women, Population and the Environment, US

References

Asdar Ali, K. (2003) 'Myths, lies and impotence: structural adjustment and male voice in Egypt', *Comparative Studies of South Asia, Africa and the Middle East*, vol 23, no 1&2, pp 321-34.

Bhatia, R., (2005) 'Ten years after Cairo: the resurgence of coercive population control in India', *DifferenTakes*, no 31, Population and Development Program at Hampshire College, http://popdev.hampshire.edu/projects/dt/pdfs/DifferenTakes_31.pdf

Burfoot, A. (1992) 'An interview with Dr Hugh Gorwill: potential risks to women exposed to clomiphene citrate', *Issues in Reproductive and Genetic Engineering*, vol 5, no 1, pp 9-12.

Cincotta, R., Engelman, R. and Anastasion, D. (2003) *The Security Demographic: Population and Civil Conflict After the Cold War*, Washington, DC: Population Action International.

Connelly, M. (2008) *Fatal MisConception: The Struggle to Control World Population*, Cambridge, MA: Harvard University Press.

Davis, M. (2002) 'The origins of the Third World: markets, states and climate', Corner House Briefing 27, www.thecornerhouse.org.uk/pdf/briefing/27origins.pdf

Ehrlich, P. (1968) *The Population Bomb*, New York, NY: Ballantine Books.

Greenhalgh, S. and Winckler, E.A. (2005) *Governing China's Population: From Leninist to Neoliberal Biopolitics*, Stanford, CA: Stanford University Press.

Halfon, S. (2006) *The Cairo Consensus: Demographic Surveys, Women's Empowerment and Regime Change*, Lanham, MD: Lexington Books.

Hartmann, B. (1995) *Reproductive Rights and Wrongs: The Global Politics of Population Control (2nd edn)*, Boston, MA: South End Press.

Hartmann, B. (2006) 'Liberal ends, illiberal means: national security, "environmental conflict" and the making of the Cairo Consensus', *Indian Journal of Gender Studies*, vol 13, no 2, pp 195-227.

Hartmann, B and Oliver, A. (eds) (2007) 'Babies, burdens and threats: current faces of population control, *DifferenTakes*, Population and Development Program at Hampshire College, http://popdev.hampshire.edu/sites/popdev/files/dt/DT_BBT_Collection.pdf

Hendrixson, A. (2004) 'Angry young men, veiled young women: constructing a new population threat', Corner House Briefing 34, www.thecornerhouse.org.uk/pdf/briefing/34veiled.pdf

Homer-Dixon, T. (1995) 'The ingenuity gap: can poor countries adapt to resource scarcity?', *Population and Development Review*, vol 21, no 3, pp 587-612.

Hudson, V.M. and Den Boer, A. (2002) 'A surplus of men, a deficit of peace: security and sex ratios in Asia's largest states', *International Security*, vol 26, no 4, pp 5-38.

Koivusalo, M. and Ollila, E. (1997) *Making a Healthy World. Agencies, Actors and Policies in International Health*, London: Zed Books.

Krause, E.L. (2005) *A Crisis of Births: Population Politics and Family-making in Italy*, Belmont, CA: Wadsworth.

Lifton, R.J. (1986) *The Nazi Doctors: Medical Killing and the Psychology of Genocide*, London: Macmillan.

Lohmann, L. (2003) 'Re-imagining the population debate', Corner House Briefing 28, www.thecornerhouse.org.uk/pdf/briefing/28reimagin.pdf

Lugton, M. with McKinney, P. (2004) *Population in Perspective: A Curriculum Resource*, Hampshire, MA: Population and Development Programme at Hampshire College, http://populationinperspective.org/

Malthus, T.R. (1993 [1798]) *Essay on the Principle of Population*, First edition, Oxford: Oxford University Press.

Maternowska, M.C. (2006) *Reproducing Inequities: Poverty and the Politics of Population in Haiti*, Piscataway, NJ: Rutgers University Press.

Meadows, D.H., Meadows, D.L., Randers, J. and Behrens, W.W. (1972) *Limits to Growth*, New York, NY: Basic Books.

Minns, R. (2006) 'Too many grannies? Private pensions, corporate welfare and growing insecurity', Corner House Briefing 35, www.thecornerhouse.org.uk/pdf/briefing/35grannies.pdf

Nair, S. and Kirbat, P. with Sexton, S. (2004) 'A decade after Cairo: women's health in a free market economy', Corner House Briefing 31, www.thecornerhouse.org.uk/pdf/briefing/31cairo.pdf

Rao, M. (2004) *From Population Control to Reproductive Health: Malthusian Arithmetic*, New Delhi: Sage Publications.

Rao, M. and Sexton, S. (eds) (forthcoming) *Rereading Cairo: Population and Gender in Neo-Liberal Times*, New Delhi: Sage Publications.

Richey, L.A. (2003) 'HIV/AIDS in the shadows of reproductive health interventions', *Reproductive Health Matters*, vol 11, no 22, pp 30-5.

Richey, L.A. (2008) *Population Politics and Development: From the Policies to the Clinics*, New York, NY: Palgrave Macmillan.

Ross, E. (1998) *The Malthus Factor: Poverty, Politics and Population and Capitalist Development*, London and New York: Zed Books.

Ross, E. (2000) 'The Malthus factor: poverty, politics and population in capitalist development', Corner House Briefing 20, www.thecornerhouse.org.uk/pdf/briefing/20malth.pdf

UNFPA (United Nations Population Fund) (2002) *People, Poverty and Possibilities: Making Development Work for the Poor: State of World Population 2002*, New York, NY: UNFPA.

USAID (United States Agency for International Development) (2008) *Balancing and the Environment to Promote Resilient Communities*, Washington DC: USAID, www.usaid.gov/our_work/global_health/pop/techareas/environment/phe_factsheet.pdf

WB (World Bank) (2004) *A Review of Population, Reproductive Health and Adolescent Health & Development in Poverty Reduction Strategies*, Washington, DC: The Population and Reproductive Health Cluster; Health, Nutrition and Population Unit, WB.

World Commission on Water for the 21st Century (2000) *A Water Secure World: Vision for Water, Life and the Environment*, Marseille: World Water Council, www.worldwatercouncil.org/fileadmin/wwc/Library/Publications_and_reports/Visions/CommissionReport.pdf

Conclusion

Nicola Yeates

Introduction

Over the last decade, global social policy has become established as a dynamic and expanding field of academic study and research. Like other globalist approaches within social science, it is contributing in significant ways to understanding of the social world and social policy formation. With its emphasis firmly on the transnational and global dimensions of social welfare provision and social policy formation, it draws attention to neglected aspects of political processes and socio-institutional formations which have marked impacts on human welfare. Global social policy also invites a consideration of whether theories, concepts and methodologies that have helped understand the making and remaking of social welfare systems and policies are still useful.

Despite its recent entry into the lexicon of social policy analysis, global social policy is having profound effects, recasting the ways in which social policy is being studied and discussed. Such is the nature of these impacts that, from the vantage point of 2008, it seems that no book on social policy is complete without attending to the 'global' dimensions of social policy in some way, no conference is complete without a 'global' panel, speaker or theme, and no social policy journal can afford to neglect the global aspects of social policy and human welfare. Therefore we can say with confidence that global social policy is now a key intellectual driver of social policy analysis.

Taking stock of this expanding field of research and scholarship, the aim of this volume was to provide a comprehensive and accessible collection of research-based chapters exploring major areas, issues, debates and themes in contemporary global social policy analysis. Each of the chapters has carefully synthesised and explained a complex set of relations and developments to provide an insightful introduction to their particular policy area or theme in a manner suitable for a non-specialist audience. At this stage in the book, it would not be appropriate to systematically summarise the various findings and conclusions of each of the 11 preceding chapters. These are already well presented at the start and end of each chapter in the form of an overview and a summary. Rather, this short concluding chapter sums up the general approach of the book and distils its main messages. It does this by looking back over the chapters in the light of the overall framework set out in Chapter One of this volume. The discussion is organised around four main themes:

- the characteristics of global social policy as a field of study and research;
- global social policy ideas, discourses, actors, agendas and practices;
- global policy actors and forces 'from above' and 'from below'; and
- the importance of history and place in understanding global social policy.

Global social policy

In Chapter One, the general approach of the book was located firmly within the tradition of globalist bodies of thought and study that attend to social systems and interactions linking different people and places around the world. While noting various distinctions and emphases arising from theoretical positions or subject areas, what matters for our purposes is the distinctive transnationalist methodology characteristic of global social policy analysis. This approach sets global social policy apart from traditional approaches to social policy: where global social policy analysts 'see' fluidity and permeability of state borders, cross-border flows of people, ideas, goods, services and the existence of collective action in cross-border spheres of governance as integral to social politics and policy, national social policy analysts 'see' the nation state as a bounded category of analysis and political action, as coterminous with society and social relations, and focus on the formation of social policy and the provision of social welfare within those national borders. As we have emphasised, there is a world of difference between bringing in 'the global' as a background feature to an analysis which otherwise privileges intranational social ties and relations and bringing in 'the global' more substantively to rethink the nature of the social world and policy formation as a globally interconnected system and set of interactions.

Although this distinction sets global social policy apart from other approaches to social policy analysis, it is also important to emphasise that global social policy analysts have much in common with those whose work is framed by methodological nationalism. After all, both share a concern with the ways in which collective action is mobilised in the interests of human welfare and with the wider social impacts of this action. Both also approach social policy as a normative subject concerned with what should or ought to be happening, as an empirically-oriented subject concerned to find out what is actually happening, and as a theoretical subject concerned to understand the 'how and why' of what is happening. But while the values and concerns are often shared, the ontological, methodological and assumptive worlds otherwise differ markedly.

Ideas, discourses, actors, agendas and practices of global social policy

Looking back across the chapters and the diverse policy areas they cover – pensions, education, employment and labour, trade, population control, housing and urban policy, health and international migration – the authors have explored key global policy ideas and discourses, the different kinds of global policy actors involved, key global policy agendas and the global dimensions of social welfare provision. *Table 12.1* picks out one or two examples from each of the chapters of how the authors have addressed these themes. The Table is necessarily selective and indicative, and you might wish to go back through the chapters to pick out other examples for yourself.

Chapter One noted how global social policy was initially confined to the practices of elite global actors and institutions in its emphasis on certain agencies and organisations such as the UN and Bretton Woods institutions. Over time, this definition has grown to encompass the agendas and practices of a wider range of global policy and social actors involved in social dialogues around global restructuring and reform processes. This more recent understanding of global social policy formation is premised on an understanding of 'embedded transnationalism' that includes, but is not restricted to, the high politics and visibly 'global' institutionalised realms of social policy formation. Thus, the examples in *Table 12.1* include the discourses and practices of:

- multilateral formations (for example, WB, ILO, UN, WTO, OECD), world-regional formations such as the European Union (EU) and others, and government agencies and departments such as USAID and DfID. Alongside these transnational organisations we must also situate various 'national' and sub-national governmental organisations and authorities with which intergovernmental organisations interact to codetermine policy formation and outcomes;

Table 12.1: Dimensions of global social policy

Chapter	Global ideas, discourses	Actors	Policy agendas and practices
2	Human rights	UN	UN Covenant on Economic, Social and Cultural Rights, Convention on Rights of the Child
	Public–private partnerships	Philanthropists, UN	GAVI
	Social solidarity	OECD, northern governments	Overseas development assistance
3	Democratic education	UNESCO	Education for All
	Lifelong learning, knowledge workers	WB	Lifelong learning skills for the global knowledge economy, individualised learning plans
4	Self-regulation	Global business interest associations and pro-business epistemic communities; IOs, eg, OECD, UN	UN Global Compact OECD Guidelines for multinational enterprises
5	International competitiveness, free trade	WTO, national and global business interest associations	Trade liberalisation treaties and laws
	Fair trade	'Anti-globalisation' and trade justice campaign/ers	Ethical consumption and investment campaigns
6	Human rights, social justice	ILO, labour movement	Core labour standards
7	Human rights	WHO	Alma Ata, Health for All
	Corporate rights	WTO	TRIPS

8	Self-help Free markets	WB, IDB, USAID, DfID	Housing-related ODA Government as enabler and the development of housing markets
9	Social solidarity Demographic crisis	ILO WB, policy coalitions of neoliberal economists, pension fund managers, governments	Declaration of Philadelphia 'New' pension reforms
10	Managed migration Kinship, obligation, reciprocity	WB, IOM, UN International migrants and diasporic communities	Healthcare worker recruitment and retention schemes, e.g. joint Caribbean Nurses Organization/ Pan American Health Organization managed migration scheme Provision of cash and care to relatives and communities in the source or home country
11	'Overpopulation' and population crisis	USAID, WB and INGOs, eg, the IPPF and the Population Council	Population control, including various fertility control measures

Notes: DfID: Department for International Development; GAVI: Global Alliance for Vaccination and Immunisation; IDB: Inter-American Development Bank; INGO: international non-governmental organisation ; ILO: International Labour Organisation; IO: international organisation; IOM: International Organization on Migration; IPPF: International Planned Parenthood Federation; ODA: overseas development assistance; OECD: Organisation for Economic Co-operation and Development; TRIPS: Agreement on Trade Related Aspects of Intellectual Property Rights; UN: United Nations; UNESCO: United Nations Educational, Scientific and Cultural Organization; USAID: United States Agency for International Development; WB: World Bank; WHO: World Health Organization; WTO: World Trade Organization.

- transnational non-governmental actors: on the one hand, global business interest associations (GBIAs), philanthropic organisations and international voluntary sector organisations directly involved in formulating and implementing policy; on the other hand, transnational advocacy coalitions and global social movements (for example, trade justice and labour movements), which are often involved in more oppositional and protest actions at the 'margins' of institutionalised policy-making machinery;
- transnational actors located outside the institutionalised realm of social policy formation, as in the existence of global families and diasporic communities. Their involvement in global social policy derives from their provision of cash and care to relatives and communities in their country of origin.

Global policy actors and forces 'from above' and 'from below'

While it is clear is that the bureaux and boardrooms of governments and intergovernmental formations are a key site of global social policy formation, there are also many other sites and policy actors of which we need to take account. So, although the institutionalised realm and the policy responses that result from them – be they in the form of debt relief measures, charters of rights or the definition of global regulatory standards – remain at the core of global social policy analysis, we have emphasised that such 'from above' forces need to be supplemented by attention to forces 'from below' in order to comprehend the political processes shaping social policy and the nature of transnational social welfare provision.

First, the book has emphasised the ways in which social formations are 'globalised' and how this globalisation generates alternative modes of welfare provision that connect people and places across national borders and territories. This was examined in Chapter Ten by Nicola Yeates where the role of migrant households and diasporic communities within transnational social policy processes was emphasised. Here, migrant remittances as a source of international financing for welfare was highlighted, together with the provision of substantial amounts of social care between geographically distant households.

A second way in which this book emphasised processes of globalisation 'from below' was through an emphasis on transnational advocacy coalitions and campaigns. Together with globalised families, these border-spanning social formations are examples of such 'grassroots' globalisation processes dating back at least as far as, if not further than, the establishment of intergovernmental organisations by international networks of governments. These 'from below' processes of global social policy formation 'from below' involve diverse social actors operating across various spheres, at different levels and on a range of scales. In the context of this book, we have looked at campaigns by social movement and non-governmental organisations against neoliberal or socially liberal forms of global social policy. These were discussed in various chapters, including Chapter Two by Bob Deacon in the context of global social governance reform, in Chapters Four, Five and Six by Kevin Farnsworth, Christopher Holden and Robert O'Brien respectively in relation to trade and labour reforms, and in Chapter Eleven by Sarah Sexton, Larry Lohmann and Nicholas Hildyard in the context of population policy.

These 'counter-currents' to the dominant tendency within global social policy formation processes are rightly emphasised, as they are part of any explanation of global social policy change. Yet confining explanations of reform (or non-reform) to non-governmental popular actions is not in itself sufficient, and this is why we have also emphasised the role of wider networks of transnational policy formations and actors – governments, professionals, experts – which also shape ideas and agendas about particular policies and policy approaches (see Chapter One). For example, Mitchell Orenstein in Chapter Nine draws attention to the significance of Harvard-trained economists, receptive governments and pension fund managers in explaining the rise of the new pension reforms and their application in the Chilean context. His discussion of the successful transfer of 'new' pension reforms in other countries around the world emphasises the importance to advocates of those reforms of securing sympathetic allies in the 'host' country in order to implement the reforms. Although domestic actors have to take account of IOs, they also have to take account of national *social* laws and agreements as well as a range of domestic actors such as the legislature and politicians, electorates, non-governmental military and domestic business interests, any of which may oppose IO-preferred reforms or win important concessions from them. Indeed, any changes in domestic regulation still needs to be explained by reference to the balance of political power nationally as well as internationally (Yeates, 2001).

All too often, transnational policy campaigns are examined only in the context of opposition to neoliberal or socially liberal global social policy, but among the most successful transnational social movements is what Leslie Sklair calls the 'transnational capitalist class' (Sklair, 2001). For this reason various chapters have also looked at the various transnational movements and campaigns in favour of neoliberal and socially liberal policy reforms. Mitchell Orenstein (Chapter Nine) is clear in identifying the sources of the 'new' pension reforms, and various other chapter authors also identify similar reform sources: Rob Hulme and Moira Hulme (Chapter Three) do so in the context of global education policy, identifying UNESCO and the World Bank (WB) as what some would regard as horses from the same stable; Kevin Farnsworth (Chapter Four) does so in his examination of the role of GBIAs in pushing for self-regulation as a response to the threat of mandatory regulation of corporate activities; Meri Koivusalo and Eeva Ollila (Chapter Seven) show how corporate interests and associations have been able to institutionalise their interests within various parts of global health policy, from tobacco control to drug pricing; Sunil Kumar (Chapter Eight) discusses how Northern donors such as the US and UK in alliance with the WB and certain intellectuals have advocated housing policy approaches that favour self-help by people with severe housing needs together with market provision; and Sarah Sexton, Larry Lohmann and Nicholas Hildyard (Chapter Eleven) discuss how Malthusian ideas have consistently defined many of the world's social problems in terms of 'overpopulation', leading to punitive and coercive responses enacted against the poorest people and women in particular. To be sure, the forces and ideas in favour of neoliberal and socially liberal forms of global social policy differ in some important respects, but they are nonetheless essentially conservative in arguing against more radical reforms that would be redistributive in impact and allow greater control by families, communities and nations over key social and political determinants affecting their lives.

The importance of history and geography

In Chapter One, I noted that two criticisms of global social policy analysis are its tendency to ignore previous enactments and formations of global social policy together with its neglect of how different places around the world both shape and are affected by global social policies. For some, the 'scaling up' of social policy analysis to a global level has resulted in 'presentist' and universalising analyses. This is why this book has emphasised the importance of both history and geography in understanding global social policy.

In terms of needing to historicise global social policy, we have shown that global social policy as a political practice dates back well before the rise of international governmental organisations (IGOs). As I discussed in Chapter One, such practices date back hundreds of years and are integral to the formation of modern nation states; they are also integral to the processes that made and remade 'national' welfare formations around the world. Far from being merely part of the background or general context, the state of welfare in today's world is in good part the product of global formations prior to the 20th century which acted as 'carriers' of social ideas, policies and practices long before the existence of present-day multilateral organisations. This theme is clearly evident across the book. In Chapter Eleven it was highlighted in the context of global population policy, one of the earliest forms of global social policy. In that chapter, Sexton, Lohmann and Hildyard discussed how the British Empire can be seen as one such global formation. They identified England as the originator of what became global ideas about 'overpopulation'. In the context of liberal economic policies, these ideas and discourses informed

Britain's response to famines overseas in the 19th century. They were also were allied to a range of policy responses to issues of poverty and scarcity during the 20th century, including measures which took the form of denying women's reproductive rights. And in Chapter Eight, Sunil Kumar traced the transnational dimensions of housing and urban policy back some 60 years to the immediate aftermath of the Second World War. He discussed the various shifts in global policy agendas and approaches that have occurred since then, showing how the nature of international housing aid and the aims of housing and urban policies have developed over time and how these changes were informed by global ideas and ideological positions.

The project of historicising global social policy is also about identifying policy paradigms and changes (or lack of them). Some scholars claim to detect a recent qualitative shift, with the emphases in the Washington Consensus (WC) on macro-economic conditions, public sector reform, getting the prices right, 'hard' conditionalities, deregulation and privatisation, giving way to a more 'humane' Post-Washington Consensus (PWC) that emphasises micro-economic conditions, private sector reform, getting the institutions right, upgrading and re-regulation, and 'smart' conditionalities. In Chapter Two Bob Deacon addressed how this shift has had an impact on the politics of global social policy generally, noting that the question being asked is not whether global markets need to be regulated but what form such regulation should take. Sunil Kumar in Chapter Eight similarly noted policy changes on the part of the WB and DfID in relation to housing and urban development support over this period.

Whether there has been any such shift and what it has meant for social policy is hotly debated, with doubts expressed as to whether any such fundamental break with the past has occurred, especially given that residualised public welfare and conservative approaches are common to both the 'old' WC and the 'new' PWC. A number of the chapters engage in this debate. Chapter Four by Kevin Farnsworth touches on this debate in his analysis of the participation of global business in the making of global social policy. He argued that IGOs have promulgated global social regulatory and policy initiatives sympathetic to corporate interests while economic priorities continue to dominate global policy decisions. Chapter Seven by Meri Koivusalo and Eeva Ollila similarly casted doubt on the 'new' global social policy in pointing to the various ways in which corporate and trade interests have permeated global health policy in recent years to the detriment of policy agendas and measures favouring comprehensive healthcare. Finally, Chapter Eleven brought out the essential historical continuity of global social policy in its emphasis on the enduring influences of Malthusian thinking that the authors argued shows little evidence of discontinuity or change over the period of the supposed decline of the WC and the emergence of the PWC: in both periods matters of intense human need and ecological crisis are constructed as issues of overpopulation rather than issues of inequitable resource distribution.

Just as history matters, so does geography. Contrary to the claims of some of the more avid globalisation enthusiasts that geography and place are less relevant now than in the past, it is clear that place remains a key social determinant that is closely tied to power. One of the key themes in global social policy is how poorer countries in Asia, Africa and South America are affected by the actions of richer ones in the region, and how the Global South is affected by powerful countries and actors located in the Global North. This attention to political and economic geography has been picked up in a number of ways in the book. For example, one of the implications of Bob Deacon's (Chapter Two) suggestion that we need to differentiate between the policy approaches and impacts of different IOs is that we can expect the impact of the EU and OECD on European social policy to be distinct from that of the WB and IMF on African social policy. In addition, both Chris Holden (Chapter Five) and Robert O'Brien (Chapter Six) noted how wealthier and poorer countries have different interests in relation to economic strategy and labour policies. Thus, developing countries often have a comparative advantage in low-skilled, low-waged, labour-intensive production and have often resisted agreements on what they regard as restrictive and protectionist international labour standards advocated by wealthier countries in the industrialised North. In Chapter Ten I similarly noted the importance of economic and political geography in the overall flow of labour migrants from poorer regions and countries towards richer ones and the apparent increase in the number of international migrants in recent decades. The flows of international migrants to these richer areas of the world forge links with poorer parts of the world through flows of people and finance (international remittances) and on a political level too with the bilateral treaties sometimes also ensuing.

Global social policy is not, then, only about what happens in poorer countries – it is also about social policies in the richer countries and the relations between them, as well as relations between poorer countries. One way in which this has been dealt with is in Chapter Ten where Yeates suggested that in so far as global social conflict and uneven development come to be manifested in the rich democracies as labour migrants, then national and global migration regimes in these countries become part of global social policy. And many of the other chapters have also highlighted how clubs of rich countries and the policies they develop and advocate for themselves can be considered part of global social policy. The policies of the OECD, an international organisation of about 30 of the world's richest countries, are a good example of this. Rob Hulme and Moira Hulme (Chapter Three) reviewed the role of the OECD in the setting of policy agendas for its member countries around education, while

Kevin Farnsworth (Chapter Four) discussed the role of this IO in formulating global corporate regulations

The importance of place in the politics of global social policy reform is ever more evident in other ways too. As Bob Deacon and other analysts have noted, there are signs that the WB recognises the importance of context in contrast to its earlier stance of 'one (policy) size fits all (countries)'. The proliferation of world-regional formations is another such indication, with groups of countries forming regionalist associations to advance member countries' economic interests (Deacon, Chapter Two; Holden, Chapter Five; O'Brien, Chapter Six). While trade and investment issues have tended to dominate the formation of these associations, social policy issues have also been part of the agenda. More generally, as Deacon (Chapter Two) points out, world-regional social governance has emerged as a credible alternative 'global' reform strategy in recent years, with advocates seeing it as a way of forging a space for Southern governments in particular, as well as civil society, to make their own policy choices. The politics of place is also evident in some of the more radical reforms advocated in global social policy, with some advocating global policy strategies of localisation, self-reliance and local economic cooperation to promote the viability of smaller-scale, localised and diversified economies that re-establish the links and connections between local economies and local populations.

Global social policy: final reflections

The main purpose of this book has been to develop a conceptual understanding of social policy in global terms. Its central premise is that social policy analysis is best understood through the lens of methodological transnationalism. Given the prevailing social policy paradigm, this approach presents important challenges as it involves rethinking the construction of fields of enquiry and revisiting conceptual, theoretical and methodological frameworks developed over many decades. Within a relatively short time it has generated much innovative work, and global social policy analysis is demonstrably offering new ways of approaching the study of the conditions and processes that have an impact on human welfare and how collective action is mobilised to address key social welfare and policy issues.

In the context of this book, we have particularly emphasised the foregrounding of global social systems, global political processes, global policy actors and global policy issues in the making of social policy – whether in national, international or supranational spheres of governance. We have identified the need for a transnationalist understanding of social policy that recognises the different spatial and scalar modes through which social policy formation occurs. Cautioning against a totalising vision of global social policy, we have emphasised the variety of forces, processes and actors involved in the making of global social policy, and stressed the need for an historically and geographically embedded understanding of global social policy formation. Indeed, rather than denying the importance of 'local' political context and economic and welfare systems, these are best understood in the context of, and by reference to, transnational and global forces and processes. In opening up social policy to these new ways of understanding social policy, we have questioned the distinctions between 'foreign' and 'domestic' arenas and policies, and what 'counts' as relevant objects of enquiry.

While current and future generations of scholars of social policy will undoubtedly continue to develop frameworks for analysing global social policy, whatever the particular subject or issue being studied, the core concern must be to identify and advocate progressive social arrangements and forms of collective action supportive of the means to social participation and social development for everyone in the world, regardless of social or national origin or place of residence.

References

Sklair, L. (2001) *The Transnational Capitalist Class*, Oxford: Blackwell.
Yeates, N. (2001) *Globalization and Social Policy*, London: Sage Publications.

Appendix

Glossary of terms

Anti-globalisation movement (also known as global social justice movement) Social movement that opposes neoliberal globalisation through summit protests and social fora. A prime instance of a global social movement.

Bilateral actors Organisations, usually governmental, representing one country in negotiations with, and activities in, another country.

Bilateralism Process of, or commitment to, forming an agreement between two states.

Bretton Woods WB and the IMF. These are the key institutional bases of the Bretton Woods system, which was set up after the Second World War to stabilise the international economy.

Burden of disease The overall impact of diseases and injuries at the individual level or at the societal level. Also refers to the economic costs of diseases.

Business/corporate power The ability of business actors and organisations to influence others so that they act in ways they would not otherwise act. Different kinds of corporate powers are sometimes distinguished: *Corporate agency power* The capacity of a business actor to influence policy making in a given direction. Mechanisms of agency power include standing for election, membership of public decision-making bodies, use of the media and direct lobbying. *Corporate structural power* The ability of firms to steer policy making towards their own ends through the simple pursuit of their own day-to-day economic interests. Power stems from the fact that decision makers depend on firms to continue to invest and make healthy profits.

Cities alliance Global coalition of cities and development partners, supporting sustainable urban development. Members include Slum Dwellers International, representatives of local authorities (such as United Cities and Local Governments, and Metropolis, the World Association of Major Metropolises) states (Brazil, Canada, Ethiopia, France, Germany, Italy, Japan, Netherlands, Nigeria, Norway, South Africa, Sweden, UK and US) and international organisations (for example, Asian Development Bank, EU, UNEP, UN-HABITAT, WB).

Civil society (also known as **civic society**) Seen as a sphere separate from state and market comprising voluntary civic or social associations, groups or organisations that represent, defend or serve the interests of their members.

Civil society organisations include advocacy groups and networks, community groups, non-governmental organisations, registered charities, self-help groups and trade unions.

Comparative advantage A theory of international trade that states that countries will gain from trade if they transfer resources between industries to specialise in the sectors in which they are the most efficient. They need not hold an absolute advantage to gain from trade. Comparative advantage stipulates that countries should specialise in the products they are the best at producing.

Competitive advantage A theory that incorporates historical and cultural factors, including the structure of industry and the level of technological development, in explaining the internationally competitive position of industries in different countries.

Comprehensive healthcare An approach that emphasises full provision of personal health services on a universal basis, with a traditional emphasis on primary healthcare. Defined in the Alma Ata Declaration, it also provides the basis for Health for All policies.

Conditionalities Attached to loans by MEIs, which include requirements to open economic sectors to foreign investment, privatise state-owned enterprises and welfare services, and remove tariff barriers and food and fuel subsidies.

Contribution A payment made to a pension plan by a plan sponsor or a plan member.

Corporate agency power *See* business/corporate power.

Corporate codes of conduct Policy statements that define ethical standards for corporate conduct. They are voluntary, have no legal standard and use a variety of monitoring and enforcement mechanisms.

Corporate social responsibility A range of business initiatives and policies that have the stated aims of contributing positively.

Corporate structural power *See* business/corporate power.

Cosmopolitan approach/cosmopolitanism The idea that all human beings, regardless of nationality, belong to a single (moral, political or cultural) community.

Cosmopolitan citizenship Citizenship that recognises the multiple identities of citizens – that is, those identities that link individuals to host locality and nation and cultural/migrant heritage – while also respecting the rights of all citizens regardless of nationality.

Cross-national attraction A conceptual framework that examines the tendency for 'northern' and 'western' nations in particular to replicate structures evident in other similarly situated countries.

Dependency theory A theory, built on Marxist principles, to explain why many Third World countries remain poor. The main argument is that they are dependent on rich industrialised countries that have sought to exploit poor countries for their resources. A key proponent of this theory is Andre Gunder Frank.

Diaspora Dispersal of people throughout the world from their original location. Originally applied to Jewish people, it now refers to any national or ethnic group with members scattered around the world.

Displacement In the context of international trade, a process whereby imported goods substitute for those produced domestically, often leading to domestic unemployment. In the context of migration, displacement refers to people who are forcibly removed from their place of residence.

Double taxation The taxation of profits within a corporation's home country and another country where income is earned. Where agreements exist, profits may be declared and taxed within either country.

Epistemic communities Networks of actors that are significant in generating and transferring knowledge about policy between policy networks.

Eugenics The belief that the hereditary traits of a population can be 'improved' through various forms of intervention. It often refers to movements and social policies of the early 20th century that were concerned with perceived intelligence factors correlated with social class. Eugenic policies have been categorised as either positive or negative, with positive eugenics aimed at encouraging reproduction among those groups of people presumed to have desirable inheritable traits and negative eugenics trying to lower or stop altogether the fertility (by means of sterilisation, family planning or abortion) of those deemed to have undesirable inheritable or genetic traits. Most of these policies have been coercive to varying degrees.

Exchange rate system A system that determines the value of one currency when exchanged with another. In 'floating' systems, it is the market that determines the exchange rate, while in 'fixed' systems this is held constant over time.

Export-oriented policy Economic policy focused on producing goods for export.

Export processing zone Area of a country where labour standards, environmental rules or tax collections are reduced in order to attract the investment of transnational corporations. Products assembled in these zones are intended for export.

Financial Sector Adjustment Loan Loan provided under the Financial Sector Assessment Programme, a joint International Monetary Fund–World Bank programme introduced in May 1999. The FSAP aims to increase the effectiveness of efforts to promote the soundness of financial systems in member countries.

Foreign direct investment Financial capital transfer from one country to another for investment in production of goods or services.

Free trade agreements Treaties between countries that commit each side to eliminating tariffs on each other's products and facilitating the exchange of goods and services.

Funded pension plans Occupational or personal pension plans that accumulate dedicated assets to cover the plan's liabilities.

G8/Group of 8 Informal forum comprising Canada, France, Germany, Italy, Japan, Russia, the UK and the US. Representatives from these countries meet to discuss a range of policy concerns.

G20/Group of 20 An informal political forum set up in 1999 to discuss issues of financial stability. It brings together industrial and emerging-market countries from different regions of the world. Members of the G20 are the finance ministers and central bank governors of 19 countries: Argentina, Australia, Brazil, Canada, China, France, Germany, India, Indonesia, Italy, Japan, Mexico, Russia, Saudi Arabia, South Africa, South Korea, Turkey, the UK and the US. The EU is also a member.

G77/Group of 77 Originally a group of 77 countries established in 1964 in the context of the first session of the UN on Trade and Development. It now comprises 132 developing country states. The group seeks to harmonise the positions of developing countries prior to and during negotiations.

GAVI Alliance (GAVI) A public–private partnership whose remit is to increase vaccination against preventable diseases in developing countries.

Global business Company or business organisation whose interests and operations extend beyond nation states and world regions to encompass the globe.

Global business interest association Associations that represent common interests of businesses worldwide, for example, the International Chambers of Commerce.

Global care chains Links and ties that connect people globally through migration to undertake paid or unpaid care work.

Global division of labour The arrangement whereby people around the world are grouped into particular types of jobs. The allocation of people to tasks can be based on ethnicity, caste, class, 'race', gender, historical or geographical circumstance, merit or talent.

Global migration regime International system of migration management involving both sending and host countries. *See also* multilateral migration regime.

Global pensions policy A policy set by transnational actors regarding government-sponsored retirement funds.

Global philanthropy Financial or in-kind support by private donors to charitable causes provided by the public sector. Sometimes used by donors as a way to avoid tax.

Global policy Policy formed by discussion between transnational actors.

Global policy actors Policy actors – such as non-governmental organisations, social movements, international governmental organisations, business organisations, governments and professional associations – that attempt to influence policy in multiple countries.

Global policy advocacy coalition Advocacy or campaigning coalition oriented around global policy reform. See also transnational advocacy coalition.

Global public goods Goods that serve the international public interest but that no one country or private actor left to itself might choose to provide – for example, the international regulation and notification of diseases. The consumption of global public goods is not exclusive to one state: it is available to many states.

Global public–private partnerships Global governance mechanisms that involve an agreement between an intergovernmental organisation (eg a UN agency) and a private agency (eg the Bill & Melinda Gates Foundation).

Global (social) redistribution The process by which funds and resources flow across state borders. Normally this occurs from richer Northern states to poorer Southern ones, such as by the means of overseas development assistance. But it also occurs from poorer Southern states to richer Northern ones, as in (for example) the subsidies to Northern health systems provided by the migration of skilled health workers trained in Southern states.

Global regulation The process whereby international actors are required to confirm to global rules, procedures and standards. Commonly discussed in the context of the need for global regulation of business actors and practices in the interests of social protection and welfare. See also global social regulation.

Global social governance The complex process of global social policy formation and implementation involving the collaboration of a number of intergovernmental and global private actors.

Global social justice movement See anti-globalisation movement.

Global social movement A social movement that is global in scale and scope. Examples include 'old' social movements – labour, peace – as well as 'new' social movements – the environment, women, human rights and development. The anti-globalisation movement is a prime example of a global social movement, as it unites various other global social movements.

Global social policy Examines how social policy issues are increasingly being perceived to be global in scope, cause and impact. The term encompasses the study of: how cross-border flows of people, goods, services, ideas and finance relate to social policy development; the emergence of transnational forms of collective action, including the development of multilateral and cross-border modes of governance and policy making; and how these modes shape the development and impacts of social policy around the world.

Global (social) regulation The process whereby the activities of transnational corporations and other global private actors are subjected to a set of rules (that may be voluntary or compulsory) to ensure that they behave in ways that enhance the social welfare of their employees, consumers or local residents.

Global social reproduction The process by which global social structures and hierarchies are reproduced from generation to generation.

Global social rights Social entitlements, such as the right to social security, normally articulated within United Nations covenants. Such rights do not currently entail the right of redress to international courts if they are not met.

Global standards Minimum common standards that are agreed on by many countries, and/or promoted by international organisations.

Globalisation A term used to denote the economic, technological, cultural, social and political forces and processes said to have produced the characteristic conditions of contemporary life. Foremost among these characteristics is a dense network of interconnections and interdependencies that routinely transcend national borders. This interconnectedness is not only said to be more extensive in scope than in previous periods, but more intensive, and the speed at which such interactions are occurring is increasing.

Globalised families *See* transnational families.

Globalisation studies A multidisciplinary field of study and research focusing on understanding globalisation processes and impacts. Sometimes referred to as global studies by those who may accept the appropriateness of a global analytical framework but who do not accept the tenets of the globalisation thesis.

Government as enabler Government role that is limited to the provision of those elements of human settlement that are beyond the capacity of individuals and households to provide, such as serviced land and networked water and sanitation.

Government as provider The direct involvement of government as a provider of services and housing.

Health status Level of health of an individual, group or population, measured according to morbidity, mortality or available health resources. More than the outcome of individual choice (such as lifestyle and diet), it is influenced by a range of social determinants of health, such as economic situation, nutritional status, education and quality of sanitation and housing.

Health system The functional expression of health policies. The formal structure that incorporates both health services and other measures whose primary purpose is to promote, restore or maintain health. Health system covers a defined population and is organised, financed and regulated by statute.

Healthcare reform A generic term for the reform of the organisation and/or financing of healthcare services. However, a particular set of changes has dominated measures on healthcare reform, following broader new public management principles, separating purchasers and providers of services and utilising market mechanisms within healthcare services.

Household internationalisation strategies Strategies by which households form international links, either through the migration of an individual member or the entire household to undertake work in another country, or through the employment of immigrants to undertake work in the household.

Housing policy A policy encompassing issues of land, physical infrastructure (such as water, sanitation, electricity, roads, drainage), housing finance, housing institutions, and the construction sector.

Individual pension fund A pension fund that comprises the assets of a single member and his/her beneficiaries, usually in the form of an individual account.

Influence mechanism The ways in which policy actors work to effect policy decisions. Examples of influence mechanisms include norms creation, persuasion and economic incentives.

Informal economy Economic activity that exists beyond formally regulated economic and legal institutions.

Institutionalise The act of ensuring that actions leading to positive outcomes, especially for the poor, become the normal practice of the state actor concerned. For example, access to and the delivery of health provision is institutionalised in the UK.

Integrated projects City-wide interventions combining components dealing with shelter, infrastructure, transport, solid waste management, business support, health, nutrition and education.

International governmental organisation (IGO) *See* international organisation.

International Labour Organization (ILO) Founded in 1919 and becoming the first United Nations specialised agency in 1946, the ILO produces international labour standards in the form of Conventions and Recommendations, provides technical assistance and promotes the development of employers' and workers' organisations. It is governed by a tripartite structure in which workers, employers and governments cooperate as formally equal partners.

International non-governmental organisation (INGO) Part of the international voluntary sector, INGOs are non-governmental organisations based mainly in western countries. They operate in a variety of countries, sometimes in cooperation with local and national NGOs, often delivering government aid in emergency situations. Recent decades have seen the growth of 'super-INGOs' such as Oxfam and Save the Children, which dominate their areas of operation.

International migrants People who, for whatever reason and for whatever duration, leave their country of birth to live in another country. International migrants include people who leave their country for economic reasons, to find or take up work or to study, as well as those who leave because of persecution, whether actual or threatened (asylum seekers and refugees). Some people emigrate without going through the formal application procedures or channels (as in 'illegal', 'irregular' or 'unauthorised' migration), whether voluntary or forced (as in smuggling and trafficking). Some people enter a country on a 'legal', 'regular', or 'authorised' basis, but their legal status may subsequently change while they are there and may move into the category of illegal/irregular/unauthorised migrant (and back again).

International migration Migration from one country to another. Also an academic approach to migration that downplays transnational aspects of migration. *See also* transnational migration.

International Monetary Fund An organisation set up in 1944 to promote international monetary stability by supervising monetary and exchange rate policies. It provides loans to countries with balance of payment difficulties.

International organisation An organisation whose members include two or more states or the organ of such an international organisation.

Lesson drawing A conceptual framework, very close to policy transfer. Rather than ideas and structures, it emphasises lessons to be drawn in framing policy.

Liberalisation The process of removing regulations and other restrictions on the operation of markets. Often used to refer to the removal of trade barriers.

Malthusianism A perspective drawing (selectively) on the 18th-century writings of English clergyman Thomas Malthus. It maintains that it is the number of people per se in any given area that causes food shortages, environmental degradation, water pollution, deforestation and so on. The obvious solution to such problems constructed this way is to reduce the numbers of these people (rather than also considering forces acting from outside the area, for instance).

Managed migration Schemes to control the migration of workers for the benefit of importing and exporting countries alike.

Mandatory pension contribution The level of contribution the member (or an entity on behalf of the member) is required to pay according to scheme rules.

Mandatory personal pension plans Personal pension plans that individuals must join or plans that are eligible to receive mandatory pension contributions.

Individuals may be required to make pension contributions to a pension plan of their choice or to a specific pension plan.

Methodological nationalism A methodological approach to studying social phenomena that focuses on social processes occuring within the confines of nation states. Does not recognise the existence of transnational processes or the effects of these processes in shaping national social structures and impacts.

Methodological transnationalism A methodological approach to studying social phenomena that moves beyond national boundaries by emphasising transnational influences and links, together with the ways in which they play out in domestic and cross-border contexts.

Migrants People who move from one country to another or from one area of a country to another (as in rural to urban migration).

Migration Movement of people from one country to another or from one area of the country to another.

Millennium Development Goals Eight development targets agreed by the members of the United Nations in 2000 that aim to halve the numbers of people living in extreme forms of poverty by the year 2015.

Mixed reforms In a pensions and social security context, these partially replace the former social security-type system with individual accounts (*see* individual pension fund). Under mixed systems, popular in central and eastern Europe, participants contribute to both a scaled-down, pay-as-you-go pension system and to an individual account, and gain benefits from both systems over time.

Modernisation theory A theory that espouses a development path for poor countries based on the experience of countries that have industrialised. In the main, this calls for investment in manufacturing in urban areas so as to absorb surplus rural labour. It has been argued that the wages earned by urban workers will be spent on consumption, thereby creating demand and more jobs. The benefits of growth would thus 'trickle down to the poor'.

Multilateral Between many organisations, committees etc.

Multilateral actor An organisation that represents many countries (for example, the WB).

Multilateral economic institutions (MEIs) Exemplified by the IMF, WB and WHO, MEIs are multilateral international organisations primarily centred towards economic objectives and concerns.

Multilateral migration regime International system of migration management involving both sending and host countries. *See also* global migration regime.

Multilateralism The process of, or commitment to, forming an agreement between many countries.

Multilevel governance The existence of levels of governance at world, world regional, national and subnational levels.

Multinational corporations *See* transnational corporations.

Neoliberal (noun) A person who believes in the untrammelled operation of the free market and a minimal role for the state in the economic and social spheres. Also used as an adjective – see, for example, neoliberal economic policy and neoliberal globalisation.

Neoliberal economic policy Economic policy resulting from neoliberalism, which favours the reduction of state involvement in economic and social regulation and supports the spread of free markets.

Neoliberal globalisation Prescription for, and description of, globalisation that emphasises the free movement of capital and a reduced role for states, including the privatisation of many state functions.

Neoliberalism A political philosophy of competitive individualism that calls for minimal state involvement in economic and social regulation. In practice, such involvement tends not to be minimal and is directed so that it benefits for-profit interests and the richer social groups. Associated with the emergence of the New Right (Reagan and Thatcher) in the 1980s and exemplified in the Washington Consensus. Sees economic liberalism as the most effective and efficient means of promoting economic development and obtaining political freedom.

Neo-Malthusianism A perspective similar to Malthusianism that advocates intervention by providing contraception and sterilisation, usually of women, to reduce human numbers by reducing the numbers of babies born.

Net emigration Refers to a situation where there is greater emigration than immigration.

Net immigration Refers to a situation where there is greater immigration than emigration.

Non-state international actors Policy actors operating in the market, community or household spheres, acting across many countries. Examples of such actors include TNCs, INGOs and households.

Notional defined contribution pension A pension system that continues pay-as-you-go financing but accounts for benefits via 'notional' individual accounts.

Overpopulation Population often denotes, or is inderstood as, not simply 'the number of people' or even a natural force, but as 'too many people' – or rather, 'overpopulation'. This term implies that too many people live within any given area. Problems with this term are that the particular area is not usually defined, nor any quantity actually calculated as to how many people are considered 'over', nor which people are 'too many'. Calculations that do determine an 'optimum population' tend not to make explicit the assumptions underpinning the results. Questions asking 'too many for what?' or 'too many for whom?' are rarely posed.

Parallel reform In the pensions context, this refers to a reform that maintains public and private systems side by side and allows individuals a choice of system in which to participate, resulting in smaller private pension systems.

Pay-as-you-go pension system An occupational or personal pension plan that accumulates dedicated assets to cover the plan's liabilities.

Pension fund The pool of assets forming an independent legal entity that are bought with the contributions to a pension plan for the exclusive purpose of financing pension plan benefits. Plan/fund members have a legal or beneficial right or some other contractual claim against the assets of the pension fund. Pension funds take the form of either a special purpose entity with legal personality (such as a trust, foundation or corporate entity) or a legally separated fund without legal personality managed by a dedicated provider (such as a pension fund management company) or other financial institution on behalf of the plan/fund members.

Personal pension plan A pension plan that does not have to be linked to an employment relationship. Such plans are established and administered directly by a pension fund or a financial institution acting as pension provider without any intervention by an employer. Individuals independently purchase and select material aspects of the arrangements. Employers may nonetheless make contributions to personal pension plans. Some personal plans may have restricted membership.

Policy borrowing A conceptual framework that is similar to policy transfer. Work in this field has focused primarily on the movement of policy between the US and the UK.

Policy convergence Process that emphasises cross-national influence, rather than direct transfer of policy structures and forms.

Policy diffusion The process by which an innovation is communicated through certain channels, over time, among members of a social system. It is a special type of communication in that the messages are concerned with new ideas.

Policy learning Refers to policy maker's desire for and use of knowledge about policy taken from other contexts.

Policy transfer Process in which policies/ideas in one setting (past or present) are used in the development of policies/ideas in another time or place.

Policy sociology A reflexive and theory-based approach to the study of policy that emphasises the role of ideas and agency in the making and remaking of policy.

Population Commonly understood as shorthand for 'the number of people' living within a specific bounded area, such as a city or country, or the world. The term 'population' became a statistical concept in 18th-century England and is now linked to many functions and factors that can supposedly be managed, such as population census, control, distribution, explosion, growth, planning, policy, pressure, survey and trend.

Population control Refers to programmes implemented by both public and private entities, state and non-state actors, that are explicitly designed to drive down the birth rates of certain groups of people, particularly in Asia and Africa, and, to a lesser extent, Latin America. Usually carried out through the aggressive promotion of sterilisation and/or long-acting contraceptives that women themselves cannot control (for instance, implants or injections rather than the Pill or condoms). Some population control programmes have called themselves family planning programmes, but population control is not the same as family planning. Family planning is a generic term encompassing many different types of birth control policies and programmes.

Population decline The rate at which the number of people in any given area is decreasing. However, the term is also used to suggest a culture or people that is deteriorating in terms of its power or importance.

Population growth The rate at which the number of people in any given area is increasing is calculated by adding up the number of births and people who have moved to the area, subtracting the number of deaths and those who have left, and expressing the result as a percentage of the initial population level.

Population policy A policy (usually) pursued by government to influence the number of people within the territory it governs. It has commonly been understood as trying to influence (usually to reduce) the number of children to whom women give birth and raise, by means of contraception or sterilisation.

Post-Washington Consensus A political consensus emanating from the recognition of the failure of 'structural adjustment policies' (*see also* structural adjustment loan). Policies consist of social funds to Highly Indebted Poor Countries and have, since the late 1990s, been extended to all countries eligible for concessional lending in the form of Poverty Reduction Strategy Papers.

Poverty Reduction Budget Support (PRBS) A form of financial aid in which funds are provided, in support of a government programme typically focusing on growth, poverty reduction, fiscal adjustment and strengthening institutions, especially budgetary processes, or directly to a partner government's central exchequer, to spend using its own financial management, procurement and accountability systems. Also known as Direct Budget Support, PRBS can take the form of a general contribution to the overall budget, often referred to as General Budget Support, or financial aid earmarked to a discrete sector (with any conditionality relating to these sectors), often referred to as Sector Budget Support.

Poverty Reduction Strategy Papers (PRSPs) Documents prepared by governments in low-income countries through a participatory process involving domestic stakeholders and external development partners, including the IMF and the WB. A PRSP describes the macroeconomic, structural and social policies and programmes that a country will pursue over several years to promote broad-based growth and reduce poverty, as well as external financing needs and the associated sources of financing.

Private pension plan A pension plan administered by an institution other than general government. Private pension plans may be administered directly by a private sector employer acting as the plan sponsor, a private pension fund or a private sector provider. Private pension plans may complement or substitute for public pension plans. In some countries, these may include plans for public sector workers.

Protection (trade) The creation of barriers to trade in order to protect domestic industries from foreign competition.

Public pension plan A social security or similar statutory programme administered by the general government (that is, central, state and local governments, as well as other public sector bodies such as social security institutions). Public pension plans have been traditionally financed through the pay-as-you-go system, but some OECD countries have partial funding of public pension liabilities or have replaced these plans by private pension plans.

Race to the bottom The thesis that in response to a perceived threat to their industrial competitiveness, states are likely to engage in behaviour that results in the lowering of social, environmental and labour standards in order to attract new or retain existing investment.

Reproductive rights/reproductive justice Women's right to control their bodies in all matters of reproduction. This includes access to contraception, but also freedom from coercion. Women from the south and women of colour have expanded the concept further to embrace maternal health and mortality, childbearing and child raising.

Scaling up The process of expanding small-scale, innovative demonstration projects to the population in question as a whole.

Scarcity Refers to insufficiency of resources, such as food, and is a key concept in Malthusianism. If attention is paid to what is actually happening in any locale, however, the causes of hunger are invariably shown to lie not in absolute scarcity – no food at all – but in socially generated scarcity – not enough food for some people in some places because other people have denied them access to food, land and water. This indicates that imbalances of power between groups of people in society generate 'scarcity' rather than 'population'. From this perspective, 'scarcity', as used in modern economics, is a means of legitimising existing inequitable social and political relationships, institutions and policies, and of blocking or diverting attention from other causes of poverty and hunger.

Sector-wide approach (SWAp) The process by which funding for the sector – whether internal or from donors – supports a single policy and expenditure programme, under government leadership, and adopts a common approach across the sector. It is generally accompanied by efforts to strengthen government procedures for disbursement and accountability. A SWAp should ideally involve broad stakeholder consultation in the design of a coherent sector programme at micro-, meso- and macro-levels, and strong coordination among donors and between donors and government.

Selective healthcare The provision of targeted or selected services so as to provide the most effective means of improving the health of people in greatest need. It was originally considered an intermediary phase before primary healthcare for all could be made available.

Shadow economy *See* informal economy.

Shelter A dwelling unit and its construction.

Shelter deprivation A term to assess the extent to which individuals and household face differential housing deficits in the five areas of: (i) durability, (ii) overcrowding, (iii) access to water, (iv) access to sanitation and (v) security of tenure.

Sites and services Involves government making new serviced land available for beneficiaries to manage and or construct their dwellings. Unlike slum improvement, site-and-service projects add to the housing stock.

Slide to the bottom A more languid version of race to the bottom.

Slum According to UN-HABITAT, a slum household is a group of individuals living under the same roof in an urban area who lack one or more of the following five conditions: durable housing; sufficient living area; access to improved water; access to sanitation; and secure tenure. Housing tenure of a slum is legally recognised. *See* squatter settlement.

Slum upgrading/improvement Slum improvement or slum upgrading was originally envisaged with environmental improvement objectives. Whenever possible, infrastructure such as water, sanitation, electricity and roads would be provided to those 'slum' or squatter settlements not deemed to occupy sites of public interest or located in areas deemed hazardous. At times this may involve the reallocation of plots in a planned manner to make service provision easier. Of significance is the fact that slum improvement does not add to the housing stock.

Social determinant of health The health effects of the social conditions in which people live and work. In particular, the ways in which underlying social inequalities and poverty affect health status.

Social protection Aims to insure workers against the risks of unemployment or sickness through a system of welfare benefits, whatever the cause.

Social security fund A social insurance scheme that covers the community as a whole and is distinct from private insurance.

Squatter settlement A form of housing tenure that is not legally recognised.

State sovereignty A doctrine that dates back several hundred years and stipulates that states are the ultimate decision-making authority in their country. The governments of states define what is in the national interest and pursue this national interest in the international arena. Thus, most states are very hesitant to empower an international body to make decisions that bind the populations of their states. Since states often have different national interests, international agreements are often difficult.

Structural Adjustment Loan Part of the Structural Adjustment Programme, a World Bank instrument prevalent in the 1980s that focused on correcting major macroeconomic 'distortions' allegedly hindering development.

Substitutive reform In the pensions context, a reform that fully replaces social security-type systems with those based on individual, funded pension savings accounts.

Targeting/targeted provision Social programmes that concentrate limited resources on the poorest and most vulnerable populations.

Trade negotiations Negotiations between governments to agree trade rules and to reduce barriers to trade. Trade negotiations involve bargaining over the concessions to be made by each government.

Trade protectionism The practice or advocacy of trade protection. *See* protection (trade).

Transnational advocacy coalition or network A group of organisations structured on a transnational basis to campaign for policy changes or wider social reforms. *See also* global policy advocacy coalition.

Transnational corporations (TNCs) Private firms that produce or sell commodities and/or services in more than one country. The largest TNCs operate in global markets in hundreds of countries around the globe. Also known as multinational corporations.

Transnational families Families that reside in different countries but which sustain active and regular links with one another. Transnational families are a major means by which transnational social structures and relations are created and maintained. Also known as globalised families.

Transnational knowledge networks A semi-coordinated alliance of scholars and professionals sharing a common understanding of an approach to a particular (policy) issue.

Transnational migration An approach to migration that emphasises its transnational aspects, that is, how migration links societies of origin and settlement through multi-dimensional social relations.

Transnational social welfare Social welfare provided on a transnational basis, linking welfare provision and outcomes between populations across countries.

Travelling and embedded policy A perspective developed from policy sociology stressing that policies that travel around the globe are contested and mediated in all countries before becoming embedded as policy settlements.

Urban policy Includes all activities within an urban area, such as urban economic development, poverty, social infrastructure (education, health, policing), physical infrastructure (transport, roads, water, electricity, sanitation), planning and the environment.

United Nations (UN) specialised agency An autonomous agency with special agreements with the UN. Several specialised agencies have normative and standard-setting functions with a truly global focus. Specialised agencies include the WHO, ILO, FAO and UNESCO.

Vernacular globalisation An approach to globalisation that emphasises the intermingling of global and local in the transformation of localities, as in 'glocalisation'.

Vertical In the health context, an approach, programme or measure that focuses on a particular disease or health issue. For example, malaria and HIV/AIDS have been dealt with through specific, stand-alone programmes. Vertical programmes often have their own funding, personnel and governance structures, separate from the main health system.

Voluntary personal pension plan Pension plan in which participation by individuals is voluntary. By law individuals are not obliged to participate or make contributions to a pension plan. Voluntary personal plans include those plans that individuals must join if they choose to replace part of their social security benefits with those from personal pension plans.

Washington Consensus A term used to denote a particular set of economic policies adopted and followed in particular by the Bretton Woods institutions in the 1980s and 1990s: the pursuit of macroeconomic stability by controlling inflation and reducing fiscal deficits; getting countries to open their economies to the rest of the world through trade and capital account liberalisation; and liberalising markets through privatisation and deregulation.

World Bank (WB) Institution comprising the International Bank for Reconstruction and Development and the International Development Association. The WB was set up in 1944 to promote economic development in the developing world through providing loans for programmes and projects for which no private finance can be found.

World Commission on Water for the 21st Century Commission established in 1998 by the World Water Council and co-sponsored by the Food and Agriculture Organization, United Nations Environment Programme, United Nations Development Programme, United Nations Educational, Scientific and Cultural Organization, United Nations Children's Fund, World Health Organization and WB to develop water and environmental policy for the 21st century.

World Health Organization (WHO) Organisation established in 1948 as the specialised UN health agency whose objective is the highest possible level of health for all peoples. It is governed by its 192 member states through the World Health Assembly.

World society theory A theory based on the existence of a global society that transcends national boundaries. It operates through a series of global cultural associations.

World Trade Organization Organisation set up in 1995 to promote international trade, with executive and legal powers recognised in international law to enforce international trade and investment law and to adjudicate in international trade disputes.

Index

A

abortion 265, 267
adult mortality rates 151, 152
advocacy coalitions *see* transnational
   advocacy coalitions or networks
Africa
   brain drain 239-40, 241
   and China 34
   education 65
   population policy 266
African Union 43
Agarwala, Ramgopal 216
Agreement on Trade-Related Intellectual
   Property Rights (TRIPS) 106, 109,
   159-60, 166
agriculture 268-9
AIDS 239, 266
Alaska 84
alcohol 150, 162
Alexiadou, N. 60
Andean Community 43
Andhra Pradesh 195-6, 263
anti-globalisation movement 37, 109, 291
   see 'from below' forces
Anti-Slave Trade Movement 17
Appadurai, A. 59
apparel industry 82
Armingeon, K. 30, 63
Arnott, M. 65
ASEAN (Association of South East Asian
   Nations) 10
   Framework Agreement on Services 117
   international migration 242, 244
   labour standards 133
   social policy 43
Asia
   international migration 231
   population policy 260
Asian Development Bank 212, 216
Australia 232
Averting the Old Age Crisis (World Bank)
   208-9, 212, 216

B

baby milk formula 83
BAE Systems 83
Baldock, C.V. 236
Ball, S.J. 59
Bangkok 197
Barr, N. 220
Bello, Walden 37, 42
Bengal 257
Berne Initiative 244

Beyeler, M. 30, 63
Bhatia, R. 264
Bhopal 84
bilateral actors 180, 181, 291
bilateralism 291
   international migration 240-1
Bill & Melinda Gates Foundation 27, 41,
   89, 162, 266
bird flu 155
Birdsall, Nancy 212
blacks 271-2
bluewashing 140, 142
Body Shop, The 89, 90
Bokros, Lajos 216
Bolivia 83
Bologna agreement 60
bottom-up perspective *see* 'from below'
   forces
BP 84
brain drain 239-40
Braithwaite, J. 162
Brazil
   IGOs 81
   pensions 210, 217-18
   trade 108
Breman, J. 182
Bretton Woods 9, 107, 211, 281, 291
   reform 36-7
   see also International Monetary Fund;
   World Bank
Brooks, S.M. 210
Brundtland, Gro Harlem 31, 164, 165
Buffet, Warren 89
burden of disease 169, 291
Burgess, Rod 186
Burma 245
Bush, George W. 265
business 74-5, 93-4
   corporate harm 79-81
   corporate social responsibility and
   corporate codes of conduct 85-90
   global business interest associations and
   social policy 90-3
   see also corporate agency power,
   corporate structural power, global
   business; transnational corporations
   Prince of Wales International Business
   Leaders Forum 139
business agency power 75, 76-7, 291
Business and Industry Advisory
   Committee to the OECD (BIAC) 78,
   91
Business in the Community 139

business power 74, 75-9, 291
business structural power 75, 76, 291-2

C

Cadbury 90
Cameron, D.R. 112
Canada
  education 64
  immigration 124, 232
capitalism 102
care 236-7, 246
Caribbean 237
CARICOM 242
cash and care 235-7, 246
Center for Law and Social Policy
  (CLASP) 10
central and eastern Europe (CEE) 210,
  212, 213, 214, 220
Chicago boys 211-12
children
  health 151, 152, 157-8
  one-child policy 209, 261-2, 267
Chile
  housing policy 192
  pensions 211-12, 214, 215, 217, 285
China 81, 113
  internal migration 232
  international migration 231
  pensions 216-17
  population policy 261-2, 266, 267
  trade 108
  unconditional aid 34, 40
Chiquita 141
churches 161, 263
Cities Alliance 196, 292
citizenship 230
  see also cosmopolitan citizenship
city development see urban development
civil society (civic society) 292
  global labour policy 126-8, 135, 142,
    143
  religious organisations 161, 263, 265
  trade 109
  see also non-governmental organisations;
    trade unions; transnational advocacy
    coalitions or networks
Clarke, J. 14
Clinton, President 265
Coca Cola 82
codes of conduct
  medical migration 240-1
  see also corporate codes of conduct
Codex Alimentarius Commission 154
coercion 214
Cohen, M.A. 189
Cohen, R. 231, 235
Colinvaux, Paul 267-8

Colombia
  Chiquita 141
  corporate harm 82
  housing policy 192
colonialism 17, 50
commercial presence 115
Common Purpose 139
Community Led Infrastructure Financing
  Facility (CLIFF) 197-8
Community Organisation Development
  Institute 197
comparative advantage 103, 137, 292
competitive advantage 103, 292
complex multilateralism 26
comprehensive healthcare 164, 292
conditionalities 214, 292
consumer groups 14, 86, 89-90, 105,
  127-8
consumption abroad 115
contraception 260, 261-2
contribution 213, 292
Convention on the Rights of the Child
  33, 157-8
core labour standards 136-8, 143
corporate agency power 75, 76-7, 291
  see business
corporate-centred social policy 74, 81, 85
  corporate social responsibility and codes
    of conduct 85-90
  global business interest associations 90-3
corporate codes of conduct 85, 138, 140,
  141, 143, 293
corporate harm 79-81, 82-4, 85
corporate power 74, 75-9, 291
corporate social responsibility (CSR) 85,
  86, 89-90, 138-40, 293
corporate structural power 75, 76, 291-2
corporations see transnational corporations
cosmopolitan approach/cosmopolitanism
  26, 137, 208, 293
cosmopolitan citizenship 230, 237, 246,
  293
Count Us In (HMIE) 65
crime 271
cross-border migration see international
  migration
cross-border trade 115
cross-national attraction 51, 53, 293

D

Davies, Phil 63
Deacon, Bob 11-12, 16, 55, 58, 61-2
decent work 132
decision making 62-4
Declaration of Alma Ata 163-4
Declaration on Fundamental Principles
  and Rights at Work 131

Declaration of Philadelphia 137, 211
defence industry 83
DeJong-Lambert, W. 57
democratic education 282
demographic crisis 283
demographic dividend 264
Den Boer, A. 270
Department of Financial and Enterprise
    Affairs (OECD) 31
Department of Health (UK) 240-1
Department for International
    Development (DfID) (UK) 181, 186,
    195-6, 198, 199, 287
  direct housing support 189
  urban ladder 192, 193
dependency theory 4-5, 181, 186, 293
Dervis, Kemal 38
determinant of health 150, 151, 157, 167,
    169, 293
developed countries 10, 30, 288
    global labour policies 129-31
    global social governance 28
    trade 35, 108-9
    see also Organisation for Economic
    Co-operation and Development
developing countries 10, 288
    brain drain 239-40
    global labour policies 129-31
    global social governance 28
    health issues 166-7, 168, 169
    housing and urban policy 181-3, 184,
    185-99
    labour standards 134, 143
    policy space 37, 39-40, 42
    population policy 261
    trade and welfare state 110-11, 113-14,
    118
    world-regional social policy 42-3
    WTO 35, 108-9
Development Advisory Committee
    (DAC) 160
diaspora 231, 293
diasporic communities 235-6, 284
Directorate for Employment, Labour and
    Social Affairs (DELSA) (OECD) 31, 34
discourse 59
Disney 142
displacement (migration) 233, 293
displacement (trade) 111-12, 293
Doha Declaration 159
Doha round 106, 108
Dolowitz, D. 51, 55
Dorn, C. 57
double taxation 79, 293
Drahos, P. 162
drugs 271

E

East African Community 242
East Asia 104, 114
Economic Commission for Latin America
    and the Caribbean (ECLAC) 40
ecology 4
Economic and Social Council
    (ECOSOC) 33, 38, 39, 245
economic globalisation 106-7, 117
Economic Security Council (UNESC)
    37, 38
economics 102-5
Ecuador 134
education 111, 285 *see also* higher
    education
    competing discourses 54
    EU 92
    global business interest associations and
    social policy 91
    policy divergence 64-5
    policy transfer 54, 55
    travelling and embedded policy 60-1
    UNESCO 56-8
Education for All (EFA) 58
Egypt 266
Ehrlich, Paul 267
embedded policy 51, 52, 59-61, 309
embedded transnationalism 13-14, 281
emigration 231, 232, 233
enabling housing policy 187-8, 297
England 65
enmeshment 3, 14, 51
epidemics 151-2, 153, 154-5
epistemic communities 6, 51, 55, 56, 294
    and corporations 81
    global pensions policy 221
    healthcare reform 165
Economics and Social Commission for
    Asia and the Pacific (ESCAP) 40
Esping-Andersen, G. 33
Essay on the Principle of Population
    (Malthus) 254, 255-6
Ethical Trade Initiative (ETI) 139
eugenics 254, 258-9, 294
European Association of Craft, Small
    and Medium-Sized Enterprises
    (UEAPME) 78
European Commission (EC) 77, 86, 138,
    199
European Economic Community 105
European Round Table (ERT) 78, 85
European Union (EU) 9, 10
    business agenda 92
    Globalisation Adjustment Fund 113
    and ILO 31
    and IMF 42
    international migration 230

labour standards 133-4
migrant workers 237, 242, 244
multilevel governance 12
 and national social policy 53
 and OECD 32
 trade 105, 109-10
 trade in welfare services 117
 WTO 108, 109
Every Child Matters (HM Treasury) 65
evidence-informed policy 62-4
exchange rate system 107, 294
export-oriented policy 104, 294
export processing zone 130, 294
extensity 3

F

Fair Globalization, A (World Commission
 on the Social Dimension of
 Globalisation) 132
Fair Labour Association (FLA) 139-40
fair trade 105, 128
families *see* transnational families
famines 256-7
farmers 127
financial markets 107
Financial Sector Adjustment Loan (FSAP)
 217, 294
Five plus Five Dialogue 244
Food and Agriculture Organization (FAO)
 127, 153, 154, 155
For Scotland's Children (Scottish Executive)
 65
Ford Foundation 266
Foreign Assistance Act (US) 260
foreign direct investment (FDI) 107, 117,
 294
France 55, 245
free markets 283
free trade 102-5, 282
free trade agreements 109, 127, 294
'from above' forces 284, 285-6
'from below' forces 284-5
 global labour policy 126-8
 global pensions policy 221
 international migration 245-6
Fujimori, Alberto 217
Fuller, Gary 270
Fundamental Principles on Rights at
 Work 141
funded pension plans 216, 220, 294

G

G8/Group of 8 27, 295
 global health policy 154, 160, 167
G20/Group of 20 27, 108, 295
G77/Group of 77 27, 39, 295
Galton, Francis 258

Gates Foundation *see* Bill & Melinda
 Gates Foundation
GAVI Alliance (GAVI) 41, 161. 295
General Agreement on Tariffs and Trade
 (GATT) 106
General Agreement on Trade in Services
 (GATS) 106, 109, 115-17, 159, 243
Geneva Convention for the Amelioration
 of the Wounded in Armies in the Field
 17
geography 17-18, 286, 288-9
 see also place
Germany 258-9
Gilbert, A. 192
Gill, I.S. 220
global business 74, 295
global business interest associations
 (GBIAs) 77, 78, 94, 284, 285-6, 295
 corporate social responsibility 85-6
 and social policy 90-3
Global Campaign for the Ratification of
 the UN Migrant Workers' Convention
 245
global care chains (GCC) 238, 295
Global Commission on International
 Migration (GCIM) 244
Global Compact 41, 86, 87
 labour standards 124, 138, 140, 141-3
Global Development Network (GDN)
 63-4
global division of labour 129-31, 295
Global Fund to Fight AIDS, Tuberculosis
 and Malaria 27, 35, 77, 89, 154, 160,
 161
 financing 168
global gag rule 265
global health governance 151-4, 169
 global public–private partnerships and
 disease-specific vertical measures 77,
 160-2
 health, the UN and human and social
 rights agenda 155-8
 healthcare financing 165
 international financial institutions and
 trade agreements 106, 109, 117,
 158-60
 OECD 160
 WHO, infectious diseases and global
 health security agenda 154-5
global health policy 150-1, 162-3, 168-9,
 287
 access to medicines 166-7
 Health for All 163-4
 healthcare reforms 165-6
 regulation, rights, redistribution and
 politics 35, 167-8
global health-related public–private
 partnerships (GHPPP) 161

global labour policy 124-5, 143, 288
  actors 126-36, 285
and housing policy 194, 199
  policy issues 136-43
global migration flows 231-4
global migration regime 230, 241-6, 295
  see also international migration
global networks 40-1
Global North *see* developed countries
global pensions policy 208, 221-2, 285, 295
  bottom-up perspective 221
  country examples 215-17
  emerging debates 220-1
  global business interest associations and social policy 91
  ILO and post-war policy 31, 55, 211
  limits 217-20
  pension reform phenomenon 208-11
  policy diffusion 214-15
  rise of new reforms 211-14
global philanthropy 89, 162, 296
global policy 296
global policy actors 281, 282-3, 296
  emerging debates 221
  forces 'from above' and 'from below' 284-6
  ideas and discourses 281-4
  pensions 208-22
global policy advocacy coalitions *see* transnational advocacy coalitions or networks
global public goods 35, 296
Global Public Policy Networks (GPPNs) 41
global public–private partnerships 26-7, 40-1, 160-2, 168, 282, 296
global redistribution 27, 34-5, 36, 296
  global health policy 149-50, 167-8, 169
  population policy 254
  world-regionalism 43
global regulation 80, 86-9, 296
  see also global social regulation; self-regulation
global social governance 26, 43-4, 208, 285, 296
  conceptualising and understanding 26-9
  international organisations and national social policies 29-34
  reform 36-43
  world-regional formations 109
  see also global health governance
global social justice movement *see* anti-globalisation movement
global social movement 284, 285-6, 296
global social policy 10, 11, 279, 280-1, 289-90, 296-7
  and business 74, 81, 85, 90-4

definitions 11-15
  forces 'from above' and 'from below' 284-6
  global redistribution, regulation and rights 34-6
  history and geography 16-18, 286-9
  ideas, discourses, actors, agendas and practices 281-4
  policy sociology 59
  policy transfer 50-1, 52-3, 65-6
  travelling and embedded policy 59-61
global (social) regulation 27, 35, 36, 297
  health 152-4, 167-8
  trade in welfare services 116
  world-regionalism 43
global social reproduction 230, 236-7, 297
global social rights 35-6, 297
  health 155-8, 167-8
  population policy 254
  world-regionalism 43
Global South *see* developing countries
global standards 114, 297
  see also labour standards
Global Strategy on Diet, Physical Activity and Health 152-3
Global Union Federations (GUFs) 126-7, 134
global warming 269
Global Warming Treaty 36
globalisation 3-4, 297
  and business power 74, 75-9
  of corporate harm 79-81, 82-4
  debates on impact and future 132
  economic 106-7
  and international migration 234, 246
  and social policy 8-11
  and trade 102
  travelling and embedded policy 52, 59-60
Globalisation Adjustment Fund 113
globalisation studies 3, 4, 16-17, 297
globalised families *see* transnational families
Globalism and Social Policy Programme (GASPP) 12
Gore, Charles 40
Gorwill, Dr Hugh 261
governance 26, 28, 196
  see also global social governance; multilevel governance
government as enabler 187-8, 191, 297
government as provider 185-7, 298
grandparents 237
Green & Black's 89, 90
Green Revolution 268-9
greenwashing 140
Gulf states 124, 245

H

Haas, E. 55, 56
Haiti 134
Handbook of Global Social Policy (Nagel) 10
harm 80
  see also corporate harm
Hartmann, B. 272
health 149-50
  and population policy 266-7
  see also global health policy
Health Action International 161
Health for All (HfA) 162, 163-4, 166, 168, 169
health status 150, 298
health systems 160, 298
health worker migration 238-41, 246
healthcare 150, 163-4
healthcare reform 160, 162-3, 165-6, 168, 298
Hendrixson, A. 271
High-Level Panel on United Nations Systems-Wide Coherence 38-9
higher education 54, 55-6, 60, 91
Hines, Colin 37
Hinz, R. 221
history 4, 16-17, 286-8
HIV/AIDS 150, 154, 159, 166, 167, 169
  global public–private partnerships 160, 161
  and population policy 266
  UN activities 155, 264
Holzmann, R. 221
Homeless International 197-8
Homer-Dixon, Thomas 268
Hong Kong 245
household internationalisation strategies 235, 298
Housing and Home Finance Agency 186
housing policy 180-1, 183, 185, 199, 286, 298
  and finance 188-9, 190
  government as enabler 187-8, 297
  government as provider 185-7, 298
  history 287
  housing markets and city development 190-4
  recent developments 194-8
  urbanisation and poverty 181-3, 184, 185
Hudson, V.M. 270
Hulme, R. 62
human rights 282
  core labour standards 136-8, 143
  health 149-50, 155-8, 163, 168, 169
  migrant workers 243
  see also global social rights
Hungary 215-16

Hunt, Paul 155-6
Hutchinson, B. 63

I

IBRD *see* International Bank for Reconstruction and Development
ICC *see* International Chambers of Commerce
ICPD *see* International Conference on Population and Development
IDA *see* International Development Association
IDB *see* Inter-American Development Bank
IFC *see* International Finance Corporation
IGOs *see* international organisations
ILO *see* International Labour Organization
IMF *see* International Monetary Fund
immigration 124, 231, 232, 233
  worker rights 126
  see also global migration flows, global migration regimes
immigration regimes (IRs) 241-2
In Larger Freedom (UN Secretary General) 38
India 81
  famine 257
  housing and urban development 189, 195-6, 197-8
  international migration 231
  population policy 261, 263-4, 266
  remittances 235-6
  trade 108
  women's deaths 266-7
individual pension fund 209, 210, 213-14, 218, 298
Indonesia 245, 262, 266
infant food 161, 162
infectious diseases 151, 154-5
influence mechanism 214-15, 298
influenza pandemics 150, 154
informal economy 125, 127, 132, 298
INGOs *see* international non-governmental organisations
  see also civil/civic society
inspiration 214, 215
Institute of Business Ethics 139
Institute of Economic Affairs 52, 62
institutionalise 198, 199, 299
integrated projects 187, 299
intellectual property rights 106, 159-60, 166
intensity 3
Inter-American Development Bank 185, 186, 188, 190, 199, 212
interconnectedness 3, 14, 51

internal migration 232, 233
International Baby Food Action Network
161
International Bank for Reconstruction
and Development 29, 34
International Chambers of Commerce 78,
85, 86
International Committee for the Relief of
the Military Wounded 17
International Confederation of Free Trade
Unions (ICFTU) 126
International Conference of Health 152
International Conference on Population
261
International Conference on Population
and Development 262-3, 265
International Conferences on Health
Promotion 164
International Convention on the
Protection of the Rights of all Migrant
Workers and Members of their
Families 244, 245
International Covenant on Economic,
Social and Cultural Rights 33, 156-7
International Criminal Court 36
International Development Association
29, 34, 162
International Federation of
Pharmaceutical Manufactureres and
Associations 162
International Finance Corporation 29, 34,
93, 134
international financial institutions (IFIs)
18, 77, 133, 134
see also International Monetary Fund;
World Bank
international governmental organisations
(IGOs) *see* international organisations
International Health Regulations 153
International Labour Organization 299
core labour standards 136, 138
decent work 194
Fundamental Principles on Rights at
Work 141
global health policy 155, 166
global labour policy 131-3, 137, 142-3
global social regulation 35
international migration 242, 244
medical migration 239-40
and national social policy 27, 31, 34
pensions 55, 208, 211, 216, 220
World Commission on the Social
Dimension of Globalisation 39
international migrants 231, 232, 233, 234,
299
international law 245
international migration 124, 230-4, 246,
300

and geography 288
global migration regime 241-6
and overpopulation 254
transnational social welfare 235-7
welfare workers and global care chain
238-41
International Monetary Fund 10, 105, 300
accountability 41-2
and business power 76, 77
exchange rate system 107
global health policy 158-9
global labour policy 134
and ILO 132, 133
and national social policy 27, 34
population policy 265
worker rights 126
and World Bank 39
and WTO 107
international non-governmental
organisations (INGOs) 17, 299
educare 64
epistemic communities 55
global health policy 161, 162, 168
religious organisations 161, 263, 265
see also non-governmental organisations
international organisations (IOs) 11-12,
26, 300
and business 76-7, 81, 85, 94
dialogue and synergy 39
epistemic communities 55
geography 288
global labour policies 131-5
GPPNs 41
and national social policy 27, 29-34,
53-4
population policy 254-5, 259-61
urban policy 194-8
International Organization on Migration
(IOM) 231, 240, 243
International Planned Population
Parenthood Federation (IPPF) 260,
264, 266
international trade *see* trade
International Trade Union Confederation
(ITUC) 126, 127, 134
intrafirm trade 107
Ireland
famine 256-7
immigration 232
migrant welfare workers 238
Italy
immigration 232
pensions 219
Iversen, T. 112

J

Jacoby, W. 214-15

James, Estelle 212
Japan 108, 266
Joint United Nations Programme on
  HIV/AIDS (UNAIDS) 155
Jones, K. 60
Jordan, G. 61
Josselin, D. 26-7

K

Kader Industrial Company 135
Kazakhstan 215
Kenya 198
Kerala 235-6
Keynes, John Maynard 62
Khor, Martin 37
Kim Dae Jung 219
Kim Young Sam 219
kinship 283
knowledge 55-6
knowledge networks 27-8, 56
  see also epistemic communities;
  transnational knowledge networks
knowledge workers 282
Korea 218, 219-20

L

labour policy see global labour policy
labour standards 35, 110-11, 113
  labour, global division of 129-31, 295
  world-regional formations and labour
  109, 281, 289
  see also core labour standards
Latin America
  housing 199
  pensions 212, 214
  population policy 260, 263
  urban poverty 182
Latinos 271
Leicester, G. 63
lesson drawing 52, 53, 300
Levin, B. 61
Liaoning 216
liberalisation 81-2, 93, 104, 300
Liebfried, S. 112
lifelong learning 64, 282
  see also education
Lingard, B. 59
Lisbon Agenda 92
local policy settlements 61-2

M

MacArthur Foundation 266
McCormack, B. 62
Madhya Pradesh 263
Madras Urban Development Projects 189
Madrid, R.L. 210
Maharashtra 263

Mahathir Mohamad 140
Mahila Milan 197
malaria 154, 160, 163, 166
Malthus, Thomas 254, 255-6, 258, 269, 272
Malthusianism 272, 286, 287, 300
  Cold War 259
  and environmental crises 267-8
  and eugenics 258-9
  export to British colonies 256-7
  see also neo-Malthusianism
managed migration 240, 283, 300
Manchester 55
mandatory pension contribution 300
mandatory personal pension plans 220, 300
Marchenko, Grigori 215
Martens, J. 41
Martineau, T. 241
Marxists 28
Médecins Sans Frontières (MSF) 161
medical migration 238-41, 246
medicines 159-60, 162, 163, 166-7, 168-9
Mediterranean 244
Menter, I. 65
mercantilism 105
Mercosur 10, 43, 242, 244
methodological nationalism 2, 8, 9, 280-1, 300-1
methodological transnationalism 2-3, 230, 280-1, 289, 300-1
Mexico 134
Migrant Workers' Convention 244, 245
migrants 20-1, 124, 237, 301
  cash and care 235-7
  global care chain 238-41
  human rights 243
  UN Conventions and Resolutions 244-5
  see also international migrants
migration 301
  see also internal migration; international migration
Migration for Employment Convention 244
Millennium Development Goals (MDGs) 32, 301
  dialogue and synergy 39
  ECOSOC 38
  and global social rights 35-6
  health 159, 168
  ITUC 126
  and medical migration 239
  regional monitoring 43
  reproductive health services 265
  slum dwellers 183, 196, 199
  task forces 40
Millennium Project 40

Mishra, R. 114
mixed reforms 213, 301
modernisation theory 181, 301
Modernising Government (Cabinet Office)
    62
mortality rates 151, 152
most favoured nation (MFN) rule 106,
    115
Movement Against Congo Colonisation
    17
movement of natural persons 115
Müller, K. 210
multilateral 302
multilateral actors 180, 181, 301
multilateral economic institutions 301
    see also International Monetary
        Fund; World Bank; World Health
        Organization
Multilateral Investment Guarantee Agency
    93
multilateral migration regime 242-4, 301
multilateral organisations *see* international
    organisations
multilateralism 114, 302
    population policy 260
multilevel governance 28, 302
multinational corporations (MNCs) *see*
    transnational corporations
Mumbai 197-8
Myanmar 245

N

NAFTA *see* North American Free Trade
    Agreement
Nagel, S. 10
nation states 286
national health policy 150
national security 267-72
National Slum Dwellers Federation
    (NSDF) 197
national social policy 28, 29-34
national treatment rule 106, 115
nationalism 139, 230
neo-Malthusianism 264, 272, 302
neoliberal 302
neoliberal economic policy 211, 302
neoliberal globalisation 74, 80, 81, 85, 302
neoliberalism 8, 18, 36, 55, 94, 302
    core labour standards 136-7
    free trade 104
    healthcare reform 165
    housing policy 188-9
    and Malthusianism 268
    OECD 30
    pensions 211-14
    UNESCO 58
Nestlé 83

net emigration 232, 233, 302
net immigration 232, 233, 302
New Labour 54, 62, 65
new managerialism 62
new pension reforms 208-14, 221-2
    bottom-up perspective 221
    country examples 215-17
    emerging debates 220-1
    limits 217-20
    methods of policy diffusion 214-15
New Public Management 62
New Zealand 232
NIEO 166
Nigeria 82, 212, 222
Nike 142
Nirman (National Slum Dwellers
    Federation, India and Mahila Milan)
    197
non-governmental organisations (NGOs)
    global gag rule 265
    global health policy 161, 167
    housing and urban development 195,
        197-8
    international migration 245-6
    labour standards 139, 140
    population policy 262, 266
    religious organisations 161, 263, 265
    see also international non-governmental
        organisations
non-state international actors 26-7
North Africa 244
North American Free Trade Agreement
    (NAFTA) 109, 113, 117, 133
Norway 232
notional defined contribution (NDC)
    pension 210, 217-18, 303

O

obesity 150, 152-3
obligation 283
Ochs, K. 50
Office of the UN High Commissioner for
    Refugees (UNCHR) 242, 245
Oliver, A. 272
one-child policy 209, 261-2, 267
L'Oréal 90
Orenstein, Mitchell 13
Organisation for Economic Co-operation
    and Development (OECD) 10, 288-9
    education 54, 64
    and global business interest associations
        77, 78
    global health policy 155, 158, 160, 165,
        166
    guidelines for multinationals 86, 87-8
    and national social policy 30-1, 32, 34,
        53, 58, 63

pensions 212, 220
population policy 265
social policy 92-3
overpopulation 254, 259, 264, 283, 286, 303
and crises 267-70
and poverty 255-7
Ozga, J. 60

P

Packard Foundation 266
pandemics 150, 154, 169
parallel reform 213-14, 303
Parsons, W. 62
partnership 215
pay-as-you-so pension systems 209-10, 213, 220, 303
peasants 127
pension funds 209-10, 216, 219, 220, 303
pensions *see* global pensions policy
People's Health Movement (PHM) 161
personal pension plan 303
persuasion 214
Peru 217
pharmaceuticals 159-60, 162, 166-7, 168-9
philanthropy 89, 162
Philippines
  housing and urban policy 198
  international migration 231, 240, 245
Phillips, D. 50
Piñera, José 215, 217
Pinochet, General Augusto 211-12
Piper, N. 244
place 17-18, 288-9
  see also geography
policy
  as discourse 59
  as text 59
  borrowing 51, 53, 303
  communities 61-2
  convergence 51, 53, 59, 304
  diffusion 51, 52, 53, 304
    pensions 211-15
  divergence 59, 64-5
  global policy 296
  global policy actors 281, 282-3, 296
  global social policy 10, 11, 279, 280-1, 289-90, 296-7
  learning 51, 62-4, 304
  network 61-2
  sociology 59, 63, 304
  transfer 50-8, 65-6, 304
    population policy 254
political mobilisation 17
politics 15
  decision making 62-4

and global social governance 28
politics of scale 28
Poor Law Amendment Act 1834 (UK) 256
population 254, 304
Population Action International 268, 271
population ageing 209
Population Bomb, The (Ehrlich) 267
population control 259-61, 304
  as counter-insurgency 267-72
  eugenics 258-9
  origins of thinking 255-7
Population Council 260, 266
population crisis 283
Population Crisis Committee 260
population decline 255, 304
population distribution 182
population growth 255, 259, 261, 304-5
population policy 254-5, 272, 285, 286, 305
  21st century 265-7
  feminist 261-5
  and health issues 158
  history 286-8
  institutions 259-61
  origins of population control thinking 255-7
  population control as counter-insurgency 267-72
Population Trust Fund 260
Portugal 232
Post-Washington Consensus (PWC) 85, 181, 195, 287, 305
poverty
  and housing 193-4
  and population policy 225-7, 258, 268
  and urbanisation 180, 181-3, 184, 185
Poverty Reduction Budget Support (PRBS) 195, 305
Poverty Reduction Strategy Papers (PRSPs) 33, 93, 132, 133, 195, 305
Power, Colin 56, 57
primary healthcare 163-4
Prince of Wales International Business Leaders Forum 139
  business 74-5, 93-4
prisoners 271-2
private pension plan 209, 305
protection *see* trade protection
protectionism *see* trade protectionism
public health 150, 159-60, 163, 167
public pension plan 209, 306
public–private partnerships *see* global public–private partnerships

R

race to the bottom 81, 110, 306

Rajasthan 263
Rao, Mohan 267
realists 26
reciprocity 283
Red Crescent 161
Red Cross 161
redistribution *see* global redistribution
regional social policy 32, 42-3
regulation *see* global regulation
religious organisations 161, 263, 265
  civil society (civic society) 292
  international non-governmental
    organisations 17, 299
  see also non-governmental organisations
    (NGOs)
remittances 235-6, 284
reproductive rights/reproductive justice
  262, 263, 306
Rieger, E. 112
rights *see* global social rights; human rights
Rio Principles on Environment and
  Development 141
Rio Tinto 142
Robertson, S. 64, 65
Rockefeller Foundation 266
Rop, Tone 218, 219
Ross, E. 258
Rowe, J.K. 138

S

SAARC (South Asian Association for
  Regional Cooperation) 43
SADC (Southern Africa Development
  Community) 10, 43
SARS (severe acute respiratory syndrome)
  150, 154
scale, politics of 28
scaling up 198, 199, 286, 306
scarcity 256, 306
Scholvinck, Johan 38
Scotland 65
Seattle 109
sector-wide approach (SWAp) 195, 306-7
security
  and global health policy 155, 167
  and population policy 267-72
selective healthcare 164, 307
Self Employed Women's Association
  (India) 127
self-help 185-6, 283
self-regulation 138-41, 143, 282
sex-selection 267, 270
Shack/Slum Dwellers Federation (SDI)
  197, 198
shadow economy *see* informal economy
Shell 82, 142
shelter 183, 307

shelter deprivation 183, 185, 307
Singapore 245
sites and services 186, 192-3, 307
Sklair, Leslie 285
slavery 17
slide to the bottom 81, 307
Slovenia 218-19
slum 180, 307
slum dwellers 183, 184, 185
slum improvement 180, 186-7, 307
Social Accountability International 139
social democracy 28, 94, 137
social determinant of health 151, 164, 308
social justice 282
Social Market Foundation 62
social policy 280-1, 289
  globalisation perspective 8-11
  rethinking theory and concepts 15-16
  and trade 104
  see also global social policy; national
    social policy
social protection 90, 308
social regulation *see* global social
  regulation
social rights *see* global social rights
social security fund 209, 308
social solidarity 282, 283
Society for the Promotion of Area
  Resource Centres (SPARC) 197
sociology 4-5, 15, 52
  see also policy sociology
Soros, George 89
Soros Foundation 55
South *see* developing countries
South Africa 81
  housing and urban development 192,
    197, 198
  medical migration 241
  pensions 212-13
squatter settlements 187, 308
Sri Lanka 245
state sovereignty 137, 140, 308
states 129-31
  see also developed countries; developing
    countries
Steiger, William 152-3
sterilisation 258-9
Stiglitz, Joseph 77, 220
Stone, D. 61-2, 63-4
Strassmann, W.P. 199
strategic demography 270
Streck, Charlotte 41
Structural Adjustment Loan 217, 308
subsidy 215
substitution 215
substitutive reform 213, 214, 308
Summers, Larry 212
swallow grandparents 237

Sweden
  housing and urban policy 181
  pensions 214, 217
  sterilisation 259
Swedish International Development
  Agency (SIDA) 181, 198

T

Taiwan 213, 222
Tanzania 266
targeting/targeted provision 91, 163-4,
  165-6, 308
Tarrow, S. 210
tax policy 79
technology 4, 111
terrorism 270-1
Texas City 84
text 59
Thailand 117, 135, 189, 197, 245
think tanks 52, 55, 61-2, 63
Thomas, Clare 138
tobacco 117
Tobacco Framework Convention 150,
  153, 162, 169
Toy Manufacturers of America 140
toys 135
trade 102, 117-18, 285
  development of trading system 105-7
  economics and welfare 102-5
  and global health policy 155, 156,
    159-60, 161, 166, 287
  global institutions and policy processes
    107-10
  global social regulation 35
  and international migration 234, 243
  and labour conditions 133-4
  in welfare services 115-17
  and welfare state 110-14
Trade Adjustment Assistance (TAA)
  112-13
trade justice 105, 109
trade negotiations 106, 308
trade protection 102, 103, 105, 306
  and welfare state 112-13
trade protectionism 35, 306
trade unions 126-7, 134
transnational advocacy coalitions or
  networks 6, 27-8, 51, 284-5, 308
  and corporations 81
  global labour policy 126
  international migration 245-6
  trade 109
transnational corporations (TNCs) 6, 74,
  77, 107, 309
  Global Compact 141-2, 143
  and global division of labour 129, 130
  global framework agreements 126-7

global health policy 162, 167, 168, 286,
  287
global labour policy 135-6, 143
  self-regulation 138-41
transnational families 235-7, 246, 284, 309
transnational knowledge networks 27-8,
  54, 309
transnational migration 309
transnational policy campaign 208-11,
  212, 214-15, 220-2
transnational social welfare 235-7, 309
transnational tobacco corporations
  (TTCs) 117
transnationalism 5, 6, 7-8, 13-14
  see also methodological transnationalism
transnationalist capitalist class 285-6
travelling and embedded policy 51, 52,
  59-61, 309
TRIPS (Agreement on Trade-Related
  Intellectual Property Rights) 106, 109,
  159-60, 166
tuberculosis 154, 160, 166
Turner, John 185-6

U

UN *see* United Nations
UNAIDS 155
UNDP *see* United Nations Development
  Programme
unemployment 111
UNESCO *see* United Nations
  Educational, Scientific and Cultural
  Organization
UN-HABITAT 188, 192, 196, 198, 199
UNHCR (Office of the UN High
  Commissioner for Refugees) 242, 245
UNICEF *see* United Nations Children's
  Fund
Union Carbide 84
Union of Industrial and Employers'
  Confederations of Europe (UNICE)
  78, 86
unions 126-7, 134
United Kingdom
  business interest associations 139
  colonialism 17
  divergence within 64-5
  education 64
  eugenics 258
  evidence-informed policy 62
  global health policy 165, 168
  global housing and urban policy 181
  housing policy 185, 188
  migrant welfare workers 124, 238-9,
    240-1
  National Health Service 116
  pensions 214

policy transfer and diffusion 52, 55
population policy 254, 256-7, 286-7
United Nations 9, 10, 27, 281
  and business power 76
  Convention on the Rights of the Child
    33, 157-8
  economic and social development 195
  and global business interest associations
    77, 78
  Global Compact 86, 87
  global health policy 155-8, 168
  global social regulation 35
  global social rights 35
  human settlements 188
  International Conference on Population
    and Development (ICPD) Programme
    of Action 262-3, 265
  international migration 242, 243, 245
  and national social policy 43
  networks, partnerships and projects 40,
    41
  population policy 260, 262, 265
  reform 36, 37-9, 43-4
  Universal Declaration of Human Rights
    141, 156
  and World Bank 39
United Nations Centre for Human
  Settlements (UNCHS (Habitat)) 188,
  194-5
United Nations Children's Fund 27, 32,
  34
  global health policy 155, 158, 163-4
  international migration 242
  population policy 260
United Nations Commission on Human
  Rights (UNCHR) 155-6
United Nations Committee on
  Economic, Social and Cultural Rights
  (UNCESCR) 33, 35
United Nations Conference on Trade and
  Development (UNCTAD) 39, 40
United Nations Convention Against
  Corruption 141
United Nations Department of Economic
  and Social Affairs (UNDESA) 27,
  32-3, 34, 39
United Nations Development Programme
  32-3, 34
  housing policy 185, 189, 190
  housing and urban policy 181
  and ILO 31
  reform 39
  trade, economics and welfare 104, 113
United Nations Economic Council for
  Latin America 212
United Nations Economic and Social
  Council 33, 38, 39, 157, 245

United Nations Educational, Scientific
  and Cultural Organization 27, 32, 34,
  64-5
  education 56-8, 285
  international migration 242
United Nations Fund for Population
  Activities (UNFPA) 260, 264, 265
United Nations General Assembly 244-5
United Nations Human Settlements
  Programme 181, 188, 192, 196, 198,
  199
United Nations Population Fund
  (UNFPA) 155, 183, 260
United Nations Secretary General 27,
  37-8, 39
  Global Compact 41, 140, 141-3
  international migration 244
  Millennium Project 40
United Nations specialised agency 151,
  309
United States
  education 65
  eugenics 258, 259
  Foreign Assistance Act (US) 260
  global governance 36-7
  global health policy 152-3, 165
  global housing and urban policy 181,
    199
  global social rights 35
  housing policy 188
  immigration 124, 232
  labour standards 139
  pensions 222
  policy transfer and diffusion 52, 55
  population policy 60, 254, 259, 260, 265,
    266, 270, 271, 272
  prisoners 271-2
  tobacco 117
  trade protection and welfare state
    112-13
  and UNESCO 57
  and World Bank 42
  WTO 108, 109
United States Agency for International
  Development (USAID)
  global health policy 162
  housing and urban policy 181, 185, 186
  pensions 212, 214, 215, 216
  population policy 260, 264-5
Universal Declaration of Human Rights
  141, 156
universalism 31, 166-7
University of Chicago 211-12
urban development 180, 181
  21st century 194-8
  1990s 190-4
urban ladder 192, 193
urban policy 180-1, 183-9, 199, 287, 309

urbanisation 180-1
  internal migration 232
  and poverty 181-3, 184, 185
Uruguay round 106
Uttar Pradesh 263

V

velocity 3
Venezuela 81, 218
vernacular globalisation 59, 309
vertical 154, 161, 310
Vertovec, S. 5, 7
Via Campesina 127
Vietnam 245
voluntary personal pension plan 209, 310

W

Wallace, W. 26-7
Washington Consensus (WC) 36, 40, 64,
  181, 188-9, 287, 310
water 269
WB *see* World Bank
welfare
  economics and trade 102-5, 110-14,
  117-18
  trade in services 115-17, 118
welfare mix 15, 16
welfare workers 238-41
West African Community 242
Weyland, K. 210
WHO *see* World Health Organization
Willetts, A. 241
women
  international migration 236-7, 245
  population policy 261-5, 266-7, 270-1,
  272, 286
  teen mothers 271-2
Woods, Ngaire 40
worker rights 126 *see also* human rights;
  core labour standards
Worker Rights Consortium (WRC)
  139-40
World Bank 9, 10, 31, 105, 289, 310
accountability 41-2, 154
  and business power 76, 77
  challenges to 81
  education 64, 65, 285
  epistemic communities 55
  global health policy 155, 158, 160, 162-
  3, 165-6
  global labour policy 134
  and Global South 39-40
  housing and urban policy 181, 186, 187,
  188, 189, 190-2, 194, 196, 197, 198,
  199, 286, 287
  and ILO 132, 133
  and IMF 39

international migration 243
  and national social policy 27, 29, 32-3,
  34, 43, 53, 54, 57, 58, 63
  New Public Management 62
  pensions 55, 208-11, 212, 214, 215, 216,
  217, 218-19, 220-2
  population policy 260, 264, 265, 266
  Post-Washington Consensus 195
  reform US 36
  social policy 93
  and United Nations
  and Via Campesina 127
  worker rights 126
  and WTO 107
World Commission on the Social
  Dimension of Globalisation 132
World Commission on Water for the 21st
  Century 269, 310
World Confederation of Labour 126
World Development Report (World Bank)
  165, 166
World Economic Forum (WEF) 10
World Health Assembly 152, 163, 240
World Health Organization 31-2, 34, 158,
  167, 168, 310
  Commission on the Social Determinants
  of Health 151
  global health governance 151-4
  global public–private partnerships 27,
  161, 162
  Health for All 162, 163-4
  healthcare reform 165, 166
  and ILO 31
  infectious diseases and global health
  security agenda 154-5
  international migration 239, 242
  population policy 260
World Health Report 161
World Population Conference 261
world-regional formations 109, 281, 289
  international migration 244
  labour standards 133-4
  social policy 32, 42-3
World Social Forum (WSF) 10, 127
world society theory 52, 310
world-systems theory 4-5
World Trade Organization (WTO) 102,
  105-6, 114, 117
  accountability 41
  and business power 76
  and global health policy 159-60, 163,
  166
  international migration 243
  labour standards 111, 131, 133, 136,
  137-8, 143
  and national social policy 27, 30, 34
  policy processes 107-9, 110
  and Via Campesina 127

welfare services 115–17
worker rights 126
Worldwide Responsible Apparel
 Production 139

Y

Yeates, Nicola 13, 53, 59, 63, 238
Young, K. 63
youth bulge theory 270–1